T'ang Transformation Texts

Harvard-Yenching Institute Monograph Series 28

Victor H. Mair

Distributed by the HARVARD UNIVERSITY PRESS, Cambridge (Massachusetts) and
London 1989

T'ang Transformation Texts

A Study of the Buddhist Contribution to the Rise of Vernacular Fiction and Drama in China

Published by the COUNCIL ON EAST ASIAN STUDIES, HARVARD UNIVERSITY

The Harvard-Yenching Institute, founded in 1928 and headquartered at Harvard University, is a foundation dedicated to the advancement of higher education in the humanities and social sciences in East and Southeast Asia. The Institute supports advanced research at Harvard by faculty members of certain Asian universities, and doctoral studies at Harvard and other universities by junior faculty at the same universities. It also supports East Asian studies at Harvard through contributions to the Harvard-Yenching Library and publication of the *Harvard Journal of Asiatic Studies* and books on pre-modern East Asian history and literature.

Library of Congress Cataloging in Publication Data

Mair, Victor H., 1943–
T'ang transformation texts: a study of the Buddhist contribution to the rise of vernacular fiction and drama in China / Victor H. Mair.
p. cm.—(Harvard-Yenching Institute monograph series; 28)
Bibliography: p.
Includes index.
ISBN 0-674-86815-3: $27.00
1. Pien wen (Buddhist song-tales)—History and criticism. 2. Chinese literature—Buddhist influences. I. Title. II. Series.
PL2365.M37 1988
398.2'0951—dc19 88-37893
CIP

À la mémoire de Paul Pelliot,
sinologue hors pair

. . . The picture-story, which critics disregard and scholars scarcely notice, has great influence at all times, perhaps even more than written literature. More people will look at pictures than at books, and, in addition, the picture-story appeals mainly to children and the lower classes—that is, to the two groups most easily misguided and most needing improvement.

Rodolphe Töpffer,
"Essay on Physiognomy"
(1845)
Tr. by E. Wiese,
Enter the Comics, p. 3

Preface

The research for this book began in the fall of 1967 when I read three histories of Chinese literature written in English, those by Lai Ming, Wu-chi Liu, and Ch'en Shou-yi. I came away from these histories with the very powerful impression that the single most important unresolved problem in the study of Chinese literature was the derivation of Tun-huang *pien-wen* 敦煌變文. Clearly these were texts of extraordinary significance for the subsequent development of popular literature in China. The discovery of the Tun-huang texts, according to Paul Demiéville ("Tun-huang Texts," p. 186), "has dated back by several centuries the origins of the vernacular literature of China, which in some respects represents one of the most fruitful and significant contributions to Chinese culture in modern times." And yet it was puzzling that no one seemed to know with any degree of certainty where they came from or how they arose. Nor was there any agreement on the size of the *pien-wen* corpus or the formal nature of the genre. Even more bewildering was the fact that the very meaning of the word *pien* had not been established. These unsettled issues relating to *pien-wen* were so intriguing that I decided to make them the central focus of my research over the next decade and more.

Among the questions to which this particular study addresses itself are the following: What are the origins of *pien-wen* and its various constituent elements (prosimetric form, relationship to pictures, verse-introductory formula, and so forth)? What does the word *pien* mean? Who were the performers of *pien*? How were they performed? Who wrote down the *pien-wen* and why did they do it? How many *pien-wen* are extant? What implications do *pien-wen* have for the subsequent development of popular fiction and drama?

As will shortly become apparent to readers of this study, in attempting to answer any of these questions, it is essential not to overlook the fundamental role of Buddhism. Indeed, part of the reason for my continuing interest in this subject is in response to the challenge issued by E. Zürcher in the preface (p. xiii) to his book called *The Buddhist Conquest of China*:

> More attention could be paid to the way in which Buddhism, as a vehicle of foreign *literary* influence, made an unprecedented impact on Chinese secular literature. In this field, cases of successful penetration (e.g. the absorption of Buddhist literary clichés, the earliest development of the "prosimetric" style, the largely Buddhist origin of the genre "edifying tales") are as notable as the cases of immunity, in which Buddhist literary patterns failed to evoke a creative response (such as epic poetry, unrhymed verse, and verbatim representation).

But, for various ideological, political, and patriotic reasons, the possibility of significant Buddhist influence on the development of *pien-wen* has frequently been denounced by scholars writing in the past half-century. Thus it will be necessary to respond to a certain number of issues that have been raised by them regarding the role of Buddhism in Chinese thought and life. Our aim will be always to achieve a *balanced view* of the impact of Buddhism on China, not one that ascribes too much shaping effect to this foreign religion, nor one that underestimates its uncanny ability to operate in diverse cultural settings.

Although it is a duty of the literary historian to distinguish between the two, both direct and indirect borrowings from the Buddhist tradition constitute influence. During the late T'ang period, Buddhism was so totally assimilated by the Chinese people at large that they were more often than not unaware of its alien origins. This fact alone makes the task of the literary historian extremely difficult when he is attempting to trace the origins of themes and forms in popular literature. For this reason, I shall proceed with caution and try to be as explicit as possible.

Since the reader of this monograph will more likely be the student of Chinese literature than the Buddhologist, it is not assumed that he or she will possess a background in Buddhist studies. Hence, to accommodate those unfamiliar with Chinese Buddhism, there are places where the student of Buddhism is sure to feel that the obvious is being stressed. My own lack of adequate knowledge regarding Buddhism may be the cause of other regrettable deficiencies.

The problems of what *pien* is and what it means have not been solved by those scholars who have confined themselves to Chinese sources. In my opinion they never will be solved unless we begin to look into Tibetan, Uighur, Sanskrit, and other sources. For this reason, I have been so bold as to look at some non-Chinese materials. Others may judge whether or not I have been amply rewarded for my efforts. I have done so only because the need to understand the meaning and history of *pien* is so compelling. So as not to waste the time of my strictly Sinological readers, I have made only minimal reference to non-Chinese materials in this book. Those whose curiosity is piqued, however, are invited to peek into my *Painting and Performance*, which gives a more complete account of many subjects only touched on here.

My boldness in encroaching upon fields in which I lack full competence has been mitigated by the unreserved assistance of numerous individuals. Şinasi Tekin's quick and expert responses to my questions regarding Uighur texts are deeply appreciated. Ahmet Evin, Erika Gilson, Margaret Feary, Francis Cleaves, and Ki Joong Song helped with Altaic languages in general. Mr. Song was also exceptionally kind in helping me to gain access to Korean sources. I am profoundly grateful for Jan Nattier-Barbaro's patient searching in the Tibetan canon for passages which I brought to her from the Chinese versions. My good friend and former colleague, Masatoshi Nagatomi, explicated in minute detail a difficult Tibetan text at my request and kept a sharp lookout for errors of interpretation in matters Sanskritic and Buddhistic throughout. Ludo Rocher graciously contributed his vast expertise in all areas of Indology, and Peter Gaeffke was always ready to share his wide-ranging erudition. In spite of a busy schedule of graduate studies, Scott Cremer never failed to answer my questions concerning Indian language, literature, and philosophy. Similarly, Hiroshi Kumamoto was able to provide expert guidance in Khotanese matters. David Utz and Wilma Heston both read the portions of this book that treat of Sogdian and Manichaean matters. Any deficiencies in these areas are entirely the result of my own inability to follow up completely on their good suggestions. Charles Benoit generously answered several of my questions about Sino-Vietnamese.

I am grateful to my former students Harry Kaplan and Masato Nishimura for having verified most of the entries in the Chinese and Japanese entries of the bibliography and to Heidi Mair and James Dudley for assistance in verifying some of the other entries. Thanks are due as well to Mira Mihelich for many kind favors. I also profited greatly from my conversations with Tseng Yung-i of Taiwan National University and Guan Dedong [Kuan Te-tung] of Shantung University about Chinese popular literature.

Though I have only recently begun to meet some of them, I feel a profound sense of respect and admiration toward the Japanese scholars whose dedicated work has inspired me to attempt these studies. Among these great students of popular Buddhist art and literature are Naba Toshisada, Kawaguchi Hisao, Kanaoka Shōkō, Iriya Yoshitaka, Akiyama Terukazu, Fujieda Akira, and Umezu Jirō.

Another scholar whose example has given me tremendous encouragement and whom I hold in the highest regard is Lien-shen Yang. Even when he was not feeling well, Professor Yang generously consented to write the characters that grace the cover of this book.

Heartfelt thanks are extended to Denis Mair and Andrew Jones for converting a horribly messy handwritten manuscript into a workable first typed draft. Without their assistance, the four typescripts that followed would not have been possible. Likewise, I consider myself most fortunate in receiving the expert editorial guidance of Florence Trefethen, who saw the book through the final stages of publication. Ann Cheng magnanimously volunteered to help in the compilation of the index and in proofreading.

I should like to take this opportunity to register my gratitude to the Harvard Graduate Society for a grant which helped to defray the cost of preparing the manuscript of this book for publication, to the University of Pennsylvania Committee on Faculty Grants and Awards for assistance in typing the final draft, and to the American Council of Learned Societies for providing the generous support, in part financed by the National Endowment for the Humanities, that enabled me to bring these protracted studies to completion.

Many libraries have provided me with important materials in the course of my research. I am particularly grateful to the Trustees of the British Library and to the authorities of the Bibliothèque Nationale (Paris) for making available to me microfilm and photographic copies of many Tun-huang manuscripts. Thanks also are due to the Library of Congress for sending me marvelously clear photostatic copies of the Śāriputra *pien-wen*. Robert Dunn, Senior Reference Librarian of the Chinese and Korean Section, has been both prompt and thorough in response to my questions. Howard Nelson, Assistant Keeper of the Department of Oriental Manuscripts and Printed Books in the British Library, obliged me by inspecting several Tun-huang manuscripts there. The hospitality and assistance of the authorities of the following institutions during the period of travel and research carried out in 1981 are deeply appreciated: Cornell University Library, British Library, Bibliothèque Nationale, the archives of the Institute of Asian Peoples (Academy of Sciences, USSR) in Leningrad, Peking National Library, and the Peking University Library. I must also register my gratitude to Eugene Eoyang and Nick Koss of the University of Indiana, who enabled me to obtain microfilm copies of many Tun-huang manuscripts. Nancy Cheng and her staff of the University of Pennsylvania Library East Asian Section have been prompt and efficient in responding to my requests. Most of all, it is to the staff of the Harvard-Yenching Library, including Eugene Wu, George Potter, Ray Lum, Deborah White, Ch'ien Ho, the late Larry Edsall, Pao-liang Chu, Daisy Hu, Sungha Kim, Rin Paik, Yukiko Pluard, and Toshiyuki Aoki, that I am in deepest debt. Without their services, this study could not even have begun; without their help, it certainly could not have been finished.

I would, furthermore, like to thank the following individuals who read this work in manuscript at various stages and who made numerous useful suggestions: Piet van der Loon, Glen Dudbridge, C. K. Wang, David Pollard, A. C. Graham, Timothy Barrett, and K. P. K. Whitaker. Above all, I appreciate Patrick Hanan's unswerving insistence on quality, reliability, and civility. His "Dutch uncle" advice has not always been easy to take, but it has contributed greatly to making this a better book. Naturally, I alone am responsible for all errors of omission and commission.

Finally, these studies would not have been possible without the cooperation and understanding of my wife, Li-ching, and son, Thomas. And, as always, the encouragement and inspiration from my entire family in Ohio were essential in bringing them to completion.

Contents

New Developments

On 1 October 1988, when the page proofs of this book were being sent to me for checking, I was in Lanchow, China, on my way back to the United States after a month-long trip to archeological sites and museums in the Soviet and Chinese parts of Central Asia. At the Kansu Provincial Museum there, I discovered a painting from Tun-huang which is of such extreme importance for this book that I am compelled at this late date to add a few brief paragraphs describing it.

The painting, finely drawn and beautifully colored, carries the actual title "Transformation on the *Sūtra Spoken by the Buddha Concerning Recompense to Parents for Their Great Kindness* (*Fo-shuo pao fu-mu en chung ching pien*)" 佛說報父母恩重經變. A lengthy inscription in the middle of the bottom portion dates it to the 3rd year of the Ch'un-hua ("Pure Transformation") 淳化 reign period of the Northern Sung dynasty, that is 992. Above the inscription is a précis of the sūtra.

At first glance, the painting gives the appearance of a *maṇḍala* with a Buddha seated in the lotus posture occupying the central position and surrounded by attendant Bodhisattvas. There are also several Bodhisattvas in a row along the top of the painting. Upon closer inspection, however, it is revaled that, on either side of the central assemblage, there are numerous scenes illustrating episodes from the sūtra in question. What is more, each of these scenes is accompanied by a cartouche with an identifying label that ends with the marker of narrative moment: ". . . at the time when" (*shih* 時). The bottom right corner presents a portrait of the Buddhist monk to whose memory it was dedicated.

According to Museum authorities, the painting itself is kept in a storeroom. Hence I was able to view only a large color photograph of it on my hurried visit. What I saw convinces me that it richly deserves thorough research, not only by scholars versed in popular Buddhist literature, but by art historians as well. For the moment, we may observe that the painting is called a "transformation" (*pien*), not a "transformation tableau" (*pien-hsiang*). It represents one of the last certifiable references to *pien* in Chinese history. Study of the format, identification of the various figures depicted, comparison with other T'ang and Sung paintings, its relationship to the obscure reference in the biography of Hsuan-tsang discussed on pp. 167–169, its connection to the illustrated sūtra from Khara-khoto described on pp. 85–86, analysis of its content vis-à-vis relevant Tun-huang manuscripts, and translation of the inscriptions, précis, and labels will require more intensive investigation. Yet, even before these tasks are carried out, we may state with confidence that this "Transformation on the *Sūtra Spoken by the Buddha Concerning Recompense to Parents for Their Great Kindness*" is of great significance both for the history of Chinese literature and of Chinese art.

On 4 November 1988, less than a week before I was set to return the corrected proofs to the publisher, Terry Kleeman called to my attention a passage in a book he himself had received from China only that very day. Entitled *Wu-chün chih* [Gazetteer of Soochow prefecture] 吳郡志 (n. p.: Kiangsu-sheng ku-chi ch'u-pan-she, 1986), this work was originally completed by the noted Sung author Fan Ch'eng-ta 范成大 (1126–1193) during the last four years of his life. In the 30th fascicle, the first portion of which deals with Taoist structures, we find (p. 454) the following entry:

> The Belvedere of Celestial Celebration, which lies in the southwest part of Long Islet 長洲 district, was founded during the Opened Prime 開元 reign period (22 December 713–9 February 742) of the T'ang dynasty. Before being damaged in the wars, its buildings were most spacious and beautiful. In 1146, the Prefect Wang Huan 王喚 had two of the verandas rebuilt. On their walls were painted a "Transformation Tableau on the *Salvation Scripture of the Numinous Jewel* [*Ling-pao tu-jen ching*]"[1] 靈寶度人經變相. He summoned artists to work on the landscapes, human

1. For a detailed study of this important text, see Michel Strickmann, "The Longest Taoist Scripture," *History of Religions* 17.1:331–354 (August 1977).

> figures, buildings, and flora. Each specialized in a particular skill and the tasks were assigned to them accordingly. The work was exceedingly fine.

This record is valuable for a number of reasons. First, it was written by a person who hailed from the time and place in question and therefore has a high degree of reliability. Furthermore, it provides significant details concerning the cooperative method used to complete the painting. Above all, it offers clear evidence that the Taoists had accepted transformation tableaux as a part of their own religion and that they were active in sponsoring them as late as the Southern Sung.

General Principles

The problematic word *pien* 變 is herein consistently translated as "transformation." The related expressions *pien-wen* 變文, *pien-hsiang* 變相, and *pien-hsien* 變現 are translated respectively as "transformation text," "transformation tableau," and "transformational representation or manifestation." *Pien* alone may mean "transformation (performance)," "transformation (text)," or "transformation (tableau)." Its precise signification on any given occurrence must be determined from context. The justification for these translations will be presented at length in several chapters of this book, but particularly in Chapter 3. When these terms are simply transcribed in this study, it usually indicates the broad or indeterminate interpretations placed upon them by the majority of scholars. Transcription is also used in cases of erroneous explanation. The translated forms are generally employed when the narrow definitions I propose in Chapter 2 are intended.

The systems of transliteration from such languages as Uighur, Khotanese, and Tibetan not being uniform, there are conflicting usages in various authorities whom I cite. Where there is a possibility of confusion, I have pointed out the necessary equivalences.

Unless otherwise indicated, citations from the standard dynastic histories are to the Kaiming (KM) edition. A list of abbreviated references may be found before the notes.

chapter one

Tun-huang and the Manuscripts

A little more than ten miles SSE of the city of Tun-huang 敦煌 in the northwestern Chinese province of Kansu lies the Howling Sands Hill 鳴沙山.[1] At the foot of the hill is a Monastery of the Three Realms (Triloka) 三界寺 beside which are to be found many conglomerate rock caves called the "Grottoes of Unsurpassed Height" (Mo-kao k'u 莫高窟), popularly known as the "Caves of the Thousand Buddhas" (Ch'ien-Fo tung 千佛洞). It was here that the manuscripts that form the major focus of this study were found. The caves were visited by Aurel Stein in May 1907 and by Paul Pelliot in February 1908. Both men recovered from Tun-huang thousands of manuscripts which they took back, respectively, to the British Museum and the Bibliothèque Nationale, where they are now housed. These are the two most important collections of Tun-huang manuscripts in the world. Large numbers of manuscripts are also to be found in Russia and China. Smaller collections are owned by libraries in Taiwan and Japan. There are, in addition, a few scattered manuscripts held by various individuals and institutions in other countries.[2]

The full story of the discovery, removal, and dispersion of the manuscripts from the Tun-huang cave where they were found is an interesting and complicated series of events which requires separate treatment.[3] For the purposes of this study, it will be necessary to make only some general observations about Tun-huang and the hoard of manuscripts found there.

In the first place, it is incorrect to say, as many often do, that Tun-huang was an isolated provincial town in terms of its relation to China. It was actually—in terms of its relation to the larger world—a most cosmopolitan city. Even the name Tun-huang (archaic **d'uən-ɣuang*) is the transcription of a foreign word, which has not been positively identified. The Greek equivalent (Ptolemaios, 6.16.6) is *Θρoava* and the Sogdian **ϑruwān* or **δruwan* (*δrw''n*).[4] Bailey has recently suggested that the name may derive from Iranian *druvāna* ("a strong, secure place; a fortress").[5] It is possible that the reconstructed aspiration in the pre-Han period pronunciation of the name was originally meant to represent the "r" of the initial consonant cluster.[6]

Tun-huang was a thriving international community, a bustling crossroads of cultural and commercial interchange.[7] Contacts with the capital in Ch'ang-an 長安 were frequent, both by governmental and religious personages, as well as by merchants.[8] Administratively, Tun-huang was not a commandery (chün 郡) under the T'ang but was itself a district or sub-prefecture (hsien 縣) and served also as the seat of the prefecture (chou 州) of Sha 沙 (that is, the "Sandy" prefecture).[9]

After a visit to Tun-huang, Joseph Needham was moved to comment thus on the wall-paintings of the Caves of the Thousand Buddhas: "These reflect the internationalism of the period by showing monks and lay people sometimes with brown or even red hair, and blue or green eyes, as well as occidental features."[10] It needs only to be added that the Tun-huang wall-paintings also reflect the internationalism of the *place*.

Many of the most renowned Buddhist translators and pilgrims stayed in Tun-huang for significant periods of time. Fa-hsien 法顯 began his journey to the Buddhist holy land at Tun-huang. And Hsuan-tsang 玄奘, on his return from India, remained there while awaiting the Emperor Hsuan-tsung's 玄宗 orders. Dharmarakṣa 法護 (c. 230–308), was born there and was known as the "Bodhisattva from Tun-huang." Kumārajīva spent some time at Tun-huang before traveling on to Ch'ang-an. Buddhist monks from Persia, Bactria, India, Sogdia, Khotan, and numerous other places would spend a period of time in Tun-huang acclimatizing themselves to China before proceeding on to the capital or elsewhere in the heartland with their manuscripts and messages.

Except for certain intervals, such as that of the Tibetan occupation,[11] when communication was impeded, there was constant communication between Tun-huang and the rest of China throughout most of the period from the Han to the T'ang. Hence there were artistic and literary influences flowing in both directions. We know, for example, of a famous cleric named Yun-pien 雲辯 ("Cumulous Debater," d. 951), who had written poems for geisha girls in Ch'ang-an and who, at the same time, had a profound effect on the type of popular lectures delivered at Tun-huang, where some of his personal documents were found.[12] We also know that pictures of the famous pilgrimage site Five Terraces Mountain 五臺山[13] (in northeastern Shansi) were common at Tun-huang,[14] which indicates that pilgrims traveled back and forth between these two sites and elsewhere in China.

Geographically, Tun-huang is situated at the crucial point in western Kansu where the northern and southern trade routes to Turkestan and western Asia branch out along the sides of the Taklamakan desert.[15] These northern and southern arms of the Silk Route, which skirted the Tarim basin, met at the Jade Gate Pass 玉門關, not far from Tun-huang. It is no wonder that Tun-huang has been referred to as China's "throat," for through it poured much from outside that nourished her. The "Biography of P'ei Chü" 裴矩傳 in the *History of the Sui*, citing the preface to his *Notes on Pictures of the Western Regions*, describes the geographic and strategic situation:

> Altogether there are three ways that begin at Tun-huang and reach to the Western Ocean. . . . Each of the various countries on each of these three ways also has its own roads for communication north and south. The Eastern Kingdom of Women[16] and the Brahman kingdoms in the south, and so forth can reach everywhere by following where these roads lead. Thus we know that, while Hami, Karakhojo, and Navapa (Pidjan) are all gates to the Western Regions, they all converge on Tun-huang, which is the location of their throat.[17]

As Grousset has so aptly put it in terms of the transmission of artistic motifs and techniques, "The culminating point of all these Central-Asiatic influences, with what they contained of Indian traditions or, through Indian Buddhism, of Graeco-Buddhist and Irano-Buddhist traditions, is to be found in Tun-huang."[18] The languages alone (Chinese, Sanskrit, Tibetan, Syriac, Uighur, Sogdian, Khotanese, Tocharian, and so forth) of the manuscripts found at Tun-huang are a good indication of the international flavor of the city. Truly, Tun-huang was a great meeting place between East and West.

Japanese scholars have been particularly fascinated by Tun-huang, not only for its romantically exotic, desert setting, but more so because it represents to them an almost tangible point of contact between Western and Eastern civilization, between Buddhist and Chinese art of all types, including literature. Many Japanese look to Tun-huang as a crucible where important elements of their own culture were forged.[19] There is even a recent best-selling novel on Tun-huang written by Inoue Yasushi.

Though the preservation of the manuscripts may be considered a miracle of sorts, it is no accident that they were preserved in Tun-huang. This was an area which had a long history of Buddhist piety and was closer to the source of Buddhism than any other part of China. The geographic location, an imminent Tangut invasion, the existence of a tightly knit, pious Buddhist community willing to collect and store away the manuscripts, and the climate, which is ideal for the preservation of paper and silk—all these factors contributed to the survival of the Tun-huang manuscripts. Thus, although I shall show that transformations (*pien* 變) were performed throughout China, it is understandable why written transformation texts (*pien-wen* 變文) happen to have been discovered at Tun-huang rather than somewhere else.

While the exact date of the discovery of the manuscripts may never be known, it seems certain that they were found sometime around the turn of the century. All the dates proposed that deserve serious consideration fall between the early summer of 1899 and the early summer of 1900.[20] The story[21] goes that a Taoist priest named Wang Yuan-lu 王圓籙, who had taken up residence at the Grottoes of Unsurpassed Height and appointed himself their custodian, was sweeping away the dust in cave 163 (Pelliot number; Chang Ta-ch'ien 張大千 no. 151; Tun-huang Research Institute no. 16; Shih Yen [Yai] 史岩 no. 401) when he felt a draft coming from a crack in the wall on the right side near the entrance. Upon breaking down the wall that had been filled in with bricks, he found the hoard of manuscripts in the adjoining room (cave no. 17 according to the Tun-huang Research Institute system). It was, as Kanaoka Shōkō has written, a veritable "mountain of waste-paper."[22] When Stein first saw the manuscripts *in situ*, he was struck by how jumbled they were.[23] This may have been due to Taoist priest Wang's handling of them. But, from both Stein's and Pelliot's accounts, one gains the impression that the manuscripts had originally been hastily deposited and that Wang had left most of them undisturbed. It would seem that they had been placed in the cave as protection from invaders.

Just as the exact date of the discovery of the manuscripts remains unknown, so does that of the sealing up of the cave. Most authorities agree, however, that the manuscripts were sealed up around the time of the Tangut (Hsi-hsia 西夏) invasions in 1035 or 1036.[24] The last dated manuscripts are from before the beginning of the eleventh century. And, even though the Tanguts occupied Tun-huang for many years, not a single manuscript among those discovered there is written in the Hsi-hsia language. At the other end of the scale, the earliest dated manuscript is from the year 406.[25] The digging of the caves themselves did not begin until after the middle of the fourth century.[26]

Estimates of the total number of extant Tun-huang manuscripts range between 20,000 and 40,000. It is fruitless to attempt at this time an accurate accounting because we still do not know the extent and provenance of the Russian holdings. According to Men'shikov,[27] there are between 10,000 and 12,000 Tun-huang manuscripts in Russia which were recovered by S. F. Ol'denburg. But this figure seems rather high and is inflated by materials from other places in Central Asia and by the separation of individual manuscripts into several parts. At any rate, since a complete catalog of the Russian holdings has never been published in any language, it is still difficult to describe their precise nature and quantity.[28] And the more than 8,000 manuscripts left in China are still inadequately cataloged.[29] The difficulty in determining the total number of manuscripts is further compounded by the fact that, in many instances, what was once a single scroll has somehow become disjoined so that one portion might be in England, say, and another in China.

For social and literary historians, the most significant manuscripts found at Tun-huang are not official government documents; nor are they precious scriptures (although these too were found in great numbers). They are notes, jottings scribblings, contracts, lists, some records of petty bureaucrats and records relating to the operation of monasteries and temples, circular notices of clubs, memoranda, copies of vernacular and classical literature, elementary textbooks, dream-divination manuals, and the like.[30] A single scroll might be composed of various scraps of paper pasted together and could thus include passages from sūtras, memoranda, songs, and so forth. The fact that many of the manuscripts have to do with inconsequential matters makes them all the more important to us now because of the rare glimpse they afford of the daily life of the common man in China during the T'ang and the Five Dynasties periods.

Of all the invaluable materials discovered at Tun-huang, the most deserving of study by students of popular literature are a group that may be designated as representing the genre called "transformation texts" (*pien-wen*). In the three-quarters of a century since their discovery by Stein and Pelliot and their introduction to the scholarly world by Kano Naoki,[31] the vicissitudes of transformation texts have been manifold. Physically they have been dispersed throughout the world, which makes it somewhat difficult to study them as a coherent body of materials. Even more trying than the physical separation of the manuscripts is the disconcerting lack of consensus among students of Chinese literature about the exact nature and significance of these texts. The chief purposes of this book are, first, to describe the *pien-wen* corpus and, second, to define the genre together with its history.

Appendix
The Szechwan Connection

The discovery at Tun-huang of a significant number of texts[32] that originated in the Szechwan area is proof that there was a developed intercourse between these two westernmost parts of China during the T'ang period. The partially Szechwanese orientation of Tun-huang culture can be demonstrated by examination of certain manuscripts. For example, one of the *Vimalakīrti sūtra* lecture manuscripts (P2292) was ostensibly written in Szechwan and then taken to Tun-huang.[33] And the 8th line of P2721, a T'ang "textbook for children,"[34] asks "What are the names of the 'three rivers' 三川?" [Answer:] "The Ch'in 秦川, the Lo 洛川, and the Shu 蜀川." To anyone familiar with traditional Chinese geography, this must seem a rather strange answer. For China as a whole, the "three rivers" always referred to geographical features around Sian or in Central China. The list of three rivers given here, however, would be meaningful only for someone primarily familiar with the Tun-huang and Szechwan regions, for they encompass an area roughly comprising the eastern part of Kansu, central Shensi, and the northern part of Szechwan. They constitute what I would like to refer to as the cultural "catchment basin" represented in a majority of Tun-huang manuscripts.[35]

The Tun-huang story of the Taoist wizard Yeh Ching-neng is full of references to Szechwan (T223ff.). In the "Introduction" to my *Tun-huang Popular Narratives*, I discuss the Szechwan connection in some detail, particularly as it relates to the story of Wu Tzu-hsu. In T alone, Szechwan is often mentioned (for example, T267.11, 420.3, and 422.8).

References to Szechwan are also frequent in the random groups of practice characters which are found scattered over the Tun-huang manuscripts. On P2249v, for example, all in one vertical line we read "Eulogized by Tsang-ch'uan [Tibet-Szechwan?], greatly compassionate śramaṇa [monk] of Ch'eng-tu prefecture. The Tathāgata approaches." 成都府大慈沙門 藏川述讚如來臨. This is followed by more practice at writing titles, including those of textbooks for children such as *Family Teachings of the Grand Duke* 太公家教 and *Important Instructions for Beginning Students* 開蒙要訓. A volume of the letters of "Brahmacārin" Wang 王梵志 is also mentioned.[36]

Recognition of the Tun-huang-Szechwan region as an area of cultural coherence may help in the solution of certain problems in the history of art and literature. For example, it was in these two places that the earliest surviving lyric verse (*tz'u* 詞) was created. And the resemblances between the narrative sculpture of Ta-tsu in Szechwan and the narrative wall-paintings of the Caves of the Thousand Buddhas merit further scrutiny. The whole question of regional cultures in China has barely been broached except by Eberhard for the southeast.

chapter two

The Corpus of *Pien-wen* and Related Genres

Our primary task is to delimit the corpus of *pien-wen*. In order to do so, we must first distinguish it from other genres of popular literature that were discovered at Tun-huang and that were current during the T'ang period.

The chaotic state of Tun-huang literary studies is reflected in one scholar's list[1] of synonyms for *pien-wen*: "Buddhist cantos" (*Fo-ch'ü* 佛曲), "sung texts" (*ch'ang-wen* 唱文), "prosimetric texts" (*chiang-ch'ang wen* 講唱文), "tales of conditional origins" (*yuan-ch'i* 緣起), "popular lectures" (*su-chiang* 俗講), "turning" or "warbling" (*chuan* 轉), and "singing" (*ch'ang* 唱). Aside from the fact that fewer than half of these terms can be validated as contemporaneous designations for T'ang literary genres of any sort, they certainly cannot all be said to mean the same thing as *pien-wen*. To use the term *pien-wen* in such an imprecise and inclusive way is strictly a modern proclivity.

Another unworkably broad categorization of *pien-wen* maintains[2] that "sūtra lectures" (*chiang-ching-wen* 講經文), "lyric texts" (*tz'u-wen* 詞文), "tales of conditional origins" (*yuan*[*-ch'i*] 緣 [起]), "rhapsodies" (*fu* 賦), "notes" (*chi* 記), "talks" (*hua* 話), "accounts" (*chuan* 傳), and "story roots" (*hua-pen* 話本) are all subcategories within it! Surely it defies all logic to assert that, as a group, these terms have any other relationship than the fact that some of them designate types of popular literature which were found at Tun-huang and are mostly Buddhist in inspiration. This information alone is of little value to the literary historian.

One of the main reasons for this terminological morass has been the tendency of scholars to include in the *pien-wen* category many other genres of popular literature simply because they were discovered at Tun-huang. This ignores the fact that there was a rich variety of literary forms current at Tun-huang during the T'ang and Five Dynasties periods. It serves no worthwhile purpose to lump them all together under the heading *pien-wen*, just as it would not make good sense to call all of the paintings from Tun-huang *pien-hsiang* 變相. Indeed, the term *pien-wen* points to an even more specific and identifiable corpus than does *pien-hsiang*.[3] The challenge we face is to determine, by observation, the identifying characteristics of *pien-wen* that will allow us to distinguish it from other genres of Tun-huang popular literature. Before this is accomplished, and so long as the nomenclature for various Tun-huang literary genres remains in such utter chaos, it will be impossible to discuss their interrelationships meaningfully.

The situation in which scholars of Tun-huang literature find themselves is one where there is not even a modicum of consensus on the basic issue of how many extant transformation texts there are. Jen Erh-pei[4] speaks of there being close to 100 *pien-wen*. Kanaoka Shōkō says that there are 100 to 130, Chou Shao-liang 127.[5] In their prefatory notes (敍例, p. 1) to T (*Tun-huang pien-wen chi*), the editors state that they consider *Record on Researches into Spirits* 搜神記[6] and *Biographies of Filial Sons* 孝子傳 to contain basic material for *pien-wen*. This implies that they hold the other 177 manuscripts collected in T under 76 titles to be, in some sense, *pien-wen* proper. One scholar has recently mentioned[7] that there are 8,102 *pien-wen* in the British Museum alone! He has obviously defined *pien-wen* as "any manuscript recovered from Tun-huang." A definition of this nature allows for such undiscriminatingly broad inclusion that it is unusable and, hence, meaningless. Until this sort of fundamental issue is clarified—whether there are 80 or 800 or 8000 *pien-wen*—rational discourse on the subject is well-nigh impossible.

Probably the first scholar to declare his dissatisfaction with the terminological morass into which *pien-wen* had sunk so deeply was Umezu Jirō in 1955.[8] Although he was severely handicapped by the paucity of published materials when he began his studies, Umezu nonetheless managed to make a number of valuable contributions to Tun-huang studies, chief among them being his insistence that no untitled Tun-huang text should be designated a *pien-wen* unless it displayed certain basic features, such as an obvious relationship to pictures. A little more than ten years before, Hsiang Ta, in his "T'ang-tai su-chiang k'ao" [An examination of the popular lectures of the T'ang period], had already distinguished the basic features of *chiang-ching-wen* ("sūtra lectures") and had clearly seen that *pien-wen* and *ya-tso-wen* 押座文 ("seat-settling texts") should be viewed as separate entities. Unfortunately, this auspicious beginning seems to have gone unheeded during the intervening years.

More recently, however, some scholars have shown an increasingly acute awareness of the problem. Among others, Chou Shao-liang has made a plea for clearer delineations of the various genres of popular literature during the T'ang period.[9] He maintains,[10] for example, that the Tun-huang story of Wu Tzu-hsu should not be considered a *pien-wen*. Though his reasoning differs from my own objections to designating that and similar texts as *pien-wen*, I agree with him wholeheartedly in decrying the imprecision with which stories are often fitted to genres. Hrdličkova, too, has noted this deficiency: "Above all, it has not yet been laid down with precision which of the large body of Tun-huang texts can really be called *pien-wen*, nor has the exact and exhaustive definition of this literary genre been so far formulated."[11]

Chiang Po-ch'ien takes the extreme position that we have no way of knowing what *pien-wen* means; nor do we have the information to determine whether it was a commonly recognized term during the T'ang and Five Dynasties periods.[12] The situation is not quite so hopeless as that, but Chiang's cautionary attitude is welcome in the face of the usual indulgent application of the term.

As an example of the confused state in which Tun-huang literature studies find themselves, let us examine the "Story of Catch-Tiger Han" (S2144). Its inclusion in T and scholarly discourse in general imply that it is a type of *pien-wen*. Although the manuscript lacks any title, this story is commonly referred to as a *hua-pen* ("story root" 韓擒虎話本).[13] This is unfortunate, first, because it is well known that the term *hua-pen* is itself among the most problematic of designations employed in the study of Chinese popular literature and, second, to the extent that calling the story in question a *hua-pen* implies anything, it suggests a generic relationship to the indeterminate corpus of Sung and Yuan vernacular stories that goes by that name. This assumption is so patently suspect that it scarcely deserves discussion. The genesis of this designation of the Catch-Tiger Han story as a *hua-pen*, however, is curious. The reasoning behind it is actually quite transparent. At the end of the story, we find this sentence: "Since the illustrated booklet [homonymous with *hua-pen*] has come to an end, [the text] as well is no longer transcribed" 畫本既終, 並無抄略.[14] The copyist had simply decided not to write down any more of the text because he had reached the final illustration. The accompanying illustrations to which he refers were most likely in a separate booklet (as they are described in the scene from the *Tale of Genji* where Ukon and Nakanokimi comfort Ukifune)[15] or, less probably, at the top of the pages of the text from which the copyist was working. Hence there is no authority for identifying the Tun-huang story about Catch-Tiger Han as a *pien-wen* or as a *hua-pen*.

The carelessness with which some modern scholars have named various works of Tun-huang literature is conspicuous in the circumstance where a piece that—except for a closing eulogy supposedly composed by Hsuan-tsung 玄宗—is entirely prose (the account of Chang Ling 張令 and the wizard, Yeh Ching-neng: S6836; T216–228) has been styled a "poem." It should be obvious that the end-title of the manuscript "Yeh Ching-neng shih" 葉淨能詩 refers only to the poem that appears at the end of the tale. The inclusion in T of the story of the wizard Yeh Ching-neng implies that it too is a *pien-wen*, a claim impossible to substantiate. The same is true of many other texts in T, but I shall not discuss each individually. Our task is to establish a positive set of standards by which to determine what can be classed as *pien-wen*, rather than to reject specific texts on a case-by-case basis.

To attack this nomenclatural problem, we might begin by saying that there are presently operative at least five different definitions of *pien-wen*, which result in corpora of five different orders of magnitude. These I shall call "the narrowest definition," "the narrow definition," "the broad definition," "the broadest definition," and "the meaninglessly broad definition." Starting with the last, we may say that it is a definition that embraces all manuscripts discovered at Tun-huang. Without further ado, we should discard it forever!

A "broadest definition" of *pien-wen* includes any and all non-canonical, non-classical, non-documentary[16] texts discovered at Tun-huang. In short, such a definition declares that any work of popular literature, be it prose or poetry or a combination of both, be it narrative or descriptive or lyrical, should be considered a *pien-wen*. Since there is no conceivable justification for such a definition and since adherence to it would seriously impede the scientific study of Chinese popular literature, it should likewise be discarded.

We must exercise careful judgement in criticizing the "broad definition" of *pien-wen*, for many responsible scholars have subscribed to it in the past. The broad definition of *pien-wen* comprises any and all narrative popular literature from Tun-huang even if written entirely in verse,[17] plus popular religious expositions such as "seat-settling texts" (*ya-tso-wen* 押座文), *chiang-ching-wen*, *yuan-ch'i*, and, in some cases, "hymns" (*sung* 頌), "eulogies" (*tsan* 讚), and suites of "cantos" (*ch'ü* 曲) as well. Throughout his book of studies on Tun-huang lyrical airs, Jen Erh-pei uses the terms *pien* and *pien-wen* loosely to apply to a variety of grouped or linked verse. Surprisingly, Jen's usage is quite conscious in that he is aware of the difficulties involved: "The meaning of *pien-wen* has still not been clarified. My opinion is that there is nothing wrong with approaching the term strictly as a literary form: 'Anything which tells a story and is composed of a combination of a variety of different verse forms and spoken language, and which is for the use of a prosimetric performer (*chiang-ch'ang-che* 講唱者) may be viewed as *pien-wen*.'"[18] Jen goes on to enumerate some of the many genres of Tun-huang literature that he believes fall under the rubric of *pien-wen*, such as *ya-tso-wen* and *yuan-ch'i*. For Jen, *pien-wen* is a basic literary form (*t'i* 體) and there are numerous applications (*yung* 用) of that form. He specifically warns his readers that it would be "obviously committing the error of being too literal-minded" if the designation *pien-wen* were restricted only to those pieces that contain it in their titles. I am not entirely convinced of the danger of such literal-mindedness, particularly when faced with the massive confusion resulting from the uncritical attitude advocated by Jen. What is the value of a definition of *pien-wen* that includes all narrative literature from Tun-huang, regardless of whether it is in verse, in prose, or is a combination of the two?[19]

The broad definition (or rather *set* of broad definitions) is one which normally results in a corpus of between 60 and 135 texts.[20] The fact that the lower and upper limits of this definition differ so widely renders it suspect and, in the long run, unsatisfactory for studies in Chinese popular literature. One thing must be recognized in regard to the broad definition of *pien-wen*: While it has a certain limited application as a tool for literary analysis, it is purely a modern scholarly convention that has no relationship whatsoever to actual T'ang and Five Dynasties usage.

A narrow definition of *pien-wen*, which I hold ultimately to be the only truly workable one, is arrived at by an attempt to understand what contemporary users of the term meant by it.

The narrow definition, the content of which I shall give detailed specifications for in the remainder of this chapter and in the following chapter, results in a corpus of less than 20 extant *pien-wen* manuscripts.[21] The majority of these texts are specifically entitled *pien* or *pien-wen* on the manuscripts.[22] A few others are included because they share certain recognizable formal characteristics with the majority of titled *pien* and *pien-wen*. There are several literary pieces from Tun-huang that have the word *pien* in their titles but that do not share the set of formal characteristics. A "narrowest definition" of *pien-wen* would exclude these pieces. A more tolerant, yet still narrow, definition would include them—but no others unless the word *pien* occurs in their titles.

Of all the Tun-huang popular literary texts, none more clearly qualifies as a *pien-wen* than that relating Mahāmaudgalyāyana's rescue of his mother from the dark regions (hell). This is a text for which there exist multiple related copies, most of which include titles specifying the work as a *pien-wen*. The following is a list of the relevant manuscripts and titles:

S2614 *Ta-mu-ch'ien-lien ming-chien chiu-mu pien-wen ping t'u i chüan ping hsü* 大目乾連冥間救母變文并圖一卷并序 (head title)[23] *Ta-mu-chien-lien pien-wen i chüan* 大目犍連變文一卷 (end title).

P3107 *Ta-mu-ch'ien-lien ming-chien chiu-mu pien-wen i chüan ping hsu* 大目乾連冥間救母變文一卷并序 (head title).

P2319 *Ta-mu-ch'ien-lien ming-chien chiu-mu pien-wen i chüan* 大目乾連冥間救母變文一卷(head title).

Ta-mu-chien-lien pien-wen i chüan 大目犍連變文一卷 (end title).

P3485 *Mu-lien pien-wen* 目連變文 (head title).

PK876 *Ta-mu-chien-lien pien-wen i chüan* 大目犍連變文一卷 (end title).

It would be incorrect to refer to the account of Maudgalyayana on PK2496 (T756–759; T[a]735–738) as a transformation text in the narrow sense since it lacks the characteristic verse-introductory formula[24] and, in many respects, more nearly resembles the anomalous "Eight Aspects *pien*" (PK3024) and "Destruction of the Transformations of Demons" (P2187).[25]

Careful examination of these transformation texts on Maudgalyāyana reveals certain specific and consistently employed identifying characteristics. Chief among these are: a unique verse-introductory (or pre-verse) formula, an episodic narrative progression, homogeneity of language, an implicit or explicit relationship to illustrations, and prosimetric structure. I shall discuss each of these identifying characteristics at greater length in succeeding chapters.

S5437 and a Peking University Library manuscript formerly belonging to Shao Hsun-mei 邵洵美 both have as their head titles "Transformation on the Han General Wang Ling" 漢將王陵變. The same title also occurs on the covers of the booklet P3627 (=P3867). P3627.2 further has the following colophon: "Transformation on Wang Ling [and His Role in] the Destruction of Ch'u and the Rise of the Han [Dynasty] in the 8th Year of the Han, One Layout. Inscribed by the Recording Officer Yen Wu-ch'eng[26] on the 16th day of the 8th month of the 4th year of the Heavenly Blessing reign period [1 October 939]." 漢八年楚滅漢興王陵變一鋪. 天福四年八月十六日孔目官閻物成寫記. The text includes the verse-introductory formula.

Another straightforward example is the account of the subduing of demons (S5511 and the copy formerly in Hu Shih's possession [originally a single manuscript]). It has the characteristic progression of the narrative, the ratio of prose to verse, the verse-introductory formula, language, and so forth. Both the head title and the end title read *Hsiang-mo pien-wen i chüan* 降魔變文一卷, but the head title on S4398v reads *Hsiang-mo pien i chüan* 降魔變一卷, which indicates that *pien* and *pien-wen* are interchangeable with regard to written transformation texts.[27] Giles says[28] that the title on S4398v does not seem to relate to what follows. This is because it includes only the introductory section of the text, and it is not apparent from this section of the text what the main theme of the story will be.

Although the Tun-huang prosimetric narrative of Wang Chao-chün 王昭君 (P2553) lacks both head and end titles, it shares the formal characteristics described above. Not only is its language and proportion of prose to verse in perfect accord with certain texts that bear contemporaneous titles or colophons identifying them as *pien-wen*; it also has the verse-introductory formula (T100.15 incorrectly gives 處若爲; the manuscript reads 處若爲陳說). But even more revealing is the clear reference (T100.12) to the setting up of more than one scroll (presumably of illustrations) to accompany the reading of the text. 上卷立鋪畢, 此入下卷. The "first scroll" and the "second scroll" here cannot refer to the literary text itself, which is manifestly on a single scroll. And *p'u* 鋪, of course, is a common designation for a "layout" of a picture or a series of pictures. We can also deduce from this notation that the first picture scroll referred to probably had more than one scene on it, since there is more than one episode preceding this point in the text. Five episodes follow the notation without mention of another picture scroll, so we may assume that the second layout had at least five scenes. Incidentally, the use of pictures here is not proof that the text was meant for performance rather than private reading. We know from the *Genji monogatari* scroll that there were separate picture books to accompany the reading of written texts. The reference to illustrations can also be construed as part of the overall attempt to provide a simulated context for the reader.[29]

The Tun-huang story about Li Ling 李陵 kept in the Peking Library, while it lacks a title, may confidently be referred to as a *pien-wen* because of its similarity in language and, particularly, in form to the majority of texts that bear that designation in titles or colophons on the manuscript. The stories of Chang I-ch'ao 張義潮

(P2962) and Chang Huai-shen 張淮深 (P3451) also fall into this category.

The following group of *pien-wen* satisfy the narrowest definition of the term:

1. "Transformation Text on Mahāmaudgalyāyana's Rescue of His Mother from the Dark Regions." S2614–Inventory 296 (here, and in subsequent lists of manuscripts, the Inventory numbers follow the hyphens), P3107–84, P2319–18, P3485–129, PK876–555, P4988v–223, S3704–319, PK3789–563, PK4085–565. T714–744; T[a]685–716.

The ultimate source for this transformation is *Sūtra of the Sacrificial Feast for Hungry Ghosts Spoken by the Buddha* 佛說盂蘭盆經, of which the authenticity is questioned. That is to say, it is presumably a "forged" text that was not translated from an Indian source. Iwamoto Yutaka's studies of this sūtra show that it may have Central Asian antecedents.

The transformation text relates how young Mu-lien (Maudgalyāyana) goes on a business trip. Not long after his return, his mother passes away. After the customary three years of filial observations, Mu-lien becomes a Buddhist monk. Having through religious practice achieved the fruits of arhatship (sainthood) and relying on the Buddha's supernatural power, Mu-lien is able to go to heaven to see his deceased father. But, when he asks his mother's whereabouts, he discovers that she has been sent to hell for her greed and disrespect shown to monks while she was alive.

Again relying on the Buddha's power, Mu-lien carries out an extensive search for his mother in hell. After witnessing many grisly spectacles of torture and suffering while bravely confronting various ogres and monsters who act as wardens in the underworld, Mu-lien locates his mother in the Avīci hell. Though he knows that his mother is being held in this most forbidding part of hell, it is impossible for him to see her at once because the gates are securely closed to mere mortals.

Yet again, Mu-lien returns to the Buddha for assistance. He is given a staff with which he is able to smash open the doors of the Avīci hell. Once inside, he systematically proceeds from cell to cell in search of his mother. It is only when he reaches the seventh cell that he finally is able to find her and witness the terrible suffering she is undergoing. Deeply troubled, he offers to endure the punishment for his mother, but this is not permitted by the chthonian authorities.

Once again, he beseeches the Buddha, whereupon the latter personally intercedes to obtain the release of all who have been consigned to hell. However, because the sinful karmic burden of Mu-lien's mother is too great, she becomes a hungry ghost. Mu-lien goes to Rājagṛha to beg for food. When he gives the food to his mother, her avarice causes it to burst into flames as she is about to eat it. The same happens when her son tries to help quench her thirst with water from the Ganges.

Mu-lien returns to the Buddha one more time for help. He is advised to stand before a stūpa in the city of Rajagṛha on the 15th day of the 7th month and to make an offering to the souls of hungry ghosts. Only then will their hunger be temporarily quelled. Mu-lien obediently follows the Buddha's instructions but is still disappointed when he attempts to make contact with his mother after she has eaten the sacrificial food for hungry ghosts.

For the last time, Mu-lien goes back to the Buddha and is told that his mother has been transformed into a black dog in Rajagṛha. The only way he can be reunited with her is to stand before a certain stūpa in that city while reciting sūtras for seven days and seven nights. This he does, whereupon his mother finally is turned back into a human being and is ultimately enabled to attain the joys of heaven.

2. "Transformation Text on the Subjugation of Demons." S5511–375 and 593, S4398v–339, P4524–207. T361–389; T[a]113–141.

This transformation text describes the contest of supernatural powers between Śāriputra and Raudrākṣa, the foremost of the six heretical masters. It is based on a story from the 10th fascicle of the *Sūtra of the Wise and the Foolish* 賢愚經, which was compiled by Chinese monks from materials gathered in Khotan.

There is a great Indian kingdom called Śrāvastī whose minister, Sudatta, does not believe in the three jewels of Buddhism. He has an unmarried son for whom he has dispatched an emissary to find a suitable match in another country. The emissary comes to a place where he finds Ānanda, a disciple of the Buddha, begging for food. Just at that moment, a beautiful girl darts out of the house before which Āndanda is begging and bows respectfully to him. The emissary inquires of the neighbors and is informed that she is the daughter of the Prime Minister, Humi.

Later, when Sudatta himself returns to arrange the marriage, he realizes through his acquaintance with Humi, who is a devout believer, the sublime power of the Buddha. The Buddha has his disciple, Śāriputra, return to Śrāvastī with Sudatta. His instructions are to construct a monastery there so that the Buddha might come to preach the law.

Śāriputra and Sudatta search diligently for a suitable site but are unsuccessful until one day they journey to the south of the city and come upon an extraordinarily pure and quiet location. Unfortunately, the land belongs to the Heir Apparent. Sudatta goes to the Heir Apparent and asks him to sell the land. The latter is unwilling to part with such a premium property, but Sudatta tricks him into selling it by convincing him that the area is haunted. The Prince agrees to complete the transaction on condition that the buyer cover the entire ground with gold. Sudatta presents himself as the buyer and, after a certain amount of wrangling, so impresses the Crown Prince with his devotion that the latter actually helps him to decorate the garden.

On their return from the garden, Sudatta and the Prince encounter the six (heretical—to the Buddhists) masters. They are upset that the Crown Prince has fallen under the influence of the Buddhists and complain to the King of Sudatta's role in what they see as a plot against the realm. The King has Sudatta and the Crown Prince brought before him. Sudatta takes advantage of the opportunity to praise the Buddha, whereupon the King asks him whether the Buddha is a match for the six masters? Sudatta replies that even the least of the Buddha's disciples can stand up to them.

The King then authorizes a contest of magical powers between Śāriputra and Raudrākṣa, the chief of the six masters, declaring that Sudatta will forfeit his life if Raudrākṣa wins. But if Śāriputra wins, the King avers that he will convert to Buddhism. This sets the stage for the exciting and vividly described contest between Śāriputra and Raudrākṣa.

After half a dozen of his best creations are destroyed by Śāriputra's transformational manifestations, Raudrākṣa admits defeat. The story ends happily with everyone, including the six masters, acquiescing in the superiority of the Buddha's power.

3. "Transformation on the Han General, Wang Ling." S5437–367, P3627 (P3667)–147, Inventory 590 and 599. T36–47; T[a]875–886.

The basis for this tale is a brief account of approximately 80 tetragraphs taken from the biography of Wang Ling in fascicle 40 of the *History of the Han Dynasty* (*Han shu*, 40.460b). The author of the transformation text has expanded this into a story that is approximately fifty times the length of the original.

The transformation text relates how the Ch'u armies of Hsiang Yü 項羽 have repeatedly defeated the Han armies of Liu Pang 劉邦. Two adherents of Liu Pang, Wang Ling and Kuan Ying 灌嬰, request permission to make a surprise attack on the enemy camp. This they do with a small party under cover of night and succeed in killing 50,000 of the Ch'u troops and wounding 200,000. Hsiang Yü is enraged and asks his advisers to come up with a plan for retaliation. He adopts the proposal of Chung-li Mo 鍾離末, which is to go to Wang Ling's hometown of Tea City (Ch'a-ch'eng) 茶城 in Sui-chou 綏州 to arrest Wang Ling and, if he cannot be found there, to bring back his mother.

Wang Ling's mother is thus brought to the Ch'u encampment where Hsiang Yü orders her to summon her son, but she refuses. She is then tortured. In the meantime, Liu Pang wishes to send a dispatch to Hsiang Yü, partly out of curiosity to learn Hsiang Yü's reaction to the surprise attack of Wang Ling and Kuan Ying. A clever messenger by the name of Lu Wan 盧綰 takes the dispatch to the Ch'u encampment and discovers that Wang Ling's mother is being held there. When he returns to the Han encampment, he reports this to Liu Pang who, in turn, informs Wang Ling. Wang Ling requests that Lu Wan be permitted to go back with him to the Ch'u camp to seek the release of his mother.

Upon reaching the dividing line between the two armies, Wang Ling has Lu Wan enter the Ch'u camp first by himself. When Wang Ling's mother hears that Lu Wan has returned, she is afraid Wang Ling will soon come too. So she falsely promises to write a letter summoning her son. This delights Hsiang Yü and he lends her his sword when she asks for it. She does this under the pretense of wanting to cut off a lock of her hair to enclose in the letter to her son, supposedly to make it more convincing. Once she gets her hand on the sword, she commits suicide in order to strengthen her son's resolve to serve the Han ruler.

Lu Wan reports the sad news of his mother's death to Wang Ling, who is naturally deeply saddened. When Liu Pang learns of the righteous death of Wang Ling's mother, he orders that elaborate sacrifices be carried out to honor her.

4. [Transformation Text on Wang Chao-chün]. P2553–30. T98–107; T[a]911–920.

This is a version of a very popular legend with a basis in history (*History of the Han Dynasty*, 9.313c). The sorrowful tale of Wang Chao-chün was often recounted in poem, story, and drama both before and after the time when the *pien-wen* was written. The *pien-wen* version occupies an important place in the development of the tale from legendary historical accounts to Yuan and Ming dramatic renditions.

The first scroll of this *pien-wen* relates how the heroine is married off to a Hunnish chieftain as part of a deal to buy peace. Though the chieftain is attentive to her and does everything he can think of to make her happy, she pines for her homeland.

The second scroll tells how the chieftain, upon seeing Chao-chün continually in tears, suggests that she go hunting with him. She ascends a mountain and, as she gazes into the distance, naturally thinks of home. Thereupon she falls prey to an illness from which she is unable to recover. She enjoins the chieftain to report her death to the ruler of China. The chieftain does so and buries her in great splendor.

5. [Transformation Text on Li Ling]. Inventory 587. T85–96, T[a]893–904.

This story ultimately derives from the well-known historical accounts in the *Records of the Grand Historian* (*Shih-chi* 史記), 109.243d and *History of the Han Dynasty*. 54.49c–492b. Li Ling's captivity among the Huns was a favorite topic of Tun-huang authors and was written up in other forms beside the transformation text (for example, T848–850).

Against insuperable odds and after the most dogged resistance, Li Ling is forced to surrender to the Huns. When he realizes there is no more hope, Li Ling tells his remaining subordinates to return to China. They are to report to the Emperor and to his mother that he did his best, that he remains loyal, and that the "barbarian ants" should be guarded against. He himself is too ashamed to face his ruler. His followers argue that there is nothing shameful in having been defeated by a force twenty times the size of his own, especially when his provisions and weapons have been exhausted. Furthermore, he has been beaten only after having killed an enormous number of the Huns. But Li Ling cannot be convinced; he finds it impossible to stand before the Emperor. Burying his valuables and insignia so that they will not fall into the hands of the enemy, he swears that he has not been disloyal to the Chinese ruler.

The foe arrives and Li Ling is escorted to the chieftain's tent. Now that he no longer has any heart to serve the Han Emperor, Li Ling declares that he is willing to shift his allegiance. The chieftain upbraids him for the incursions he has made and mentions the intransigence of Su Wu 蘇武, who has been sent off to a remote place to herd sheep. The chieftain briefly recounts the history of the relationship between the Chinese and his people. In this passage and elsewhere in the text, the author anachronistically includes elements drawn from T'ang experience with the Eastern Turks. In obsequious terms, Li Ling throws himself upon the mercy of the Hunnish chieftain and offers to serve him. The chieftain is impressed with his peculiar combination of humility and bravery and awards him an official position among his advisers and outfits him with a complete set of Hunnish clothing.

Of the 1,000 survivors from Li Ling's army, 400 make it back to the Han court. The Emperor correctly surmises that Li Ling has been captured. He calls before him the historian Ssu-ma Ch'ien 司馬遷 and Li Ling's wife and aged mother. He orders Ssu-ma Ch'ien to determine from the color of the wife's and mother's faces whether Li Ling is alive or dead. Having completed his physiognomical examination, Ssu-ma Ch'ien declares that there is no aura of death on their faces and hence that Li Ling is alive "among the barbarians." The Emperor is outraged that a general of his would surrender to Huns and orders the execution of Li Ling's mother and wife. Recalling the illustrious contributions of Li Ling's grandfather, Li Kuang 李廣, in fighting the Huns, Ssu-ma Ch'ien begs the Emperor for clemency and offers himself as surety. The Emperor thereupon releases the wife and mother.

The next year, China sends a force of 50,000 men under Kung-sun Ao 公孫敖 to seek the release of Li Ling and Su Wu. Among Kung-sun Ao's aides is a general by the name of Li Hsu 李緒 who had once been defeated by the Huns and instructed them in tactics. The results are devastating for Kung-sun Ao, whose forces are decimated by the skillful Hun attack. The Chinese commander asks who is now in charge of tactics in the Hun armies and Li Hsu declares that it is none other than Li Ling. When Kung-sun reports to the Emperor this excuse for his own failure, the Emperor is extremely angry. He has Ssu-ma Ch'ien castrated and Li Ling's wife and mother suffer a bloody execution in the horse-market. The sun and moon dim their light while branches of trees snap and break in sympathy over this injustice.

The following year, an embassy led by Wang Chin-ch'ao 王進朝 is sent to the Huns to determine whether Li Ling is still alive. When Li Ling receives a letter from Wang Chin-ch'ao that confirms the rumors of his mother's death, he is grief-stricken. In a meeting with Wang Chin-ch'ao, he insists that, though he has surrendered to the Huns, in his heart he is still loyal to the Han Emperor. Wang Chin-ch'ao is understanding, but can do nothing to assuage Li Ling's distress. Li Ling reiterates that he surrendered against his will and that it was always his intention to return to China. The transformation text ends with Li Ling's ringing declaration that the Emperor has been unfair to him.[30]

6. [Transformation Text on Chang I-ch'ao]. P2962–70. T114–117, T[a]931–936.

A contemporaneous tale of a local hero, this fragmentary account relates the expulsion of the Tibetans from the area around Tun-huang.

An outstanding feature of this text is the vivid portrayal of the battle scenes. The long pursuit of the fleeing Tibetan soldiers and the triumphal return to Tun-huang of Chang I-ch'ao's army are effectively described. Another episode describes the punishment in the 10th month of 856 by Chang I-ch'ao of bands of Uighurs and Tuyughuns who had been marauding in I-chou 伊州. The final episode of the fragment details the disruption by dissident Uighurs of the attempted investiture of a presumably friendly chieftain by a mission from the T'ang court. A straggler from the mission reports this to Chang I-ch'ao and he prepares to set out in pursuit of the offenders. Before he does so, however, news comes on the 5th day of the 8th month in the year 857 that Uighurs have again attacked I-chou. The text breaks off at this point.

7. [Transformation Text on Chang Huai-shen.] P3451–126. T121–127; T[a]941–947.

Another contemporaneous tale of a local hero, this fragmentary account relates the achievements of Chang Huai-shen, the nephew of Chang I-ch'ao and his successor as leader of the "Returning-to-Righteousness Army." Like the Chang I-ch'ao transformation text, it too emphasizes the fighting spirit of the Chinese troops and their valor in battle.

The tale begins by relating Chang Huai-shen's accomplishments in subduing various Tibetan and Uighur groups in the vicinity of Tun-huang. The Emperor is so impressed with Chang Huai-shen's contributions to the enlargement of Chinese influence that he sends a mission of nine messengers, including three officials of relatively high rank, to thank him for his services. When Chang Huai-shen reads the Emperor's congratulatory letter, he faces east (toward the capital) and weeps with gratitude. Together with the emissaries from the capital, Chang Huai-shen worships an image of Hsuan-tsung 玄宗 (r. 712–756). Though Tun-huang has been cut off from the heartland for more than a hundred years, the local Chinese authorities have kept this portrait as evidence of their loyalty. The emissaries are deeply moved by this evidence of the persistence of Chinese civilization amidst a sea of "barbarians."

> After several days of banqueting and celebrating, the mission must return to the capital. But no sooner have the emissaries left the area than the Uighurs revolt. Like ants, they have gathered by the shores of a lake to the west of Tun-huang called West Paulownia (also mentioned as the site of a military encounter in the Chang I-ch'ao transformation text) and Chang Huai-shen suspects they are getting ready to wreak havoc on the Chinese. He decides to take swift and decisive military action to forestall any such eventuality. After his crack troops inflict much carnage upon the Uighurs, Chang Huai-shen returns triumphantly to Tun-huang. The text ends with a panegyric recounting of Chang Huai-shen's role in reopening the Kansu corridor to Chinese influence.

Among those texts that include the word *pien* in their titles but do not share the formal characteristics of the above works is the "Causal[31] Transformation on a Maiden in the Women's[32] Palace of King Bimbisāra [Named] 'Intends to Create Merit' Who Is Reborn in Heaven for Having Given Her Support to a Stūpa." 頻婆沙羅王后宮綵女功德意供養塔生天因緣變. The text presented by the T editors on T764–769 is actually a composite work. The title and the first third of the account are from S3491v–314 (the middle third is missing) and the last third is from P3051–79. There are several curious features of this text which require mention. First, it begins with the same "seat-settling text" as another text in the same category, the "Destruction of the Transformations of Demons" (P2187–11, T344–345b). Second, the title is repeated in abbreviated form, after the "seat-settling text" and a brief prose bridge in praise of the reigning authorities, as "The Occasion[33] of 'Intends to Create Merit' Being Reborn in Heaven for Having Given Her Support to a Stūpa" 功德意供養塔生天緣 without any mention of *pien* or *pien-wen*. (Compare the *Huan-hsi kuo-wang yuan* discussed below.) Third, the distinctive verse-introductory formula occurs only once (T767.12). Fourth, the verse in the first third is a combination of hexasyllabic and heptasyllabic lines, while that in the final third is a combination of pentasyllabic and heptasyllabic lines (typical of the majority of *pien-wen* according to a narrow definition). Fifth, the first part bears fewer vestigial marks of descent from oral narrative than does the final part. On the basis of all these features, I would refer to this work—certainly as assembled by the T editors—as a "mixed" or "hybrid" transformation text. Even the final one-third (from P3051) does not share all of the formal characteristics.

Except for two short poems,[34] the Tun-huang story of the extreme filial piety of the legendary Shun as a boy is written entirely in prose. Unless one assumes that the verse has simply been omitted,[35] this poses problems for a definition of *pien* or *pien-wen* that specifies the prosimetric form as an essential characteristic. The two manuscripts, S4654–354 and P2721–52, respectively, have a head title and an end title which identify the story as *Shun-tzu pien i chüan* 舜子變一卷 and *Shun-tzu chih-hsiao pien-wen i chüan* 舜子至孝變文一卷. The text also lacks the pre-verse formula and any other implicit or ostensible references to illustrations. The language and style resemble less those of the majority of works I have been considering than they do those of the wholly prose narratives such as the story of Ch'iu Hu 秋胡 and Hui-yuan 惠遠 (this latter is simply designated on the manuscript [S2073–283] as a "Tale [*hua*] of the Honorable [Hui-]yuan of Lu Mountain" 廬山遠公話).[36] The Shun-tzu text differs so radically from the first group of *pien-wen*, in fact, that we are tempted to declare either that it constitutes a case of mislabeling or that it represents a loose usage of the term.[37]

On both P3645–150 and S5547–382, the story of the Crown Prince of the Liu house during the Former Han dynasty carries the actual head title 前漢劉家太子傳. This title also occurs later on P3645.[38] The designation as *chuan* 傳 seems proper, since this is a wholly prose account of certain events surrounding the fall of the Western Han dynasty at the hands of Wang Mang 王莽. Yet, *after* several marginally related anecdotes,[39] an end title[40] is given on P3645 (劉家太子變一卷) which identifies it as a *pien*. Here, too, we are dealing with an apparently loose application of the term.[41]

Another text of this type deals with the eight aspects[42] of the Buddha's life. On the back of PK3024–560 (the text occurs on the front and in a seemingly different hand) are written the three characters *pa-hsiang pien* 八相變. In spite of the reassurances of the T editors (T342n1), I am suspicious of the authenticity of such titles written alone on the backs of scrolls.[43] It should be noted that the author himself, in a discussion of the title of his work, does not refer to it as a *pien* (T342.5). The rather cryptic reference reads as follows: "I have just[44] spoken to you the 'Eight Manifestations of the Tathāgata' 如來八相[45] but could not exhaust its sources during the 3rd month[46] of autumn. Roughly according to the title, I have revealed the subject and set forth its main points." The remainder of the writing on the manuscript is a clear reference to a particular session at which this text was delivered (the sun is setting in the west, the good audience has been seated for a long time, and so forth). Even assuming that the three characters on the verso are actually contemporaneous with the text on the recto, we can only say that this text represents an unusual variant of the *pien* genre. Like the abbreviated Maudgalyāyana transformation text (P2319), it frequently resorts to the formula "and so on and so forth" 云云. It is also prosimetric, but the verse portions give the impression of being greatly shortened. The usual verse-introductory formula in this text is "At that time, what words did he say?" 當爾之時, 道何言語, or the temporal phrase alone. This indicates an affinity with *avadāna* and *nidāna*[47] rather than the first list of *pien-wen*.

Similar to the so-called "Eight Aspects *pien*" on PK3024 is the "Destruction of the Transformations of Demons" 破魔變一卷 (end title) on P2187–11. Its head title reads "Seat-Settling Text for the Defeat of the Transformations of Demons" 降魔變[48] 押座文. We may discount the significance of the head title at once because it refers only to the opening section and not to the main text.[49] Though the verse is not so compressed, it too occasionally invokes the formula for abbreviation 云云. Likewise, its usual verse introductory formula is "At that time, what words did he say?" or variations thereof. A most intriguing feature of this work is that it is a veritable hybrid combining the dramatic and narrative modes. On the one hand, we frequently encounter such tags as "the damsel" and "the Buddha" followed by direct discourse (usually in verse), as though this text were meant to serve as the script of a play. On the other hand, the voice of the storyteller persona is prominent in the prose sections.[50]

It would appear that, thus far in our examination of the *pien-wen* corpus, we are dealing with two separate groups of texts. The first group of 7 texts (20 manuscripts) fits a tighter or narrower definition which includes the following elements: a specific verse-introductory formula, a connection with picture storytelling,[51] prosimetric form, heptasyllabic verse, vernacular language, and so forth. About half of the 20 manuscripts in this group bear titles that identify these stories as *pien* or *pien-wen*. In the second group of 5 texts (8 manuscripts), each lacks one or more of the above elements. At the same time, at least one manuscript for each of the 5 texts is designated as a *pien* or *pien-wen*, although most of these designations are questionable owing to their placement on the manuscript, the fact that there are alternative titles, or for some other reason. The first, larger group is coherent and distinctive; the second, smaller group consists of texts that share no common features aside from being labeled (albeit problematically) as *pien* or *pien-wen*. Given these circumstances and the limited data available to us, it would seem that the safest procedure is to accept the narrow set of criteria that applies to the first group as constituting an operating definition for transformation texts. Even though it may be argued that the term *pien-wen* also applies a bit more widely for one reason or another, the narrow definition is a useful working tool for purpose of description and analysis.

We may now turn to examine a number of other texts that have been mistakenly identified as *pien-wen*, if we follow this operating definition. The Tun-huang version of the Tung Yung 董永 story (S2204) is written almost[52] entirely in heptasyllabic verse. The T editors suggest (T113n1) that, because of the strangely disjointed nature (see, for example, T111.2–3) of the text, the prose sections have been omitted from what may have originally been a prosimetric narrative. The language is also comparable to the verse portions of the works that fit the operating definition. However, since the manuscript shows on connection with and makes no reference (implicit or otherwise) to pictures, it cannot—as it now stands—properly be called a *pien-wen*.

The lack of the characteristic verse-introductory formula, the occasional employment of verse other than heptasyllabic, the relatively more polished style, the higher proportion of prose (for example, T17.1–19.5 and the long section from T25.5 to the end), and the comparatively frequent literary allusions (see the annotations to my translation in *Tun-huang Popular Narratives*) all disbar the Tun-huang story of Wu Tzu-hsu (P3213–100, S6331–428, S328–241, and P2794–56) from qualification as a *pien-wen*[53] according to our working definition.

The Tun-huang prosimetric story of Meng Chiang-nü 孟姜女 (P5039–231), which lacks both head and end titles, in diction, style, form, and tone is similar to the Wu Tzu-hsu story. It should not, by any narrow definition of the genre, be referred to as a *pien-wen*.

The story of the apprehension of Chi Pu 季布 for his tirade against Liu Pang 劉邦, which the T editors label (T51.1) a *chuan-wen* 傳文, should probably better be referred to as a "lyric text" (*tz'u-wen* 詞文). The basis for the T editors' designation—although they nowhere specify this—is probably S5441–370, which carries the head title "Text of the Story of the Capture of Chi Pu in One Scroll" 捉季布傳文一卷. S5439–368 is a booklet with the end titles "Song of Chi Pu in One Scroll" 季布歌一卷 and "Song of Chi Pu" 季布歌. This alone makes clear that it is a song and not a prosimetric narrative. The contemporary designation applied to it on several of the manuscripts (S2056v–282 [head title], P3386–118 [end title], P3697–157 [subtitle], and so forth; cf. T51.2 and 71.5) is *tz'u-wen*. The author actually refers to himself as a "lyricist" (*tz'u-jen* 詞人) at the end of the piece (T71.3). Given these contemporary references to the work as belonging to the genre of *tz'u-wen*, plus the fact that it is written entirely in verse (virtually[54] all heptasyllabic), there is little justification for designating it as a *pien-wen*.

Other texts that have been misrepresented as *pien-wen* are: the brief story of the Crown Prince's attainment of the Way on P3496–132 and PK8579–585 (primarily in verse with prose headings beginning "at that time" used to introduce the *gāthās* [see T317–318]), and different portions of the same story on S4480v–345, S4128–330, S4633–352, S3096 (all entirely in prose, see T320ff);[55] PK833 (T761–762), an incredibly powerful expression of purgatorial regret for misdeeds while living in which a *preta* ("hungry ghost") flogs its own corpse; the fragmentary text on P3128–87 that is unmistakably related both to the class of texts that use the formula "What words did he say?" (see T814.10 and 815.1: 道個甚言語也) and that ends with the lecturer exhorting his auditors to "come back early to listen the next morning when they hear the bell"; a fragmentary Taoistic piece on sickness and death (S4327–

337; T817); and a piece, wholly in prose, about a monk named Shan-hui (善惠 Sādhumatī [?]) (S3050–308; T819–820).[56]

There are also several other Tun-huang genres that have been confused with *pien-wen*. The most important is that of sūtra lectures (*chiang-ching-wen* 講經文). I have argued elsewhere[57] on the necessity of and means for separating these two genres. Neither should be considered a subdivision of the other. Not only do they have strikingly different forms; their social and performance contexts are quite dissimilar.

The characteristics of the Tun-huang popular religious literary genre known as *yuan-ch'i* are determinable because at least one manuscript (P2193–12) exists with this designation in the title, the *Maudgalyāyana yuan-ch'i* 目連緣起. It is more overtly moralistic than *pien-wen* and lacks the verse-introductory formula. Su Ying-hui states[58] that *pien-wen* are amplifications of *yuan-ch'i* but offers no evidence to support this claim. *Yuan-ch'i* means "(tale of) conditional origin," "conditional causation," "co-dependent origination," or "conditioned co-arising." The Chinese expression derives from Sanskrit *pratītya-samutpanna*, *pratītya-samutpāda*, *pratyayaudbhava*, and so forth. As literary genres, these texts are more properly referred to as *avadāna* and *nidāna*.[59]

From the ending of the "Maudgalyāyana *Nidāna*" (P2193), we know that this type of popular religious narrative was presented on the day before a sūtra lecture:

> Today I've proclaimed for you this matter,
> Come early tomorrow morning to hear the real sūtra.[60]

This interpretation is reinforced by the ending of another, untitled, *avadāna* or *nidāna*:

> Stand before the steps with your palms joined together and take a *gāthā*,
> Tomorrow when you hear the bell, come early to listen.[61]

What the preacher might say the next morning during the reading of the seat-settling text and before the actual sūtra lecture is something like this:

This morning I intend to speak on this profound sūtra;
I only wish that compassion will visit us here,
So that the sins of the audience who listen to the sūtra will be wiped clean.[62]

Similar to the *yuan-ch'i* but more like certain sūtra lectures than like *pien-wen* is a text designated on the manuscript (split into a fragment formerly owned by Lo Chen-yü and P3375v–115) as a *yuan* ("occasion," *pratyaya*). This is the "*Nidāna* on the King of Abhirati" 歡喜國王緣 (end title, T780.14). It is noteworthy that the same musical notations that mark the verse portions of this text ("cantillate" [*yin* 吟], "slant" [*ts'e* 側], "break" [*tuan* 斷], and so on)[63] also occur in one of the lectures on the *Vimalakīrti sūtra* (formerly in the possession of Lo Chen-yü-588, T634ff).

Another text with the same musical or prosodic notations is the "Autumn Cantillation, One Text" 秋吟一本. The prose portions occupy a minor percentage of this piece which is rather more descriptive than narrative. In regard to the possible significance of the notations, it should be remarked that there are repeated references in this piece to *gāthā* (偈 "stanzas") and *stotra* (讚 "eulogies"), and that it is immediately preceded on the manuscript (P3618–144) by a Sanskritic hymn.[64]. Hence, one possible assumption to be made is that the notations are expressive of certain types of Indic psalmody as rendered in the Chinese language. The respectful references in Tun-huang popular religious texts to "Brahmanic sounds" 梵音 / 語云 are frequent (for example, T504.7, 605.2, 646.2, 652.4, and so on). It would seem that the Buddhist community there and elsewhere[65] considered it a sacred language and sought to mimic its intonations.

There can be no doubt that portions of sūtra lecture services were sung. Ryūkoku 龍谷 University manuscript 021.1–26.1, which has as its actual title "Causation and Occasion (Skt. *hetupratyaya*, *nidāna*, or *avadāna*) of Prince Siddhārta's Cultivation of the Way" 悉達太子修道因緣 is a case in point.[66] It is interesting to observe, in regard to the musical qualities of popular lectures, that the following note is set off from the rest of the text almost as though it were a series of directions:

In any event, the Master of the Law who gives lectures and holds discussions is rather like a music official 樂官. Each time, he must modulate the tunes to be used with lyrics 調置曲詞. That which he pronounced just now was the "Prince Siddhartha Seat-Settling Text." Let us watch as the Master of the Law explains the meaning.[67]

The musical ability of the assistant to the sūtra lecturer is brought out in the following portion of a lecture on the *Amitābha-sūtra* (P2955–69):

> The cantor-*ācārya*[68] is a man of great virtue,
> His tones are clear and he can modulate them;
> With a pleasant sound, he descants gracefully in the *kung* and *shang* modes,
> Now I request him to sing aloud [the next passage from the sūtra].[69]

Note that there is also every likelihood that the verse portions of the oral antecedents of *pien-wen* were also sung in performance. All the evidence provided by other Asian analogues and by study of later historical developments deriving from *pien-wen* points to this conclusion. It is well-known that heptasyllabic verse,[70] which is the typical *pien-wen* verse length, may be readily sung to canto (*ch'ü*) and lyric meters (*tz'u*) by using such techniques as padding words, repetition of syllables, and so on.

A key text for understanding the relationships among the various popular Buddhist literary genres designated as *pien*, *yuan*, *yin-yuan*, and *yuan-ch'i* is the series of related manuscripts (S4511–347, P3048–78, S2114v–286, P3592–139, and P2945v–68) which present the story of the ugly girl who, because of her faith in the Buddha, is transformed into a beautiful woman. In form, the text as assembled by the T editors (T787–800) has a strong resemblance to the so-called "Eight Aspects *pien*" and the "Destruction of the Transformations of Demons" discussed above. All three texts employ the verse-introductory formula "At that time, what words did he say?" and the formula for abbreviation 云云. The proportion of verse to prose and the narrative style are also similar. The head title on S4511 is "The Causation and Occasion of Vajrā, the Ugly Girl, One Text" 金剛醜女因緣一本, on S2114 is "The Occasion of the Ugly Girl Vajrā," 醜女金剛緣, and on P3048 is "The Conditional Origin of the Ugly Girl" 醜女緣起. The sources of the Tun-huang story in *The Sūtra of One Hundred Occasions* 百緣經 and *The*

Sūtra of the Treasures of Assorted Jewels 雜寶藏經 are, respectively, entitled "Occasion of the Ugly Daughter of King Prasenajit" 波斯匿王醜女緣 and "Occasion of the Ugly Girl Raktikā (or Retti[?])" 醜女賴提緣.[71] But here the appellation *yuan* ("occasion") is less a literary designation than it is a doctrinal one. Hence, we may observe that, while the Tun-huang stories designated as *yuan* are derived from the sections of the *nidāna* and *avadāna* (metaphorical, illustrative) literature in the Mahāyāna canon dealing with causation, the term itself becomes fixed as a literary designation in Tun-huang usage. The parallels with the doctrinal and literary significations of *pien* are valuable in our attempts to understand how the latter word functions in the milieu of Chinese popular and folk Buddhism.

One last, but important, observation about the Tun-huang story of the ugly girl which needs to be made is that, at the end of P3048, the following six characters are found: 上來所說醜變. Grammatically, this text breaks off in mid-sentence ("The transformation of ugliness which was told above..."). It is, therefore, impossible to construe *pien* here as a generic designation. It refers, rather, quite literally to the miraculous transformation of the ugly girl into a beautiful woman (T798.1ff).

The final category of Tun-huang popular literary texts to be discussed is *ya-tso-wen* 押座文 ("seat-settling text").[72] S2440–293 includes six different seat-settling texts, most with titles positively identifying them as such. All end with a phrase indicating that they are to be followed by the singing, with an attitude of reverence, of the title of the sūtra to be lectured on that day. Thus, it is virtually certain that *ya-tso-wen* were meant primarily to function as a sort of introit for religious services in which the main item was a sūtra lecture. The oral quality of these texts is obvious from such directions as "repeat" 重述 (T830.15), "say aloud 'Bodhisattva Buddhaputra'" 念菩薩佛子 (T829.4), and so forth. The existence of numerous texts of a homogeneous nature and purpose having the designation *ya-tso-wen* is adequate proof that it should be considered as a fixed, discrete genre of T'ang period popular Buddhist literature and not as a subtype of *pien-wen*.

Appendix
On Dating

Most of the dated transformation-text manuscripts bear colophons that place them within the period of the Five Dynasties. These late dates for the copying of the texts, in the majority of cases, have no bearing on the question of when the various transformations themselves were originally composed. The earliest transformation texts are datable by internal evidence to the reign of Emperor Hsuan-tsung (712–756).[73] Several examples of the dating of the Tun-huang popular narratives are given here. A few of the texts mentioned cannot be considered to be *pien-wen* according to either the tight or the more lenient definition of the term. They are included nonetheless because they bear certain affinities with *pien-wen* or have frequently been confused with them.

On the basis of a place name ("the modern Ch'eng-fu district" 今城父縣是也) in the Tun-huang Wu Tzu-hsu story, Hsieh Hai-p'ing dates it to sometime between the years 676 and 712.[74] The latitude of the date indicated by this place-name is actually much greater, namely 636–884 (based on the *Tu shih fang-yü chi yao* [*Essentials of Geography for Reading the Histories*] 讀史方輿紀要). There are other grounds, however, for dating the story to the first quarter of the eighth century.[75] While this may be true of the content of the story in its original recension, stylistically it is a much more mature work and should probably be dated to the late ninth or early tenth century.[76] Hence, I concur with Liu Hsiu-yeh who believes[77] that the Wu Tzu-hsu story—as we now have it—was written later in the T'ang period. The style is rather more literary than the normal transformation text and the story reads somewhat like a classical tale (*ch'uan-ch'i*).

Although the extant copy of the "Transformation Text on the Extreme Filial Piety of Shun as a Boy" was written down during the Five Dynasties period, its composition was probably originally T'ang. This may, in part, be deduced from the list of books therein that the boy Shun was said to have read, a list that is compatible with the curriculum of classical studies during the T'ang. The same conclusions may be drawn regarding the Tun-huang story about Ch'iu Hu.

The "Destruction of the Transformations of Demons" (P2187), in spite of the 944 date in the colophon, must have originally been written during the Later Liang 後梁 (907–923). We can deduce this from the manner in which that dynasty is referred to on T354.13.

Both from their manifestly topical nature and from internal evidence (T115.9, 116.10, 117.2, 124.8ff), the composition of the transformation texts on Chang I-ch'ao and Chang Huai-shen can be dated respectively to not long after approximately 856[78] and 862 (probably sometime between 874 and 880).[79]

The composition of the Wang Chao-chün transformation text is easily datable to approximately 775, since the heroine was given to the "barbarian" chieftain in 33 B.C.[80] and died in 25 B.C. The text mentions (T105.13) that a period of 800 years had elapsed since then.[81] Although we may assume that this is a round number, it does give us a fairly accurate date for the Tun-huang story. The Wang Chao-chün transformation text also contains names of cities and places that were current during the Sui and T'ang. And the relations with the Turks described therein are not so very different from those which existed around the early part of the T'ang.

According to Nicole Vandier-Nicolas, the style of the illustrated scroll of Śāriputra's magic contest with Raudrākṣa (P4524) dates it to the eighth or ninth century.[82] This is in conformity with our expectations of when such a transformation scroll would have been current.

The interested reader should consult Lo Tsung-t'ao, *Tun-huang chiang-ching pien-wen yen-chiu*, Chapter 5, for extensive discussion of the dates of 17 Tun-huang popular literary texts of various types. Kanaoka Shōkō, *Tonkō shutsudo bungaku mokuroku*, provides basic information for each datable manuscript included therein. It should be reiterated as a general caveat for those who deal with Tun-huang texts that date of composition and date of copying are two entirely separate matters. The majority of the dates that are determinable are of copying. In terms of literary history, dates of composition, though harder to establish, are far more important.

In general, we may aver that the narrowly defined group of transformation texts were composed between the first quarter of the eighth century and the third quarter of the ninth century. The more broadly defined list and related texts would stretch this period about a half-century at both ends. Most of the extant manuscripts for both types were copied during the Five Dynasties (roughly the first half of the tenth century).

chapter three

The Meaning of the Term *pien-wen*

The meaning of the character *pien* in *pien-wen*, as distinct from the delineation of the genre, is one of the most refractory problems in the study of Chinese literature. There are almost as many definitions as there are scholars studying the subject. The problem is only exacerbated by the confusion over the corpus of *pien-wen*, as described in the preceding chapter.

There is no point in reviewing systematically all the various scholarly views on the meaning of the word *pien* because this has already been done expertly by Kanaoka,[1] Hrdličková,[2] and Lanciotti.[3] But, in order to reveal certain currently held misconceptions concerning the nature of transformation texts, I shall refer to representative opinions, paying particular attention to explanations not treated in depth by Kanaoka, Hrdličková, and Lanciotti. I wish to emphasize that I mention and discuss these various explanations not for the purpose of minimizing the contributions of their authors but to make clear that the views of earlier scholars have not been overlooked. The meaning of the term *pien-wen* is obviously a very thorny problem. A satisfactory understanding can be arrived at only by taking into account the full range of previous scholarship.

Among the more common explanations of the meaning of *pien* is that it has to do with the *change* from prose to prosimetric form.[4] The most that can be said for such an explanation is that it is simple. A more bizarre explanation belonging to the same school is the assertion that "because it was *changed* (*pien* 變) from oral to written text (*wen-tzu* 文字), it was therefore called a '*changed* text' (*pien-wen* 變文)."[5] One scholar, considering the "change" to have taken place in exactly the opposite direction, refers to *pien-wen* as an "oralization" of a written tale,[6] a view that has no philological basis. A related view maintains that *pien-wen* got its name because it refers to a "change" from one literary form (for example, Buddhist sūtras or historical records) to another (the prosimetric).[7] These texts are also said to be called *pien-wen* because the original sūtras have been changed into popular lectures.[8] Similarly, according to this opinion, *pien-hsiang* are sūtras that have been turned into paintings.

This brings us to the most frequently encountered explanation of *pien-wen*—that it means "popularization." Cheng Chen-to was the first to propose such an interpretation. In his *Illustrated History of Chinese Literature*, Cheng held that "*pien-wen* means almost the same as *yen-i* 演義 ('extended interpretation,' 'historical romance'). That is to say, classical stories were retold and transformed 變化 to make them more easily understood by the people."[9] This is but a rewording of Cheng's earlier interpretation of *pien* as *pien-keng* 變更.[10] As a corollary, *pien-hsiang* would be a form for popularizing the sūtras by changing them into pictures. Elsewhere,[11] however, Cheng seems to be saying something quite different when he declares that *pien-wen* is the proper designation for the alternating style and that sūtra lectures (*chiang-ching-wen*) are a sub-category of it.

Cheng's views have been adopted by the majority of students who have written on the subject.[12] The chaos that such an explanation can lead to is evident in the statement that "'*Pien-wen*' is for the purpose of popularizing the Buddhist sūtras and *changing* (*pien*) them into popular lectures (*su-chiang* 俗講); this is the definition of the word *pien*."[13] *Pien-wen* and *su-chiang* are two separate entities; it is not easy to see how one could have become a part of the other.

Because it is too vague and philologically unsound, the explanation[14] that *pien-wen* are called such because they "evolved" (*yen-pien* 演變) out of the sūtras similarly cannot be accepted. A related (but ultimately incomprehensible) view asserts that *pien-wen* means "the altered form of a text" (文的變體).[15]

It has been suggested that the name *pien-wen* "may derive from the fact that they are made up of alternating verse and prose."[16] But this is impossible because *pien* by itself never means "alternating."

One student makes the far-fetched claim that *pien* ultimately refers to the *change* of Indian Buddhist artistic models into Chinese ones.[17] This causes him to assert that *pien* originally arose in the Northern Wei, a claim for which there is no substantiation.[18].

Falling into what I would call the "evasive school" of explanation are those who translate *pien-wen* into a foreign language but, in doing so, fail to illuminate it accurately. One such scholar says that "technically the Chinese terms means literally, 'changed composition or writing,' indicating a slight deviation in the telling of a story from the version recorded in a Buddhist sutra."[19] The same scholar also referred to *pien-wen* as "revised versions."[20] And another says that "These T'ang texts are so-called *pien-wen*; changed texts, i.e. literary texts rendered in the colloquial language."[21]

One of the most inventive attempts to explain the meaning of *pien-wen* is Lo Tsung-t'ao's assertion[22] that it is derived from a Six Dynasties technical term in music and in poetics that may be rendered roughly as "variation" or "modification."[23] Lo's professed intention in propounding this ingenious explanation is to find a Chinese source for the word. But there are several flaws in his argument, among them the fact that even the musical term cannot be certified to be free of Indian influence. At the least, we must admit that its origins are not well known. Secondly, Lo fails to make any convincing connection between *pien-ko* 變歌 ("modified song") and *pien-wen* other than that they happen to have the same morpheme in their names. Chou I-liang has demonstrated the historical improbability of any connection between these *pien-ko* in the balled tradition and *pien-wen*.[24] Tseng Yung-i has cast further doubt on Lo's argument in a critical article.[25]

Hsiang Ta had earlier made a suggestion similar to Lo Tsung-t'ao's, though not with such conviction.[26] All the poems and ballads that Hsiang cites in support of his suggestion use the word *pien* in a musical sense (for example, the "Tzu-yeh Variation" 子夜變 and the "Joyful Hearing Variation" 歡聞變 preserved in the *Collection of Ballad Poetry* [*Yueh-fu shih-chi* 樂府詩集]). They bear no resemblance, either in content or in structure, to any of the known *pien-wen*. Most of the specific pieces Hsiang refers to are actually nothing more than pentasyllabic quatrains. It is difficult to see how there can be any significant evolutionary relationship between these Six Dynasties "variations" and the T'ang period Buddhist *pien-wen*.

On the basis of one newly proffered bit of evidence, two Soviet scholars have recently once again argued for a purely Chinese meaning for the term *pien-wen*.[27] They cite Kuo P'u's 郭璞 (276–324) gloss on the word *chü-hsu* as it is found in Ssu-ma Hsiang-ju's 司馬相如 (c. 179–117 B.C.) "Rhymeprose on the Imperial Hunt" 天子游獵賦. The gloss reads: 距虛即蛩蛩, 變文互言耳. But surely this usage has no bearing whatsoever on the expression *pien-wen* as it is employed in the titles of T'ang period popular literary texts. N. Egami's serviceable translation should be adequate to establish that the characters as used in Kuo P'u's gloss are functioning in a quite different manner. "The *chü-hsü* is identical with the *ch'iung-ch'iung*, these being different phrases and words used interchangeably."[28] As I shall demonstrate below, only when the Buddhist nuances of *pien* are taken into account can we make full sense of the expressions *pien-wen* and *pien-hsiang*.

Sawada Mizuho maintained that *pien* had something to do with *Jātaka* stories, that is, stories of the Buddha's former lives.[29] His reasoning was that the Buddha had experienced many *changes* in his former existence. I consider this a justifiable connection but an unacceptable explanation of the meaning of the word *pien*.

One writer referred to *pien-wen* as "monastery chants and recitations."[30] This is an inaccurate description because it links these texts too closely to religious establishments. Another has called them "Buddhist narrative poems,"[31] but this is surely wrong because *pien-wen* are not poems.

It has been fashionable, both in French and in English,[32] to refer to *pien-wen* as "chantefables." This is actually not an attempt to render *pien*, but to indicate the narrative form. Nevertheless, because the disadvantages of this common usage are legion, we should perhaps reassess its appropriateness as a means of identifying *pien-wen*. In the first place, there are numerous genres other than *pien-wen* in Chinese literature that might qualify as "chantefables". Second, the French word properly refers to a unique specimen, *Aucassin et Nicolette*, although students of comparative literature have used the expression to designate any work that alternates between verse and prose. Third, the word *chantefable* expresses nothing of the semantic content of *pien*. And, fourth, it fails to convey any idea of the place in the evolution of literary genres occupied by *pien-wen.* We should strive to discover an English equivalent that circumvents all of these drawbacks.

Pelliot's opinion on the meaning of *pien-wen* is worth citing in its entirety for its air of caution and uncertainty:

> I doubt that *pien-wen* is "altered texts." Cf. the meaning of *pien* and *pien-hsiang* for the "scenes" illustrating episodes of Buddhist sutras, and the Japanese use of the term *hengō*[*hensō*?]. The Buddhist use is the most ancient one, and may apply to "episodes" as a transitory aspect of a permanent truth. But I am not prepared to express any positive view on the point. In literature, could not *pien* have finally come to mean the literary form of the tale, a mixture of written and popular language, or of prose and verse? "Altered" seems to be misleading. Could not "changing text" be adopted?[33]

It appears that Pelliot was tentatively on the same path of exegesis as those who erroneously interpret *pien* to mean "alternating [between prose and verse portions]."

Waley's rendering of *pien-wen* as "incident-text,"[34] though helpful in that it directs attention to the content of these stories, is inadequate because it conveys next to nothing of what I shall show to be the strong Buddhist connotations to the term.

De Visser translated *Jōdo hensō* 淨土變相 as "Phases of (Amitābha's) Pure Land."[35] More recently, Crump has referred to *pien* in titles as "episodes" and *pien-wen* as "episode texts."[36] The de Visser and Crump renderings provide some indication of the narrative nature of the paintings and texts concerned but fail to convey what I consider to be the actual semantic content of *pien*

Yü Chien-hua, in his annotations to *A Record of Famous Painters of Successive Dynasties*, says that "to paint a story from the Buddhist sūtras as a picture is called *pien.*"[37] More exact is Acker's commentary on the same text:

> The terms *piēn*[*sic*] 變, *piēn-hsiáng*[*sic*] 變相, *chīng-piēn*[*sic*] 經變 all refer to paintings illustrating the paradises of *particular* Buddhas, *particular* hells, or as in the case of Vimalakīrti some *particular* incident or happening described in a sūtra, all this in contradistinction to the esoteric maṇḍala which is a sort of representation of the whole universe,

its various Buddhas and divinities symbolizing different aspects of existence.[38]

This is in fundamental agreement with my notion that a *pien* is the representation (whether verbal or pictorial or sculptural) of a narrative moment or locus or a succession of narrative moments or loci.

So far as it goes, the formulation that "a *pien-wen* is the text for a *pien-hsiang*"[39] is a correct explanation. But it does not indicate that there is a distinction between oral *pien* and written *pien*[-*wen*]. Nor does this type of circular formulation indicate anything of the Buddhist antecedents of the word *pien* itself.

I consider one of the most convincing interpretations of *pien-wen* to be Paul Demiéville's rendering of *pien* as "scene." This interpretation has the marvelous advantage of being directly applicable both to *pien-wen* ("text of a scene") and to *pien-hsiang* ("figure[s] of a scene"),[40] a mandatory requirement for any explanation of the word. Demiéville's rendering is also highly *visual* in its semantic content, which fits both *pien-wen* and *pien-hsiang* perfectly. The only defect in this rendering is that it does not convey the necessary Buddhist resonance.

A Uighur scholar who is also familiar with Chinese sources, Annemarie von Gabain, holds that *pien-wen* and *pien-hsiang* have a Central Asian origin (we shall see later that there is some validity to this claim). She accurately renders the two terms in German as *Verwandlungsgeschichten* and *Darstellung der Verwandlungen*.[41]

Ono Genmyo, more than seventy years ago, had already provided a valuable discussion[42] of the meaning of *pien* in relation to art. It would appear that few later scholars consulted his work. Naba Toshisada was probably the first to declare[43] that *pien* (more frequently) or *pien-wen* were the records of expanded expositions of paintings that were sung and spoken. This discovery represented a breakthrough in *pien-wen* studies for, as we shall see below in Chapters 4 and 6, it is impossible to understand the true nature of transformations without recognizing their essential relationship to pictures. It was Umezu Jirō who established this relationship irrefutably and gave it a theoretical underpinning. His explanation of *pien* as a Buddhist technical term meaning "a story as shown in some concrete form like a picture"[44] has approximately the same strengths and weaknesses as Demiéville's. Shih Chih-ts'un 施蟄存 was also headed approximately in the right direction when he said[45] that *pien* means "Chinese (?) painting" 國畫 and that it must be a transcription of some foreign word.

One way to think of the term *pien-wen* is that it is an abbreviation of *pien-hsiang chih wen* 變相之文 ("[explanatory] text for a transformation tableau").[46] This is helpfully suggestive because it highlights the crucial relationship between *pien-wen* and *pien-hsiang*. But it is an inadequate interpretation for two major reasons: The definition *pien-hsiang chih wen* is not validated in contemporaneous sources, and it is not provable that any of the extant *pien-wen* were ever actually intended for use in the oral explanation of *pien-hsiang*.[47] The available evidence indicates that they were primarily intended for private reading. The relationship between *pien-wen* and *pien-hsiang*, as we shall see, is far more complicated than that expressed by the formulation *pien-hsiang chih wen*.

To retreat one step further, according to Mochizuki,[48] *pien-hsiang* means *pien-hsien chih hsiang* 變現之相 ("the appearance of manifestation through transformation").[49] While I have not seen it so defined in T'ang texts, this is a useful way of approaching the term. The Sanskrit equivalent of *pien-hsiang* in its original sense ("having a transformed appearance; changed; altered") is *vipariṇata*, for which the Tibetan equivalent is *rnam par gyur ba*.[50] *Pien-hsiang* in the sense of "[artistic] representation of [a supernatural] transformation" is a derivative and more specialized application.

A number of scholars have attempted to interpret *pien* as "strange", not as "transformation". In the opening pages[51] of his article entitled "Miscellaneous Notes from Reading *pien-wen*," Sun K'ai-ti assembled an impressive array of occurrences (dating mostly from the Six Dynasties through the Sung) of the word *pien* where it clearly meant "strange, unusual, extraordinary." He concluded that this was the sense of the word in the terms *pien-wen* and *pien-hsiang*. James J. Y. Liu followed Sun in translating *pien-wen* as "texts of (tales of) the unusual."[52] Liu Ta-chieh has a similar understanding of the term. "*Pien-wen*," he states, "is also abbreviated as *pien*. *Pien* means 'strange'; *pien-wen* thus means the prosimetric recitation of a strange story."[53] And Průšek is in agreement with this view when he renders *pien-wen* as "texts relating strange incidents."[54]

Many strange incidents mentioned in the Buddhist collection of stories called *Pearl Grove in the Garden of Dharma* (*Fa-yuan chu-lin* 法苑珠林) are referred to as such and such a "[miraculous] transformation" (*pien* 變, *pien-hua* 變化, or *shen-pien* 神變).[55] Some of these events were taken from earlier collections such as Kan Pao's 干寶 (fl. 318) *Records of Researches into Spirits* (*Sou-shen chi* 搜神記) but were not there regularly designated as *pien*. Since *Pearl Grove in the Graden of Dharma* was compiled by Tao-shih 道世 in 668, it would seem that around the beginning of the T'ang period Chinese authors were becoming increasingly familiar with *pien* in the sense of "strange incident" (more specifically, "supernatural transformation").

Pien in the sense of "strange" appears to be a post-Buddhist usage, that is, one not encountered until after the entry of Buddhism into China.[56] But more thorough analysis is required before we may declare that *pien-wen* simply means "strange text" or *pien-hsiang* "strange appearance" with no stronger Buddhistic overtones.

It is necessary to recognize, in the first instance, that *pien* in the sense of "unusual" or "strange" is itself an extension of the word in its Buddhist technical sense of "transformation." To lay Chinese unfamiliar with the finer points of technical usage but familiar with basic Buddhist concepts which had been widely disseminated throughout the populace by the middle of the Six Dynasties, it is understandable that supernatural "transformation" or "transmutation" (*nirmāṇa*, *pariṇāma*, *vikāra*, *vikṛti*, and so on) might be interpreted as something "strange." This is especially true considering the widely differing philosophical presuppositions that existed in pre-Buddhist China and in India.[57] In Buddhist philosophy, *pien* may mean the actualization or realization of cognition, hence creative mentation in the most concrete possible sense, or even conjuration. We create the world as we are perceiving it. Confronted with such an alien concept, it is not at all surprising that many Chinese found it "strange." The T'ang *Continued Biographies of Eminent Monks* 續高僧傳 has a curious story about ghosts "producing various transformations" 作諸變現 during the Liang period (502–556). It also refers to their manifestations as "strange transformations" 怪變.[58]

Before the introduction of Buddhism, the word *pien* in the classical Chinese language meant "change," "evolution," "movement," "modification," "alteration," "variation," and, as derivatives of one or another of these meanings, "incident," "disturbance," "eclipse," "rebellion," and so on.[59] It was only after the introduction of Buddhism to China that the character also took on the added meaning of "(supernatural) transformation" and the secondarily derived notion of "strange (event)." Let us examine, now, something of the history of the word *pien*, in order to see how it was adapted to suit the purposes of Buddhism.

The character *pien* seems not to have been found on oracle-bone inscriptions or bronze inscriptions; hence it is of relatively late invention. "The meaning of the drawing is uncertain, but it contains two hanks of silk, and Hsu Shen [許愼, in his etymological dictionary, *Shuo-wen chieh-tzu* 說文解字 (A.D. 100)] said that it meant 'to bring into order,' as in spinning or reeling. The radical, placed below, shows a hand holding a stick, signifying movement, action."[60] Hsu Shen's explanation is most curious, since one of the meanings of the character is "disorder" (that is, "change from the norm"). It is futile, however, to attempt to gain an understanding of the etymology of this character from its shape in the stone inscriptions where it first appears around 320 B.C. For, both then and now, the top part of the character has a primarily phonetic value (Karlgren, *GSR* 178 **blwân*, **bli̯wan*, **mlwan*, **slwan*, **pli̯an*).

In pre-Buddhist usage, according to Manfred Porkert:

> *Hua* 化 denotes a fundamental and essential change—a transformation. However, sometimes one also encounters the word *pien*, denoting external, momentary, or apparent change. A *locus classicus* for this distinction is in the *Kuan-tzu* 管子 49/270:[61] "The exemplary man (*sheng-jen*) changes (*pien*) in accordance with the times without transforming [the essence of his being]." 聖人與時變而不化. This in turn permits us to understand the passage in the *Huang-ti nei-ching su-wen* 黃帝內經素問 66/583:[62] "When the beings take rise (*sheng* . . .), this is called *hua* (transformation); when the beings have reached their full development (in Chinese *chi* 極 "to arrive at the ridge or summit") [and consequently have taken on a different appearance], this is called *pien* (change)."

> 物生謂之化, 物極謂之變. The terms *pien* and *hua* seem to suggest the idea of complementary antonyms [*sic*]. In the passage of the *Su-wen* 66/583 just quoted above where yin and yang are called the father and mother of change and transformation (*pien-hua*), the compound *pien-hua* may be understood as a composite of synonyms and therefore be translated by "changes"; yet, on the other hand, the parallelism between yin/yang and *pien/hua* shows that *pien* and *hua* can be conceived as the two aspects of an action polarized in turn—*pien* as its iterative, active, *hua* as its perfective, structive aspect.[63]

Joseph Needham also has a long and helpful disquisition[64] on "Change, Transformation, and Relativity." It is evident, as Needham says, that "there is no strict frontier between the words."

In certain cases, it may be necessary to render pre-Buddhist *pien* as "change [leading to transformation]." For example, in the *Book of Change*, we read:

> Thus water and fire contribute together to the one object; thunder and wind do not act contrary to each other; mountains and collections of water interchange their influences. It is in this way that they are able to change and transform 變化, and to give completion to all things.[65]

Yet in no case of which I am aware does the pre-Buddhist concept of *pien* mean or imply "transformation from nothing to something." Nor have I encountered it in the sense of "magically creative power to conjure." It refers rather to changes from one state of being or matter to another; a thing *becomes* some other thing. The pre-Buddhist *pien* never implies a discontinuity or break with reality (illusion), which is the very essence of *nirmāṇa*. So resistant was early Chinese philosophy to the notion of discontinuous metamorphosis that Kung-sun Lung-tzu 公孫龍子, in his chapter entitled "On Comprehending 'Change'" 通變論, actually makes an elaborate attempt to disprove through logic the possibility of transformation of entities and their constituent parts.[66]

No proponent for an indigenous origin of *pien* as a performing art has yet to mention a passage from the *History of the Han*,[67] where the term occurs in a context of conjuration and theatricals. This is from the biography of Chang Ch'ien 張騫, the great explorer of the Western Regions, and most likely refers to entertainments from Central Asia. Hulsewé and Loewe suggest that the term might be rendered as "theatrical scene, act."[68] A close examination of the text, however, reveals that the correct translation is as follows: "[Every] year [they] increased the *varieties* of the wrestling and strange performances" 角氐奇戲歲增變. This is well within the expected pre-Buddhist range of meaning for the word.

Even where we are dealing in classical Chinese contexts with change from one state to another, there is always an evolutionary continuity as in this famous passage from the *Chuang-tzu*:

> The seeds of things have mysterious workings. In the water they become 爲 Break Vine. On the edges of the water they become Frog's Robe. If they sprout on the slopes, they become Hill Slippers. If Hill Slippers get rich soil, they turn into 爲 Crow's Feet. The roots of Crow's Feet turn into maggots and their leaves turn into butterflies. Before long the butterflies are transformed 化 and turn into insects that live under the stove; they look like snakes and their name is Ch'ü-t'o. After a thousand days, the Ch'ü-t'o insects become birds called Dried Leftover Bones. The saliva of the Dried Leftover Bones becomes Ssu-mi bugs and the Ssu-mi bugs become Vinegar Eaters. I-lo bugs are born 生 from the Vinegar Eaters, and Huang-shuang bugs from Chiu-yu bugs. Chiu-yu bugs are born from Mou-jui bugs and Mou-jui bugs are born from Rot Grubs and Rot Grubs are born from Sheep's Groom. Sheep's Groom couples with bamboo that has not sprouted for a long while and produces 生 Green Peace plants. Green Peace plants produce leopards and leopards produce horses and horses produce men. Men in time return again to the mysterious workings. So all creatures come out of the mysterious workings and go back into them again.[69]

On the other hand, the post-Buddhist neo-Confucians had a clear concept of discontinuities in the process of change. There is no mistaking Chu Hsi's (1130–1200) understanding of the difference between *pien* and *hua* because he repeats it so many times. *Hua* is change viewed from an evolutionary point of view; *pien* is change seen from a transformational vantage.[70]

One T'ang author, who also had strong Buddhist predilections, did grapple with the meaning of *pien* in the expression *pien-hsiang*. That is the poet, Wang Wei 王維 (701–761), who wrote a "Eulogy on a Transformation [Tableau] of the Western Paradise of Amitābha [Buddha] Painted on the Stūpa of the Temple of Filiality and Duty by the Grand Secretary of the Imperial Chancellery, Tou Shao, for His Deceased Younger Brother, [Tou I 竇繹], the Late Husband of the Imperial Princes [Ch'ang-shan 常山], with Preface" 給事中竇紹爲亡弟故駙馬都尉于孝義寺浮圖畫西方阿彌陀變讚并序.[71] Wang must have recognized that he was dealing with a difficult and unusual usage of the word *pien* for, in a preface that is nearly four times as long as the eulogy, he launches into a discussion of the term. His explanation deserves our closest scrutiny.

Wang begins by quoting from the *Book of Change*: "[(The sage) perceives how the union of] essence and breath form things, and the [disappearance or] wandering away of the soul produces the change [of their constitution]" 游魂爲變.[72] Wang then quotes from a "Biography" which, upon investigation, turns out to be that of the Han Prince Yuan of Ch'u: "The vital energy of the soul reaches everywhere" 魂氣則無不之.[73] This leads Wang to conclude: "Thus do we know that the spirit is reborn"[74] 固知神明更生矣. He then elaborates: "Supported by the Way,[75] it is transformed into a perfect body[76] 則變爲妙身 and goes to a happy land." And, in the eulogy itself, Wang speaks of "evolving through change" 憑化而遷 and "ceaseless rebirth"[77] 轉身不息. Eventually, it is hoped that the deceased "will escape from the six paths of reincarnation"[78] 將免不息.

In effect, Wang Wei connects *pien* with the revolution of the cycle of metempsychosis (*saṃsāra-parivartana*) and looks upon the paradise of Amitābha as a place where one can achieve a final transfiguration to a steady state of spiritual existence no longer subject to the vagaries of *saṃsāra* and the six paths of reincarnation. Unfortunately, this explanation does not and cannot satisfy the use of the word *pien* (=*pien-hsiang*) in the title of his eulogy where it surely signifies a painting of the Western Paradise. There are many other related expressions that refer to similar representations, for example, *ching-t'u pien-hsiang* 淨土變相, *hsi-fang ching-t'u pien-hsiang* 西方淨土變相, *ching-t'u man-t'u-lo* 淨土曼荼羅, *ching-t'u chuang-yen pien* 淨土莊嚴變, and so on. It would appear that Wang, in spite of his vast learning in Chinese texts (including Buddhist ones), was not philologically equipped to deal with the fundamental concept behind *pien* in the sense of "transformation scene or tableau."[79] Forced to rely on a largely irrelevant passage from the *Book of*

Change, together with all the materialist baggage of its exegetical tradition, Wang Wei is led astray upon the paths of metempsychosis. With the textual interpretation provided by the poet, it is impossible to grasp the basic notion that paradises such as the Western one are said to be "*transformationally manifested* by the Buddha." 謂佛所變.

If it is impossible to find *pien* in classical, pre-Buddhist texts with the meaning that it carries in the terms *pien-wen* and *pien-hsiang*, we must turn to examine Buddhist sources directly to see whether there is any appropriate usage which might help to explain its semantic content. Although he has not revealed the sources for his conviction, Liu Ts'un-yan has stated that he knows "for certain that the Chinese character 變 (*pien*) in the term 變文 (*pien-wên*) originally meant *shên-pien* 神變 or supernatural powers as exhibited in awe-inspiring miracles."[80] This identification of *pien* with the obviously Buddhist *shen-pien* has led Kenneth Ch'en to call *pien-wen* "texts of marvelous events"[81] (probably a rendering into English of 神變之文). Lili Ch'en, likewise, seems to be accepting the same interpretation when she defines *pien-wen* as "a narrative depicting the marvelous incident of [such and such] . . . ."[82] Waley, too, may once have entertained such an interpretation when he referred[83] to *pien-wen* as "wonder-writings."

Chou Shao-liang[84] and Chou I-liang[85] have also recognized that the *pien* of *pien-wen* means *shen-pien* ("miraculous transformation"). In the words of Chou Shao-liang: "'*Pien-wen*' take stories dealing with miraculous transformations 神變 from the Buddhist sūtras and elaborate them into written works for the purpose of guiding the common people and converting the masses."[86] He goes on to say that, when one takes a miraculous transformational event from a sūtra and makes it into a picture, it is called *pien-hsiang*, and when it is expressed in literary form, it is called *pien-wen*. As for the non-Buddhist stories among the *pien-wen*, says Chou, their form is the same as that of the Buddhist *pien-wen* because they are modeled on them. I believe that this analysis is essentially correct, with the proviso that the sources of the "miraculous transformations" were not necessarily restricted to the fixed corpus of Buddhist texts but were also sometimes witnessed during individual religious experience. More specifically, Fu Yun-tzu connects[87] *pien* with the "miraculous transformations" used by the Buddha in preaching the law (說法 [*dhārmi kathā*] 神變) that are so often mentioned in the sūtras.

Shen-pien may be used to render Sanskrit *prātihārya* ("sham, illusion, delusion, magic, jugglery, sorcery"),[88] *ṛddhi* ("supernatural or magic power"),[89] *vikurvaṇa* ("the ability to assume various shapes"),[90] and so forth. Also note 神變示導 *ṛddhi-prātihārya* and 神變相 *mahā-nimittaṃ-prātihāryam*. Closely allied expressions in Chinese Buddhist terminology include:

神通	*ṛddhi, ṛddhi-sampad, abhijñā* ("supernatural knowledge");
神通力	*vikurvā, vikurvaṇa(-prātihārya), nirmita-adhiṣṭhāna-abhisamaya, ṛddhi-bala* [BHS], *ṛddhyānubhāvena* ("by means of miraculous power");
神通變化	*ṛddhi-vikurvita, vikurvāṇa*;
變化神通	*nirmāṇa-ṛddhi* ("supernatural power of transformation," cf. *T*[3]1.157a).[91]

Regardless of their knowledge of the various Sanskrit antecedents which have become compressed in this term, it is clear enough what Chinese Buddhist meant by *shen-pien*. Basically, it is a miraculous transformation (that is, appearance or manifestation) performed by a Buddha or Bodhisattva for the edification of sentient beings. Not only is the transformation in and of itself an impressive display of the abilities of the enlightened one who performs it and hence an effective device to encourage those who witness it to be receptive to his teachings, but, for those whose wisdom is sufficiently advanced, it is also a none-too-subtle affirmation of the illusory nature of all existence. If the enlightened one can so effortlessly produce such marvelous—but insubstantial—entities, there are profound ontological implications which, being directly perceived, need not be expressed verbally.

A very common trick for one possessed of such supernatural powers is to rise up into space and hover there while causing water and fire to issue from his body. This is exactly what Śāriputra does in the "Transformation Text on the Subduing of Demons" after his defeat of Raudrākṣa. These powers also enable their possessor to cause flowers to rain down, the earth to shake, lightning to flash, distant places to be illumined, and so on. The executor of *shen-pien* can also change his own person into an infinite number of beings, as does Monkey in his battles with the Heavenly Hosts in *Journey to the West*. It should, too, be mentioned that most of these activities are things that shamans do in performance. This will be of importance later when we discuss the social position and identity of those who were *pien* performers.

The motif of rising up into space and manifesting various (usually 18) manifestations is frequently encountered in Buddhist literature. For example, in the *Aśokarāja-sūtra* (?) 阿育王經,[92] we read the following: "Using his miraculous strength,[93] like a goose-king[94] flying up into space, in an instant the monk then rose up out of the iron cauldron into space and manifested the 18 transformations." And, in the Svagata story as told in *Divyāvadāna*, reference is made to the "18 transformations or miraculous powers" 十八變. Since these are met so frequently in Buddhist canonical texts as well as in popular literature, it is worth our while to study them in some detail in order to gain a better understanding of the Buddhist notion of transformational powers. Kenneth Ch'en has provided[95] the Chinese equivalents and English explanations of the Sanskrit terms:

1. *kampana*	振動	ability to move any object, even the worlds
2. *jvalana*	熾然	ability to emit fire from body
3. *spharana*	流布	ability to emit light that can illuminate the innumerable worlds
4. *vidarśana*	示現	ability to cause beings in all the *gatis* [states of sentient existence], Buddhas, Bodhisattvas, and devas, to be seen
5. *anyathī-bhava-karaṇa*	轉變	ability to change the nature of an object into something different
6. *gamanāgamana*	往來	ability to go anywhere, through the walls, mountains, water, air, and so forth
7. *samkṣepa*	卷	ability to roll anything, even the Himalayas, into a minute size
8. *prathana*	舒	ability to enlarge minute objects to gigantic proportions

9.	*sarva-rūpa-kāya-praveśana*	衆像入身	ability to store up swarms of people, mountains, or earth within the body
10.	*sabhāgato-pasankrānti*	同類往趣	ability to enter any group, assume their forms, shapes, and voices, preach to them, then disappear
11.	*āvirbhāva*	顯	ability to magnify body a thousandfold
12.	*tirobhāva*	隱	ability to disappear
13.	*vaśitva-karaṇa*	所作自在	ability to cause living creatures to become subject to his will
14.	*para-ṛddhy-abhibhava*	制他神通	ability to control the *ṛddhi* [supernatural power] of those below him in rank
15.	*pratibhāna-dāna*	能施辯才	ability to equip sentient beings with fluency in expression
16.	*smṛti-dāna*	能施憶念	ability to cause one who has forgotten the dharma to remember it again
17.	*sukha-dāna*	能施安樂	ability to bestow joy on listeners
18.	*raśmi-pramokṣana*	放大光明	ability to send forth light to all creatures in all worlds

The transformational powers on this list are many and varied. Encountering these and other miraculous abilities of Buddhist saints for the first time must have been a heady experience.

The centrality of the concept of transformational manifestation of illusory states of reality in Buddhist doctrine can be shown easily by reference to several specific passages from the Chinese *Tripiṭaka*. In the short *Sūtra of the Former Lives of the Buddha Siṃhacandra* (?) 師子月佛本生經, translated anonymously sometime between A.D. 350 and 431, there is a story[96] set in the city of Rājagṛha where Buddha is at the head of a host of bhikṣus and bodhisattvas. One of them, named Vasumitra, roams around in the bamboo grove, frolicking like an ape. He takes hold of a bell and puts on a dance-drama 作那羅 (*naṭa*) 戲. A crowd gathers to watch him, which spurs him to greater heights. With an ape-like cry uttered from the top of a tree where he has climbed, he summons 84,000 golden monkeys and performs various transformational manifestations 作種種變現

for the pleasure of his assembled audience. All of this hocus-pocus is not only tolerated but is encouraged by the Buddha, for it puts the crowd in a receptive mood to hear his doctrine.

The efficacy of thaumaturgy for conversion is a commonplace in Buddhist books. In the words of the *Divyāvadāna*, "A magical feat quickly wins over the minds of worldlings."[97] Wonder-working is also effective in restoring the faith of errant souls. This is illustrated by the story of the king in the *Lotus Sūtra*[98] whose two sons, Pure Treasury 淨藏 and Pure Eyes 淨眼, showed him all sorts of supernatural transformations 現種種神變 in order to pry him away from his attachment to heretical teaching.

Piety, the transformation of a deity, and art which captures it are all brought together in an anecdote recorded in *A Buddhist Gazetteer* 釋迦方志, compiled by Tao-hsuan 道宣 (596–667), founder of the Vinaya sect: "Of old, there were two poor men, each of whom donated one piece of gold toward the painting of an image of the Buddha. They requested the appearance of a supernatural transformation (請現神變), whereupon the image appeared with the body divided in two above the chest and joined as one below."[99]

A modern devotee has described his experience of witnessing the appearance of Kuan-yin thus:

> As though to illustrate the truth of divinity with innumerable aspects, the Bodhisattva startled me by manifesting herself in a veritable whirl of transformations, appearing now as Avalokita with eleven heads, now as the mirror-bearing, many-armed Chên-T'i, now as the horse-headed Hayagrīva, now as Tara, now as a terrifying wrathful-seeming deity not unlike Yamantaka, the blue, bull-headed Conquereor of Death, now as the handsome youth Manjusri—all of these alternating with many unnameable forms, male and female, horrendous and sublime, one merging into another like the changing patterns in a child's kaleidoscope![100]

The optical simile is particularly noteworthy.

There can be no doubt that one of the meanings of *pien* is "conjuration through transformation." Even today, *pien hsi-fa* 變戲法 is a common way to refer to the performance of magic.[101] In the *Śākyamuni Genealogy* 釋迦譜, it is said of a tree that has been conjured up, "This transformation (*pien*) was done/made by

Raudrākṣa." 此變乃是勞度差作.[102] It is highly significant that similar language appears in the "Transformation Text on the Subduing of Demons."[103] It is, further, demonstrable that *pien* in such contexts stands for *shen-pien*. In a passage from the *Pearl Grove in the Garden of Dharma* (*Fa-yuan chu-lin* 法苑珠林) dealing with the same matter (that of conjuration) in the very same story, we read: "Then Śāriputra and Raudrākṣa each manifested supernatural transformations" 各現神變.[104] The received Chinese Buddhist meaning of *pien* operative in such cases is "to make something appear" or "to produce one thing from another." Compare the cognate expressions 變作,[105] 變化, 變現,[106] and so forth.

The building of the Jetavana garden and the contest of supernatural powers between Śāriputra and Raudrākṣa, the subject of the illustrated transformation scroll P4524, is one of the most frequently depicted in Tun-huang wall-paintings.[107] The oldest of these is in cave 9 of the Western Caves of the Thousand Buddhas 西千佛洞 and dates from the mid-sixth century. It also occurs at the nearby Cliffs of the Ten Thousand Buddhas. 萬佛峽,[108] which date from the ninth or tenth century or perhaps a little later.[109] The canonical sources for the contest—none of which are in Pāli—are to be found in the *Mūlasarvāstivādavinayasaṅghabhedakavastu* 根本說一切有部毗奈耶破僧事 (*T*[1450]24.141aff), the *Mahā-sammata-sūtra* 衆許摩訶帝經 (*T*[191]3.968ab), and the *Sūtra of the Wise and the Foolish* 賢愚經 (*T*[202]4.418b–420c). Comparison of the sources with the account as depicted in Tun-huang art and popular literature reveals that a certain amount of adaptation and expansion has occurred in the latter.[110]

In the story of the magic contest between Śāriputra and Raudrākṣa as given in the *Mahā-sammata-sūtra*, the heretics declare, "We shall display our [ubiquitous] supernatural powers" 我現神通.[111] This indicates a kind of loose equivalence between *shen-pien* and *shen-t'ung* 神通.

A better understanding of the Buddhist meaning of *pien* as "conjuration," "illusory appearance," and so on can be gained from the following extended passage taken from the *Sūtra of the Wise and the Foolish*:

> Among the Six Heterodox Teachers, there was a disciple named Raudrākṣa, who was well versed in the techniques of illusion 幻術.

With an incantation,[112] he created 呪作 before the great crowd a tree that, of itself, grew to large size. Its shade covered the assembly; its branches and leaves were luxuriant; its flowers and fruits were extraordinary. The crowd of people all said, "This transformation 變 was created 作 by Raudrākṣa!" Then Śāriputra, by means of his supernatural power, created 以神通力作 a whirlwind which blew so hard that it uprooted the tree. The tree toppled to the ground and smashed into tiny pieces of dust. The crowd of people all said, "Śāriputra's the winner! This time, Raudrākṣa was no match for him!"

Again, with an incantation, he created a pond. On all four sides of the pond were the seven types of jewels.[113] In the middle of the water were growing all sorts of flowers. The crowd of people all said, "This is Raudrākṣa's creation 所作!" Then Śāriputra magically created 化作 a great six-tusked white elephant. On each of its tusks there were seven lotus blossoms and on each blossom was a jade girl. The elephant slowly ambled over to the side of the pond and drew all the water into its mouth causing the pond to disappear at once. The crowd of people all said, "Śāriputra's the winner! Raudrākṣa's no match for him!"

Again he created 作 a mountain decorated with the seven types of jewels. On it, there were springs and ponds, as well as trees and bushes full of flowers and fruit. The crowd of people all said, "This is Raudrākṣa's creation 作." Śāriputra then immediately magically created 化作 a guardian spirit of irresistable strength. With his adamantine mace,[114] the spirit pointed at the mountain from afar and it was destroyed at once, leaving not a trace. Everyone in the assembly said, "Śāriputra's the winner. Raudrākṣa's no match for him."

Again, he created the body of a dragon which had ten heads. From space, it rained down all sorts of jewels. Thunder and lightening shook the earth, startling the great crowd. The crowd of people said, "This too is Raudrākṣa's creation 作!" Śāriputra then magically created a golden-winged king of birds[115] which slashed, tore, and devoured it. The crowd of people all said, "Śāriputra's the winner! Raudrākṣa's no match for him!"

Again, he created a bull. Its body was tall and large; it was stout and sturdy. With its thick hoofs and sharp horns, it scraped the ground and bellowed loudly as it came racing forward. Then Śāriputra magically created a lion king which rent it to pieces and ate it. The crowd of people exclaimed, "Śāriputra's the winner! Raudrākṣa's no match for him!"

Again, he transformed his body into 變其身作 a *yakṣa* demon. Its size was enormous; flames shot from its head. Its eyes were as red as blood;

> its four teeth were long and sharp. Flames issuing from its mouth, it bounded forward. Then Śāriputra changed himself into 自化其身作 the Mahārāja Vaiśravaṇa. The *yakṣa* was terrified and wanted to retreat at once. Fire sprang up on all four sides so there was no place to escape. Only on Śāriputra's side it was cool and there was no fire. The *yakṣa* submitted right away by throwing himself on the ground in an attitude of profound reverence[116] and begging plaintively that his life be spared. As soon as he felt shame, the fire disappeared. The crowd cried out in unison, "Śāriputra's the winner! Raudrākṣa's no match for him!"
>
> Then Śāriputra's body rose up into space and manifested the four imposing forms of demeanor in walking, standing, sitting, and lying. Water came forth from the upper part of his body and fire came forth from the lower part. He sank down in the east, leapt up in the west; sank down in the west, leapt up in the east. He sank down in the north, leapt up in the south; sank down in the south, leapt up in the north. Or, by manifesting 現 his major body, he filled up all space and, then again, he would manifest his minor body. Or he would divide his single body into hundreds, thousands, millions, and trillions of bodies and then once more make them into a single body. He would be in space and then suddenly on the ground. He walked on the land as though it were water and on the water as though it were land. When he finished creating 作 these transformations 變, he returned with light steps[117] to his original seat. Then, seeing his supernatural power, the great crowd of the assembly rejoiced together. Śāriputra then began at once to discourse on the dharma.[118]

Thus we see that the wonderful transformations created by Śāriputra all serve as a prelude for religious instruction. This is a commonplace in Buddhist texts, whether more popular, as here, or more sophisticated, as with the *Lotus Sūtra*.

The magic contest between the Tīrthyas (heretics) and Śāriputra is also described in the *Saṅghabheda*[*ka*]*vastu* of the Vinaya (statutes) of the Mūlasarvāstivādins. Fortunately, the Sanskrit original of the *Saṅghabheda*[*ka*]*vastu* does exist and we can gain some knowledge about the type of language involved in dealing with transformational manifestations. Where the Chinese translation by I-ching (A.D. 635–713) gives 外道化爲七頭龍王. 舍利弗化爲大金翅鳥. 從空飛下食龍而去. (*T*[1450]24.140c), the Sanskrit has *tena śataśīrṣo nāgo nirmitaḥ*; *āyuṣmatā śāriputreṇa garuḍa nirmitaḥ*, *yenāsāv apahṛtaḥ*.[119] The idea conveyed by both the Chinese and the Sanskrit is that the heretic conjured up a seven-headed dragon and that this was destroyed by a roc-like bird conjured up by Śāriputra. The key word in the Sanskrit account is *nirmita*, which recurs repeatedly just as 化[作/爲] does in the Chinese. *Nirmita* is the past passive participle of *nirminati* which in BHS means "creates by magic[al transformation]"[120] and goes back to the Sanskrit root √*nir-mā*.[121] 化[爲/作] could mean either "created through transformation" or "transformed themselves into." The corresponding verb in the Śāriputra transformation text is *hua-ch'u* 化出, which I have regularly translated as "conjure up" and which literally means "transform out," that is, "produce through transformation." The nouns in both the Chinese canonical scripture and in the transformation text referring to the transformational products or creations of Śāriputra and Raudrākṣa are *shen-pien* 神變 ("spiritual transformation"), *shen-t'ung pien-hsien* 神通變現 ("supernatural transformational manifestation"), or simply *pien*.

The Buddha, deep in meditation, manifests many wonderful apparitions in preparation for preaching the *Lotus Sūtra*. Maitreya Bodhisattva reflects on this: "O how great a wonder does the Tathāgata display!" *Mahānimittaṃ prātihāryaṃ batedaṃ tathāgatena kṛtam*.[122] It is interesting to remark on how the various Chinese translators of the *Lotus* interpreted this sentence. Dharmarakṣa (c. 223–300), who translated it in the year 286 as the *Cheng-fa-hua ching* 正法華經 gives "Now the World-Honored has attained the true, correct understanding." 今者世尊如來至眞等正覺.[123] Kumārajīva (344–413), who translated it in the year 406 as *Miao-fa lien-hua ching* 妙法蓮華經, gives "Now does the World-Honored One display an appearance so marvelous."[124] 今者世尊現神變相.[125] Dharmagupta and Jñānagupta, who rendered the text into Chinese in the year 601, called it *T'ien-p'in miao-fa lien-hua ching* 塡品妙法蓮華經 and rendered the line in question exactly as Kumārajīva did.[126] If it is possible to draw any conclusions from the chronology and comparison of these and other translations, it is that the notion of *prātihārya* was not easily expressible in the Chinese language until the meaning of *pien* had been sufficiently expanded to accommodate it.

Another passage from the *Lotus Sūtra* brings together the notion of dramatic performance with that of transformational illusion and therefore deserves our closest scrutiny. The Buddha is describing to Mañjuśrī the proper conduct of a Bodhisattva-mahāsattva. There are certain types of people that he must avoid, including wrestlers, vendors of pork, poulterers, deer-hunters, butchers, *actors*, *dancers*, and so forth.[127] The Sanskrit compound expression for the last two types mentioned is *naṭa nṛttakān*[128] (from √*nat*, "to represent anything [dramatically]; perform; dance" and √*nṛt*, "to act on the stage; represent; dance about").[129] Kumārajīva renders[130] this as 那羅等種種變現之戲, which may be literally Englished as "various kinds of transformational manifestation performances [put on by] *naṭas* [that is, dancers/actors], and so forth."[131] Apparently, Kumārajīva understood *nṛtta* to mean something like *prātihārya* ("transformational appearance") for he uses *pien-hsien* 變現, the usual translation for the latter Sanskrit term, to render it. Even in Buddhist Hybrid Sanskrit, acting is sometimes thought to have a delusive nature. The *Mahāvyutpatti* (no. 2837) lists, under the heading *māyādayaḥ* ("*māyā* [illusion], etc."), the expression *naṭaraṅgaḥ*. This literally means "theatrical stage" but it is used as a symbol of deceptive or illusory character.[132] We read,[133] for example, in the *Śikṣāsamuccaya* (quoting the *Sāgaramatisūtra*) that a Bodhisattva's speech should not be "fictitious" or, more literally, "stage language" (*na naṭaraṅga-vacanaḥ*). Whereas *naṭa* and *nṛtta* actually mean approximately the same thing ("actors and dancers"), Kumārajīva's translation functions partly as a gloss intended to convey the implicit connotations of the Sanskrit terms and so seems to say more than the original. It is significant, none the less, that a connection has been made in a Chinese Buddhist text between transformational manifestation and dramatic performance. This has a direct bearing on the nature of Sino-Indian dramatic narrative.[134]

As to the use of supernatural transformations to convert infidels, there is an interesting story in the *Notes on Monasteries of Loyang*.[135] A Serindian merchant brings a monk named Vairocana before the King of Khotan. The monk asks the Buddha to send his disciple Rāhula there and the latter transforms himself into the Buddha in mid-air. The King is so much impressed that he is immediately converted. He proceeds to construct a temple in which he has painted an image of Rāhula.

A passage from *Journey to the West* shows how the later folk Buddhist tradition took delight in the spectacular and dazzling qualities of supernatural manifestations:

> Seeing that the demon[136] was becoming savage, Monkey now used the method called Body Outside the Body. He plucked out a handful of hairs, bit them into small pieces and then spat them out into the air, crying "Change!" 變. The fragments of hair changed into several hundred small monkeys, all pressing round in a throng. For you must know that, when anyone becomes an Immortal, he can project his soul, change his shape and perform all kinds of miracles. Monkey, since his Illumination, could change every one of the 84,000 hairs of his body into whatever he chose.[137]

In China, the Buddha's most noted disciples were Śāriputra (for his wisdom) and Maudgalyāyana (for his magical abilities) in distinction to India where Ānanda (for his extensive experience) was the clear favorite. And, in the folk Buddhist traditions of China, Maudgalyāyana was even more popular than Śāriputra, while the latter was often himself depicted as something of a conjurer. One of the reasons for Maudgalyāyana's vast popularity in China, aside from the fact that his story nicely complemented native teachings on filial piety, is that he functioned as a sort of patron saint of prestidigitators. For the populace, visual effects were more convincing than doctrinal disquisitions.

It would be improper to discredit an Indian Buddhist origin for the word *pien* on the grounds that not all *pien-wen* have Buddhist themes. This is to ignore the obvious: *pien-wen* in China has a history of its own. It began as an Indo-Buddhist phenomenon but gradually became secularized, first to the extent that the form could be employed to tell non-Buddhist stories, and second to the extent that the Buddhist-tinged name nearly dropped out of use altogether though the form survived.[138] Because of the apparent Buddhist origins of *pien-wen*, we ought to seek to determine whether there is an exactly corresponding term in Indian languages.

Hrdličkova's suggestion[139] that the *pien* of *pien-wen* is the Chinese equivalent of Sanskrit *pariṇāma* is not far from the mark. *Pariṇāma*, usually rendered in Chinese as 轉變, means "change" or "evolution." As a figure of speech, it expresses a feeling, emotion, intention, or thought that is actualized (brought into reality).[140] In philosophy, it refers to the alteration from one condition or the development into another. This constituted an essential element in the teachings of the Dharmalakṣana school (法相 or 唯識 *Vijñānamātra*[*vāda*]; *cittamātra*), which held that all things are dependent on mind-evolution, being neither real nor unreal in and of themselves. We must ultimately reject *pariṇāma* as the equivalent of *pien* in *pien-wen* and *pien-hsiang*, however, for it never means, in an active sense, "create the illusion or appearance of," "conjure up," "manifestation of a divine being," and so on—all meanings which *pien* in these contexts conveys.

Kuan Te-tung was of the opinion[141] that *pien* is a transliteration of *maṇḍala*. Note also Dolby's translation[142] of *pien-wen* as "Mandala texts," which shows that he accepts Kuan Te-tung's interpretation of the expression. It is likely that Kuan was prompted to make this equation between *pien* and *maṇḍala* because of earlier remarks such as that made by Nagasawa Kikuya: "It is said that *pien-wen* originally specified the inscription on a *maṇḍala*."[143] Shionoya On had also declared that *pien* is probably a Buddhist term and gone on to say that *pien-hsiang* is like *maṇḍala* and *pien-wen* is similar to the explanations which accompany a *maṇḍala*.[144] Yet no one has substantiated the equation between *pien* and *maṇḍala* with reference to any text or inscription. There are, furthermore, more immediate objections which must be raised against it.

Because of the fact that it occurs in combination with *wen* and *hsiang* and also because of other textual associations, it is evident that *pien* in the contexts that concern us is being used for its semantic content rather than employed for purposes of transliteration. And, even if it were exceptionally so employed, it is highly unlikely that it would simultaneously be used to convey a meaning.[145] But, on the assumption that it were being used to convey a meaning, *pien* was already firmly established in the Buddhist technical vocabulary as a translation for Sanskrit words that had to do with supernatural transformation. It is almost inconceivable that it would also be made to imply circularity, which is the root meaning of *maṇḍala*. Finally, there are numerous other standard renderings of *maṇḍala* in Chinese (for example, 曼荼羅, 蔓陀囉, 滿荼邏, and so on). It is virtually impossible that a totally unrelated word such as *pien* would have been used only in the case of "**maṇḍala* text" and "**maṇḍala* tableau."

We must also, in discussing the proposed equation between *pien* and *maṇḍala*, point out that these terms refer to two largely separate entities in Chinese Buddhist art. Art historians, however, have used the two terms somewhat interchangeably. Close examination[146] of T'ang texts, however, reveals that Chinese Buddhist authors normally tended to make a distinction between the two forms. We cannot, of course, expect that the dividing line between *maṇḍala* and *pien-hsiang* can ever be made completely clear for, in truth, the two merge into each other. While the *maṇḍala* side of the scale is more related to devotion, worship, ritual, and meditation, the *pien* side has more to do with the illustration of narrative episodes, whether individually or in series. A given painting may include elements of both and hence, to a greater or lesser degree, may fulfill a dual function. A *maṇḍala* is primarily a place, site, location, arena, or object used to assist in religiously oriented concentration which leads to spiritual enlightenment. The Chinese translation, 道場 ("way-arena," cf. "bema"), of Sanskrit *bodhimaṇḍala* is most revealing in this regard. A religious *pien*, on the other hand, is primarily intended to portray a scene or incident (or, more often, a series of scenes and incidents) of didactic import. Hence we should not confuse *pien* and *maṇḍala*, nor should we equate the two.

We may thus, in one sense, consider *pien* to be "the appearance, manifestation, or realization of a deity in a narrative context." This not only makes it qualitatively different from a *maṇḍala*, but also from a plain *hsiang* 像 (*pratirūpa*, *pratirūpaka*, and so forth) or *ch'ü* 軀 that is but an image of a deity. Presumably, the religious *pien* storyteller was thought to be able to cause the epiphany of a deity or deities in a narrative context. His counterparts, the Indonesian *dalang* and the Rajasthani *bhopo*, at any rate, are certainly credited with such ability.[147]

In discussing the possible Sanskrit antecedents of Chinese Buddhist *pien*, it is necessary at this stage to issue a general caveat concerning the equation of Buddhist technical terms in different languages. As Régamey has shown very clearly, it is dangerous to equate terms from Sanskrit, Tibetan, and Chinese even when they are found in parallel passages from the same text: "When, in two parallel passages, two expressions are found which correspond with each other in a sentence, these expressions are noted as equivalent even when the proper meanings of those words have very little in common. These discrepancies are interpreted as the result of the artificial character of Buddhist translations and as a proof that there existed no fixed Buddhist terminology in Chinese, whereas they very often constitute divergencies made on purpose or simply misreadings."[148] There is almost never an exact one-to-one correspondence between a Chinese Buddhist translated text and its original Sanskrit source, whereas it is often more nearly possible to achieve approximate equivalence for many Tibetan translated texts and their Sanskrit originals. A striking example of a complete misunderstanding and mistranslation of an entire scripture is entertainingly described by Brough in his "The Chinese Pseudo-Translation of Árya-Śūra's Jātaka-mālā." Even when a Sanskrit original or a highly literal Tibetan translation exists with which to check the Chinese, one should always offer equivalences of technical terms circumspectly and tentatively. There did exist a more or less fixed Buddhist terminology in Chinese but it was naturally Chinese first and Sanskritic only secondarily. Naturally it also changed over time so that, at different periods of history, the same Sanskrit word or concept might be rendered by several Chinese expressions.

The relationship between Chinese Buddhist and Sanskrit technical vocabulary is no simple matter. In some cases, there may be equivalence between items (for example, 阿槃陀羅 and *avāntara* ["intermediate"]). In other cases, one Sanskrit word may be rendered by many quite different Chinese expressions (e.g. 怛他揭[or 蘖] 多, 多陁 [or 他] 阿伽度 [or 陀 or 馱], 怛闥 [or 薩] 阿竭, 荅荅蓦達, 怛佗議多, 多他阿伽陀[耶], 如來 and Tathāgata ["Thus-come," an epithet for a Buddha]). Some Chinese technical Buddhist terms may actually be a conflation of several nearly synonymous Sanskrit terms (for example, 性 and *svabhāva*, *prakṛti*, *pradhāna*, and so forth). And many technical terms in Chinese Buddhism have no analogues in Sanskrit (for example, Zen *kōan* 公案). I consider *pien* as an artistic or literary genre to be in the next-to-last category, that is, although it has definite Sanskritic antecedents, *pien* is not equal to any single Sanskrit word or term.

One of the very few texts in the Chinese Buddhist canon that includes the word *pien* with the approximate meaning "picture (of a transformational or supernatural event or deity)" is the *Mūlasarvāstivādavinayakṣudrakavastu* 根本說一切有部毘奈耶雜事 (text no. 1451 in *T*24). This text was translated in full by I-ching in the year 703 from manuscripts that he himself had brought back from India.[149] The crucial passage[150] in which the important reference to *pien* occurs may be summarized as follows: After the elder, Anāthapiṇḍika 給孤長者, had completed the construction of the Jetavana garden, he felt that it would be appropriate to decorate the buildings with colorful paintings. And so he went to the Buddha to ask his advice. The Buddha told him to follow his own inclinations. Thereupon, he collected the necessary materials for painting and called together artisans to carry out the work. But, when the artisans asked him *what* they should paint and *where*, Anāthapiṇḍika replied that he did not know and that he had better go ask the Buddha again. The Buddha then proceeded to explain, in precise detail, both the subject matter and the location of suggested paintings.

In this context, the word *pien* occurs twice (*T*24.283b, lines 3 and 8) with the probable meaning of "supernatural event(s) [pictorially represented]." In its first occurrence, the suggested painting is designated as a "*pien* of great supernatural power" 大神通變.[151] Unfortunately, although numerous fragments of the Sanskrit *Mūlasarvāstivādavinaya* survive,[152] there are none corresponding to this passage.[153] The Tibetan version,[154] however, which dates to around the beginning of the ninth century, follows the extant Sanskrit fragments closely and may be considered a reliable substitute for the lost portion of the original sūtra.[155] For "*pien* of great supernatural power," the Tibetan here reads "a great *cho-hphrul*,"[156] which is a standard translation of Sanskrit *prātihārya* (cf. *prātihāra*, "magician") and *ṛddhi*.[157] The second occurrence of *pien* is in the expression "*pien* of hell" 地獄變. The Chinese expression means "manifestation" or "representation" 變[現] (Sanskrit *prātihārya*) of [the sufferings in] hell (Sanskrit *naraka*). Unexpectedly, the Tibetan here reads *dmyal-baḥai-rabs*, which means "a hell family," that is, a "lineage" or "hierarchy" of the arrangement of hell.[158] It is impossible to determine, on the basis of available materials, whether the Chinese or the Tibetan more accurately represents the original Sanskrit. What matters is that we have been able to identify in a Chinese sūtra ultimately derived from a Sanskrit source the word *pien* occurring with the probable meaning of "[pictorial representation of] supernatural event(s)."

Chou I-liang, referring to the Chinese text, states[159] that this seems not to be a normal Chinese usage of *pien* and suggests that it has a Sanskrit antecedent. The word which he mentions as a possibility is *citra* ("picture" 畫). This a commendable guess but one which can be justified neither etymologically nor textually. *Citra* also has the following meanings, which I give with their established Chinese translations: "variegated" (種種[不同], 雜類, 雜飾), "strange" (有殊), "wonderful" (希奇, 妙色). These compounds also give an indication of the types of Chinese translations normally used to render *citra*: *citra-kāra* ("painter" 畫師), *citra-kara* ("painter" 畫匠), *citra-gṛha* or *citra-śālā* ("a room painted with pictures" 畫室), *citra-darśana* ("variegated-eyed" 現見種種法), *citra-paṭa* or *citra-paṭṭa* ("painting" 采畫, 畫像, 錦).[160] To the best of my knowledge, *citra* was never translated into Chinese as *pien*.

Wu Hsiao-ling has a suggestion similar to Chou I-liang's. Wu offers *vicitra* ("variegated," "brilliant") as the Sanskrit equivalent of *pien*.[161] He maintains that *vicitra* includes the meanings "strange" and "supernatural" and indeed it does. But I have not been able to confirm that it occurs in contexts with the meaning "[pictorial representation of] supernatural/transformational [event(s)/deities(s)]" which it must if it is to match Chinese Buddhist *pien* in the sense under discussion. Another interesting observation[162] by Chou on the *Mūlasarvāstivādavinaya* passage is that, since it refers both to *hsiang* 像 *and pien* 變, the two must be different. "It is probable that the subject of a *hsiang* is a person while the subject of a *pien* is an episode (lit. 'event' or 'matter' 事)." This ties in very well with my contention[163] that *pien* by its very nature has narrative qualities.

The longest passage in the Pāli canon describing the construction and decoration of the Jetavana garden and monastery that I have been able to locate is *Cullavagga* 6, 4.10:

Then the householder Anāthapiṇḍika, thinking: "This Prince Jeta is a distinguished, well-known man; surely the faith in this *dhamma* and discipline of well-known men like this is very efficacious," made over that open space to Prince Jeta. The Prince Jeta built a porch[164] on that open space. The householder Anāthapiṇḍika had dwelling-places made, he had cells made . . . porches . . . attendance halls . . . fire halls . . . huts for what is allowable . . . privies . . . places for pacing up and down in . . . halls in the places for pacing up and down in . . . wells . . . halls at the wells . . . bathrooms . . . halls in the bathrooms . . . lotus ponds . . . . He had sheds made.[165]

Nowhere is there a mention of pictures being painted; hence it is impossible to make any claim about the Indic equivalent of *pien* on the basis of this passage. The account as given by the Mūlasarvāstivādins has all the earmarks of a later elaboration of a canonical legend.

In a discussion of the possible evolution within Buddhism of *caraṇa citra* ("rambling," "strolling," or "improvised pictures") into wall-paintings, Barua cites a legend from the *Divyāvadāna*[166] which I have also been able to locate in the Chinese version of the *Mūlasarvāstivādavinaya*.[167] The Buddha suggests that, in order for the other disciples to become as effective preachers as Mahāmaudgalyāyana, certain paintings should be affixed to the monastery where they dwelled. (One wonders whether Mahāmaudgalyāyana may not himself have used pictures in his preaching. At any rate, his ability to conjure images is undisputed, since he was preeminent among the Buddha's disciples for his magical powers 神通第一.)

The wheel of life with five divisions should be represented on the doorway (of the Veṇuvana monastery), showing the five destinies of men, namely, those typified by the infernal creatures, the brute, the departed spirits, the gods and the human beings. In the lowest division are to be shown the infernal creatures, the brute world and the departed spirits; in the upper division the gods, men and the four continents (Pūrvavideha, Aparagodānīya, Uttaraku and Jambudvīpa); in the middle parts Passion, Hatred, and Delusion,—Passion in the form of a pidgeon, Hatred in that of a serpent, Delusion in that of a boar, as well as the Buddha-image, the circle of Nirvāṇa, and the chance-born beings, the last as rising and falling in the form of the rope-and-bucket of a well; while surrounding all is to be engraved the Buddhist Wheel of Life, divided into 12 segments and revolving forwards and backwards. The representations must set forth concrete examples of the different ways and actions leading persons along these destinies. The Wheel of Life must be accompanied by the inscription recording the two verses urging—

> "Proceed, O man, come out and flock to Buddha's standard,
> Shatter Death's legion, as elephant tramples house of reed,
> not hard."[168]

Where the Sanskrit text has *kārayitavyam* or *kartavyā* (literally, "what has to be done," translated by Barua as "represented," "shown," and so forth), the Chinese gives *hua* 畫 ("paint"). And, where the Chinese text, apparently for clarity's sake, is compelled to use *hsiang* 像 ("image"), *hsiang* 相 ("appearance") and *hsing* 形 ("form"), the Sanskrit omits similar expressions altogether. In spite of the obvious similarity to the decorations stipulated for the Jetavana monastery in the *Mūlasarvāstivadavinayakṣudrakavastu* where the word *pien* 變 does occur with the meaning "transformational (representation)," it is totally absent from this passage.

After an extensive search, I have not been able to discover in any Indian language, ancient or modern, an expression that corresponds exactly to the Chinese "*pien-wen*." Though *pien* surely means "transformation(al manifestation)" in the sense of "(pictorial) representation," it does not equal *śaubhika*, *yamapaṭa*, *maṅkha*, or any of the many other words in Indian languages for picture storytelling.[169] The conclusion that I, therefore, have been forced to reach is that the Chinese, when confronted with these mysterious transformational shadows, coined the expression themselves. But, in so doing, they chose a Buddhist technical term of respectable pedigree, one already established as a translation of *nirmāṇa*, *prātihārya*, and related concepts. The Chinese Buddhist technical term *pien*, which is markedly different from earlier usages of the graph in classical contexts, would seem to be a conflation of a number of Indian Buddhist concepts. We may not say that it is exactly equivalent to any single Sanskrit term. The passage of Buddhism through Central Asia alone means that, in many cases, certain residues of languages there would have become attached to the technical vocabulary that was transmitted to China.[170] *Pien-*

wen is thus the embodiment of an intercultural nexus: It is neither simply Indian nor Chinese, yet it is paradoxically both Indian and Chinese.

Having established that *pien* in the terms *pien-wen* and *pien-hsiang* means "transformation," I shall now proceed with a general discussion of Buddhist ideas of transformation in order to put these two literary and artistic genres in a larger context. For someone totally unacquainted with Buddhist metaphysics, the concept of transformation here referred to may, perhaps, be crudely characterized as "realization" in the musical sense that one begins with the mere *idea* of a melody and *actualizes* it in performance. Similarly, in Buddhist philosophy, the mind conceives of something and then, through cognition, brings it into (illusory) being.

Conze's analysis of the use of magic sounds in Tantrism is helpful in understanding how visualization (which is what a *pien* performance attempts to achieve) may be accomplished through pictures:

> Each word can be analyzed into its syllables, and according to the Tantra, different syllables not only correspond to different spiritual forces or deities, but a syllable, or letter, can be used to conjure up a deity, and therefore it can, in a sense, be called the "germ" of that deity, just as a grain of wheat contains the plant in itself. It seems logical to assume that if one can, as the first step, dissolve oneself into emptiness through concentrated thought, then it must also be possible to conjure up from emptiness the entire world of phenomena. With the help of certain sounds—such as AM, HUM, SVAHA—one does actually create the deities out of the void.[171]

The ability to achieve these feats is premised upon the basic Indian idea that all phenomenal existence is an illusion. A most sustained and revealing example of the Buddhist understanding of the illusory nature of all dharmas may be found in the *Bhadramāyākāravyākaraṇa*, *The Prophecy Concerning the Illusionist Bhadra*. The translators mentioned in the Tibetan colophon, Jinamitra Prajñāvarma and Ye-śes-sde, worked in the ninth century.[172] Régamey refers to this text as "the Sanskrit version."[173] There are two available Chinese translations of this work which I shall refer to in the notes as Ch. 1 and Ch. 2. The first translation, attributed to Dharmarakṣa (fl. 266–300), is called (*Fo-shuo*) *huan-shih jen-hsien ching* (佛說) 幻士仁賢經.[174] It is usually preferable for its understanding of the original but has occasional gross errors. The second Chinese translation was done by Bodhiruci sometime between 693–713. It is called *Shou huan-shih Pa-t'o-lo chi hui* 授幻師跋陀羅記會.[175] It is generally laconic but sometimes provides quite intelligent interpretations. There also exist a Pāli and a Khotanese version of the tale.[176]

The *Bhadramāyākāravyākaraṇa* is the 21st of the 49 Mahāyāna texts included in the Ratnakūṭa section of the Tripiṭaka. It is a description of a magic contest between a famous conjurer named Bhadra and the Buddha himself, who engages in the contest in order to convert his opponent. Bhadra seeks to embarrass the Buddha by having him attend a magnificent banquet complete with splendid trappings and trimmings that is situated on a garbage dump. After decisively defeating Bhadra, in the first instance, by causing the creation of an even more magnificent courtyard and banquet attended by 30,000 gods led by Śakra and, in the second, by not allowing Bhadra to withdraw his illusory creation when he realizes his error, the Buddha then seizes upon this opportunity to teach that the world is but an illusion:

> "The enjoyments (*upabhoga*) and gains (*paribhoga*) of all beings, Bhadra, are created by the magic of the deed (*karmamāyā*), this order of monks is created by the magic of the *Dharma* (*dharmamāyā*). I am created by the magic of wisdom (*jñānamāyā*), the Universe containing three thousand thousands of worlds is created by the magic of all the productions (*abhiniṣpatti*, *abhinirvṛtti*); and the entire reality (*sarve dharmāḥ*) is created by the magic of the complex of conditions (*pratyayasaṃbhara*)."[177]

In the end, Bhadra is thoroughly convinced that all is "universal Illusion."[178] The same vision of the world as a magic show or series of conjuror's tricks is repeated as an extended parable in the *Kālakārāma Sutta*.[179]

An individual who is thoroughly enlightened about the true nature of the world possesses an abundance of impressive abilities. As examples of the various magical powers it was thought those who had achieved the higher levels of meditation were capable of exercising, I cite the following from Buddhaghoṣa's *Visuddhimagga* (xii):

1. The magical power of sustained resolution
   a. Having been one, he becomes many; having been many, he becomes one.
   b. He becomes visible or invisible.
   c. Right through a wall, a rampart, or a hill he glides unimpeded, as though through empty space.
   d. He dives into the earth and out of it.
   e. He walks on water without sinking into it.
   f. Cross-legged he floats along like a bird on the wing.
   g. Even the sun and the moon, powerful and mighty though they be, he touches and strokes with his hands.
   h. Even as far as the world of Brahma he has power over his body.
2. The power of miraculous transformation.
3. The power of producing mind-made bodies.[180]

The Buddha himself is naturally thought to possess such abilities. According to Conze:

> In the Hinayana, already, the Buddha was credited with the miraculous power of conjuring up an appearance of himself, a "*nimitta-Buddha*," which preached elsewhere, while he went begging. The Hindu Gods also had such powers. So we read in the Digha Nikaya that Brahma Sahampati, when he appears in the assembly of the "*Gods of the Thirty-three*," manifests himself in a material body. "*For his shape, as it naturally is, is unbearable to the sight of these Gods.*"[181]

It is significant that so many Indian words dealing with supernatural manifestation were rendered in Chinese by expressions employing various combinations of *pien*. Closely related words (although they come from entirely different Sanskrit roots) in this complex of meanings are *pien-hua* 變化 (*nirmāṇa*, "transformation"), *pien-hsien* 變現 (*prātihārya*, "manifestation"), *pien-hsiang* 變相 (*vipariṇata*, "changed aspect"), *shen-pien* 神變 (*prātihārya* or *vikurvita*, "spiritual/supernatural transformation/manifestation"), plain *pien* 變 (*vikṛti* or *vyakta*, "something manifested through transformation"), and the Chinese Buddhist expression *pien-hua* 變幻 (**nirmāṇa-māyā* [?], "transformational illusion").[182]

It is not surprising that transformation and illusion would ultimately be combined in Chinese literature to form a single expression. In the "Rhapsody on the Lamps of the Pagoda in the Center of the Ou 歐 River"[183] 江心埣(=塔)燈賦 by the Ming writer Wang Kuang-yun 王光蘊, it is said that the lamps display "multicolored[184] spiritual evocations through transformational illusion, emit manifold emblazonry[185] that soars on high." 神五色於變幻, 嘘七寶而騫騰.[186] These lines are embedded in the very center of a text that is heavily laden with crystalline and vitreous images, with lightning, rainbows, flickering flames, shadows, reflections, and other optical phenomena, as well as with manifestations of the Buddha. This complex of images and concepts is consonant with other Indian-influenced religio-literary traditions throughout Asia.

The notion of transformational manifestation is so pervasive in Buddhist thought that it can scarcely be overstressed. In the *Lotus Sūtra*, we read of the three transformations of the Buddha-realm (*san-pien t'u-t'ien* 三變土田) by Śākyamuni on Vulture Peak: the revelation of the world, the vast extension of that world, and a still vaster extension. For this and similar reasons, the Buddha is sometimes thought of as the "Great Magician"; one might almost say that his is the greatest illustrated story being performed. And he seems to do this, at times, out of sheer pleasure or sport (*vikrīḍita* 遊戲[神通] or 神變). The transformations of the Bhutatathatā 眞如, in fact, are so unlimited as to be inconceivable (*acintya-pariṇāminī* 不思議變). For purposes of propagating the Buddha-truth, he is able to assume any sort of metamorphic body (*nirmāṇa-kāya* 化身 or 變化身 or 應化身, the third of the "three bodies," *trikāya* 三身).

It is more than a passing curiosity that both the Chinese and the Tibetan Buddhists chose what was etymologically the very same word to stand for the complex of concepts in Sanskrit that have to do with illusory transformation. That is, as Simon has pointed out,[187] Tibetan *sprul* ("to juggle [that is, perform tricks of illusion], change") and Chinese *biann* [*pien*] (Karlgren, *GSR*, p. 67, no. 178, o: **pli̯an*/*pi̯än*-) are essentially the same word.

Rolf Stein's analysis[188] of a cluster of words in Tibetan all centering on the concept of transformation is helpful in understanding the relationship between illusion and creation. He mentions the binomes *rju-'phrul*[189] (where *rju* is related to *rjun* "dream"), *čho-'phrul* (the meaning of *čho* is uncertain but it probably has to do with engenderment or production) and *sgyu-'phrul* (= Skt. *māyā* or "illusion").[190] The common element in all these binomes is the noun or adjective *'phrul* ("[having] magical/supernatural/transforming ability"). The causative of *'phrul* is *sprul* ("to change [the subject itself or anything or anyone] into [something else]"; "to emanate"; "to produce the appearances or illusions of [corresponding substantives]"). What is most revealing is that Tibetan *sprul* in all of these cases means exactly the same as Chinese *pien*! Rolf Stein expatiates[191] on Walter Simon's proposal that *sprul* and *pien* be considered as both equivalent and etymologically related in these two Sino-Tibetan languages. They each have approximately the same range of pre-Buddhist meaning and, more curious still, were utilized by Tibetan and Chinese respectively to cover virtually identical sets of technical vocabulary. Both *sprul-sku* and *pien-hua shen* 變化身, for example, mean *nirmāṇa-kāya* ("transformation body").

There is a group of Chinese terms centering on Sanskrit *pratibimba* ("image") that express the notion of shadows or reflections without any true existence. These are *ying-hsiang* 影像 ("shadow-image"), *ching-hsiang* 鏡像 ("image in a mirror"), and *se-hsiang* 色像 ('image of a form [*rūpa*]"). Two other related expressions are *ying-hsien* 影現 ("the epiphany or manifestation of the shadow," that is, "the temporal Buddha") and *ying-t'ang* 影堂 ("a hall where there are images, pictures, or objects of worship"). In all of these expressions, we see the concatenation of shadow, manifestation, and representation of a deity.

It is most thought-provoking that several medieval (late Six Dynasties through Liao) orthographies of the word *pien* include the *shan* 彡 radical (no. 59) which is a component in many characters expressing reflection or shimmering brilliance. Those unusual forms of *pien* that I have culled from various sources[192] include 𢒱, 䝤 (= 𢒡 or 影), 𢒤, and 𢒰. It appears that *pien*, for a certain period which coincides roughly with the time when *pien-hsiang* and *pien-wen* were current, was understood by some as a visual or optical phenomenon. What is perhaps even more interesting is that there exist two characters with the radical 彡 (𢒈 [pronounced 方未切]

and 㣎 [pronounced the same as 浮]), the meaning of which is not known but which may well have some relationship to the Buddha since the phonetic element in each case was used to transcribe the sound of his name into Chinese.

The following group of Sogdian words (except for three or four of Manichaean origin, all are from Buddhist texts) also indicates a close connection between transformational manifestation and visual phenomena: *pδ'yškyn* or *pδ'štkyn* ("apparent," "appear spontaneously"), *pδ'yš* ("appear," "[to] show"), *'ndyš-* ("[to] show"), *'nδysn* ("reflection"), *fδys* ("vision"), *βδ'yp(')* ("radiance, brilliance"), *'βδ'ys* ("appearance, apparition, vision," used to translate Chinese *ying* where it equals Sanskrit *chaya* with the meaning "shadow, silhouette, form, image"; cf. Parthian *'bdys-* ["show"]; parallel to *prγšnh*, *nγšnh*, and *'γšnyrk*; the latter glossed in Middle Persian as *nīšān* ["sign, mark"], cf. *hsiang* 相 with the meaning of Sanskrit *lakṣaṇa* or *nimitta*)[193] *'βδ'ymtyh* ("transformation, magic," used to translate Chinese *hua* 化 with the meaning of Sanskrit *nirmita* which is also rendered in Chinese by such relevant expressions as *hsien-hua* 現化 ["appear through transformation"], *ying-hua* 應化 ["responsive transformation"], *ju-huan* 如幻 ["as though an illusion"], and, of course, *pien-hua* 變化 ["transformation"]). Buddhist Sogdian was current during approximately the same period of time as were transformations in China.

When discussing shadow-play traditions in other societies, for comparative purposes, we should keep in mind all of the nuances of the Chinese word *pien*. An early word for shadow-play in Arabic, for example, *sha'wa̱da*, has a strikingly similar range of meaning with Buddhist *pien*: "fascination(s); a kind of play; legerdemain, or sleight-of-hand; making a thing to appear different from what it really is; showing a man what has no real existence; making what is false assume the form of what is true."[194] Not only are these meanings reminiscent of Buddhist *pien*; they recall even more the Indian concept of *māyā* that lies in the ontological background of *pien*. It is equally interesting to note that another Arabic word for "shadow-play" and "magic lantern," *khayāl*, primarily signifies "imagination, shadow, phantom."[195] In examining the evolution of picture storytelling into shadow and puppet plays that seems to have taken place in India, Indonesia, China, and elsewhere, it will be helpful to recall these fundamental affinities and resemblances between illusion, transformation, and the power of creative imagination.[196]

For China, the concatenation of illusory transformation, optical phenomena,[197] and outlawed or suspect (to the establishment) popular religious movements can be seen as far back as the Sui period:

> In the year 613, when the Emperor (Yang-ti 煬帝) was at Kao-yang 高陽,[198] there was a man from T'ang 唐 district,[199] Sung Tzu-hsien 宋子賢, who was good at illusory arts. Every night there was a glow of light from the second floor of his apartments. Through transformation, he could make an image[200] of the Buddha 能變作佛形 and styled himself "Maitreya Appearing in the World." [201] He would hang a large mirror in his hall and would depict on plain paper snakes, beasts, and even human figures. When people came there to worship, he would turn the mirror sideways causing shapes of future rebirths[202] to be seen or projecting the images of snakes on the plain paper. Tzu-hsien would abruptly tell them that this was sinful karma.

This account in the *Sui History*[203] goes on to relate how, through worship centered on this optical chicanery, Sung incited large numbers of his followers to take part in a design against the Emperor. The plot leaked out, however, and government forces were sent to subdue the rebels, not without first having to penetrate an imaginary ring of fire that Sung had magically created to protect himself.

In spite of the fact that this account reeks of Confucian prejudice and distortion, it affords us a glimpse of the power of alleged transformational manifestations. This account also adumbrates the social status of an early religious movement that relied on transformational illusions to rally the populace. It is no wonder that the establishment would seek to suppress such movements and that orthodox Buddhists (who were usually part of the establishment or, except in times of widespread anti-Buddhist persecution, were at least on the fringes of it) would make strenuous efforts to dissociate themselves from all such activities. As we shall see in the latter part of Chapter 6, all these facets of *pien* came together in conjunction with Manichaean cults.

chapter four

Form, Formula, and Features of Transformations

In Chapter 2, we considered the question of how many extant *pien-wen* there are. This involved distinguishing *pien-wen* from other types of Tun-huang popular literature. In so doing, certain identifying features of *pien-wen* were mentioned, such as the pre-verse formula, the prosimetric form, and a necessary relationship to illustrations. This chapter will describe these features and their functions in detail.

The basic transformation-text verse-introductory formula may be conceived of as "[Please look for a moment at the] place [where] × [occurs]. How [should I] present [it]?" [且看][1] × 處, 若爲[2] 陳[說]?[3] The best way to begin our investigation of this formula is with a discussion of the origins of the word *ch'u* as it is used here. I should preface my remarks with mention of the recent discovery of the existence of virtually the same formula in an Indian picture-storytelling genre known as *paṛ vā̃caṇo*. Because the Indian tradition is still a living oral performing art, the formula does not occur with such obligatory regularity as in *pien-wen*, nor is it of such a standardized form. The resemblance between the *pien-wen* and *paṛ vā̃caṇo* pre-verse formulas suggests that they serve the same purpose, function in a virtually identical fashion, and are almost certainly related to each other through some common ancestor.[4]

There is compelling evidence that the use of the word *ch'u* in the verse-introductory formula is linked to inscriptions on paintings identifying individual scenes. Several occurrences of *ch'u* at the end of a narrative label on the Tun-huang wall-paintings have been mentioned by Kawaguchi Hisao. He has recorded[5] two inscriptions from cartouches of a wall painting depicting scenes from the

Buddha's life that are on the east wall of Tun-huang cave 102 (Pelliot number; Tun-huang Institute no. 76): "The place where the Crown Prince, in the Himalayas, has his hair shaved off" 太子雪山落髮處 and "The place where he bathes in the river with lotuses (?) growing out of the mud" 泥連(→蓮？)河澡浴處. I recorded the following inscriptions from the right portion (at the top) of the east wall of the same cave during my 1981 summer trip to Tun-huang:

> The place where he bathes in the Hiraṇyavatī River.
> 凞(=熙)連河澡浴雳 (probably the same as Kawaguchi's second inscription).
>
> The place where the Crown Prince undergoes six years of austerities.
> 太子六年苦行雳
>
> The place in the Himalayas where the Crown Prince cuts off his hair [and becomes a monk] (the same as Kawaguchi's first inscription).
> 太子雪山落髮雳
>
> The place where he teaches and converts five brothers.
> 教化昆季五人雳
>
> [The place where] the Crown Prince crosses the city wall in the middle of the night.
> 太子夜半逾城 (no *ch'u*)

I also spotted in the lower left corner of the north wall of cave 17 *bis* (Pelliot number, 156 in the Tun-huang Institute numbering system; dating from the late T'ang) these three characters: 飛鳴處 ("The place where [it?] is flying and singing.")[6] The west wall of cave 117 (Tun-huang Institute no. 61; a Sung painting) depicts the miraculous events associated with Mañjuśrī at Five Terraces Mountain (Wu-t'ai shan 五臺山, Pañcaśīrṣa or Pañcaśikha). One of the cartouches reads: "The place where a golden bridge is made to appear through transformation." 化金槗(=橋)現虜(=處).[7]

A cartouche on a ceiling painting in the corridor of cave 108 (Tun-huang Institute number, late T'ang [?]) bears the following inscription: "This is the place where the Dharma Master T'an-yen went into reclusion at the Mountain (that is, Monastery) of One Hundred Ladders (in Khotan)." 此是百梯山延法師隱處.[8] It is unlikely that *ch'u* here specifies the actual location where T'an-yen was a recluse because "Mountain of One Hundred Ladders" tells us that. Hence *ch'u* must be functioning in a more abstract way. As we shall see momentarily, its purpose in such situations is to designate an event in a narrative sequence.

Tun-huang manuscript P3317 confirms this interpretation of *ch'u* ("place") functioning as a market of narrative locus. It is a list of 118 events in the Buddha's life based on *nidānas* from the third and following fascicles of the *Buddhacarita* 佛本行經集經第三卷已(→以)下緣起簡子目號. These short tags, averaging approximately ten characters in length, each end in the word "place" (*ch'u*). They would have been suitable for cartouches on a transformation tableau or for the first part of pre-verse formulas in a transformation text dealing with the life of the Buddha. They are written in an undistinguished hand.

S6320 is a long strip of paper with an inscription honoring Vaiśravaṇa 毗沙門 and Dhṛtarāṣṭra (?) 樓略叉 that ends in *ch'u*. It is probably a label for a painting, a statue, or a temporary altar.

A wood-block print text from Kiangsu,[9] dating to c. 1104 and entitled *Dhāraṇī sūtra* 陀羅尼經, includes illustrations. Among the inscriptions for these illustrations is the following: "This is the place where the official borrows money from the Abbot of the Monastery of Pervading Light and the Abbot orders the little monk to divide it up and give it to him." 官人從普光寺主借錢, 寺主令小和尙分付處.

A set of transformation tableaux illustrating the *Lotus Sūtra*,[10] probably dating from the end of the Northern Sung or the beginning of the Southern Sung, has cartouches with inscriptions describing the events depicted; one of these ends with the word *ch'u*.

Kameta Tsutomu has compiled a list[11] of the identifying inscriptions of scenes on Japanese narrative picture scrolls depicting the founding of the Avataṃsa ["Garland"] school of Buddhism 華嚴緣起. Many of these inscriptions end with the word *tokoro* ところ ("place").[12] Some of the scrolls date from the early thirteenth century (c. 1227–1231).

There is preserved in Japan an important illustrated scroll entitled *Bussetsu Mokuren kyūbo kyō* [*Sūtra on Maudgalyāyana's Saving of His Mother*] 佛說目連救母經.[13] A colophon at the end states that it is a reprint of the same type of scripture printed in the 5th month of 1251 in Yuan China.[14] The reprinting itself was undertaken on a date equivalent to 15 July 1346 in Kyoto. The scroll has the format of a fully illustrated plain tale (*ch'üan-hsiang p'ing-hua* 全相平話) with pictures on the top and a popularized version of the scripture on the bottom. We should also note that the scroll dates from the same period as that of the greatest popularity of *p'ing-hua* ("plain tales" or "expository tales" 評話). It is, furthermore, not insignificant that the subject of this scroll is also the most popular of all Tun-huang transformation texts. What is particularly interesting about this scroll, however, is that there are cartouches on the pictures and that the inscriptions therein usually consist of a short description of the scene depicted that ends with the word *tokoro* 処 (處 "place"). For example, "The place where preparations are made for the Feast of Hungry Ghosts" 造盂蘭盆処 and "The place where Maudgalyāyana's mother receives the precepts in front of the Buddha and is reborn in heaven" 目連母於佛前受戒得生天処, and so on. Surely this usage has a direct relationship to the *ch'u* in the verse-introductory formula of transformation texts.[15]

Even more revealing is what happened to this market of narrative locus in later Japanese popular fiction. There is a genre of storybooks for women and children known as *otogi zoshi* お伽草子 that is closely linked to a tradition of picture recitation. One such story is entitled "Shichinin bikuni [Seven nuns]" 七人比丘尼.[16] In the 1635 edition of this story, the following statement occurs just before an illustration: "This is the place (*tokoro*) where they set off for an unknown destination with the young master Fujiwara, 12 years of age, at the head of their party." The 1682 version eliminates the direct linkage between text and picture by omitting the word *tokoro*.[17] The number of pictures in the latter text was also reduced and later storybooks would forgo them entirely. This is but one item of specific evidence demonstrating how popular written narratives gradually grew out of a tradition of picture recitation.

An anonymous twelfth-century narrative hand scroll in the William Rockhill Nelson Gallery of Art is entitled "Picture of [Chao Yü's] Pacification of the Barbarians South of Lu" 瀘南平夷圖.[18] The various scenes are labeled thus: "This section depicts the matter of X" 此段畫X事. Here *shih* 事 functions in a similar fashion to *ch'u* in Buddhist paintings by marking a discrete narrative event depicted as part of a series.

An illustrated *Pulsŏl Amita-gyŏng* 佛說阿彌陁經, published in Korean in 1572, consists of pages that are one-half picture and one-half text, very much in the fashion of printed plain or expository tales (*p'ing-hua*). Each picture has an inscription which describes its contents and ends with the word *vyūha* 莊嚴. Hence, "[This is] the spiritually adorned scene in which X [happens]." In this case, *vyūha* is used in the same way as *ch'u* (*tokoro*) on Buddhist narrative paintings in China and in Japan.

In the "Transformation on the Han General, Wang Ling," there is an extremely important textual problem relating to the meanings of *pien* and *ch'u* which must be discussed in depth. This occurs on T36.11. I will first translate the passage following the Peking University Library manuscript (p. 9, lines 3–4) formerly owned by Shao Hsun-mei: "[This is] the place where the two generals took leave of the king and went to destroy the encampment. From this picture [lit. 'layout' or 'spread'] is thence the beginning [following the unannounced emendation of the T editors; the manuscript has 'division'] of the transformation." 二將辭王便往斫當(=營)處從此一鋪便是變功 (Tun huang orthographical form of 切→初 [?]). S5437 has "... the place where they destroy the encampment. With this one turn [of the picture scroll] is thence the beginning of the transformation." 斫營處從此一輭(=轉)便是變初. P3627 has "... a layout of the place where they destroy the encampment is thence the beginning of the place (→ transformation)." 斫營處一鋪便是處(→變)初. Comparison of the three versions leads me to the conclusion that there was some semantic overlap between *ch'u* and *pien*, because they cannot be confused orthographically or phonically.[19] This overlap, plus the simultaneous occurrence of *p'u* 鋪 ("pictorial/illustrative layout/spread") in the same sentence, offers strong supporting evidence for my contention that both *ch'u* and *pien* have intimately to do with pictures. The fact that the end title of P3867 (T47.2) also includes the word *p'u* in combination with *pien* is further evidence of this connection.[20]

In cases where the word "look" (*k'an* 看) precedes it, *ch'u* in the transformation-text pre-verse formula cannot but be considered as a (vestigial) reference to a picture or, perhaps more accurately, a part of or a point on a picture. For a reader of written transformation texts without accompanying picture scrolls, the simulated context would have evoked the meaning "place [on a painting]," hence "[visualized] scene." But the extended meaning comes simply to be "place or point in a narrative context." The shift to a temporal signification is evident.

That the notion "place" in narrative contexts can have a temporal meaning is also known from the fact that Japanese *tokoro* 處 has both spatial and temporal facets. In Japanese "epistolary style" (*sōrōbun* 候文) and in certain other styles, *tokoro* has a very intriguing sequential usage. Since at least the year 1016 it has been employed as a conjunction which serves to connect the narration of a given clause with its succeeding clause.[21] The Manchu word *ba* ("place") has also developed many similar idiomatic usages, among them that of "when."[22] The development of this usage of *tokoro* and *ba* seems to have been as follows: "at the [narrative] locus where X happened" > "at the [narrative] moment when X happened" > "after/when X happened, then Y occurred." The first stage resembles very much the transformation text usage of *ch'u* as a narrative sequential marker and might conceivably have been influenced by it.

About the same time as this usage of *tokoro* arose in Japan, *ch'u* in China also begins to function as a mark of narrative sequence in the written, colloquial language. This is evident from Zen historical records and dialogues as well as from such neo-Confucian texts as the *Classified Conversations of Chu Hsi*.[23] That this peculiar usage of *ch'u* and *tokoro* as narrative sequential marks developed in a popular Buddhist environment seems obvious. For *ch'u* in Tun-huang texts other than *pien-wen* with the denotation "locus (here, of course, not pictorially illustrated)" but still with a temporal or sequential connotation, see T441.10, 525.12, 623.11, 652.15 [in the past], and so on.

This usage of *ch'u* in the sense of "time when" also occurs sporadically in *shih* 詩 poetry as early as the middle of the eighth century.[24] It becomes even more frequent in Sung lyric meters (*tz'u* 詞) and Yuan drama. It may be noted that the first appearance of this usage in poetry follows upon its introduction in Buddhist narrative contexts. Some poems even replicate the pairing of *shih* ("time when") and *ch'u* found in Tun-huang wall-paintings.

In the *Śikṣāsamuccaya*, compiled by Śāntideva during the seventh century,[25] there are two occurrences[26] of the word *viṭhapana*, which may be of value in explaining the connection between illusory creation (that is, representation) and place (locus). In both instances,[27] Sanskrit *māyā* is rendered in Chinese by Dharmakīrti as 幻化 and *viṭhapana* as 處. As such, I believe that Edgerton is justified in rendering *viṭhapana* in BHS as "*fixation, establishment, creation, making*; especially with implication of something illusory and fleeting." Significantly, *viṭhapana* has also been expressed in Chinese as "transformational manifestation" (*pien-hsien* 變現). This is helpful in our efforts to understand the original meaning of *ch'u* in the *pien-wen* pre-verse formula. I should also point out that there is a direct parallel between this transformational aspect of *ch'u* in the *pien-wen* formula and the notion of "place" that occurs in the Indian *paṛ vā̃caṇo* verse-introductory formula mentioned at the beginning of this chapter.

Pien and *ch'u* repeatedly recur as linked philosophical terms in Hsuan-tsang's 玄奘 (594–664) translation of Vasubandhu's *Vijñaptimātratāsiddhi* [*Viṃśatikā*] (*Wei-shih erh-shih lun* 唯識二十論; *The Treatise in Twenty Stanzas on Representation Only*.)[28] They usually stand respectively for *pariṇāma* ("transformation") and *āyatana* ("abiding place") in the original Sanskrit text. *Āyatana* is understood as the result or impression of the transformational process.

The variations of the pre-verse formula in the "Transformation on the Han General, Wang Ling" (T38.10 . . . 處謹 [carefully] 爲陳說; 39.11–12 而 [and] 爲轉[29] 說;41.3 處若爲 [how] 陳說; 42.4–5 遂 [thereupon] 爲陳說; 43.6 若爲陳說; 45.10 而爲轉說; and 46.12 處若爲陳說)[30] allow us to conclude that the actual interrogatory force of the formula is almost nil. Compare also T99.15 . . . 處有 ["there is," but perhaps an orthographical error for 若] 爲陳 of the Wang Chao-chün transformation text. It is at most a perfunctory utterance that probably derives from such storyteller's phrases as "How should I put it?" "How does it go?" or "This is how it goes."

An interesting variant of the *pien-wen* pre-verse formula is to be found in a fragmentary manuscript dealing with the Crown Prince's (that is, the Buddha's) achievement of the Way that is kept in the Nara Art Museum 寧樂美術館.[31] It is not certain that this manuscript is from Tun-huang but it does bear a strong resemblance to many texts recovered there. The formula in question reads thus: "How can it be explained? [This is] the place where the seer examines him for the auspicious marks of a Buddha." 若河(→何)解說？仙人占相處.[32] Notice how it presents a curious reversal of the usual *pien-wen* verse-introductory formula.

It is apparent that *ch'u*, both at the end of inscriptions on paintings and in the transformation-text verse-introductory formula, means approximately "[narrative] locus [pictorially represented or visualized]." This interpretation is substantiated by the frequently encountered parallel, Buddhist usage in texts and on paintings of *shih* 時 as "[narrative] moment [pictorially represented or visualized]."[33]

The expression "the time when . . ." (*shih*) is often used in inscriptions. For example, in cave 106 (Tun-huang Institute no. 72), there are scenes from the Mahāsattva Jātaka. One of the inscriptions reads: "At that time [lit., The time when at that time!], [Mahā]sattva decided to sacrifice himself and, unhesitatingly, removed his clothing and hung it on the branch of a tree." 尔時薩埵决定捨身而無疑悔即脫衣服掛在樹枝時. Note what appears to be a redundancy of *shih*. I believe, however, that in the second occurrence it is functioning as a quasi-ablative grammatical inflection. "The place where . . ." (*ch'u*) in similar inscriptions can be considered the same sort of device used as a quasi-locative. This is a resourceful invention that has other parallels in the development of the Chinese language under the impact of Sanskritically expressed Buddhism.[34]

In cave 9 of the Western Caves of the Thousand Buddhas 西千佛洞, in the middle of the right wall on the south side, there is a painting of the biography of the Buddha in a former life as Śāmaka 睒魔. This cave includes paintings from the early T'ang, Sung, and Uighur periods as well as the only Sui painting of Śāriputra's contest with the Six Heretics. Śāmaka was "a bodhisattva born to a blind couple, clad in deerskin, slain by the king in hunting, restored to life and to his blind parents by the gods."[35] An inscription on the painting reads[36] as follows: "Śāmaka led his blind father and mother . . . . [This is] the time when he made a grass hut and picked sweet fruits to nourish his parents." 睒子將盲父母....作草屋採甘草供養父母時.

Many other examples[37] of *shih* being used as a mark of narrative moment can be found at Tun-huang. On the east wall of cave 10, there are altogether 11 panels which illustrate the story of the construction of the Jetavana Garden. Each of the panels bears an inscription that ends with the marker *shih*. The first panel, for example, reads as follows: "The time when the elder Sudatta took leave of the Buddha and was about to go towards the city of Śrāvastī to build a monastery, and the Buddha told Śāriputra to construct the monastery with Sudatta so he took leave of the Buddha." 須達長者辭佛 將 向舍衛國 造 精舍, 佛 告 舍利弗共 須 達 建告(→造)精舍, 辭佛之時.[38] In cave 98 there are even more detailed inscriptions of the magic contest: "The time when the heretic, Raudrākṣa, produced through transformation a great tree and asked Śāriputra how many leaves it had and how deep its roots were." 外道勞度差變作大樹問舍利弗其葉數其根深淺時. "The time when Śāriputra, after having answered how many leaves there were, conjures a great snake which pulls up the tree." 舍利弗答葉數訖, 化作大蛇拔樹時. "The time when the Wind Spirit angrily releases his wind to blow at Raudrākṣa." 風神鎮(→震？)怒放風吹勞度差時. "The time when the heretics, blown by the Wind, anxiously cover their faces." 外道被風吹急遮面時, and so on.[39] In each case, the inscription ends with the narrative sequence mark *shih*.[40] Although I have translated this as "the time when" in English, the sense of this mark is actually far less explicit. In an almost nonverbal way, it means, rather, something like "X [sequential *event* which *occurred* at a given] *time* [is here *depicted/explained*]." When similar inscriptions bear the narrative sequence mark *ch'ụ*, we should interpret thus: "X [sequential *event* which *occurred* at a given] *place* [is here *depicted/explained*]." The italicized words represent the primarily implicit semantic content of 時 and 處. The "event" portrayed may not be simply a single incident but may actually consist of several disparate incidents compressed into a larger entity. The given "time" and "place" are hence correspondingly stretched to include the total span of durational or spatial occurrence.

One of the most interesting wall-paintings with inscriptions of this type is to be found in cave 128 at Tun-huang. It is rather large and dates from the "high" T'ang period. On the north wall, there is a series of narrative paintings, one of which is about Chang Ch'ien's 張騫 mission to the Western Regions during the reign of Han Wu-ti (140–87 B.C.). The inscriptions read as follows:

> The time during the former Han when Chung-tsung (!) obtained a golden man[41] but no one knew its name, so he sent the Marquis of Extensive Vision, Chang Ch'ien, to [the kingdom] of Fer [ghana][42] in the Western Regions to inquire about its [that is, the Buddha's] name.

> The time when the Martial Emperor (Wu-ti) of the Han led his hosts to punish the Huns and obtained two golden men that were more than ten feet tall; he had them placed in the Sweet Springs Palace; the Emperor considered them to be great deities and often went to worship them.[43]

An unusual usage of the narrative sequence mark *shih* may be seen in cave 300 at Tun-huang. Here we find[44] portraits of devotees, each with identifying inscriptions that end in *shih*. This usage seems to transcend both the primary meaning ("time") and secondary significance ("narrative moment") of *shih*; it appears, rather, to have evolved to the point that it functions here simply as a tag to end the inscription.

An anonymous eighth-century silk banner (36.8 × 17.6 cm)[45] from Tun-huang preserved in the British Museum depicting scenes from the life of the Buddha also employs the narrative sequence mark *shih*. Altogether, there should be four scenes of the Crown Prince going out of the palace gates on his white horse and observing an old man, a sick person, a corpse, and a monk (*bhikṣu*). Only the first two survive. Of these I translate the first as an example of the usage of *shih* in the inscriptions of such banners: "[This is the] time [in the narrative sequence which depicts] that time[46] [when the] Crown Prince[47] went forth from the east gate of the city-wall and, seeing an elderly man, asked about the primary and secondary causes[48] [of old age.]" 爾時太子出城東門觀老人問因緣時. The second inscription has an identical form.

At Haystack Mountain 麥積山, near the town of T'ien-shui 天水 in southeast Kansu province,[49] I did not discover a single instance of *pien* as a generic term in all the inscriptions affixed to the wall-paintings there. Nor did I observe any occurrences of *ch'u* as a marker of narrative locus. I did, however, note 19 instances (caves

126, 127, and 160) where *shih* serves as a marker of narrative moment and 15 instances (cave 110) where it functions simply as a tag to end inscriptions designating donors and devotees. Given the dates of these wall-paintings (mostly Northern Wei, 386–534), such findings are not surprising.

The same *shih* occurs at the end of a fragmentary explanatory inscription on a silk drawing[50] of the Buddha recovered from Toyuk in Central Asia. It is impossible to determine with absolute certainty whether this represents a borrowing of a device that had developed in China proper or a Chinese adaptation in areas bordering on Central Asia of Sanskritic, Iranian, or Turkic narrative inscriptions. The generally earlier date of the Central Asian inscriptions, the fact that Buddhist art and literature entered China *from* the west, and other evidence that I present in the chapter of *Painting and Performance* dealing with Central Asian influence on *pien* storytelling all point to the latter possibility as being the more likely of the two.

The use of *shih* as a narrative sequence mark can also be found in manuscripts. S4527 has a description of the contest between Śāriputra and the six heretics in which individual narrative moments are marked *shih*, for example: "The time when the wind breaks the strings of the canopy and the heretics try to tie them down" 風吹幄帳繩斷, 外道卻欲繫時, "The time when the wind is about to blow the canopy over and the heretics take a ladder and think what to do" 風吹幄帳欲倒, 外道將梯想時, and so on. This is probably a list of scenes that are keyed to a set of narrative illustrations.

A set of inscriptions on a wall-painting in cave 76 (Sung period) at Tun-huang attests to the functional relatedness of *ch'u* and *shih*. At the bottom left of the east wall may be found the following inscription: "The time when the five mendicant monks [*bhikṣu*] listen to the preaching [that is, the turning of the Wheel of the Law or *dharma-cakra*] of the Four Noble Truths [*catvāri ārya-satyām*]" 五比丘聞四諦法輪時. As noted above on p. 74, at least three other inscriptions on the same wall end in *ch'u*. Here it is clear that *shih* and *ch'u* have coalesced into an identical usage, that of marking an event in a narrative sequence.[51]

It is thought-provoking to consider that the episodes in the

"Sūtra of the Crown Prince's Attainment of the Way" 太子成道經 are labeled on P2299 as "Such-and-such an appearance (*hsiang* 相)."[52] When we remember that these very scenes were acted out by a troupe of dancers (as is evident from S2440v);[53] when we recall that 11 out of the 15 extant chapter titles of the *Tale Interspersed with Poetry on Tripiṭaka of the Great T'ang Dynasty Retrieving the Buddhist Sūtras* 大唐三藏取經詩話 are labeled as *ch'u* ("narrative locus");[54]and when we reflect on the genetic relationship between *pien-wen* with its succession of *ch'u* and *pien-hsiang* with its succession of *shih* ("moments")—we can see that *hsiang* in some cases may refer to the episodes of a narrative dramatically represented, just as *ch'u* and *shih* may refer to the episodes of a narrative pictorially, sculpturally, or verbally represented.

At Bhārhut (in India), many of the sculptures have identifying labels inscribed on them. Yet, as Barua tells us:

> The Barhut artists were not very judicious in their use of the labels. For in the same row of [c]oping-panels one finds that, if a scene in one panel is inscribed, the one in the next panel is not. . . . And yet in reviewing the sculptures . . . one is apt to feel that in theory all were intended to be labeled, the omissions being due to oversight or negligence on the part of the artists. Thus, if the Barhut examples are worth . . . anything, they seem to indicate a transitional stage when the practice of labeling the sculptures became optional.[55]

Bhārhut is fairly early (third-second century B.C.). Later, it became the custom not to affix labels to Buddhist sculptures and frescoes such as at Bodh Gaya, Sāñcī, Mathura, Taxila, Amarāvatī, Sarnath, Karle, and Ajaṇṭā.

Of the narrative statuary at Bhārhut that is provided with labels describing the scene depicted, we find, for example, that a medallion carving is labeled with the words "Anāthapiṇḍika dedicates Prince Jeta's Garden after purchasing it with a layer of crores [ten million piece of gold]" *Jetavana Ȧnādhapeḍiko deti koṭisaṃthatena Keto*.[56] A small coping-panel reads "The Jātaka-scene relating to Mahādeva." *Maghādeviya-Jātakaṃ*.[57] And a small bas-relief has the tag "A Jātaka-episode of the Kinnaras." *Kiṃnara -Jātakaṃ*.[58] Nowhere in any of these inscriptions known to me do we find a word like "the place [where] . . ." (*ch'u* 處)[59] or "the time [when] . . . (*shih* 時). My inclination, as expressed less explicitly above, is to believe that these latter are Chinese inventions and that they were intended: (1) to approximate, respectively, the locative and ablative cases in inflected Buddhist languages, and (2) to designate narrative moment and locus.

I am here making no claims about the handling of Sanskritic case endings in the scriptural tradition because the usage of *shih* and *ch'u* under discussion would have arisen in the popular realm.

Among the texts discovered by Kozlov at Kharakhoto was a *Fo-shuo pao fu-mu en chung ching* [Sūtra spoken by the Buddha concerning recompense to parents for their great kindness] 佛說報父母恩重經.[60] This is an apocryphal sūtra, printed xylographically, that dates from the beginning of the twelfth century. Preceding the fragmentary text is an illustration which represents the deeds of a filial son performed for the benefit of his parents. The various scenes are labeled with inscriptions that constitute revealing evidence of the deterioration of the understanding of the meaning of the word *ch'u*. On the right side of the illustration are seven inscriptions that read as follows:

The place where he circumambulates Mount Sumeru for his parents.
爲[父母遶]須彌山處

The place where he slices off some of his flesh for his parents.
爲父母割肉之處

The place where he gouges out his eyes for his parents.
爲父母剜眼睛之處

The place where he cuts out his heart and liver for his parents.
爲父母割心肝之處

The place where he smashes his bones for his parents.
爲父母打骨處

The place where he submits to the wheel of swords for his parents.
爲父母受刀輪之處

The place where he swallows iron pellets for his parents.
爲父母吞鐵丸之處

On the left side, the inscriptions read as follows:

Receiving and observing for his parents the precept (*śīla*) concerning sacrifice.
爲父母受持祭戒

Worshiping the Three Jewels (*triratna*) for his parents.
爲父母供養三寶

Dispensing alms and doing good works for his parents.
爲父母布施修福

Copying out scriptures for his parents.
爲父母書寫經典

Reciting the scriptures for his parents.
爲父母讀誦經典

Seeking forgiveness for the wrongdoing of his parents.
爲父母懺悔罪愆

It would appear that late Sung artists had partially forgotton the significance of the marker, *ch'u*, retaining it vestigially only in connection with specific scenes of suffering in hell. This is not surprising, since the Maudgalyāyana story was by far the most popular transformation text and would have linked the usage of *ch'u* more or less permanently in the minds of those who were familiar with it.

We must now consider the difficult question of whether or not the pre-verse formula in transformation texts should be counted as straightforward evidence of orality. On the one hand, such a formula is ostensibly less straightforward than the direct addresses to the audience which we encounter so frequently in some of the sūtra lectures. On the other hand, it would appear that the pre-verse formula is an attempt to convey the impression of an oral context, hence the transformation texts may, to greater or lesser degree, be said to derive from oral literature. In considering the degree of orality of a given transformation text, it is necessary to examine it on the basis of the following criteria: frequency of corrections, deletions, additions, and so on; whether these are by the original scribe or by others; indications of immediacy; gaps in the text; imperfect rhyme patterns; lines obviously missing from the verse sections; poor or hurried quality of the calligraphy; irregular spacing of lines; illogical sentences and passages; *non sequiturs*; needless repetitions; lack of a colophon stating that the text is a copy; and so on. I have already discussed the significance of revisions of a text by subsequent hands.[61]

The most obvious evidence of immediacy in transformation texts in general would seem to be the verse-introductory formula. Of the many variations of this formula, I consider the extended forms ("*Look* at the place where X occurs; how shall [I]explain it?") to be relatively stronger evidence of close relationship to a spoken presentation. But this a very complicated issue and I shall return to it later. Gaps in the text indicate either that the recorder fell behind in his transcription, that he (or they) had faulty recollection of the oral event, or simply sheer negligence on the part of the copyist. The same holds for imperfect rhyme sequence, missing verse, illogical passages, false starts, and other comparable features. As for the presence of a colophon stating that the manuscript is a "copy" of a given text, this is direct proof that there must have been at least one other intermediate written stage between the oral event(s) and the manuscript in question. It is logical to assume that there would be a tendency for all but one of these criteria gradually to be refined out of a text with each successive copying and rewriting. The nearer an orally derived text is to its source of inspiration, the more fluid and unstable it will be because the oral exemplar changes with each retelling. Conversely, a text that has been written, rewritten, and copied several times gradually takes on a fixed form. The exception, as we shall see, is the pre-verse formula which would, after regularization, be retained as a conscious attempt to maintain the appearance of orality.

No one of the criteria mentioned in the previous paragraph by itself may be taken as evidence of orality. If, however, a large number of these features are discovered in a given text, the probability of closeness to an oral event is enhanced. Judged by these standards, none of the transformation-text manuscripts I have examined approach the less sophisticated sūtra lectures as being demonstrably derived from or related to an oral setting. Indeed, some of the transformation texts are rather well written and virtually free of revisions. Texts such as the Tun-huang Wu Tzu-hsu story or the "Tale of the Honorable [Hui-]yuan of Lu Mountain" 爐山遠公話,[62] again judged by these standards, are even further removed from the original oral event(s) which, presumably, were their inspiration, though they may only have existed as written texts from their very beginning.

The overall impression one gains from the available data is that the majority of transformation texts, evolutionally speaking, were already several generations removed from the seminal oral performances that led to their birth. Conversely, the less sophisticated sūtra lectures have all the earmarks of being in the first generation of descendants from their original oral parent(s). Few Tun-huang manuscripts of popular literature that I have examined rival Taiwan 32[63] in respect to outright messiness. It is also significant that the quotative formula ("Please sing" or "Now I shall begin singing") appears only infrequently in the less sophisticated sūtra lectures, whereas it occurs with fixed regularity in the more polished ones. Likewise, I have deep reluctance to admit the transformation-text verse-introductory formula as evidence of direct derivation from oral performance on the grounds that it is too obligatory. No other form of storytelling with pictures anywhere in the world that I am aware of employs this kind of formula *with such fixed regularity*. The very fact that it is required with such constancy smacks of literary convention rather than oral improvisation. This is not to deny, however, that the verse-introductory formula in all likelihood is a reflection and stylization of actual phrases customarily but not compulsorily employed by picture storytellers. Storytellers' phrases in Ming and Ch'ing vernacular short stories, even more so than the verse-introductory formula of transformation texts and the quotation formula of the more polished sūtra lectures, are stereotypic. In the very conscious effort to convey immediacy through these and other devices which constitute the "simulated context," the true nature of such late stories as written literature is revealed.

The second of the chief identifying features of *pien-wen* is their prosimetric arrangement. The typical form of Tun-huang transformation texts consists of an alternation between prose and verse sections. There may be variations among different texts in the proportion of verse to prose and in the manner in which they are employed. For example, in the Maudgalyāyana transformation, there are more verse lines than prose lines. The prose portions introduce the basic substance of the story, whereas the verse repeats and expands, emphasizing salient details. By contrast, the prose portions of the Śāriputra transformation take on much greater prominence in relation to the verse, while in the Li Ling transformation there is a fairly even balance. The Wang Ling transformation at times uses the verse to carry a large amount of the narrational burden but at other times relegates it virtually to a minor role of recapitulation or comment. The same may be said of the prose portions in the Wang Chao-chün transformation. But, regardless of the amount of prose and verse in the various Tun-huang texts and the nature of the relationship between them, prosimetric alternation is characteristic of most works labeled *pien-wen*. What is perhaps more important is that this form is also characteristic of many other popular literary genres that appear in China *after* transformation texts. It must be reiterated that the prosimetric form did not enter China solely in the guise of *pien-wen*. There were numerous other genres of Buddhist literature, both classical and vernacular, that used the typical Indian alternation between prose and verse. These genres began to enter China as early as the second century and had an impact on various levels of culture.

I have decided to follow the Prague school of Sinology in using the English word "prosimetric(al)" rather than the French *chantefable*. In the first place, although students of comparative literature have used the latter word to refer to any narrative work that alternates between verse and prose, it originally signified a specific type of medieval French narrative. In fact, the term occurs only once in medieval French literature, at the end of the thirteenth-century *Aucassin et Nicolette*: "*No chantefable prent fin*" (Our *chantefable* comes to an end). It apparently means "[piece to] sing-speak" and derives from the nominal form of the Middle French verbs *canter* ("to sing") and *fabler* ("to relate").[64] On the other hand, "prosimetric" has a known Latin derivation (*prōsimetricus*) that fits the purpose for which we intend to use it. And, while obsolete for the last 300 years, it was long ago adopted into the English language. According to Thomas Blount's *Glossographia* (1656), "prosimetrical" means "consisting partly of Prose, partly of Meeter or Verse."[65] The alternation of prose and verse may be referred to in Sanskrit as *miśrakam* ("mixed; not prose; various; manifold").[66] In Tibetan, the equivalent of *miśrakam* is *spel-ma*.[67] This term is inaccurately and misleadingly translated in the Chinese section of the *Mahāvyutpatti* (no. 1456) as "long and short lines" 長短句, that is, "lyric verse" 詞.[68] *Campū*, a term of obscure origins dating from the tenth century A.D., was used by Daṇḍin in *Kāvyādarśa* (i. 31)[69] to designate the alternating prose and verse form of narrative. But the alternation of prose and verse in Indian narration is so pervasive that rarely do literary critics find it necessary to give it a special name.

One other preliminary observation regarding my use of the word "prosimetric" needs to be made. While it is permissible to describe *pien-wen* as prosimetric in form, it must be emphasized that this in no sense is a translation of the term itself. I have discussed the problem of the meaning of *pien-wen* as "transformation text" at length in Chapters 2 and 3.

The first problem concerning the prosimetric narrative form is, naturally, its origin. Careful consideration of the available evidence leads to the conclusion that it was not present in Chinese literature before the introduction of Buddhism. But the issue of the origins of the prosimetric form in China has been so hotly debated that we cannot ignore the counterclaims of those who insist that it has a native source. I shall begin by reviewing their arguments.

Though half-a-century ago Buddhist importation was considered to be the most reasonable explanation for the sudden and unprecedented appearance of extended prosimetric narrative during the T'ang period, some later scholars have begun to disavow all possibility of Buddhist influence. As a result, various theories have been propounded to account for the native origins of the prosimetric form. Thus Lu K'an-ju, while taking Hu Shih to task for having suggested[70] a Buddhist origin for the prosimetric form, names[71] the *Book of Change* 易經, *Conversations of the States* 國語, the pre-Ch'in philosophers, and the metrical *tz'u-fu* 辭賦[72] as prosimetric in form. In fact, says Lu, every period of Chinese history had this form. Yet examination reveals that none of the works mentioned by him bears any resemblance to prosimetric narrative. Lu also inexplicably mentions several Sung-period popular performing arts (for example, the medley and "The Pedlar") as prosimetric genres having no possible connection with Buddhist *gāthā*. As a matter of fact, there is definite, contemporaneous proof that the verse portions of transformation texts (which preceded the Sung dynasty!) were referred to by the same name (*gāthā*) as those in sūtras. This proof is found in a note which follows the title of P2319, "Transformation Text on Mahāmaudgalyāyana Rescues His Mother from the Nether World." This is an abbreviated version of the story, and the purpose of the note is to explain one way in which the abbreviations are consistently made. "Each of the verses (*gāthā*) [is cut short] after two or three lines by the notation 'and so on and so forth.'" 其偈子每槭[73]三兩句後云ㄋ是.

But it was Ch'eng I-chung who mounted[74] the most serious and concentrated challenge against the Indian origins of prosimetric narrative:

> We do not at all reject cultures that come from abroad, but rather all along have constructively and creatively absorbed the strengths and special features of foreign cultures. But the culture of our race has its own traditions; all influences from abroad must combine with the traditions of the race before they can produce a beneficial result. This literary form, *pien-wen*, is mainly composed of parallel prose and heptasyllabic poetry which are determined by the special features of the Han [Chinese] language. Is it possible that this most authentic form of the people could have been transmitted from India?! The origins of *pien-wen* as a type of prosimetric literature can be found far back in the *fu* 賦 of ancient times.[75]

Ch'eng confuses the separate components (prose and verse) of the prosimetric form with the combined form itself. The highly speculative nature of his reference to *fu* ("rhapsody" or "rhyme-prose") is also obvious when, in listing a long series of ancient *fu* titles, he says that they were "perhaps" ("maybe," "likely," "possibly") narratives in direct discourse. A look at the cited *fu* shows that they are largely ornate and embellished examples of parallel prose, are not primarily narrative but descriptive, and contain no extensive dialogue. In short, they do not resemble transformation texts in form, content, or style. Ch'eng is even less sure of himself when discussing later *tsa-fu* ("miscellaneous rhapsodies" 雜賦), which he says he "feels" had a close relationship to *pien-wen*.[76] This attempt by Ch'eng to find a thoroughly Chinese pedigree for transformation texts is not convincing. The *tsa-fu* he cites (by Ts'ai Yung 蔡邕 [133–192] and Chao I 趙壹 [fl. 178]) are mostly quadrisyllabic with a Ch'u style song or pentasyllabic poem appended at their end. In any case, it is puzzling that Ch'eng claims a basic prosimetrical structure for these pieces. His argument becomes even less satisfactory when, advancing forward in time, he declares that the minor *fu* of Six Dynasties authors resemble *pien-wen* still more closely. He cites Yü Hsin's 庾信 (513–581) "Spring Rhapsody," but examination reveals that it is constructed of four-six (parallel) prose with a heptasyllabic poem tacked on at beginning and end.

When tested, Ch'eng's fragile but influential hypothesis concerning the structural affinities of *fu* and *pien-wen* collapses *in toto*. It is well known that the narrative element in *fu* is scanty. Its most characteristic use is for long and elaborate descriptive pieces, such as those that describe imperial hunts, capitals, natural and urban scenery, and sometimes for philosophical reflection or discourse. Another weak point in Ch'eng's argument centers on the fact that all of the *fu* that he cites, even the ancient ones, were written by well-known literati. This contradicts his own later stress[77] on *pien-wen* as coming from the people. Finally, as a self-contained specimen of Ch'eng's erroneous premises, I quote the following sentence: "The main reason for saying that *pien-wen* came from India is that they elaborate stories from the Buddhist sūtras and, since Buddhism comes from India, *pien-wen* too can only come from India."[78]

Su Ying-hui's attempts[79] to establish *fu* as the progenitor of *pien-wen* fare no better when submitted to critical analysis. His argument is replete with contradictions, such as when he declares within the space of two lines that, on the one hand, the origins of *pien-wen* are "very early" and, on the other, that [T'ang?] monks are to be given credit for spreading this "new literary form." Su even goes so far as to invent a hypothetical "folk" *fu* from the Han and Wei periods as the putative ancestor of *pien-wen*.

An even more strained attempt to find a Chinese origin for the prosimetric form is that of Yang Yin-shen,[80] who adduced tomb epitaphs and obituaries as the native forerunners of the combination of prose and verse characteristic of *pien-wen*. Aside from the obvious facts that these were always in classical Chinese, did not alternate between prose and verse, and were not intended to be narratives, Yang's deduction is irrelevant to a discussion of the origins of *pien-wen* except to say that the Chinese literary environment, of which tomb epitaphs and obituaries were a part, was not predisposed to the rejection of the Buddhist innovation or, more precisely and positively, to the importation of the prosimetric narrative form. As a matter of fact, beyond *fu* ("rhymeprose" or "rhapsody"), it is easy to name many other genres of early Chinese literature that either stand midway between prose and verse or mingle the two in various ways: *chen* 箴 ("admonition"), *ming* 銘 ("commemorative inscription"), *sung* 頌 ("ode"), *tsan* 贊 ("eulogy"), *lei* 誄 ("obituary"), *tiao* 弔 ("condolence"), and *chi-wen* 祭文 ("sacrificial text"), to name only a few. Strangely, none of the proponents for a Chinese source for the prosimetric form have mentioned these genres. Yet inspection of typical examples reveals that it would be to no avail anyway because they simply were not used to advance a narrative through alternation of prose and verse sections the way genuine prosimetric literature does.

Two additional sources for a native prosimetric tradition have been adduced by Chang Hung-hsun.[81] The first is the *Spring and Autumn Annals of Wu and Yueh* (*Wu Yueh ch'un-ch'iu*). Chang claims that it stands as an example of early prosimetric storytelling. The latter claim (that it is an example of early storytelling) cannot be tested, and the former (that it is prosimetric) cannot be sustained because the verses in this historical narrative are short, occur only very sporadically, and do not carry the narrative.

Chang's second hypothetical proof of an early prosimetric tradition in China is taken from the first chapter of the *Biographies of Illustrious Women*. Here we find the statement "Of old, when a woman was pregnant. . . , at night they would have a blind [entertainer] recite poetry and tell of proper matters." 古者婦人妊子... 夜則令瞽誦詩道正事.[82] Chang suggests that this refers to a prosimetric performance, but such an interpretation is not justified on the basis of the cited passage alone, and no ancillary evidence is forthcoming.

As a specimen of the confusion that results from insisting upon a wholly native Chinese source for the prosimetric form, I cite *A History of Chinese Folk-Literature* collectively written by the students of the class of 1955 of the Chinese Department at Peking Normal University. They begin their discussion of the subject by stating, "We believe that the prosimetric form did not begin with *pien-wen* but that it had its own source of development in China."[83] As examples of these Chinese "sources," they mention "Southeastward Flies the Peacock" 孔雀東南飛 and the "Ballad of Muklan" 木蘭詩.

Aside from the fact that the quoted statement implicitly accepts the foreign origins of *pien-wen*, what are its merits? In the first place, no responsible scholar would say that the origin of the prosimetric form in China was *pien-wen* alone. The importation of this new form into China was a highly complicated process which involved, among other elements, the translation of sūtras and the oral performance of folk narratives. The students of the class of 1955 have here called upon a straw man whose claims—and hence their counterargument—must be disqualified. Second, "Southeastward Flies the Peacock" and "Ballad of Muklan" are pentasyllabic narrative poems (which themselves are not entirely free of the suspicion of foreign influence) and hence have no direct bearing on the question of the importation of the prosimetric form per se into China.

Perhaps sensing the weakness of their argument, the students of the class of 1955 then proceed to withdraw and make a more equivocal statement about the possibility of Indian influence:

> In the process of the development from verse to the combination of prose and verse, we do not at all deny that the form of Indian Buddhist prosimetric sūtra lectures which use verse and prose side by side had a certain influence, but this influence could take effect only upon a pre-existent Chinese foundation. . . .[84]

If by "pre-existent Chinese foundation" the authors mean "the Chinese languages and their inherent stylistic capabilities," no one can take exception to this statement.

If the various proposals for a Chinese source of the prosimetric form do not stand up under scrutiny, what may be said of those that suggest an Indian origin? Not surprisingly, they fare much better. The prosimetric form is so common a characteristic of Sanskrit sūtras and their Chinese translations that it would be tedious to list all examples. Chinese scholars working on *pien-wen* in the second quarter of this century were well aware of this, and it is only natural that they should have made a connection between the two.

Thus Cheng Chen-to, noting that the alternation of verse and prose for narrative purposes was absent in Chinese literature before the T'ang period, declared[85] that the most workable hypothesis for the introduction of this new form was that it entered in the wake of the translation of Buddhist literature. Liang Ch'i-ch'ao had earlier noted the unique Indian proclivity for the alternate use of prose and verse in his study of the relationship between Buddhist translations and Chinese literature. The prosimetric form is as characteristic of Indian Buddhist literature as parallel prose is of Chinese classical literature. In adapting the foreign form to their own needs, the Chinese fused these two originally disparate literary modes into a new one.

There can be little objection to Cheng Chen-to's statement that "the origins of *pien-wen* definitely cannot be found in native [Chinese] writings."[86] In discussing the mysteriously sudden appearance of the prosimetric form in Chinese literature, Cheng Chen-to has offered these eminently sensible words of advice: "But a new literary form certainly cannot just fall from the clear blue sky; if it is not the creation of a native genius, then it must be the importation of foreign influence."[87]

Hsiang Ta, in his study entitled "On Buddhist Cantos of the T'ang Period" (Lun T'ang-tai Fo-ch'ü 論唐代佛曲),[88] has tentatively established the nature of the foreign influence which was operative in the development of Tun-huang popular literature. Ch'en Kuo-ning holds that the form of *pien-wen* was imported from India and cites[89] the *Jātaka-mālā* of Aśvaghoṣa (→ Āryaśūra) as an example of its early use for narrative purposes there.

In an attempt to explain the origins of prosimetric literature in China, Hrdličková has focused on the translation of Buddhist sūtras: "If we want to gain a proper understanding of [the] development of *shuo-ch'ang wen-hsue*[*h*], we have to go back to the translations of Buddhist sūtras in Chinese, in which prosimetric form appears for the first time in Chinese literature."[90] Hrdličková is able to offer unimpeachable evidence that the written prosimetric form was, indeed, introduced from India through the medium of Buddhas sūtras. Hrdličková's article[91] has shown that the translation of Buddhist literature was the genesis of the prosimetric form in China. Even though a whole cache of late Han or Six Dynasties prosimetric narratives might one day be discovered (granted this is virtually an impossibility given the preponderant shape of the development of Chinese narrative), it would still not obviate Buddhist influence. All that needs to be added to what Hrdličková has written is the qualification that prosimetric literature was in all probability also concurrently being introduced to China in the oral realm. There is, however, no convincing way to demonstrate this conclusively for the time before the T'ang period.

In an important but almost wholly ignored article, Chi Hsien-lin has specified the possibility of Tocharian texts having functioned as an intermediary stage in the introduction of the prosimetric form to China:

> This form is not of Chinese but of Indian origin. The *Mahavastu* and the *Lalitavistara* are among the many works written in this style. The *Pancatantra* is also in verse and prose.
>
> China had access to this form through translations of Buddhist scriptures and through the ancient languages of Central Asia. Several versions of the tale of the carpenter and painter exist in Chinese translations of sutras, all of them in prose; but in ancient Tocharian the same story is in verse and prose. As ancient Tocharian served as a bridge between China and India, it may also have been instrumental in introducing this genre to China.[92]

Chi's suggestion leads us directly back to India and a discussion of the origins, place, and function of the prosimetric form there.

Pischel has outlined the typical form of Indian narrative literature as having verse of a fixed character and prose that functions primarily as interstitial connective between the separate units of verse:

> The hymns in dialogue of the Ṛgveda and other works also, as the Suparṇādhyāya, are almost incomprehensible in the form in which they have come down to us. The connection between the separate verses is very loose, often quite impossible to discover. To understand it we need a connecting text, which in some cases is given in prose by the Brāhmaṇas, works explanatory of the Vedas. Later works, such as the Mahābhārata and the Purāṇas, sometimes contain the entire narrative, but then often in a very different form. On the ground of similar cases in Irish literature, Windisch first threw out [i.e., advanced] the

> suggestion that originally only the verses were unchangeable, and that the reciters connected them by means of prose narrations. This view is undoubtedly correct. It is borne out by the name of the rhapsodist *granthika*, i.e., joiner or connector. The prose narrations were in general rigidly fixed only as regards their contents; their development in detail was left to the judgment of the rhapsodist. Originally it was precisely the same with drama. The classical drama of India has a peculiar construction, the prose being continually interrupted by stanzas in various metres. Such stanzas in pre-classical times formed the "fixed capital" of the player. As regards the prose the greatest freedom was left to him. This is the case up to the present day in the popular plays. Popular plays have never been written down in India. The manager gives his actors a short summary of the contents of the piece they are to act, and leaves the development of it to their talent for improvisation. We have literary imitations of popular plays in Bengal and Nepal, all of which have the same characteristics. The verses are fixed: only suggestions are given for the prose, and these in the Nepali pieces are in the dialects of the country.[93]

Thus we see that, from the earliest known and most sacred literature of the Indian people down to more recent and popular entertainments, it has always been the verse portions of a literary work that are relatively fixed and the interjacent prose passages that are more fluid.[94]

Gokuldas De has shown[95] conclusively that the original form of the *Jātaka* consisted of a verse or verses embodying some episode from the Buddha's past lives. The moral of the episode was implicit in the verse but was made more apparent through the addition of a prose narrative that varied according to circumstances. As a collection of selected verses, the *Jātaka* go back approximately to the time of the Buddha. In many instances, however, they have adopted and adapted stories current before the Buddha's birth.

In the long tradition of the creation and transmission of the stories about the Buddha's former births in the *Jātaka*, there are many phases that are instructive for students of transformation texts. One of the most important conclusions of scholars concerning this rich body of stories composed of various combinations of prose and verse is that the verse portions have always been the most stable parts. Ratilal Mehta has reviewed the scholarship on the subject and gives the following synoptic explanation:

> Originally both prose and verse of the *Jātakas* came down orally; but naturally the prose had a less stable form than the verse, being more exposed to changes and enlargements, so that when the canon was composed, and subsequently when it was written down, in the 1st century B.C. . . . only the verses retained their original form, whereas the rendering of the prose was at first entrusted to the reciters who could recite the verses more faithfully than the prose, and it was only at a later period committed to writing by Commentators.[96]

Hence, there is nothing mysterious about the manner in which folk literature is composed:

> Authors of folklore have always remained anonymous: the story originates in the mind of one man: he composes the verses and puts them afloat among the folk: in course of time these verses become the common possession of the whole folk: the verses are thus preserved, with very rare modifications: the prose which is only a commentary on these verses changes from mouth to mouth, until it settles in the form in which it is finally committed to writing. This is, in general, the life-story of a folk-tale. The same can be said with regard to the *Jātaka* stories.[97]

Likewise, a similar process of birth and growth can be imagined for transformations and transformation texts. In this regard, it is significant that only the verses are written on the back of the illustrated Śāriputra scroll (P4524). It is the verses that are the central, stable core of a prosimetric folk narrative in the Indian tradition and in other Asian traditions influenced by it. In modern times, many Chinese storytellers still insist that "the song" is inviolate and cannot be changed.[98]

The relationship between the transformation text and *Jātaka* traditions is not simply one of parallels and correspondences regarding the development of the prosimetric form. These two traditions must also be considered as related because they were both Buddhist teaching devices and both were illustrated with pictures. The *Jātaka*, already in the third and second centuries B.C., were portrayed in the bas-reliefs on the stone walls of Bhārhut and

Sāñchī, in the second century A.D. at Amarāvatī and at Ajaṇṭā. Fa-hsien, in the fifth century, saw 500 *Jātaka* represented by figures at Abhayagiri in Ceylon and Hsuan-tsang saw them depicted on many stupas during his pilgrimage to India. The *Jātaka* were also an important source of imagery for the wall-paintings at Tun-huang.

The third of the chief identifying characteristics of *pien-wen* is a close connection with illustrations. The very nature of the first identifying characteristic, the pre-verse formula, discussed at length at the beginning of this chapter, points to this relationship. But there are many other items of evidence which can be adduced,[99] including some of the contemporaneous literary references I cite in Chapter 6. By no means do I wish to rule out the possibility that pictures could also have been used in conjunction with sūtra lectures and other evangelistic performances by monks. What I emphasize is that the use of pictures was mandatory for the folk, oral antecedents of transformation texts in the strictest or narrowest sense. As so aptly put by Kanaoka Shōkō, "*pien-wen* cannot exist apart from pictures."[100]

The illustrated scroll (P4524) of Śāriputra's contest of supernatural powers with Raudrākṣa is the most important item of primary evidence for the organic connection between genuine *pien-wen* and pictures.[101] In the first place, the very story of Śāriputra's contest[102] with the Six Heretics is perfect material for the transformation text *par excellence*. For the business of both the contest and the genre is to create illusory objects and states of being. We should note, parenthetically, that there is a long Indian tradition of intellectual and religious debates' being described in terms of contests of supernatural feats or accompanied by them.[103] The theme of an opponent's pitting his magical conjurations against those of another is frequent in later Chinese popular literature as well.[104] The six scenes[105] represented on the illustrated Śāriputra scroll perfectly correspond to the incidents narrated in the matching transformation text (part on S5511 and part formerly in Hu Shih's possession, also S4398, P4615, and a copy formerly owned by Lo Chen-yü):

	Six Heretics	Śāriputra
Conjuration	mountain	warrior (*vajrapāṇi*) with club
	water buffalo	lion
	pond	white elephant
	poisonous dragon	gold-winged bird (*garuḍa*)
	yellow-headed ghost	Vaiśravaṇa Mahārāja
	tree	wind

Needless to say, Śāriputra beats his rival in this unfairly organized contest. Since he is always permitted to "go" second (and last), it is easy for him to top anything his frustrated opponent can produce. The verses on the back of the scroll are virtually identical to those in the corresponding sections of the transformation text. It is also noteworthy that they are different from any verses in the canonical source of the story, "Sudatta Builds a Monastery" 須達起精舍 in the tenth fascicle of the *Sūtra of the Wise and the Foolish* 賢愚經. This would seem to indicate that they have an independent, perhaps folk, origin. Be that as it may, if anything were to be written on a performance scroll, it is understandable that it would be the verses. This we already know from the whole prosimetric tradition in India where the verses are relatively fixed and the prose passages tend to be improvised anew with each session.

The language of the cartouches on the wall-paintings at the back of Tun-huang cave 146 correspond rather closely to that in the "Transformation Text on the Subjugation of Demons" 降魔變文 which relates the magic contest between Śāriputra and Raudrākṣa.[106] It would appear that the cartouches and the text are related by more than the fact that they have the same story. The common ground to which I refer is the intimate connection which both have with transformation illustrations.

The very title of S2614 (dated 921) is proof of the close connection between transformation texts and pictures: "Transformation Text on Mahāmaudgalyāyana's Rescue of His Mother from the Dark Regions, With Pictures, One Scroll, With Preface" 大目乾

連冥間救母變文并圖一卷并序. The two characters for "with pictures" have been marked out with ink. Since there are no pictures anywhere on S2614, it is puzzling to consider what may have been the actual relationship of the missing illustrations to the text. It is conceivable that it was originally intended to paint the pictures on the so-called verso of the scroll but that, for lack of funds, inability to locate a suitable artist, or for some other reason, the work was never completed. This seems unlikely, however, for at least two reasons. The first is that the writing on the nominal verso of the scroll, which consists of lists of monks in various Tun-huang monasteries, appears from examination of its placement to have been written prior to the transformation text. Hence, there never would have been any space available on the alleged verso for the pictures. The second is that the transformation text, being complete with both prose and verse, must have been intended for reading rather than for oral presentation. This is in contrast to the illustrated Śāriputra scroll (P4524), which has pictures on the front and *verses only* on the back. Just as with the S5511-Hu Shih Śāriputra transformation text, one simply would not expect to find pictures on the back of a scroll intended for private reading instead of public performance. Though the manuscript lacks the pictures, it does not lack the preface which, apparently, extends from the beginning up to "Long ago, when the Buddha was in the world...."[107]

Although the pictures that were intended to accompany S2614 have long since become separated from it or were, perhaps, never executed, we are obliged to take the words in the title ("With Pictures") at face value. If we do, it is inevitable that we ask ourselves such questions as who purchased and owned these scrolls? For what purpose did they want them? In this regard, it is possible to detect a parallel with certain later illustrated texts derived from oral performance. What, for example is the *raison d'être* for the Ming dynasty *Playscript about Maudgalyāyana Rescuing His Mother and Exhorting Her to Goodness*?[108] Surely actors would not require such an elaborately designed and profusely illustrated script? The pictures, together with the text, can most plausibly be explained as serving the purpose of reminding the reader what a real performance of the play was like. The printed version allowed the owner of the *Playscript about Maudgalyāyana Rescuing His Mother and Exhorting Her to Goodness* to reanimate his recollection of the words and movements of the players or to imagine what they might be—and in the convenient privacy of his home, at that. The demand for written transformation texts with pictures such as S2614 might be explained similarly.

That S2614 was intended for reading rather than for performance is partially evident, as I have said, from the inclusion of the prose passages together with the verse passages. The conclusion which would appear inescapable is that a separate scroll of pictures was produced (or there were plans for such a scroll) for the convenience and delectation of the reader of the transformation text (hence the words "With Pictures" in the title) but that it was subsequently lost or never procured (hence the inking out). A passage from *The Tale of Genji* amply demonstrates that picture books were used in conjunction with private reading of fiction during the late Heian (late ninth to twelfth centuries):

> The princess took out illustrations to old romances, which they examined while Ukon[109] read from the texts. Absorbed now in the pictures and facing her sister in the lamplight, Ukifune[110] had a delicate, girlish beauty that was perfection of its kind. The quiet elegance of the face, with a slight glow about the eyes and at the forehead, was so like Oigimi[111] that Nakanokimi herself was paying little attention to the pictures.[112]

This scene, as portrayed on the *Tale of Genji Picture Scroll* (*Genji Monogatari emaki* 源氏物語繪卷), vividly and accurately depicts how picture scrolls or books might be used privately for entertainment in conjunction with a separate written text.[113]

A tenth-century collection of Buddhist stories entitled *Sanbōe* (*kotoba*) [(Explanations of the) pictures of the three jewels] 三寶繪(詞) provides further confirmation of this practice in medieval Japan. In his introduction, the author, Minamotono Tamenori, says that he composed the book in order to console an unhappy princess. He states that the book was meant to explain the meanings of picture-scrolls illustrating the stories.[114]

It is important to note, in connection with the problem of the title of S2614, the title given on P3107 which is "Transformation Text on Mahāmaudgalyāyana's Rescue of His Mother from the

Dark Regions, One Scroll, With Preface" 大目乾連冥間救母變文一卷并序.' The resemblance is unmistakable. Although only the beginning of P3107 is preserved, it is clear that it belongs to precisely the same lineage of copies as S2614. But there is no mention of pictures, neither in the title nor in the text. The conclusion that must be drawn is that pictures were not originally intended to be a part of this class of manuscript. The pictures mentioned in the title of S2614 would have been produced independently of the transformation text and were thus liable to become separated from it. The back of P3107 carries the notation "Transformation Text on Mahāmaudgalyāyana; One Scroll. Precious Preserve."[115]

Another manuscript of the Mahāmaudgalyāyana transformation, PK876, has blank spaces alternating with portions of the text.[116] These appear to have been intended for pictures that the owner of the scroll was unable to procure. If such be the case, it would indicate even more forcefully than does S2614 that there was a desire on the part of some transformation readers to look at both text and pictures. The illustrated transformation *manqué* on PK876 would have had its pictures facing the reader, an unsuitable placement for performance.

One rather important Tun-huang manuscript which appears not to have been mentioned previously in discussions of *pien-wen* and *pien-hsiang* is the fragmentary P5019. The verso is a crudely drawn picture. On the right side is a person carrying a back pack. His hands are raised to support the straps of the pack. It appears that the pack is quite heavy. He is shown leaving through the gate of a (city? courtyard? defense?) wall on top of which is a tiny flag. Another similarly equipped figure is entering the gate from the left. At the bottom left there is a structure that seems to be in the process of construction. Perhaps the men are carrying stones to build the uncompleted wall. The picture continues on toward both the left and right before the fragment breaks off. The recto, which may well be the corresponding text for the pictures (cf. the format of P4524), is written in heptasyllabic verse but also includes several lines with four syllables. Since this text specifically mentions the "King of Ch'in" 秦王 and his mass conscription of workers to build the Great Wall as protection against the "barbarian" nomads, it is possible that this is part of a transformation dealing with Meng

Chiang-nü 孟姜女, although neither she nor her husband, Ch'i Liang 杞梁, is mentioned by name in it. The text deals mainly with the sufferings and sorrows of the workers. The geographical locations mentioned in it are compatible with the story of Meng Chiang-nü. It should be recalled that the fragment (P5039) of the Meng Chiang-nü story printed in T32–35 is not a *pien-wen* in the narrowest sense that I have given the word because it lacks the verse-introductory formula.[117]

At the beginning of S5511 (the opening part of the "Transformation Text on the Subduing of Demons"), there is a drawing of a man holding a pole with a larger object attached to the end of it, perhaps a banner or a fan or large drum-beater.[118] The picture is unmistakably drawn on a separate piece of paper that was later joined to the beginning of the text fragment. Perhaps the drawing may originally have come from a narrative picture scroll. Hence, it is conceivable that the individual responsible for pasting this picture to the beginning of S5511 had obtained a set of illustrations for the "Transformation Text on the Subduing of Demons" and that he had intended to cut them up and splice them into the text itself at appropriate intervals.[119] That this never actually happened is obvious from the fact that the manuscript formerly in Hu Shih's possession, which takes up where S5511 leaves off (and is actually part of the same original manuscript), shows no traces of pictures throughout its entire length. The tear that caused these two parts of what should be a single manuscript to become separated may in some way be related to the attempt to join the pictures to it. There are two additional facts about the surviving picture fragment that require attention. The first is that it is torn off (on the right side) close to where it joins the text (on the left side). The second is that the picture faces the reader. This latter fact is particularly significant since it means that the fragmentary scroll as it is now constructed was probably *not* intended for performance before an audience but for individual or, at most, intimate group viewing.

I have so far not been able to discover any hard and fast pictorial evidence of transformation performances during the T'ang period. Among the more tantalizing bits of evidence encountered is from Tun-huang cave 70 (Pelliot number; Tun-huang Institute 217) in the middle section at the bottom of the left wall.[120] During a trip to Tun-huang in September 1985, I examined closely the figures of several men on this section who are holding up scrolls. At least two of these scrolls appear to have designs on the verso side, particularly that of the man under the tree facing left. It is of the utmost importance to know whether this impression is corroborated by similar scenes elsewhere. Scholars who have ready access to all of the Tun-huang caves would be performing a great service if they closely examined the paintings of this cave and other caves for evidence of storytelling and lecturing. Let us hope that all of the inscriptions in the cartouches at Tun-huang and other cave sites in China will be recorded accurately and quickly before they vanish forever.[121]

Appendix
The Indian Hypothesis

Many of the most characteristic features of *pien-wen* discussed thus far in our presentation seem to point to an Indian (or partially Indian) origin for the genre. These include the Buddhist content of the earliest examples (Chapter 2), the meaning of the term *pien* itself (Chapter 3), and the prosimetric form of the texts (Chapter 4). Perhaps these apparent affinities are only accidental and should therefore be discounted out of hand. After all, the concept of cultural diffusion has fallen into disrepute of late, and we would be well advised to steer clear of any hint of borrowing unless there is ironclad evidence to demonstrate that it actually exists. Yet, even though the above-mentioned grounds for an Indian background may be only circumstantial, they certainly loom large enough to invite consideration.

When we examine the fourth characteristic feature of *pien-wen* (its relationship to pictures), however, we find ourselves confronted once again with signs of Indian antecedents. In pursuing the forerunners of Chinese picture storytelling, the investigator is inexorably drawn to India, even against his own will. The case for some sort of Indian influence on the development of *pien* as a type of picture storytelling actually almost builds itself. The evidence that has accumulated is massive and can no longer be ignored. Since there is far too much of it to offer in the present monograph, I shall content myself here with a brief resumé of some of the more salient points. For a full, documented treatment of all of the subjects touched upon in the remainder of this appendix, the reader is invited to examine the author's *Painting and Performance*: *Chinese Picture Recitation, Its Indian Genesis, and Analogues Elsewhere.*

What is the origin of the "Indian hypothesis"? Put simply, it would appear to be the inevitable result of attempting to trace back in time and space the Chinese tradition of picture recitation. That there existed such a tradition can no longer be denied. One of the most surprising discoveries in this regard is the fact that *pao-chüan* 寶卷 ("treasure scroll") performers from the Ming to the middle of this century often used pictures to illustrate their narratives. There are hard data as well for picture storytelling during the Sung and Yuan periods. The representative T'ang genre of picture recitation (*chuan-pien* 轉變) was indubitably the oral predecessor of the *pien-wen*. If we attempt to find the forerunners of oral *pien* picture recitations, however, we are drawn to Central Asia. No clear-cut proof of a pre-T'ang Chinese tradition of picture recitation has yet been adduced, although vague, speculative attempts have been made to link the T'ang tradition to pictures associated with the *Classic of Mountains and Seas* (*Shan-hai ching* 山海經) and the *Songs of the South* (*Ch'u-tz'u* 楚辭). The Central Asian data, on the other hand, are unassailable. There are, in fact, several graphic depictions of picture recitation among the wall-paintings at Kyzil in Eastern Turkestan.

The problem with the Central Asian evidence is that most of it points back to India. Much as we might wish to avoid following the trail of *pien-wen* to the land of the Buddha, that is where it leads us. Once we have arrived in India, the manifestations of picture recitation are simply overwhelming. There are frequent references to a wide variety of picture reciters in religious scriptures, political and grammatical treatises, novels, plays, and commentaries that date back as far as the fifth century B.C. The picture reciter was such a common figure in the early Indian landscape that this was a favorite disguise of spies.

The picture showman has thrived throughout Indian history. We are fortunate in possessing extremely detailed ethnographic descriptions of these performers for the last hundred years. I might add that they are still active in various parts of the subcontinent and that extensive video recordings have been made of their performances. We know the social (namely, low), economic (poor), and religious (lay) status of Indian picture reciters. We have precise information about their mode and range of activity, their relationship to the painters of the scrolls they used, and the manner in which they learned their trade. More important, we have learned that they are normally illiterate, that the shape of their narratives is determined by various oral and pictorial formulaic devices, and that printed versions of their tales are the products of local scribes and publishers. All of this rich body of data either corroborates our sketchy understanding of oral transformation performers or, if we accept the Indian hypothesis and apply it judiciously, helps to flesh it out.

One way to test the hypothesis is to find out whether Indian picture storytelling traditions were transmitted to other areas of the world and, if so, whether there are any obvious analogies between T'ang-period oral *pien* and these transplanted traditions. It turns out that, here again, the hypothesis would appear to be confirmed.

The Indonesian term for nearly all types of dramatic representation is *wayang*. Without delving into the striking etymological resemblances between this word and *pien*, let me say simply that one type of *wayang*, namely *wayang bèbèr*, corresponds almost exactly to what we can glean from the historical and archeological record about oral *pien*. In fact, *wayang bèbèr* scrolls closely resemble, in size, shape, and arrangement of scenes, the sole surviving transformation picture scroll (P4524). Most competent authorities agree that *bèbèr* is the earliest type of *wayang* and that it may date back to approximately the T'ang period. All of these resemblances are striking enough, but we could dismiss them if we chose to on the grounds that that is all they are—adventitious similarities. What we cannot dismiss so lightly, however, is the testimony of two trustworthy early Ming travelers to Java who witnessed *wayang bèbèr* performances and stated that they were "exactly like ... *p'ing-hua* ('plain tales' or 'expository tales')." This would seem to indicate, first of all, that certain oral *p'ing-hua* (in particular, those that were presumably the forerunners of the Yuan period illustrated printed texts also styled *p'ing-hua*) may have employed pictures and, second, that they may be connected in some fashion with oral *pien*.

There is strong evidence to indicate that Indian picture storytelling traditions also traveled west to Persia. The same word *parda* (= Sanskrit *paṭ*) was used in Iran to designate the painting used by the storyteller to illustrate his tale. Even more convincing is the fact that Iranian picture storytellers customarily prefaced their performances with an "Indian *rāga* (*rāk i-hindī*)." I have also succeeded in identifying early picture storytelling traditions in Egypt, Turkey, Italy, France, Switzerland, Germany, and most other European countries. The chronology of the earliest historical records of picture storytelling in these countries would appear to vouch for a gradual spread westward out of India and then northward into Europe.

Many of the West Asian and European traditions of picture recitations show striking parallels to what we have been able to piece together about *pien*. Here I mention only that the Chinese picture storyteller's "Please look at the place . . ." (*Ch'ieh k'an . . . ch'u*) is echoed around the world and all seem to go back to an Indic "*dekhã̄ . . . para/mē*."

The Indian hypothesis is advanced solely because no more convincing explanation for the sudden appearance of transformations during the T'ang period has been forthcoming. We must emphasize that it remains a working hypothesis and is meant to be neither more nor less than that. We have not been able to establish any definite textual or archeological connection between *pien-wen* and a specific Indian example of picture recitation during the T'ang period or just before it. And yet there is a large body of evidence that points toward some sort of linkage between the oral antecedents of *pien* and Indian picture storytelling. Given the nature of the materials we are dealing with and barring any spectacular new finds that would reverse the presently perceived configuration of the development of *pien-wen*, the Indian hypothesis is a compelling argument. Since the form, early content, name, and structural rationale of *pien-wen* all show signs of Indian influence, it seems logical to conclude that the genre as a whole may have arisen through contact with Indic sources. This does not mean that *pien-wen* were imported lock, stock, and barrel from India. Considering that India and China are separated by thousands of miles of deserts, jungles, mountains, and oceans, such a conclusion would be absurd. The very fact that *pien-wen* are written in Chinese belies a total Indian source for the genre. All that the Indian hypothesis argues for is the recognition that inputs from the South Asian subcontinent were partly, perhaps fundamentally, responsible for the rise of *pien-wen*.

chapter five

Performers, Writers, and Copyists

One problem concerning Tun-huang popular literature that has most intrigued scholars is to what degree it has an oral provenance. Since the performers and scribes neglected to leave an explicit record of how they worked, we shall never be able to say with certainty exactly what process of transcription was involved. But there is much that can be inferred from the Tun-huang manuscripts themselves and from parallel cases in other literatures where we do have fuller evidence.

There are at least the following possibilities which might serve to explain how and why transformation texts came to be written down:

1. They were promptbooks, *aides-mémoire*, or scripts copied by the storytellers themselves for use in performance.

2. They were composed by someone else for the storyteller to deliver.

3. They were essentially apprentice's notes, hence they were intended for professional training purposes.

4. They were taken down *during* performance by an auditor (or auditors) for personal use or for someone else who wished to have a record of the performance.

5. An auditor wrote out the story from memory *after* an individual performance—again, for his own use or for someone who engaged him specifically for that purpose.

6. Though obviously a product of an oral *ambiance*, transformation texts are, strictly speaking, written literature, conceived, executed, and enjoyed in the study.

In order to determine which of these possibilities is the most likely, let us turn to some general observations, drawn from various traditions of storytelling and drama around the world, on the relationship between oral performance and written text.

A written text may grow up in the milieu of oral literature and be thoroughly imbued with its spirit. But it has not been demonstrated that performers of oral literature in China or elsewhere ever restricted themselves to exact reproduction of any given text. For, in the first place, no text can possibly prescribe all of the sound effects, gestures, asides, and so on, that are the stock in trade of even the least skillful performer. Judging from the evidence provided by numerous other Asian traditions of storytelling with pictures and of its cousin, the shadow-play,[1] the transformation performer would probably not have relied on a text. Those responsible for the writing of texts are most often members of the audience. Those who transcribe oral folk literature and thus begin the process of transforming it into popular written literature are very seldom the performers of oral literature themselves. The performers, in the majority of traditions that I have investigated, are generally functionally illiterate. As Barbara Ruch states, "Oral literature usually implies illiteracy on the part of the producer of a story, on the part of the audience, or both."[2] In the vast majority of oral traditions, transcription is perforce done by semi-literate or literate afficionados and merchant-purveyors of commercial texts.

Waley has offered the following cautionary note in regard to the relationship between the oral and written traditions:

> We must not . . . in dealing with societies where both exist, attempt to make too sharp a distinction between the two. Wherever texts exist at all, even if they are accessible only to a small minority, *the two sorts of tradition are bound to infiltrate one another*. A Mongol peasant who tells the story of Buddha's life may have learnt most of the episodes orally from other members of the tribe, who also learnt most of them orally. But he may very well have learnt other episodes from a Lama who has read them in a book. And the same Lama, should he write a book, would be likely enough to incorporate in his story folk-lore elements belonging to an oral tradition. A Majorcan peasant who tells one stories about the Moors has probably never read a book about the Moors or, indeed, any book at all. But much of what he tells could ultimately be traced to printed texts.[3]

In a discussion of the relation between folk storytellers and individuals who were capable of writing down stories to be read, Hrdličková makes clear the vitally creative role of the former:

> Especially in the towns, the relations between folk storytellers and literati were often very close, so that the work of the latter also exercised its influence on this branch of folk art, especially as regards subject-matter. Certainly, however, it would be a mistake to take as a starting-point for the study of the storytellers' material only a knowledge of literary fixed productions and assume that these works were written for the use of storytellers who memorized them and modified them only in unsubstantial details. Such a conception would imply that the true creators were, above all, the authors of these texts, who alone were able to give the story content and shape, while the storytellers' contribution was of secondary importance. If we penetrate more deeply into the true character of the storytelling art and make a closer acquaintance with the methods of training its practitioners, we realize that the direction of the process was reversed—that folk artists were not dependent on written texts, but rather the contrary was true, and that in this exceptionally strong stream of folk creation are to be found the origins of those works which today, although denied recognition by the literati in the past, form an integral and valuable part of Chinese literature.[4]

Amin Sweeny, who has studied the Malay shadow-play exhaustively, discovered that performers very rarely use written texts. And, even in the uncommon cases when they do, these texts are by no means in such a state that someone else could read them as a finished narrative:

> There are perhaps 5% of *Wayang Siam* dalangs who possess written records of part of their repertoire.[5] These manuscripts were all made by the owners themselves, and their sources were almost entirely oral. In all cases examined, dalangs owning such writings hand down their repertoire in oral form and the written record appears to be more for the dalang's personal reference than for the benefit of pupils although there is the possibility of a pupil being allowed to copy them.[6] *Further, in half the manuscripts examined, the writing was so hurried and so many details left to memory, that there would be little chance [for] anyone but the owner of finding them completely comprehensible.* There is, moreover, no known tradition of writings being handed down from teacher to pupil, and the fact that a majority of dalangs are illiterate or semi-illiterate seems to account for this ....[7]

H. I. R. Hinzler carried out an intensive study of the performance techniques of one high-prestige Indonesian *dalang* (shadow-play performer). Several very significant facts emerge from this study. In the first place, although the *dalang* was partially literate and could note down portions of Old Javanese texts that were suitable for use in his plays, he never consulted his notes before—much less during—a performance. He learned his plays by oral transmission largely from his teacher. While the *dalang* also made reference to stories contained in Sanskrit texts, his knowledge of these stories was derived from oral sources, and he never wrote them down. Most remarkable of all, according to Hinzler, "The *dalang* was surprised to hear the recording [of his performance]. He could not imagine or remember that he had spoken all these words. He was not even able to fill in the unintelligible passages."[8] The reason he could not do so was that he was supposedly possessed during performance. Ironically, the *dalang's* son (who was also his apprentice) could fill in most of the gaps. In the end, however, there remained passages that it was impossible to transcribe.

Choe Sang-su has pointed out[9] that Korean puppet players are usually farmers or part time farmers. It is unlikely that, in premodern times, such individuals would have attained sufficient literacy to compose texts based on their performances that would be satisfying to an audience of readers. Some few Peking shadow-play performers do possess rudimentary scripts, while others transmit their stories only orally.[10]

Until very recently, performers of Chinese folk theater normally did not use scripts. Occasionally there did exist texts of some of the plays they presented, but these were written down by "play enthusiasts" or "fans" (*hsi-mi* 戲迷), not by the actors themselves. The transcription, if that is what it should be called, occurred *after* the performance and was done by partially literate individuals who were *not* members of the elite segments of society. The elite, as a matter of fact, tended scrupulously to avoid attendance at such folk plays (in distinction to more formal performances put on by prestige troupes). Much more rarely, the texts may have been dictated by the actors to the same sort of scribe who would transcribe them from memory after performance. Naturally, a text taken down from dictation would more closely resemble what really occurs on the stage than one dependent on the recall of the scribe. But neither method would be completely faithful to the plays as given in live performance.[11]

The fullest historical account of the use of written materials in connection with Indonesian *wayang* plays[12] is that of Pigeaud. Several of the points he makes correspond exactly to what is known of traditions elsewhere in Asia:

> Probably Javanese wayaŋ play performers relied on orally transmitted tradition for the contents of their plays up to the beginning of the renaissance of classical letters in the eighteenth century. Some men of letters perhaps borrowed plots from the Sĕrat Kaṇḍa compendiums in order to make new plays. But then, the Sĕrat Kaṇḍa tales themselves were based on ancient tradition of professional story-tellers and wayaŋ play performers.
>
> In the eighteenth and nineteenth centuries Javanese dalaŋs became familiar with the use of books containing concise prose notes on the plots of wayaŋ plays. Such books were called *pakĕms*, manuals. In many cases the notes were so concise as to be almost incomprehensible for outsiders. In the middle of the nineteenth century some wayaŋ *pakĕms* were amplified and worked into prose tales, sometimes even containing texts of the conversation of the personages. Lastly, some complete texts of wayaŋ plays were written.[13]

But Pigeaud does not indicate that they were written by the performers themselves. That would be highly unlikely, since most of them were illiterate or only partially literate. Indeed, two paragraphs later, Pigeaud mentions the important role of Dutch scholars in encouraging Javanese authors to write about *wayang*:

> In the nineteenth and twentieth centuries much attention has been given by Dutch scholars to wayaŋ art and wayaŋ literature. They rightly considered the wayaŋ as one of the most important features of Javanese culture, leaving its mark in all domains of Javanese life. Therefore Dutch scholars stimulated Javanese authors to write treatises on the art of the wayaŋ play performer. No doubt the interest shown by nineteenth and twentieth-century Dutch scholars was instrumental in enlarging Javanese literature on wayaŋ.[14]

I suspect that the Dutch scholarly activity was one of the chief reasons why the *pakĕms* (handbooks) and *lakons* (play plots) came to be written down in a form accessible to individuals other than the *dalangs* themselves.

In discussing the subject of the evolution of folk and popular literature from oral to written forms, we must ask some basic questions about the motives of the individuals responsible for this transition. Did the performers themselves feel a need for something written to serve as a reminder of the contents of the stories they told? Would they have been interested in the printing and publishing of their stories? But, if the answers to these two questions are negative (as we shall see they generally are), who then was responsible? And why did they wish to transcribe the storytellers' wares?

A brief, but important, study of this problem may be found in Ssu Su's "Do Storytellers Have Promptbooks?"[15] The majority of performers interviewed by Ssu over a period of several years informed him that they transmitted their stories (including words, modulations of voice, gestures, expressions, and so on) orally and that they did not make use of promptbooks. But they also admitted that occasionally some parts of their stories had written texts and that these were usually the *verse sections* (N.B.). The storytellers stressed that the verses had to be memorized perfectly—not a word was to be changed. On the other hand, they allowed themselves much more flexibility in the spoken prose sections. This is in perfect agreement with historical experience and practice in the Indian prosimetric storytelling traditions.

According to Ssu Su, in cases where there were partial promptbooks, they were usually hand-copied by the performer himself on account books, scraps of paper, and so on:

> Because of the limitations of their cultural level, miswritten characters, wrong characters, and displaced characters as well as sentences that are ungrammatical or illogical are exceedingly numerous. Add to this the messy handwriting and it all makes it difficult to finish reading such texts.[16]

These conditions naturally contributed to keeping each storytelling tradition a secret known fully only to the performers themselves. But this was precisely what the storytellers wanted.

Some of the promptbooks seen by Ssu Su simply mentioned chapter headings and the main incidents within each. Never were directions for gestures, music, and so on described in detail. If there were any attempts to do so, they were always greatly simplified and abbreviated, perhaps because of the limitations of literacy. Only rarely did these promptbooks follow an established written text such as Lo Kuan-chung's 羅貫中 (Yuan period) *Romance of the Three Kingdoms* 三國志演義.

One other point stressed by Ssu Su is that, if they ever did note anything down in written form, the storytellers guarded it jealously and even denied outright that it existed. This is in harmony with what is known of storytellers the world over, including German *Bänkelsänger* ("bench-singers") and puppeteers. The last thing a performer wanted to see was his secretly transmitted tradition made public, since such an exposure threatened his capacity to earn an income from it. Those who wished to have the texts copied down and distributed were entrepreneurs outside the group of storytellers themselves. The ironic fact is that the demand for written forms of storytellers' narratives comes chiefly from those who are fond of the stories but desire a more permanent record than can be gained by attendance at an actual performance. Ruth Sawyer, a master storyteller in her own right, explains that "there is a kind of death to every story when it leaves the speaker and becomes impaled for all time on clay tablets or the written and printed page."[17] It is no wonder that traditional oral performers were unwilling to have their stories transcribed or recorded. Their very livelihood was at stake. All of this has a bearing both on the reasons for the appearance of transformation texts and the rapid disappearance of the form in the Sung period.[18]

The commercial motivation for the writing down of oral and vocal performances by scribes is convincingly established by Catherine Stevens in her study of Peking drumsinging (*ching-yun ta-ku* 京韻大鼓).[19] Enterprising businessmen would transcribe a given performance, then sell or rent their *hand-copied manuscripts* at temple fairs.[20] These texts were made without the consent and perhaps even without the knowledge of the drumsingers themselves. The simple fact that there was an economic demand for such texts brought them into existence, not any authorial urge on the part of the drumsingers. Certainly their own instincts would have precluded, if not prohibited, any attempt to publish their most private property. Pischel notes[21] that early German itinerant puppet troupes took oaths among themselves never to write down a word of their plays lest they fall into alien hands. The Rajasthani *bhopo* (picture storytellers) and *paṛ* painters, too, are highly secretive about the transmission of their traditions and craft.[22] To make their unique performances accessible in written form to large numbers of potential paying customers would be, in some measure, "to break their rice-bowl." But, no matter how threatening such unauthorized transcription and copying may have been, the singers were defenseless against the indefatigable efforts of the merchants to make a profit on their wares. Indeed, merchants displayed considerable competitive acumen in searching out the most entertaining stories, revising them, and hawking their finished product. Stevens mentions one famous individual who was active for a very long period of time beginning in the late eighteenth century named "Hundred-book Chang" (she refers to him as "Omnibus Chang").

In special cases, however, it would appear that ballad-singers and picture storytellers were themselves sometimes involved in the sale of printed materials relating to their performances. The commercial aspect of Japanese *etoki* ("picture explanation"), for example, is instructive for the study of picture storytelling elsewhere. The Kumano *bikuni* (so-called "nuns") would often carry extra copies of the pictures they explained as a way to make money. What is even more interesting is that they sometimes also sold booklets that consisted of simplified written versions of their oral narratives. Ruch's remarks[23] on the commercial activities of *etoki* correspond to what Brednich has to say[24] about the German *Bänkelsänger* (more precisely, their forerunners) who supported themselves by the sale of newspaperlike broadsheets, or Archer[25] about the Bengali *paṭuā* ("picture reciters") whose crude mythological scenes were purchased in the thousands by pilgrims, especially from stalls near the shrine of Kālīghāṭ. Yet, in no case known to me were storytellers engaged in the sale of the complete texts of their performances. Usually what they purveyed, if anything, were the barest outlines of their stories or perhaps just some of the song verses, or maybe a picture of one of the major episodes. This actually served to attract listeners who might want to hear the full versions.

Regardless of who exactly was responsible for doing the work of publication and making the sales, we are probably justified in postulating that the rise of printed popular literature in the Sung period had its roots in a similar combination of entertainment and commercial impulses.

The *Record of the Retrieval of Sūtras by the Tripiṭaka Dharma-Master of the Great T'ang Dynasty* (*Ta T'ang San-tsang Fa-shih ch'ü-ching chi* 大唐三藏法師取經記), for example, was "Printed by the Chang Family of the Central Entertainment District" 中瓦子張家印.[26] In his preface to the text, Wang Kuo-wei held that this is proof that it originated in Hangchow. There was, indeed, during the Sung period, a Hangchow Central Bazaar or Entertainment District as well as a bookseller surnamed Chang.[27] Průšek, however, is skeptical and reminds[28] us that other cities had Central bazaars and that Chang was a very common surname. But, no matter which city this work was printed in, we at least learn from its colophon that there were printers active in the same quarters where storytellers told their stories. This is confirmed by a Ming writer, Yeh Sheng, who has noted[29] the commercial incentives for gathering and publishing pictures and texts related to popular entertainment.

Korean *p'ansori*[30] are performed by *kwangdae*, who alternate between sung (*ch'ang*) and spoken (*aniri*) passages. They do not employ pictures, but these storytellers—who are accompanied by a single drummer—often employ gestures, which makes the performance, like transformations, intermediate between oral narrative and drama. The *kwangdae* are interesting for our present purposes because of the fact that, although they did have some mnemonic aids of their own, the *p'ansori* texts that were printed and sold to the public were written by outsiders of the *kwangdae's* profession.

One final note on the subject of who is responsible for writing down stories that were originally orally performed. Blindness has often been a trait of performers of oral literature throughout the world. The greatest bard of antiquity, Homer, is commonly supposed to have been sightless. Blindness was a mark of singers in many parts of medieval Europe.[31] This was certainly true as well of *biwa* (balloon guitar) singers in old Japan and *erh-hu* (two-stringed fiddle) storytellers in Ch'ing-period China.[32] Even today, many Cantonese ballad-singers and storytellers are blind.[33] A printed text would obviously have little significance for them. And yet their ballads and stories have come to be written down—by fans, by publishers, and by scholars.

In addressing the problem of the reason for the existence of the transformation-text manuscripts, we must not discount the possibility that they represent various points of development on a continuum ranging from oral to written. It would seem to be incontestable that transformation texts bear some relationship, however tenuous, to oral performances. Though highly imaginative, by and large transformation texts show a low level of literary polish. The frequent occurrence of homophonic error is an indication (though by on means proof) that the individuals who wrote down the transformation texts were more strongly influenced by oral renditions of stories than by written ones. Countless examples could be cited to indicate that the sound rather than the shape of a given character was usually uppermost in the mind of the scribe.[34] But how, then, are the less frequent orthographic errors to be explained? In the first place, the individuals who transcribed the transformation texts and other types of Tun-huang popular literature were obviously at least partially literate. Hence it is not unlikely that a scribe who had heard a given piece performed a number of times might also have read various popular and classical versions of the same story. As such, he would also have had in mind—even when transcribing what he may have considered to be a unique performance—certain visual recollections of the various texts relating to the story he had previously encountered. Total recall of a given performance, even one that the transcriber heard only moments before he began to write it down, is impossible. There are simply too many small details and happenings involved in a three- or four-hour performance for a transcriber to catch everything. Inasmuch as there were no developed stenographic,[35] mechanical, or electronic means available to make a verbatim transcription of any single performance, it was inevitable that written versions would be composite in nature because *all* previous encounters with the story at hand—whether oral or written—would be operative, to greater or lesser degree, in the mind of the transcriber. Therefore, it may be concluded that not one of the Tun-huang manuscripts of popular narratives accurately represents any single performance. I say this in spite of the fact that there are remarks recorded on some of the manuscripts that are ostensibly directed to an actual audience.

It is important, in this connection, to recall Patrick Hanan's concept of "simulated context." After a series of studies[36] in which he demonstrated that the corpus of extant vernacular short stories from the Ch'ing period and earlier are primarily written literature,[37] Hanan went on to account for the apparent marks of orality that many of these stories bear. His definition of this concept is as follows:

> "Simulated context" means the context or situation in which a piece of fiction claims to be transmitted. In Chinese vernacular fiction, of course, the simulacrum is that of the oral storyteller addressing his audience, a pretense in which the author and reader happily acquiesce in order that the fiction can be communicated.[38]

More specifically, "simulated context" refers to the phrases, devices, and techniques employed by an author or editor of vernacular short stories to create the atmosphere of a storytelling event. Thus, many vestiges of orality in fiction dating from the Sung through Ch'ing were shown to be part of the craft of the authors, who were attempting, whether consciously or unconsciously, to create the semblance of oral literature. The conventions of this craft required that certain formulaic expressions be employed which had all the appearance of deriving directly from oral performance. But it must be emphasized that, in the rare instances where outsiders have been privileged to examine the few genuine promptbooks of practicing storytellers (be they from Africa, Persia, Indonesia, or twentieth-century China) that do exist, the formulaic expressions are among the first elements to be left out. Such expressions serve no purpose when it comes to reminding the performer of the *content* of the tale he is about to perform (the performer has very different types of devices for that function). They operate, rather, in an automatic fashion as transitions to punctuate the performance, largely *for the audience*. They occur as reflex actions of the teller in performance, much as a hornist knows by instinct and practice where to breathe in a piece of music without marking the places or as a coloratura soprano knows by training and talent how to embellish a passage without specifying the notes ahead of time. The existence of numerous transparently formulaic expressions in a short story may be regarded as an indication that the work was intended for a reader and not for a performer. A performer would not need such markers; indeed, he would find them to be an encumbrance. On the other hand, an author who was attempting to duplicate or simulate a performance for a reader would regard them as essential.

This is not, of course, to deny that—in an evolutionary or developmental sense—there is a meaningful connection to be made between these vestiges of orality and their origin in actual storytelling. It is, in fact, one of the major purposes of this study to push back the limits of vernacular fiction to the time when it merges with the performing arts from which it was born. Needless to say, storytelling has continued in China up to the present day, and it is clear that authors of fiction from all periods have relied upon it as a rich source of themes, motifs, language, and even formulaic expressions. However, as I have pointed out before, formulaic language does not necessarily imply orality. Buddhist sūtras are highly formulaic, as are Ming and Ch'ing novels, but these are clearly written forms of literature. It would seem, rather, that obvious and recurrent formulaic expressions in written texts are *ipso facto* attempts to recapture a lost orality, that is, they are evidences of secondary orality.

To return to the reasons for the existence of popular narrative literature among the Tun-huang manuscripts, except for P4524 (the illustrated Śāriputra scroll) which was probably the property of a performer, it was written down for the purpose of being read—not necessarily by the larger public—just as were the later short stories. The common designation of the group of texts we are studying, after all, is *pien-wen*; surely *wen* is meant to refer to a category of written literature. What appear to be obvious evidences of orality are attributes of an effort to create a simulated context. Yet it must be conceded that the greater frequency of homophonic errors over orthographic errors indicates that certain of the transformation texts may be closer to spoken literature than to written literature.[39]

Another important type of evidence which indicates how closely these texts are related to the performing arts is the existence, in many cases, of multiple copies of the same story. While these copies may differ in details, when there is sufficient correspondence on the grosser aspect it is possible immediately to recognize individual manuscripts as variants of a single, basic tale. The most compelling explanation for this phenomenon is that there was a circumscribed body of tales which was standard fare for the transformation performers, but that these tales would be modified slightly with each telling and with each teller. Someone who assumed the task of preparing a written version would have been exposed to the stuff of that tale on countless occasions during his life. He may have heard it (or parts of it) from his uncle or mother, older brother or sister, friend or acquaintance, not to mention the numerous storytellers who would have recounted it for him.

It is well known that many storytellers and, indeed, many genres of storytelling have a repertoire consisting solely of one item, the Mongolian tale of Gesar[40] being a good example. Under such circumstances, it is the business of the storyteller to rework, recapture, and revivify the basic stuff of the story. To depart too far from the conventional mode of presentation would bring censure rather than praise. A scribe who transcribes what he may consider to be a unique performance is, in actuality, transcribing a tradition, a tradition that has been homogenized, digested, and assimilated through long practice on the part of the storyteller and his comrades and through repeated exposure on the part of the scribe. The tale belongs to no one, and there are no totally unique performances. Though a given performer may be especially renowned for his renditions of a particular tale, that tale is by no means his personal property. Afficionados of Peking opera are alert to spot, and criticize, singers who render a passage in an unconventional way. Complaints such as "That's not the way it's supposed to be sung!" are heard far more frequently than comments to the effect that "This is really an interesting and unusual new way to sing it!"

Where there are multiple copies of the same transformation, we are not permitted to conclude for certain that any one of these is the original and that the others have been taken from it. So long as there are a substantial number of phonetic errors, we must assume that the transcriber had in mind (chiefly derived from oral renditions) the sound of the story as well as its shape (stylized in various written versions).[41] However, even when there are phonetic, orthographic, and other differences between two manuscripts (such as between the Maudgalyāyana story on S2614 and on P3485), it is still possible to identify them as representations of the same basic tradition. This is possible because, in spite of the differences, it is clear that the intention of the individuals responsible for the manuscripts was to relate the same story in approximately the same way. For this reason, the editors of T relied on no less than nine different manuscripts in establishing the recension of the Maudgalyāyana transformation text given on pages 714–744. There are legitimate complaints that such an editorial policy offers scholars only composite texts and that any serious research still requires that the originals themselves be consulted.[42] But, in another sense, there is some justification for emphasizing that the authors or scribes of all nine manuscripts were attempting to record the same basic story and, therefore, that the similarities are more important than the differences. Where the variants are few in number, it is even possible that one copyist was working from the text of another.

On the other hand, although they deal with the same subject, it is impossible to collate P2193 (T701–712) and PK2496 (T756–759) with the group of nine manuscripts referred to above, for it is apparent that the differences are greater than the similarities. Indeed, these two manuscripts represent separate traditions, P2193 being a highly moralistic retribution story (that is, a "tale of conditioned origins" *yuan-ch'i*) focusing on Maudgalyāyana's mother and PK2496 (mislabeled by the T editors as a *pien-wen*) being a straightforward exposition of the Maudgalyāyana story written in a rather prosaic fashion.

Having discussed the complicated relatedness of multiple copies of the same transformation text, I should like now to consider some possible reasons for their differences. The copies are never identical, there being always at least some minor variations among the individual manuscripts. Occasionally, there may even be changes in the basic structure of the narrative. It has been asserted[43] that the existence of multiple copies of a given *pien-wen* is proof that they were written down for professional use. This is not necessarily true, since the demand for written versions of favorite oral narratives would be far greater and would more readily account for numerous copies of the same transformation text were that demand to have originated from potential readers rather than potential performers. Just at the time the transformation texts were being written down, marginally or newly literate and affluent social groups, such as the Buddhist laity and merchants, were beginning to come into prominence. The difference (often negligible) from manuscript to manuscript may be attributable to the facts that the scribes and copyists were not themselves professionals, that they were influenced by repeated (but not identical) performances, and that there was bound to be a certain amount of variation because these are handwritten, not printed, texts with which we are dealing.

It is highly doubtful that P2319, an abridged Maudgalyāyana transformation text, could ever have been intended for performance. For it is the verse portions that have been consistently reduced in length from what they are in S2614. Below the title of P2319, we find the following remark: "Each of the verses (*gāthā*) [is cut short] after two or three lines by the notation 'and so forth and so on.'" 其偈子每緎[44] 三兩句後云ろ是. Yet the verse, as we have seen, was the most important element of the narrative for the performer. The P2319 transformation text on Maudgalyāyana thus stands at a curiously opposite pole from the P4524 transformation text on Śāriputra, which gives *only* the verse portion on the verso of the illustrations. Various techniques are used to abbreviate the prose portions of P2319 as well.[45] For example, when Maudgalyāyana arrives at the Avīci hell, P2319 declares that "the horrors therein cannot be fully described" 此中惡事說不可盡. But S2614 proceeds to attempt the impossible:

> Swords and lances bristled in ranks, knives and spears clustered in rows. Sword-trees reached upward for a thousand fathoms with a clattering flourish as their needle-sharp points brushed together. Knife-mountains soared ten-thousand rods in a chaotic jumble of intercon-

> necting cliffs and crags. Fierce fires throbbed, seeming to leap about the entire sky with a thundrous roar. Sword-wheels whirled, seeming to brush the earth with the dust of starry brightness. Iron snakes belched fire, their scales bristling on all sides. Copper dogs breathed smoke, barking impetuously in every direction. Metal thorns descended chaotically from mid-air, piercing the chests of the men. Awls and augurs flew by every which way, gouging the backs of the women. Iron rakes flailed at their eyes, causing red blood to flow to the west. Copper pitchforks jabbed at their loins until white fat oozed to the east. Thereupon, they were made [to crawl up] the knife mountains and enter the furnace coals. Their skulls were smashed to bits, their bones and flesh decomposed; tendons and skin snapped, liver and gall broke. Ground flesh spurted and splattered beyond the four gates; congealed blood drenched and drooked the pathways which run through the black clods of hell. With wailing voices, they called out to Heaven—moan, groan. The [roar] of thunder [shakes] the earth—rumble, bumble. Up above are clouds and smoke which tumble-jumble; down below are iron spears which jangle-tangle. Goblins with arrows for feathers chattered-scattered; birds with copper beaks wildly-widely called. There were more than several ten-thousands of gaolers and all were ox-headed and horse-faced.

All of this vivid and gory detail is omitted from P2319.

There are at least two possibilities that might account for why P2319 is so scaled down, particularly in the verse. The prospective owner of the scroll may not have been willing or able to pay a copyist to reproduce the entire transformation text but still was attracted enough by it to want something more permanent than the performances themselves. The writing, while fairly neat and done on lightly ruled paper, is somewhat hurried. And there are a noticeable number of additions to the text, which seems to indicate that the owner of the scroll or his friends supplemented from their own recollection certain details that the scribe had omitted. The other possibility that comes to mind is that the prospective owner may previously have managed somehow to obtain a scroll, illustrated perhaps, of the verse portions of the transformation text and now wished to complement this with the prose portions. This is rather doubtful, however, for several reasons. In the first place, if the prospective owner of P2319 were primarily interested in obtaining the prose complement, would he allow a drastic reduction in the scope of the prose itself? Second, it is most unlikely that any performer would have been willing to part with an illustrated scroll of the P4524 type that bore only the verse. Such scrolls, as is clear from the Indonesian and Indian evidence, were jealously guarded by the performers, who handed them down from generation to generation. This may also account for the crossing out of "With Pictures" in the title of S2614; they were simply unavailable.[46] In any case, P2319 gives the distinct impression[47] of having been copied from another written text that was itself already at some remove from the oral realm.

We are particularly fortunate in knowing the names of two individuals associated with the most important manuscript (S2614) of the Maudgalyāyana transformation text. Both names occur at the end of the manuscript, one in the colophon and the other, by another hand, separately. The colophon reads:

> Written on the 16th day of the 4th month in the 7th (*hsin-ssu*) year of the Pure and Bright (Chen-ming) reign period by a lay student 學郎 of the Pure Land Monastery, Hsueh An-chün 薛耍(安)俊.

The date given is in accordance with A.D. 26 May 921. Below that we read 張保達文書, which Giles[48] takes to mean "Composition by Chang Pao-ta." Does Giles mean to imply by this that Chang Pao-ta was the author of the Maudgalyāyana transformation text? From what is known of the tradition of oral performance associated with the *pien-wen*, we may safely rule out such a possibility. Furthermore, *wen-shu* 文書 cannot mean what Giles says it does. The expression has nothing to do with authorship. It means, rather, "document; official dispatch; secretary who writes such a dispatch; archives; and so forth." Hence we must understand that Chang Pao-ta is the keeper or owner of the manuscript which was copied by Hsueh An-chün. That is to say, S2614 was originally "Chang Pao-ta's book."

I have been unable to discover any additional references to Chang Pao-ta in the Tun-huang manuscripts. Hsueh An-chün's name, however, occurs on at least two other manuscripts. One is P2054, a "General Exhortation to the Four Orders[49] to Cultivate and Practice the Way According to the Doctrine Following the Hours of the Day" 十二時普勸四衆依教修行 by Chih-yen 智嚴.

The colophon states that it was

> transcribed 書 by the student 學子 Hsueh An-chün on 17th day of the 5th month in the 2nd (*chia-shen*) year of the Equiluminous (T'ung-kuang) reign period [21 July 924]. The faithful disciple, Li Chi-shun 李吉順, was responsible for this recitation to encourage goodness.[50]

It may be that Hsueh An-chün and Li Chi-shun collaborated in the preparation of this manuscript, the latter reciting and the former copying down. In any event, it is valuable to know what other types of manuscripts Hsueh was involved in copying and also to know that, though he was a secular student in a Buddhist monastery, he associated with the declared faithful.

Hsueh An-chün is also mentioned twice in the colophon of PK8668, which is an exhortation to observe the precepts.[51] Although Hsueh An-chün is not here identified as a lay student studying at the Pure Land Monastery, the two individuals with whom he is associated in this colophon are so identified. The manuscript, dated the 21st of the 1st month (equivalent to 13 February 920), would appear to have been for Hsueh An-chün's personal use 扎(=札?)用.

I have dwelt at length on Hsueh An-chün because I believe it is important, in order to understand why transformation texts came to be written down, to know as much as possible about those who are in any way associated with these manuscripts. In the case of the Maudgalyāyana transformation text on S2614, it is significant that the manuscript was transcribed by a lay student in a Tun-huang monastery and owned by someone who, to judge from his name, was probably also a layman.

Another transformation text that was definitely copied by a lay student is that on the Han general Wang Ling 王陵.[52] Thus we see that students were involved in copying transformation texts on both secular and religious subjects.

At least one extant transformation text was copied by a lay student for pietistic reasons. This is the PK876 fragment of the Maudgalyāyana transformation text of which the colophon reads as follows:

> On the 5th day of the intercalary 6th [*sic*][53] month in the 2nd, *ting-ch'ou*, year of the National Rebirth of Peace and Prosperity (T'ai-p'ing hsing-

kuo) reign period [that is, 22 August 977], the lay student Yang Yuan-shou[54] of the Manifest Virtue Temple, having pondered the matter by himself, made a vow to create blessings by writing in full this *Transformation on Maudgalyāyana* in one scroll. It is his determination that, in the future, together with Śākyamuni Buddha,[55] he shall be reborn[56] a Buddha once[57] he encounters Maitreya.[58] If, later, there are individuals[59] who, expressing a similar faith,[60] write out in full the *Transformation on Maudgalyāyana*, and similarly maintain the power of their vow,[61] they will avoid falling upon the three[62] paths[63] of hell.

It is especially interesting to note that Yang Yuan-shou not only decided to copy the *Transformation on Maudgalyāyana* for his own spiritual welfare but exhorted others to do so. This same name, Yang Yuan-shou, also appears in a circular of a lay religious association (S5631) dated in accordance with 8 February 980 (?)[64] as that of "announcements secretary" 帖社官.

Two of the manuscripts (in booklet form) of the "Transformation of the Han General Wang Ling" bear inscriptions mentioning petty government officials. The colophon of P3627.1 was inscribed on the 16th day of the 8th month in the 4th year of the Heavenly Blessing reign period (in accordance with 1 October 939) by the Recording Officer, Yen Wu-ch'eng 孔目官閻物成. Yen Wu-ch'eng's name also appears on P3272v in connection with the title of "emissary" 使頭. He delivered a letter concerning banditry and theft in a *ting-mao* year (907 ?) to a responsible official. The cover and two otherwise empty pages of the manuscript formerly owned by Shao Hsun-mei 邵洵美 and now kept in the library of Peking University bear several notations written in a different hand from the text. These are as follows:

1. The 9th month of the *hsin-ssu* year (A.D. 921?).
2. The 3rd year of the National Rebirth of Peace and Prosperity (T'ai-p'ing hsing-kuo) reign period (A.D. 978). So Ch'ing-tzu 索淸子.
3. Inscribed by So Ch'ing-tzu, lay student of the Recording Officer 孔目官學仕郎.[65] If, later, someone should read this aloud, please do not find fault.[66]

It is obvious that So Ch'ing-tzu expected others, who would have their own opinions on what was the correct story, to read his manuscript.

It is noteworthy that several of these manuscripts bear colophons that refer to the position of "recording officer," "bibliographic secretary," or "archivist" (*k'ung-mu kuan* 孔目官 or a variation thereof).[67] We may not assume, however, that holders of this position in Tun-huang were appointed by the central government of even that their duties were identical to central-government appointees. In two instances, the title occurs in close association with the standard designation of a lay student resident in a Buddhist monastery (*hsueh-shih lang* 學仕郎). It is likely that this was a local appointment and that the authorities in Tun-huang borrowed the nomenclature of the central government.[68]

Another secular piece, copied by an official surnamed So, is the "Names of the Hundred Birds" 百鳥名 (S3835). This manuscript is dated to the 12th month of a *keng-yin* year (A.D. 930?) and signed by the Chief Escort So Pu-tzu 押牙索不子.

On the back of P3485 ("Maudgalyāyana Transformation Text") is a notation that this manuscript was "recorded by Chang Ta-ch'ing" 張大慶記. We are most fortunate in having been able to identify the same name on another Tun-huang manuscript, S367, which consists of topographical and historical notes on cities in Turkestan under Chinese influence. The colophon to S367 reads:

> On the 25th day of the 12th moon of the 1st year of the Luminous Beginning (Kuang-ch'i) reign period [2 February 886], when the An-wei-shih-fu [Assistant Commissioner] of Ling-chou, Minister of State, arrived with his suite at the *chou*, Chang Ta-ch'ing, in attendance on the Assistant Commissioner, made a copy of this document to serve as a record.[69]

This information is important in that it helps give some idea of the status of one more individual who may have been responsible for the writing down of a transformation text, and also because it provides an approximate date for the time when it was copied.

Two manuscripts on religious subjects not belonging to the transformation-text genre are a lecture on the *Sūtra of Deep Gratitude to Parents* 父母恩重經 (P2418) and the "Conditional Origins (*Nidāna*) of Maudgalyāyana" 目連緣起 (P2193). Both bear the names of individuals who are clearly not lay Buddhists nor secular students. The latter has an inscription which states that it is a true copy of Chieh-tao ("Way of Differentiation [*dhātu*]") 界道眞本記.[70] The former was copied on the 7th day of the 8th month of the 2nd year of the Heavenly Completion (T'ien-ch'eng) reign period (5 September 927) by I-chueh 一乞 ("Once Awakened"). A note that immediately precedes the inscription reads "To Instruct [Cf. Skt. *parikṣeptṛ* (instructor)] the Populace, the Sixth" 誘俗第六.

A semi-vernacular narrative (S548v) of Prince Siddhārtha's attainment of the Way has the following colophon:

> On the 19th day of the 8th moon in the *chia-wu* year, the 5th of the Extended Resurgence (Ch'ang-hsing) reign period [30 September 934], the monk Hung-fu of the Lotus Platform (Lotus Throne) Monastery recorded the copying of the foregoing. Kept for reading and recitation by the monk Hui-ting. His friends are asked not to take it away. 長興伍年甲午歲八月十九日蓮臺寺僧洪福寫記諸耳. 僧惠定池(for 持?) 念讀誦, 知人不取.[71]

This would seem to be fair indication that at least some Tun-huang manuscripts were passed around for reading by others than the owner himself.

Another religious piece (S1, see also P3361), the "Seat-Settling Text by the Late, Great Teacher Yuan-chien ('Full-Orbed Mirror') on the Twenty-four Exemplars of Filiality," which consists of 107 heptasyllabic lines, was composed by the Recipient of the Purple,[72] Yun-pien ("Cumulous Debater"), the Great Master of the Full-Orbed Mirror, Recorder of Monks[73] from the Right Side of the Thoroughfare. Yun-pien is known to have died in the year 951[74] and to have spent some time in Lo-yang where he wrote poems in the company of geishas.[75] In all likelihood, though not named, Yun-pien is also responsible for the "Seat-Settling Text by the Great Teacher, Recorder of Monks from the Right Side of the Thoroughfare" (S3728).[76]

It would be pointless to give here an exhaustive list[77] of all the names associated with these manuscripts for, already, a definite pattern has emerged. The overall impression one gets from reviewing the information available on the individuals mentioned in the various colophons and inscriptions is that many of the transformation texts were copied by a body of lay students[78] who had not yet passed their examinations and who were enamored of popular storytelling. Some considered it an act of piety to have religious stories copied out, even though these were decidedly noncanonical. On the other hand, canonical texts and lectures on them tended to be copied by individuals who were more directly affiliated with the Buddhist faith. In no case is the name of the author of a transformation text known to us for certain.[79] Nor is it likely that any should be, because the oral and collective nature of composition would militate against any single person's being designated the creator of a given transformation text.

In general, we may observe that genuine transformation texts, regardless of the subject matter, exist in manuscripts that were copied by lay students or other lay persons. The same holds true for other types of popular narratives that do not deal with religious subjects. But sūtra lectures and popular narratives with a pronounced religious content that are not transformation texts tend to be associated with monks and others who have taken obviously religious names.[80] Monks might, however, occasionally be involved in the transcription of secular (mostly non-narrative) literature. P3579.2, for instance, is a collection of poems by Po Chü-i and others. Dated the 20th day of the 2nd month of the year 877, it was copied by a monk of the Ling-t'u Monastery 靈圖寺比丘寫.

While searching for any bit of information regarding the copyists of the Tun-huang popular narratives, I was led to the registers of monks and nuns affiliated with the monasteries and nunneries of that area.[81] Although some of the same monasteries and nunneries appear in the registers as in the colophons of the popular narrative manuscripts, in no case has it been possible to identify individuals listed in the registers with those monks who were responsible for copying various manuscripts of popular literature. This may be attributable to the fact that the registers and the manuscripts date from different eras. But it may also partly be due to the diverse geographic origin of the manuscripts and their copyists.

The colophons to various Tun-huang manuscripts reveal many other interesting facts about who did the copying, how they did it, and for what purpose. P2825, for example, is a copy of the *Family Instructions of the Grand Duke* (*T'ai-kung chia-chiao* 太公家教). The colophon, written on the 15th day of the 1st month of the year 850, states that the text was "read by the student Sung Wen-hsien and written by An Wen-te" 學生宋文顯讀安文德寫. This indicates that oral transcription was involved in the writing of this text and, thus, that a high incidence of purely homophonic errors cannot be ruled out even if an already existing copy was utilized.

Several colophons in the corpus of Tun-huang popular literature are charged with a vivid sense of immediacy. The "Destruction of the Transformations of Demons"[82] (P2187) bears the following:

> On the 10th day of the 11th month in the 9th year of the Heavenly Blessing (T'ien-fu) reign period [28 November 944], blowing on my brush which had frozen from the cold, I write this inscription.[83]
>
> Written by the Buddhist *śramaṇa* of the Dharma and Vinaya, Yuan-jung ("Vow-splendid"),[84] who resides in the Pure Land Monastery.

At the end of the lecture on the *Vajracchedikāprajñāpāramitā-sūtra* (P2133v):

> Copied behind the refectory on the X day of the 1st month in the 6th year of the True Brightness (Chen-ming) reign period [920]. Ch'ing-mi[85] ("Pure-esotericism") has accordingly inscribed it.[86]

The colophon of the transformation text on Śāriputra's subduing of demons, though it includes no name, helps to elucidate the fact that this type of literature was collectively inspired, performed, transcribed, and revised: "If anyone who reads this sees a part that is incorrect, I pray that he will correct it forthwith."[87] It would have been impossible for others to make the corrections here invited if the story, as transcribed, did not have broad currency. This particular colophon is also one of the grounds for my belief that transformation texts were meant to be passed around and read.

The last line of the story of the capture of Chi Pu reads: "All that I have said is written up in the *History of the Han*; Do not say that the lyricist has sung untruly." (T71.4) A fully satisfying interpretation of this line is difficult to achieve. It does indicate, however, that this text—not a *pien-wen*—had some connection with an oral rendition and was written down by someone who was aware of the classical source of the story.

"The Story of the Crown Prince of the House of Liu during the Former Han" (P3645) seems to have been written by a moderately educated individual. Several times, classical texts are quoted and the language tends more to the literary than most Tun-huang popular narratives.

It is virtually certain that the P2794v manuscript of the Wu Tzu-hsu story was copied from another written text by someone who was only partially literate. Ungrammatical sentences and mis-written characters abound. There are many instances where the copyist jumps from the middle of one sentence to the middle of another without making any adjustments or indications in his writing (for example, from 18.10.4 to 8.12.11 and from 16.2.3 to 16.2.25, 合). A probable explanation for this is that his eye skipped ahead. Elsewhere, the manuscript is garbled and repetitive, the work of a negligent or inexperienced copyist. The interspersed practice characters indicate that the latter is the more likely case.[88]

One of the lectures on the *Vimalakīrti-nirdeśa sūtra* (P2292) bears the following informative colophons:

> On the 9th day of the 8th month in the 10th year[89] of the Broad Governance (Kuang-cheng) reign period [25 September 947], I wrote down this manuscript of the twentieth scroll at the Zen Temple of Serene Truth in West Szechwan [?].[90] Just as I finished the writing, it became dark. I don't know how I'll get back to my village.
>
> Now 48 years old, I am holding a lecture at Ying[91]-ming ("Responsive Brightness") Monastery in the prefecture. It is exceedingly hot.[92]

It would appear that this manuscript was for the personal use, in worship services, of the owner. The second colophon refers to a specific time and place when the contents of the scroll were presented to an audience. The mention of the age of the writer of the colophon, in particular, gives one the impression that the manuscript was a private possession. And the remark about the heat vividly conveys a sense of immediacy to the lecture itself.

The "Causal[93] Transformation on a Maiden in the Women's Palace of King Bimbisāra [Named] 'Intends to Create Merit' Who Is Reborn in Heaven for Having Given Her Support to a Stūpa" (P3051) has the longest colophon of all the Tun-huang popular narratives. Not only does it tell the names of both the author[94] and the copyist; it gives explicit reasons why the former undertook to compose it:

> The Law of the Buddha is broad, its power of salvation boundless. Whosoever pursues the Way with all his heart will certainly reap a reward. But I, Pao-hsuan ("Protector-proclaimer") 保宣, among those who adhere to the gate of immateriality,[95] am of little art and, within the Brahmanic temples, am barren of talent. I am indisposed to a thorough understanding of the teaching of the sūtras and, in philosophical discussions,[96] lack penetrating knowledge. I have impulsively demonstrated my shortsightedness by piecing together the reasoning of esotericism. Not fearful of shame, I have gathered[97] these very profound parables of causation.[98]
>
> Personally inscribed by the Zen monk, Fa-pao ("Dharma-protector") of the Three Realms[99] Monastery on the 20th day of the 4th month in the 3rd (*kuei-ch'ou*) year of the Broad Docility (Kuang-shun) reign period of the Great Chou dynasty [4 June 953].

Other manuscripts from the same monastery that were written at approximately the same time are: "*Nidāna* on the King of Abhirati (?)" 歡喜國王緣 (P3375v), which bears an inscription written by the Monk Chieh-ching ("Preceptively Pure") on the 6th day of the 7th[100] month of an *i-mao* year (27 July 955?); and copies of letters between the famous Western Han captives of the Huns, Li Ling 李陵 and Su Wu 蘇武 (S173), by Chang Ying-chün 張英俊, a lay student 學士郎, dated in accordance with 19 July 975.

The survey of this second group of colophons on manuscripts of Tun-huang popular literature confirms the pattern we saw emerging from examination of the first and from other types of evidence. To wit, overtly religious texts such as sūtra lectures seem to have been written, copied, and owned by individuals who employed them in connection with actual worship service. The individuals involved tend, furthermore, to be professional *religieux*. Transformation texts and other genres of Tun-huang popular narratives, on the other hand, appear to represent an early stage in the development of the written story that was meant for reading but that ultimately derived from an oral context. Those involved in the production of such texts are largely local, lay intelligentsia who might, however, display a personal predilection for Buddhism.

During his travels to India (672 *et seq.*), the famous pilgrim I-ching observed that there were two categories of non-clerical pupils in the Buddhist monasteries, the *mānava*, who studied chiefly Buddhist works and who wished themselves eventually to become monks, and the *brahmacārin*, who pursued secular studies and had no intention of changing their way of life.[101] "In the monasteries of India there are many 'students' who are entrusted to the Bhikshus and instructed by them in secular literature."[102] There is no reason why a similar system of education should not have been transferred to Buddhist monasteries in China. Indeed, Zürcher gives[103] evidence that, already in the fourth century, the monastery had developed the secondary function of an institute of secular learning and education. And it is known for a fact that many lay students during the T'ang period repaired to Buddhist precincts to pursue their secular studies.

This practice of pursuing a secular course of studies in the monasteries was most popular after the K'ai-yuan ("Epochal Beginning") reign period (December 713–February 742).[104] Tun-huang was one of the favorite places for students to gather.[105] The frequent occurrence in the Tun-huang manuscripts of such terms as *hsueh-shih* 學師 ("Instructor"), *hsueh-lang* 學郞, *hsueh-shih-lang* 學士 (or 仕) 郞, and *hsueh-sheng* 學生 (the last three terms all designating student status) attests to this.[106] The famous rescuer of Tun-huang from the clutches of the Tibetans, Chang I-ch'ao, was himself such a student. P3620 includes an untitled song and the following colophon: "The 25th day of the 3rd month of 815 (or 827). Written by the student, Chang I-ch'ao" 未年三月二十五日學生張議潮写.[107]

Although Chang I-ch'ao was not awarded his own full biography in either of the two T'ang histories,[108] enough has been gleaned from various sources to allow Lo Chen-yü[109] and Hsiang Ta[110] to compile extensive biographical accounts of him. Chang I-ch'ao's most famous exploit is the expulsion of the Tibetans from the Kansu corridor. Tun-huang had fallen to them in the year 781. An early, brief account of Chang I-ch'ao's recapture of Tun-huang from the Tibetans in 848 may be found on S3329.[111] Chang profited from internal dissension amounting to civil war which had erupted among the Tibetans after the death of their king, Glaṅ Darma in 842.[112] In the same year that he recaptured Tun-huang, he founded the "Returning-to-Righteousness Army" (Kuei-i chün 歸義軍), which remained the main force in the area until the arrival of the Tanguts sometime around 1030.[113] For his services, Chang was greatly honored by the central government and revered by the local Chinese populace. We know from S3329 that, after his military successes, Chang immediately sent a report to the Emperor in Ch'ang-an by one Kao Chin-ta 高進達 and some others. Thereupon the Emperor awarded Chang the title of President of the Ministry of War and conferred upon him a marquisate with the rank of 10,000 households 授兵部尙書萬戶侯.[114] He then served for a time as the military governor of the Ho-hsi region 河西節度使. In 867, Chang himself went to Ch'ang-an and died there in 872. Among his posthumous titles is that of Honorary President of the Ministry of Officials and Marquis of Ho-hsi with 10,000 households 檢校吏部尙書河西萬戶侯.[115]

Chang I-ch'ao was himself an enthusiastic supporter of Buddhism. We have already seen how he must have pursued some of his early studies in a monastery under the tutelage of monks. In 860, he dedicated cave 156 (Pelliot no. 17 *bis*) at Tun-huang. Paeans of praise are heaped upon him in the "Destruction of the Transformations of Demons" (T345.9, 345.11, 354.13, and 355.8). We know that, in the 3rd month of the year 863, he presented to the Emperor an exegetical work written by a monk named "Dharma-faith" (Fa-hsin 法信) from the area which he governed.[116] The noted Tun-huang clerical leader "Enlightenment-truth" (Wu-chen 悟眞) wrote two series of poems, "Passing of the Five Watches" (*wu-keng chuan* 五更轉) and "The Twelve Hours" (*shih-erh shih* 十二時) to praise him.[117] It is not at all surprising, then, to discover that Chang had been a lay student in one of the Tun-huang monasteries as a youth.

The educational establishment at Tun-huang was far more elaborate than the terms *hsueh-shih*, *hsueh-lang*, and so on alone can convey and included, as well, various professorial, administrative, and examinational authorities.[118] As I have demonstrated earlier in this chapter and more fully in my article on "The Making of Written Vernacular Narrative," many of the manuscripts containing popular literature recovered from Tun-huang were copied by individuals from these circles. Buddhist monasteries in Central Asia were likewise centers of education, both theological and secular;[119] it is probable that the Indian educational patterns were transmitted through this area into China.

In China proper, the schools sponsored by Buddhist monasteries (*ssu-hsueh* 私學) were essentially private academies (*ssu-shu* 私塾).[120] The studies undertaken there were by no means restricted to Buddhist subjects and might be entirely secular in nature:

> In the 4th month of the year 831, I pursued my studies at Hui-shan ("Grace Mountain") Monastery[121] and remained there for three years. Those works which I recited include: *The Tso Chronicle of the Spring and Autumn Period*, *The Odes*, *The Changes*, Ssu-ma Ch'ien's and Pan Ku's histories, "Encountering Sorrow" by Ch'ü Yuan, *Chuang-tzu*, *Han-fei-tzu*, letters, notes, and several hundred poetical compositions.[122]

In the Tun-huang story of Ch'iu Hu (S133), when the anti-hero takes leave of his wife to go into the mountains in preparation for becoming an official, the books he takes with him are the following (note the order listed): the *Classic of Filial Piety*, the *Analects*, the *Book of History*, the *Chronicle of Tso*, the *Kung-yang* and *Ku-liang* [Chronicles of the Spring and Autumn period], the *Mao* [recension of the] *Odes*, the *Records of Ritual*, the *Chuang-tzu*, and the *Literary Selections* [*Wen-hsuan*] (T155.6). Since the *Wen-hsuan* is included in this list, the Tun-huang story of Ch'iu Hu must have been written later than the first quarter of the sixth century, when Hsiao T'ung 蕭統 (501–531) compiled it. Ch'iu Hu actually receives his learning at the hands of old Taoist adepts who are "well-versed in the *Nine Classics* and understand clearly the *Seven Bibliographies*". It would have been anachronistic to have Ch'iu Hu study with Buddhist savants, since he was a man of Lu 魯, and his story was first written down during the Han dynasty. We may understand this as partially indicative of the T'ang popular (the manuscript is rather poorly written and replete with errors) conception of literati education.

The Tun-huang story of Shun as a boy has the hero study first the *Analects* 論語 and the *Classic of Filial Piety* 孝經, then the *Mao* [recension of the] *Odes* 毛詩 and the *Records of Ritual* 禮記 (T131.8 and 132.5).

In a discussion of preaching (*ch'ang-tao* 唱導) from Chapter 13 of the *Biographies of Eminent Monks* by Hui-chiao 慧皎, the following suggestions to utilize different approaches for different audiences may be found:

> As for the first five groups,[123] it is necessary to speak incisively of impermanence[124] and to discourse trenchantly of repentance.[125] For[126] rulers and elders[127] it is necessary to cite popular allusions and interweave set phrases. For the numerous mass of commoners, it is necessary to point to events and construct shapes, to speak directly of what is seen and heard. For mountain folk and desert dwellers, it is necessary to use neighborly words and reproach with terms of guilt. When each of these variations 變態 arises from the situation at hand, it may be said that one knows both the time and the audience.[128]

The pedagogical idea being conveyed here is that the method of preaching should be suited to the person to whom it is directed. This is actually an explicit advocacy of the concept of *upāya* ("skill-in-means").

An awareness on the part of T'ang-period Buddhist teachers of differing levels of literacy and their attempts to alleviate the difficulties of those with minimum proficiency is evident from such documents as S2577.[129] The main contents of this manuscript consist of the eighth scroll of the *Lotus Sūtra*. But the manuscript also bears an extremely interesting and enlightening note:

> For beginning readers of this sūtra who do not recognize sentences, I[130] have punctuated it, though I have paid no attention to paragraphs; nor have I mentioned the beginning and end of sections. Most of the sentences consist of four characters. I only punctuate those sentences that have other than four characters. But, for those sentences that have four characters, I never add punctuation. Passages that are set off and the ends of lines are also used to distinguish new sentences.[131] In this fashion, too, separate distinctions have been made. Those who see this later, please do not blame me for[132] mispunctuation with vermilion [re]marks.

The author's final sentence indicates that some manuscripts would be passed around to an indeterminate number of readers. Compare the similar remarks at the end of S548v (on Prince Siddhartha's attainment of the Way) and the Peking University

Library manuscript formerly owned by Shao Hsun-mei ("Transformation on the Han General Wang Ling").[133]

From P2249v,[134] we know that even someone who was newly or partially literate would try his best to write the names of Buddhist saints who figured prominently in the transformation texts. The first line of a set of practice characters on this manuscript is "Mahāmahāmahāmahāmahāmaudgalyāyana, first in supernatural [abilities]" 大大大大大目乹連神 (*sic*) 第一. Several lines later, *g'i̯än* 乹 (that is, *ga*) is written five times in a row. And, again, "Mahāmaudgalyāyana, first in supernatural abilities" 大目乹連神通第一. Other practice titles given are those of the writings of Brahmacārin Wang[135] 王梵志書集 and of the famous book of homilies called "Family Instructions of the Grand Duke" 太公家教 (three times).

Inside a statue of the influential Tun-huang monk, Hung-pien 洪䛒, a bag containing his ashes was discovered. It was wrapped in crude paper on which were written a child's practice writing in a mediocre hand together with a teacher's comments.[136]

Other evidence of more widespread low-level literacy in the T'ang than we are wont to assume comes from the Arab travel account entitled *'Aḫbār aṣ-Ṣīn wa l-Hind*, written in 851. In it we learn that "Poor or rich, small or great, all the Chinese learn to trace out the characters and to write." And "In each town there is a school and a schoolmaster to instruct the poor and their children; [these schoolmasters] are provided for by funds from the Treasury."[137] While the unwieldiness of the Chinese writing system prevented all but a very small precentage of individuals from attaining mastery of the written language, the contemporaneous evidence I have adduced indicates that there were various levels of literacy, ranging from those who could not even write their own names, through those who recognized a few graphs, to those who could read and write several hundred of them with difficulty, and so on. We may thus assume that an incipient reading public for popular literary texts existed during at least the latter part of the T'ang. This would have constituted a powerful stimulus for the copying of such texts. It would also have served as a harbinger of the full flowering of popular printed literature during the Sung and later periods.

Having gained some idea of who wrote down the transformation texts and who might have read them, we must now attempt to determine what type of individuals performed the transformations that served as their inspiration. We may begin by a discussion of what is known of the *modus operandi et vivendi*.

One of the most commonly held misconceptions about transformation texts is that they were the texts, records, promptbooks, or *aides-mémoire* used in connection with actual oral delivery. The usual formulation is that "transformation texts are the *hua-pen* 話本 (or *ti-pen* 底本) for popular lectures 俗講."[138] Not only does this fly in the face of all that we know about the techniques and methods of storytellers generally, which are observable in many countries today or are ascertainable through examination of historical documents; it is simply not borne out by scrutiny of the Tun-huang transformation-text manuscripts themselves, nor is it supported by any other Chinese source known to me. Any formulation that posits the employment of transformation texts in popular lectures (that is, lectures for laymen given by monks) is perforce made suspect by the fact that the former often have an entirely secular theme while the purpose of the latter was obviously religious. The contention that secular stories were told by properly ordained monks to attract audiences for their sermons is not convincing. No one has yet demonstrated satisfactorily that such a practice ever occurred in the T'ang period.

In his article called "An Informal Talk on the Origins of *pien-wen*" (Man-t'an pien-wen te ch'i-yuan), Chou Shu-chia delves into the *Biographies of Eminent Monks* (*Kao-seng chuan* 高僧傳) in an attempt to find the roots of sūtra lectures. But it is necessary to reiterate that there is no demonstrable direct relationship, much less equivalence, between sūtra lectures and transformation texts (or rather their oral predecessors). Furthermore, the individuals who presented these two types of oral literature were of entirely different social and religious status. The men who were included in the *Biographies of Eminent Monks* were ordained; the tellers of transformations were folk entertainers and lay devotees who had no recognized status in the Buddhist ecclesia. The relationship between lay transformation performer and ordained sūtra lecturer bears many striking parallels to that between the red-head (*fa-shih* 法師) and black-head (*tao-shih* 道師) priests of the Taoist tradition.[139]

It has, nonetheless, been repeatedly asserted by numerous students of Chinese popular literature that eminent Buddhist monks were involved in popular lectures, and the leap is then made from this to the further (and untenable) assertion that those who gave popular lectures also performed transformations. The first assertion deserves serious consideration because known Buddhist pedagogical practices during the T'ang period would have encouraged it; the second is unacceptable because there simply has been no satisfactory proof adduced to support it. Both assertions center around the person(s) of Wen-shu 文淑 and/or Wen-hsu 文溆. I advisedly write "and/or" because it has never been shown that Wen-shu and Wen-hsu are the same individual, as has frequently been alleged. Without doubt, by far the most crucial passage for those who wish to connect Wen-hsu and/or Wen-shu with transformation performances is the following from the T'ang author Chao Lin's *Record of Tales of Causation*:

> There was a monk, Wen-shu, who held public talks for large crowds. He made a pretense of lecturing on the scriptures but it was all licentiousness and crudity. Dissolute persons egged him on and supported him. Doltish men and loose women liked to listen to him. The auditors packed themselves in. The temples respected and honored him, calling him a reverend.[140] The schools,[141] in imitation of his tunes, made songs and cantos. The common lot is easily tempted, but those Buddhists who know the truth and are versed in literature thoroughly despise him.[142]

In the first place, there is no reference in this passage to transformations. Second, it seems obvious that this man, Wen-shu, is not portrayed as a genuine monk but that he is held by Chao Lin to be an impostor. Third, competent Buddhists themselves rejected him. It is essential that all three of these points be kept in mind as we survey some of the other important sources on Wen-shu and/or Wen-hsu.

The next item of evidence is taken from Tuan An-chieh's *Miscellaneous Register of Ballads*, under the heading that deals with the lyric meter (*tz'u-tiao* 詞調) "Wen-hsu-tzu" 文溆子:

> During the Ch'ang-ch'ing ("Lasting Celebration") reign period [821–824], there was a monk, Wen-hsu, who gave popular lectures (*su-chiang*) and was a talented reader of sūtras. His lilting voice stirred the villagers. The musician, Huang Mi-fan 黃米飯 ["Yellow Rice"?], composed this tune on the basis of his intonation in the recitation of Avalokiteśvara.[143]

The attitude of Tuan An-chieh toward Wen-hsu is so diametrically opposed to that of Chao Lin toward Wen-shu that we can scarcely believe them to be the same individual, unless we assume an extremely high degree of subjectivity on the part of the two observers. The fact that the tunes of both were adopted by musicians may, however, lead some to equate the two individuals. I, personally, am not so inclined because of other data available for our consideration.

According to Chang Yen-yuan's *A Record of Famous Paintings of Successive Dynasties*, at the Bodhi Temple in Ch'ang-an, "On the east wall of the Buddha hall, there is a Bodhisattva who turns his eyes to look at people 轉目視人.[144] The Dharma Master Wen-hsu, for no reason at all, had an artisan lay on colors and so spoil it."[145] These two sentences by no means warrant the identification of Wen-hsu as an explainer of transformation tableaux. In fact, Tuan Ch'eng-shih, who also records this incident in his *Notes on Monasteries and Stūpas*,[146] specifically identifies Wen-hsu as a "monk who gave popular lectures" 俗講僧 (which tallies with what Tuan An-chieh says of him), not a transformation performer. Ono Katsutoshi, in his annotations to the passage in question, has the following note:

> The *Hsueh Chin T'ao Yuan* edition and the *Chin Tai Pi Shu* edition both have 文漵 Wen-hsu, whereas the *Wang Shih Shu Hua Yuan* edition and Tuan Ch'eng-shih's (段成式?–863) *Sze T'a Chi* 寺塔記 (Chi-ku-ko edition) give his names as Wen-shu 文淑.[147]

Ono goes on to quote from an entry in *Ennin's Diary* for the 9th day of the 1st month in the year 841. I here offer the translation (with a slight modification) of the relevant portions by Reischauer:

> An Imperial order was sent to seven monasteries in the left and right streets to hold lectures for laymen 俗講. Three of the places [are]

in the right streets: the Hui-ch'ang-ssu had Wen-hsü 文漵 Fa-shih, who is a Court Priest, a Debater of the Three Teachings, a Reverence Granted the Purple, and a Personal Attendant Priest, lecture on the *Lotus Sutra*. He was the foremost Priest to give lectures for laymen in the city. I have not yet obtained the names of lecturers at the Hui-jih-ssu 惠日寺 and the Ch'ung-fu-ssu 崇福寺.[148]

The very high status and great dignity of Wen-hsu are thus confirmed by Ennin, one of the most serious and reliable reporters of the religious scene during the T'ang period. His observations are supported by other evidence.

Both the *Extensive Register of Great Tranquility* and *Diffuse Notes from the Ward of Blue-Green Fowl* quote a passage from *Mr. Lu's Miscellaneous Talks* (*Lu Shih tsa-shuo* 盧氏雜說) about Wen-hsu.[149] It is clear from this account that the Dharma Master of great virtue (*bhadanta*), Wen-hsu, was a man of high rank and esteem, for he had won admittance to the palace. He committed an offense, however, and was banished. When this happened, his disciples gathered up his books and continued to lecture in the manner for which he was famous. The Emperor Wen-tsung 文宗 (r. 827–840), who was something of a musician himself, adopted Wen-hsu's "sound" as a canto and called it "The Master Wen-hsu" 文漵子. This account is in substantial agreement with that given[150] for the origin of the lyric meter of the same title in the *Miscellaneous Register of Ballads*.

Unfortunately, the problem of Wen-shu and/or Wen-hsu[151] is compounded by the fact that, if they were indeed two different individuals, they must have been contemporaries or near-contemporaries.[152] And the problem is further exacerbated by the anti-Buddhist bias of Hu San-hsing's commentary to the *Comprehensive Mirror for Aid in Government*. Ssu-ma Kuang had written under the *chi-mao* day of the 6th month of the year 826 that "the Emperor paid a visit to the Temple of Nascent Blessings (興福寺 [in Cultivation of Virtue Ward 修德坊]) to watch the *śramaṇa* Wen-hsu give a popular lecture."[153] Under the year 826, the *Unified Chronology of the Buddhist Patriarchate* 佛祖統記 (ch. 42) has this entry: "The Emperor paid a visit to the Temple of Nascent Blessings to watch the *śramaṇa* Wen-hsu 文敍 lecture on a sūtra. The Emperor declared that he was good."[154] Hu's comment on this event belittles Buddhist evangelism to such a degree that even the sober and well-intentioned discussion of the doctrine is made to have a base purpose: "When the Buddhists preach, it is in the category of talking about emptiness, but the popular lectures cannot elaborate the meaning of emptiness. All they do is make the people happy and then invite donations." Hu, writing approximately 500 years after the historical event, displays here not his knowledge but his prejudices. Still, his words carried influence and anyone reading about Wen-hsu with Hu's commentary as a guide would tend to think that the eminent monk was quite unscrupulous.

This is a crucial issue (namely, whether Wen-hsu is Wen-shu), for upon it hinges so much of the argument that eminent monks were involved in supposedly disreputable transformation performances. Naba Toshisada made a thorough study[155] of the relevant materials and came to the conclusion that it is likely that Wen-hsu was the famous monk who gave lectures for laymen and Wen-shu the entertainer who regaled mixed audiences with suggestive songs. On the basis of presently available evidence, it is not valid to claim with any certitude that Wen-hsu told risqué stories in the presence of mixed crowds. Nor is it possible to say with any assurance that Wen-shu, who did tell such stories, was an eminent monk who lectured before emperors. Above all, there is not a shred of evidence linking either Wen-shu or Wen-hsu—whoever they might have been—to the performance of transformations. Even supposing that Wen-hsu and Wen-shu were the same person, the whole issue may actually be said to be irrelevant to the study of transformation performances and transformation texts, since neither Wen-hsu nor Wen-shu can be shown to have had any connection with these forms of oral and popular literature. I have discussed the issue at such length only because it is taken for granted by most students of Chinese popular literature that he/they did.

The possibility of confusion between monk and picture storyteller is, however, a real one and is partly due to the desire of the storyteller to be granted a higher degree of respectability than his profession is customarily accorded. For an example from a later period, the "Taoist storyteller," T'an Erh-yin 談爾音, in *The Gallant Maid* (*Erh-nü ying-hsiung chuan* 兒女英雄傳) by Wen K'ang 文康

(fl. 1868) only pretends to be a priest. He actually has no credentials as a Taoist but is simply a storyteller (though one with a very checkered past) who dresses up like a priest because that is a customary garb for the profession he has assumed. In India, beggars of various sorts who carry about a religious icon and tell stories concerning it often attempt to pass themselves off as holy men or women. For example, Haraprasād Sāstri, writing sometime before 1911, stated that "The so-called Brahmins who beg with the image of Śītalā in their hands and come from Howrah and Mīdnapore districts are all Dharmaghariā yogis."[156] A Soochow *t'an-tz'u* ("strum lyric") performer, Yang Pin-kuei, has his main character, a fortuneteller, come on "*in the garb of* a Taoist priest." It is clear that this is only a guise.[157] A comparable phenomenon in medieval Japan has caused some confusion regarding the social status of *etoki* (picture storytellers). For similar reasons, modern interpreters of T'ang transformation performers have consistently, but erroneously, referred to them as monks. If they were "monks," they were so only in a highly qualified sense.[158]

On the verso of PK2496 is a list of sums received by monks in payment for certain chanting which they had done. Because the recto of the scroll is a fragment of a prosimetric vernacular narrative (not a transformation text) about Maudgalyāyana rescuing his mother, Jaworski reasons as follows:

> Nous pouvons en déduire que les donateurs, payant les frais des messes et d'offrandes pour le repos des âmes en peine, demandaient également aux moines l'exécution des *pien-wen*, comme de nos jours encore, ils engagent des troupes d'acteurs pour donner des représentations théâtrales. Pendant l'été 1935 j'ai eu l'occasion, à Harbin, d'assister à une représentation de *Mou lien kieou mou hi* [目連救母戲], donnée aux frais d'un riche marchand pendant la fête d'Avalambana.[159]

As I have often pointed out elsewhere in this study,[160] there is no hard-and-fast evidence that it was actual monks who were the performers of transformations. The contents of the recto and verso of PK2496, as is usual with Tun-huang manuscripts, bear no necessary relationship to each other. Furthermore, we know that funeral dramas in many parts of Taiwan are not normally performed by genuine (in the sense of "ecclesiastically ordained") monks or priests but by actors who, admittedly, sometimes pass themselves off as quasi monks or para-priests. Laurence Thompson refers to one such troupe as "actors who specialize in funeral rituals playing the roles of ordained Buddhists and various supernatural characters at a country wake."[161] He calls such actors "priests" (in quotes), not simply priests. This assessment is supported by Susan Naquin's study of late Ch'ing and early Republican period funeral ritual in North China.[162] Among the list of various professionals who participated in funerals, she includes opera troupes, acrobats, and storytellers. Priests and their lay assistants *are* involved in liturgically oriented rituals carried out at memorial services (*fa-shih hsi* 法事戲) that may display some theatrical features. But proto-dramatic performances (such as the Taiwanese Hoklo *Khan-bông-koa* 牽亡歌) and full-fledged drama such as the various Maudgalyāyana plays put on in conjunction with funerals are presented by amateur players or professional acting troupes.[163] Gary Seaman refers to this type of service as "drama-*cum*-ritual."[164]

Jaworski's own experience in China—indeed, his own statement here—should have alerted him to the fact that religious entertainment, like religious art, is most often provided by laymen whose professional or semi-professional occupation it is, rather than by monks or priests. Put differently, it might be said that religious entertainers—in distinction to ordained experts in charge of formal, doctrinal instruction and ritual—are neither members of religious orders nor of the priesthood. This does not preclude their associating very closely with monks or priests. It is plain in Taiwan today, for example, that the two types of individuals—the professional religious and the lay devotee—work closely together at many points of contact with the people. We may observe, as has Hans-Dieter Evers[165] for Ceylon, that each social stratum except the very lowest has its own type of religious specialist, "the Bhikku (buddhist monk), the Kapurāla (in Ceylon sometimes called 'peoples' priest'), and the Edurā ('exorcist')." It is only the first, however, for whom there are standards of ordination that are acceptable to the establishment.

The most thorough study of Chinese funeral performers is that of Gary Seaman, who has written extensively and made several films[166] about troupes in the Taiwanese town of Puli and villages in its surrounding basin. The Taiwanese word for the actors in these funeral dramas is *sai-kong* 師公, which in this context means roughly something like "master of ceremonies." The funerals in the Puli basin are almost exclusively in the Buddhist tradition. While it would be possible to hire in Taoist ritual experts from Hsinchu, Taipei, or other places where they are active, these individuals are seldom seen around Puli.

Among the Puli Buddhists there are two ritual traditions, the Lunghua 龍華 ("Dragon Flower") and the Sabun 沙門 ("Śramaṇa"). Funeral dramas by groups using the Dragon Flower ritual tradition are performed by professional actors, that is, they have not undertaken vows of abstention from lay or secular life which would distinguish them from the rest of the populace. Their only distinction is the ability to perform the rituals and read the texts of the Dragon Flower Tradition. About a half-dozen of these men are well known enough for their abilities in this regard to have established their own *toa* 壇 ("altar"). By doing so, they have proclaimed that they will undertake, for a fee, to organize an entire funeral for a client family. Their entrepreneurial skills are much more important in this matter than are their ritual abilities or knowledge, for they can always hire other people who have such knowledge and ability but who lack the business sense, connections, or paraphernalia to organize a funeral. Individuals of the Sabun tradition do organize funerals, and they are usually recognizable as celibate Buddhist monks and nuns from the surrounding Buddhist temples or alternatively members of the various "at-home" Buddhist sects in the area who have families but who have undertaken to live up to some of the prohibitions of the *saṅgha* rules.

Nearly all of the Dragon Flower groups perform funerals as a supplementary profession. Only about a half-dozen who have their own ritual paraphernalia and who make it a point to operate as organizers clearly depend in large part for their livelihood on the funeral business. As groups or as individuals, these funeral professionals will travel wherever the price is right or where there is a demand for their services, but the constraints of demand and social networks usually keep those from Puli operating within the Puli basin.

The social status of the *sai-kung* is rather poor.[167] A typical insult hurled in their direction is that they "eat the rice of the dead," meaning primarily that they make their living off the misfortunes of others. There is also much unseemly competition for the "contracts" to perform funerals, which involves waiting around for someone who is terminally ill to die. This disreputability does not necessarily extend to the monks of the Sabun tradition, since they (in Puli, at least) apparently do not seek out mortuary business but do perform funerals at the special request of the bereaved family. Hence we find that, while the Dragon Flower specialists who put on funeral dramas may on the surface appear to be monks, they are actually professionals whom local inhabitants readily distinguish from true monks and nuns.

Returning to the T'ang period, in order to differentiate clearly between transformations and formal religious discourse held by monks for lay audiences, we must study the latter in some detail. The term "popular lecture" (*su-chiang* 俗講) appears[168] for the first time in the *Continued Biographies of Eminent Monks* (*Hsu Kao-seng chuan* 續高僧傳), compiled by Tao-hsuan (596–667) in the year 645. In 629, Shan-fu 善伏, a future monk, had been introduced to a Confucian academy by the Prefect of Ch'ang-chou (in modern Kiangsu). But he was always out listening to "popular lectures" during the day and reflecting on Buddhist doctrine during the evening. For this he was reprimanded by the learned doctors (*po-shih* 博士) who were his teachers.

There is no lack of primary sources for the study of the precise nature and content of popular lectures. P3849v contains two texts[169] which outline the steps for carrying out a popular lecture (the words *su-chiang* actually occur in the first of the two) service which focuses on a *Vimalakīrti Sūtra* lecture. The service, which is conducted chiefly by a Master of the Dharma (*fa-shih* 法師), begins with a recitation of the "Sanskrit" (*fan* 梵). The Bodhisattva is invoked twice and then the "seat-settling [text]" (*ya-tso* 押座) is chanted. Various stages of the sūtra lecture itself are described, including an "ornamentation" (*chuang-yen* 莊嚴, *alaṃkāraka*) and the invocation of the Buddha. After the sūtra lecture is finished, the ten "perfections" (*shih po-lo-mi-to* 十波羅蜜多, *pāramitā*) are explained. Hymns praising the Buddha are chanted and vows are made. The Buddha is once again invoked and vows are made to transfer the merit of the service to others, after which the congregation disperses. P3770[170] carries the actual title "Text for the Ornamentation and Transfer of Merit (*pariṇāmana*) of a Popular Lecture" 俗講莊嚴迴向文. S4417 also gives the order of service for popular lectures. In the third section of fascicle 3 of Yuan Chao's 元照 (1048–1116)[171] "Records of Copied Materials to Aid in Behaving according to the Four-Fold Vinaya" 四分律行事抄資持記 entitled "Chapter on Explaining to and Leading the Common People" 釋導俗篇,[172] lectures for laymen are also described in terms similar to those of the Tun-huang orders of service. The Taoists, finding these methods of religious instruction effective, borrowed them from the Buddhists and used them for their own purposes.[173]

From an examination of these primary texts and other sources, it becomes clear that *su-chiang* ("popular lecture") is the name for a religious service that may include various types of liturgical and exegetical texts (such as invocations and sūtra lectures) but *not* transformation texts. This is further evidence that the individuals responsible for the performance of transformations and those responsible for holding religious services were distinct.

After intensive investigation[174] of the subject, Fukui Fumimasa-Bunga concluded that the practice of popular lectures (*su-chiang*) has an Indian origin. Indeed, even though Buddhist services were held in Chinese, there was still an effort to maintain an Indian aura about them. On P3334, for example, there is an inscription that accompanies a "Preaching Text for Śrāvakas" 聲聞唱道(＝導)文. One line in the inscription says that "the master of precepts who [sings] Indian [style] sounds mounts the high platform" 梵音戒師昇高座.

It is more in agreement with the chronological and evolutionary development of Chinese popular literature to say that the historical and other non-Buddhist transformation texts were an extension of a religious form into the secular realm than to say that Buddhist priests consciously used secular storytelling as a drawing card for their religious lectures. What evidence is available points to lay performance of religious transformations and to their early secularization, a widening out into a larger public for performance by individuals who were entertainers rather than monks. By "early," I mean that the evidence for the broad currency of secular transformations in China shows that they appeared no later than seventy-five years after religious transformations (both in the eighth century). Hence, the "drawing-card" assertion is strictly hypothetical. We should, therefore, dispense with the notion that Buddhist monks told risqué stories to pack in their audiences and then blithely switched to more pious subjects. There may well have been, as certain Confucian critics claimed, "monks" who told off-color stories, "priests" who were acclaimed for their musical talent, and entertainers who told captivating tales about religious subjects. But it is essential that none of these be confused with Buddhist evangelists and lecturers whose purpose, first and foremost, was to convey the substance of Buddhist doctrine. The ends of their evangelism/entertainment ought to be recognized for what they were. Or, to put it differently, exceptions should not be made the rule.

The section on evangelism (*ch'ang-tao* 唱導) in Hui-chiao's (497–554) *Biographies of Eminent Monks* 高僧傳 provides ample documentation of the dedicated purpose of Buddhist preachers to discount decisively any rumor of their rampant impropriety. What all of this leads to is the recognition that entertainment and evangelism were two separate activities pursued by two different groups. Naturally, an evangelist might be somewhat entertaining in his presentation and an entertainer might effectively convey some religious truth. Though the dividing line was, at times, rather hazy (especially when the entertainer purposely affected some traits of the evangelist), these were essentially separate professions.

There were, admittedly, monks called Populace-Converting Dharma Masters 化俗法師, who specialized in preaching to the common folk, and "traveling monks and nuns" 游[行]僧, who went from village to village preaching. Yet, here again, we should be wary of equating either of these two types with popular entertainers. The former usually restricted themselves to the exposition of sūtras and the latter were limited in their activity by strict government regulation.[175]

It is noteworthy that, in the *Biographies of Eminent Monks*, which contains accounts of the lives of nearly 500 monks, I have not been able to uncover a single mention of *pien* or *pien-wen*. This implies that either: (1) *pien-wen* (or its oral precursors) had not developed by the Liang period; or (2) *pien* was not performed by eminent monks. Actually, both of these statements are probably true. It is not possible to document the existence of transformation performances and texts before the T'ang period; nor is there any proof that, even in the T'ang, eminent monks were responsible for them. Similarly, I have not come across any reference to *pien-wen* as a genre in the various continuations of the *Biographies of Eminent Monks* for later dynasties.

Further, with regard to the social status of transformation texts, nowhere in my reading of the Chinese *Tripiṭaka*[176] do I ever recall having encountered the genre term *pien-wen*. Since the phenomena is Buddhistic and was demonstrably widely current during the T'ang period,[177] we are forced to conclude that it had no canonical or scriptural status and that, being a product of folk and popular cultures, it was ignored by the elite monks who compiled and edited the canon and the various individual texts that constitute it. And yet we cannot ignore the fact that *pien* performances began as folk, religious entertainment of a quintessentially Indo-Buddhist kind.

chapter six

Evidence for the Existence of Transformation Performances

There are two contemporaneous references to transformations in the T'ang period that have been cited by most competent authorities on the subject. The first is a poem by Chi Shih-lao 吉師老 entitled "Watching the Girl from Shu Perform[1] the 'Transformation on Wang Chao-chün' 昭君變."

Before this charming woman donned her pomegranate skirt,
Her home, she says, was by the bank of the Brocade River;[2]
Her red lips know how to unravel events of a thousand years,
Her clear word mixed with sighs tell a tale of autumn sorrows.[3]

Where her penciled eyebrows join, there seems the southern moon of Ch'u,
But when she opens her picture scroll, there are clouds beyond the northern passes;
Having told fully the regrets of the fair lady in those days of yore,
Her thoughts turn from Chao-chün to her countrywoman Wen-chün.[4]

Although we do not know the details of Chi Shih-lao's life, this poem most likely was written in the middle or late T'ang, as were the majority of poems in Wei Hu's collection where it appears. It certainly dates from before the early tenth century when Wei completed his compilation.

The poem describes the performance of a transformation on the story of Wang Chao-chün by a female entertainer from the Szechwan area. The details of Chao-chün's selection as a palace beauty during the reign of Yuan-ti (48–33 B.C.) and her subsequent fate of being given to the Hunnish chieftain to procure peace are well known and need not detain us here. Nor need we dwell on the checkered love of Ssu-ma Hsiang-ju 司馬相如 (d. 118 B.C.) and Cho Wen-chün 卓文君 (also from the Szechwan area) in the last line which is, after all, only a way of saying that, having finished her performance, the girl thinks of her own plight. What is important for our purposes is the wealth of significant primary data concerning the nature of transformation performances that can be gleaned from the poem. In the specific instance here recorded, it is noteworthy that there is but a single performer and that the performer is a woman. It is also essential to note that she is not a Buddhist *religieuse*, but a professional, secular entertainer. That she is from Szechwan may also be significant in terms of the connection which that area had to Tun-huang and thence to Central Asia (see the "Appendix" to Chapter 1). She would appear to be wearing a distinctively colored dress. Her most important piece of equipment is a picture scroll, although we cannot tell whether it is hand-held or placed in a stationary position during performance. At any rate, this corroborates the other evidence I have assembled in this study which demonstrates that transformation performances utilized narrative picture scrolls.

Since there exists a Tun-huang transformation text on Wang Chao-chün (P2553),[5] this poem also raises the fundamental question of the relationship between orally performed transformation and written transformation text. While there may have been verses or other prompt-words written on the back of her scroll as with P4524 (the illustrated Śāriputra transformation) and P5019 (Meng Chiang-nü transformation [?]), it is doubtful that a singing-girl from the banks of the Brocade River in Szechwan could have written her own text. Be that as it may, the emphasis in this poem is on the visual aspects of the performance (the beauty of the performer, the scenes depicted on the scroll and her ability to bring them to life) as well as the aural ones (her sandalwood-shaded lips "tell fully" the tale of the heroine). The people attending this performance, including Chi Shih-lao, obviously are enjoying a multimedia event; they have not come to witness a reading.

The extant transformation text on Wang Chao-chün can be dated confidently on the basis of internal evidence[6] to the late eighth or early ninth century.[7] Nemoto Makoto has attempted to show that it was written down sometime between 772 and 780.[8] In any case, oral transformations of the type described by Chi Shih-lao surely were the forerunners of the written transformation text that has come down to us. Since the written transformation text on Wang Chao-chün may be from a slightly earlier time than that of Chi Shih-lao's poem, it is evident that the transition from oral performance to written text did not immediately lead to the demise of the former. It seems, rather, that both types could exist simultaneously for a time, although the oral performance is manifestly primary.

There are additional grounds for holding that entertainers from the Yunnan-Szechwan area who specialized in the Wang Chao-chün story were active throughout China before the transformation text came to be written down. A poem by Wang Chien 王建 (Advanced Scholar c. 775) called "Watching the Szechwanese Entertainer" 觀蠻妓[9] begins "As she is about to tell the story of Chao-chün, she knits her penciled brows" (cf. line 5 of the Chi Shih-lao poem) and ends with an appreciative youth in the audience throwing her money and shouting "Bravo! Bravo!" I have translated *man* 蠻 (usually "southern barbarian") as "Szechwanese" (coming from Szechwan) on the basis of Chang T'ai-yen's explanation[10] of the usage of the word in the Szechwan area. Yunnan was called by the inhabitants of Szechwan *man-ti* 蠻地 ("southern barbarian land"), and maids in Szechwan, possibly because many of them had Yunnanese tribal backgrounds, were referred to simply as *man* 蠻, while males slaves were called *man-nan* 蠻男 ("southern barbarian men"). The appellation is patently derogatory in a social-class sense and was applied even to individuals of low status who did not come from Yunnan. Unfortunately, Wang Chien's short poem focuses on the singing ability of his performer and makes no mention of a painted scroll or of transformations.

Still another piece of contemporaneous evidence regarding the Ming-chün (that is, Chao-chün) transformation may be found in a poem by Li Ho (790–816) about the beauty and talent of a girl surnamed Cheng. She had been a singing-girl who came to Loyang and became so admired there that a scion of the noble Hsu family took her as his favorite. Li Ho wrote a poem for her entitled "A Song for the Young Gentleman Hsu's Lovely Lady Cheng" 許公

子鄭姬歌. The penultimate quatrain of the poem has been translated by Frodsham as follows:

On a long scroll of costly paper,
The ballad of Ming-chün.
Gliding from note to note, her song
Pierced the sapphire clouds
Vanity-patches on her cheeks,
She trod the eastern road—
Now the long-browed girls of the gay quarters
See very few guests.[11]

長翻蜀紙卷明君
轉角含商破碧雲
自從小靨來東道
曲裏長眉少見人

Although the girl Cheng is not here said to have "penciled brows" as were the performers in the poems by Chi Shih-lao and Wang Chien, it is significant that she is able to attract the patrons of the "long-brows." But the key words, for the purpose of our discussion, are those of the first line: *ch'ang fan Shu-chih chüan Ming-chün*. Frodsham follows Saitō and Suzuki[12] in understanding this to refer to a *yueh-fu* ("Music Bureau") ballad. However, such an understanding presents the seemingly insuperable difficulty of there being no verb in the entire line. Numerous other interpretations have been put forward to explain this line. Wang Ch'i (fl. 1758) believed that it refers to the lady Cheng's artistic talent while the succeeding line refers to her singing abilities.[13] But since she was an entertainer, there is no necessary reason to assume that she was accomplished in painting. Furthermore, nowhere else do we find that Cheng was good at painting. Indeed, the line in question can only yield such a meaning after a certain amount of violence has been done to it. Wu Cheng-tzu (Sung) states simply that 翻 is equivalent to 番, "a time, a turn" (by which he must mean 幡 or 旛, "pennant, streamer, banner") and hence that *ch'ang fan* means 長幅, "a long strip."[14] Yet this does not really explain the line. Yao Wen-hsieh seems to indicate that *Ming-chün* refers to a melody (*ch'ü* 曲) and *fan* to the singing of it.[15] This, however, strays too far from the original wording of the line. Ch'ien Yin-kuang 錢飲光 felt that the line "appears to mean that, for long periods of time, she would spread out for her enjoyment the picture of Ming-chün" 似以明君圖長在手展玩耳.[16] This interpretation commendably makes mention of a picture but incorrectly has the line signify a pastime of Cheng rather than her renowned ability to entertain. Ch'iu Chi-chen 丘季貞 claimed that *ch'ang fan Shu-chih* means "record a tune" 乃錄曲也 and that *chüan Ming-chün* means "to be written inside a booklet" 書於册內[17] but, given the usual semantic content of the words in question, this flies in the face of all logic.

It has been necessary to treat the commentaries to this single line of poetry by Li Ho at such exhaustive length to discover whether any of them point to a performance of song in which illustrative pictures are employed. It would appear that none have interpreted the line in this fashion. Yet, given the more explicit reference to such renditions discussed above in connection with the Chi Shih-lao poem and the very words of the line itself,[18] the conclusion that Li Ho is here describing Cheng's use of transformation pictures seems almost unavoidable. Thus the line should be interpreted "She unrolls the long strip of Szechwan paper, spinning a tale of Ming-chün"[19] or some such.

The second important contemporaneous reference to transformations in the T'ang that has frequently been cited by students of the subject is an exchange of repartee between Po Chü-i (772–846) and another poet, Chang Hu 張祜. It appears, among other places, in two T'ang sources and one encyclopedia.[20] The differences among the three texts raise some very significant questions that have hitherto been overlooked. I shall translate the relevant portion of the passage as it is recorded in the *Extensive Register of Great Tranquility* (*T'ai-p'ing kuang-chi*) and compare it with the other two texts.

Po Chü-i assumed the position of Governor of Soochow sometime after the latter part of the 3rd month in the year 825.[21] Chang Hu, whom he had never met before, came to visit him.

> Po said, "I have long admired your excellent reputation and recall your poem of legal interrogation."[22]
>
> Surprised, Hu asked, "To which poem are you referring?"
>
> Po replied: "'Where was the belt inlaid with mandarin ducks

> thrown?/ To whom[23] was the gauze blouse decorated with peacocks given?'[24] If these are not legal interrogations, what are they?"
>
> Chang nodded and smiled faintly. Then he looked up and answered, "And I recall your 'Maudgalyāyana Transformation.'"
>
> "What?" asked Po Chü-i.
>
> Chang replied: "'Above he traveled to the end of the blue heavens, below he went to the Yellow Springs,/ But in neither of these boundless places did he find her.'[25] If these are not lines from the 'Maudgalyāyana Transformation,' what are they?"[26] Whereupon together they had a joyful banquet to end the day.

The anecdote as related in the *Extensive Register of Great Tranquility* and in *Topical Poetry* (*Pen-shih shih*) differs only in minor details. The *T'ang Gleanings* (*T'ang chih-yen*) account differs radically from both of these and deserves separate translation for purposes of comparison:

> The retired scholar Chang recalled a "Silkworm Thorn Branch[27] Poem" of his, saying: "'Where was the belt inlaid with mandarin ducks thrown?/ To whom was the gauze blouse decorated with peacocks given?'"
>
> Po Chü-i called these lines "legal interrogations."[28]
>
> Chang Hu got back at him, saying: "I'm guilty of the 'legal interrogations' charge and I don't deny it. But you, too, have your *Maudgalyāyana Sūtra*. The words of your 'Song of Lasting Sorrow' [written in 806] go like this: 'Above he traveled to the end of the blue heavens, below he went to the Yellow Springs,/ But in neither of these boundless places did he find her.' Do you mean to say that this is not about Maudgalyāyana looking for his mother?"

We must first ask why *T'ang Gleanings*, which the *Extensive Register of Great Tranquility* declares itself to be citing, has *Maudgalyāyana sūtra* 目連經 and "Maudgalyāyana looking for his mother" instead of "Maudgalyāyana Transformation" 目連變. A probable answer to this question can be arrived at by making an examination of some of the various editions of *T'ang Gleanings* available to us. The *Ya-yü t'ang ts'ung-shu* [Collectanea from the Hall of Elegant Rain] 雅雨堂叢書 (1756) version[29] has "Maudgalyāyana Transformation" and "Maudgalyāyana looking for his mother" at the two crucial points mentioned above. The *Hsiao-yuan ts'ung-shu* [Whistling Garden collectanea] 嘯園叢書 (1883) version[30] follows the *Hall of Elegant Rain* text. The *Hsueh-chin t'ao-yuan* [Seek the source of the ford of learning] 學津討源 version[31] edited by Chang Hai-p'eng 張海鵬 (1755–1816), however, is the same as that of the modern edition I have used. Both *SPPY* and *TsSCC* also follow the *Seek the Source* version. The explanation that comes to mind for why some editions retained "Maudgalyāyana Transformation" and others did not is this: Faced with a word they did not understand, some editors simply exchanged it for one they did, while others left the text intact.

In spite of the textual differences involved, what does this anecdote tell us about the nature and history of transformation texts? First, it is significant that two highly educated poets would be so thoroughly familiar with the Maudgalyāyana transformation as to use it comfortably for the substance of a joke. We have, however, no definite way to discover whether their acquaintanceship with the Maudgalyāyana transformation was made through personal observance of oral performances or through reading of written texts. My own inclination is that they acquired knowledge of transformations primarily through attendance at actual performances. Whatever the case may be, it is certain that there were in the early ninth century traditions of transformation stories sufficiently solidified as to be quotable. Second, this incident occurred in Soochow in the year 825, indicating that transformations were well established throughout much of China before that time. The time-frame squares well with other available data regarding the period of currency of transformations. Third, transformations were such common currency that they could be considered on the same level as "legal interrogations."

Wang Shih-chen 王世禎 (1634–1711), the early Ch'ing poetry critic, knew of the anecdote concerning Po Chü-i. Without comprehending exactly the meaning of "Maudgalyāyana Transformation," he was astute enough to realize that it was derogatory if applied to someone's poetry 固是謔語, 然亦詩之病.[32]

Kuo Shih 郭湜 (T'ang), in his *Unofficial Biography of Kao Li-shih*,[33] offers a very interesting account which proves that transformations were performed even for the Emperor himself. The context of the account is determined by Kao Li-shih's efforts to relieve Hsuan-tsung's 玄宗 boredom after he returned—without his beloved "Honored Consort" Yang 楊貴妃 (719–756)—to Ch'ang-an from his disastrous flight to the Szechwan area. The time of this account is approximately the year 760:

> Every day, the ex-Emperor and Kao would personally oversee the sweeping out of the courtyard, the cutting of the grass, and the trimming of the shrubs. Or there would be sūtra lectures, discussions of doctrine,[34] performances of transformations 轉[35] 變, and storytelling 說話.[36] Although these were far from being proper literature, it was hoped that, in the end, they would cheer His Highness's feelings.

What is most striking about this account is the forthright recognition that the products of popular culture might very well be useful and appealing to members of the ranks of elite society. The rather early date (in terms of the verifiable development of transformation performances and transformation texts), as well as the fact that Kao Li-shih was a devout Buddhist (note that two of the other three genres mentioned are explicitly Buddhist), should not be overlooked in attempts to interpret this passage.

In the *Extensive Register of Great Tranquility*,[37] there is recorded an extraordinarily graphic description of the drawing power of transformation performances. This account is extremely valuable for historians of Chinese folk culture because it not only gives an indication of the types of individuals who flocked to these performances but the sometimes nefarious motivation of those who sponsored them:

> . . . When Yang Kuo-chung 楊國忠 (d. 756) was Military Governor of Chien-nan 劍南,[38] he summoned envoys to go the long distance to Lu-nan 瀘南.[39] Provisions were few and the road was dangerous; often none would return. His Chien-nan operatives each year would order Sung Yü 宋昱 and Wei Huan 韋儇, as imperial representatives, to compel the prefects and district magistrates to levy troops. The men knew they would surely die, so the prefects and district magistrates could not fulfill the commands. Therefore, they resorted to a stratagem whereby, under false pretenses, they would order monks to hold a vegetarian feast or perform[40] transformations along important roads. 詐令[41] 僧設齋, 或于要路轉變. They would bind those among the crowd who were without relatives or were poor and put them in a secret room. Then they would issue them coarsely made clothes and, having

formed them into ranks wearing cangues, would quickly send them off to the campaigns.

This passage tells us several important things about transformations. First, it once again corroborates the Szechwan connection I have repeatedly stressed. Second, it shows that this form of entertainment was presented not in temples but on public thoroughfares. Third, we learn that it was enormously popular; it was a type of performance that even the poorest people would flock to. Fourth, we find that transformations were probably perceived as Buddhistic (though of a suspect sort) by the people. Fifth, the attraction of transformations was well enough known to the authorities that they chose to exploit it to their own ends.

Hsueh Chao-yun, in his *Biographies of Illusionists*,[42] has a story about one "Graduate Li" 李秀才. Li is chided by a monk who says, among other things, "How can you expect anything good of those who hanker after tavern banners and play around at transformation arenas (*wan pien-ch'ang* 玩變場)?" I have not seen attested elsewhere the phrase *wan pien-ch'ang* and am uncertain of its exact meaning. But the fact that it occurs in a story dealing with illusionism opens up the possibility that it may point to the existence of localized centers where transformations (but perhaps it refers more generally to illusionary tricks of magic) were regularly performed during the T'ang. If this is what it actually means, it is significant that a monk has spoken ill of such places. Sūtra lectures, by contrast, were delivered in the "lecture courts" 講院 of temples and monks encouraged Buddhist laymen to go to them often.[43]

In his *Miscellany of Rarities*, Tuan Ch'eng-shih records an account of a strange happening that makes a connection between illusionism and a specific transformation tableau:

> During the Great Calendar reign period (766–779), there was a magician who came from the south and stopped at Bald Mountain Monastery. He was fond of wine and, before long, became a bit intoxicated.
>
> Because of a major vegetarian feast that was being held in the monastery, several thousand people had gathered. Suddenly, the magician said, "I have a trick that can take the place of the pleasure afforded from 'Pebble Toss.'" Whereupon he mixed up some colors in a vessel.

> He pranced about and rubbed his eyes. Slowly he muttered several dozen words of incantation. Then he sipped up the liquid and spat it out repeatedly on the wall, thus creating a "Transformation Tableau of Visiting Vimalakīrti in His Illness."維摩問疾變相. The many colors stood out as though freshly painted. It was more than a half a day before the colors gradually began to fade. By evening they had all disappeared except for a flower on Śāriputra's silken cap that had been decorated with chrysanthemums. After two days it was still there.[44]

It is noteworthy that the magician who creates this spectacular transformation of Vimalakīrti comes from *outside* the monastery and is not a Buddhist monk.

Another item of evidence for the broad circulation of transformations in China is that a line from the verse portion of the Maudgalyāyana transformation was quoted verbatim in the recorded sayings of a Zen master.[45]

The disputable piety of "monks" who were overly fond of transformations is plain from the following incident, which probably happened c. 947.

"Deaf Monk" Li

> There was a monk of Later Shu times (925–965) named Tz'u-yuan 辭遠 and surnamed Li 李 who was from the Monastery (*ārāma*) of the Three Sages in Kuang-tu District 廣都縣 [southeast of modern Hua-yang District 華陽縣 in Szechwan]. He had a slight amount of learning [or "was slightly literate" 薄有文學] but could memorize and recite a lot. His master, called Ssu-chien 思鑒, was a stupid person. Tz'u-yuan often belittled his teacher by saying, "What a pity that I am a disciple of this monk!" Whether sitting or walking, he was always mumbling the "Transformation on Madame Spirit of the Earth" 后土夫人變. The master would try to stop him but that would only make him do it all the more. He was completely unsupportive of his master.
>
> One day, while he was loudly performing [literally, "turning" or "warbling"] the transformation 轉變, a hand came out of nowhere and cuffed him on the ear so that he became deaf. For more than twenty years, until the "Incipient Treasure" reign period (968–976) of the present (Sung) dynasty, he stayed in the Well of Righteousness Monastery in Ch'eng-tu.[46]

After this decisive supernal punishment for his transgressions, Tz'u-yuan is unlikely to have continued "turning" transformations.

If he had, in all probability he would not have been permitted to continue to stay in a monastery for the next twenty years of his life.

About 150 years later, the still-suspect text was no longer called a "transformation" but simply a "lyric":

The Disrespectfulness of the
"Lyric on the Spirit of the Earth"
后土詞瀆慢

Shao Yen 邵衍, style Chung-ch'ang 仲昌, was a man of Chin-ling [Nanking]. He was sincere and fond of learning, never wearying of it his whole life long. On 4 June 1110 at the age of 82, he passed away without an illness. One day not long before his end, he looked at his nephew, Huang Tzu-wen 黄子文, and said: "Your old uncle will bid you farewell tomorrow. On a night in the past, I dreamed that a person in yellow clothing [that is, a monk or a priest] summoned me to a government office. The attendants were stern. Leaning on the table as he sat, a man with cap and robe like that of a king said to me, 'The "Lyric on the Spirit of the Earth" transmitted in the world is too disrespectful. Why do you keep a copy of it?' Whereupon he ordered the person in yellow clothing to lead me past several city gates. We stopped at a palace and I turned my head to look at it. Its gold and jade hallways were captivating but they were silent; no human voices were heard there. In a moment, someone suddenly called out 'Shao Yen' from amidst the curtains. 'The Emperor orders that, for you to have a perfect form, you must extirpate the "Lyric on the Spirit of the Earth" which has been transmitted in the world. How will you accomplish that?' I responded by saying that those who transmit it should die. The one who called out to me replied, 'All right.' And so I assumed my duties that very day. Having received the order, I went out the door. I stumbled and awoke. What I had dreamed was extremely clear. Now I want the members of my family and you, my nephew, to know that this lyric may no longer be transmitted. Remember it! Remember it!"

Tzu-wen did not really believe him. The next day before dawn, he went to see his uncle. "Nephew, just listen long enough to hear this ode of mine," Yen said to Tzu-wen. Thereupon he raised his voice and sang aloud:

> "Although everything is over now,
> What use to repeat it whenever you meet someone?

This morning I shake my sleeve with displeasure,
I have to catch the wheel of a bright moon."

He died as soon as he finished these words.

Tzu-wen is my niece's husband. I used to go on outings with Yen.[47]

A widespread cult, complete with images and shrines, developed around the figure of "Madame Spirit of the Earth." This in itself was sufficient to evoke the wrath of the Confucian watchdogs of culture. Even worse was the blasphemous nature of the central cult figure. In the first place, she represented a sort of transvestitism of a respectable deity. Furthermore, she had the audacity to "seduce" a human being named Wei An-tao 韋安道 When he took her home as his wife, so the story goes, Wei's parents were displeased. They hired two monks and a Taoist priest to exorcise her but she would not bow to them. Finally, the father ordered An-tao to get rid of her. She obliged him by leaving and taking An-tao with her to the realm of spirits.

It is clear from all of this that Madame Spirit of the Earth was considered by the guardians of propriety to be an unwelcome aberration. Other, more brutally male-chauvinist types thought that she could be used to attack their nemesis, Empress Wu:

> Upon first reading the *Tale of Madame Spirit of the Earth* 后土夫人傳 written by people of the T'ang,[48] I detested its slanderous disrespectfulness. When I saw Ch'en Shih-tao's 陳師道 (1053–1101) remarks in his *Poetry Talks* to the effect that ". . . the people of the T'ang recorded the story of [Madame] Spirit of the Earth in order to ridicule Empress Wu," I said that Empress Wu was not worth ridiculing. And to use the Spirit of the Earth for this purpose was simply being too blasphemous. Later incorrigibles proceeded to put the story to music [referring to the "Lyric on the Spirit of the Earth"] with the result that ignoramuses took it to be true.[49]

Since neither the "Transformation on Madame Spirit of the Earth" nor the "Lyric on the Spirit of the Earth" has survived (small wonder!), it is impossible to determine what the relationship between the two of them was or how they compared to the classical *Tale of Madame Spirit of the Earth*. For stylistic reasons, the last may have been somewhat less objectionable than the other two forms of the story, which would help to account for its preservation in the face of their loss. In any case, if these remarks of three Sung scholars are an indication of the moral outrage and cultural indignation surrounding the subject of a single mid-tenth-century transformation, it is not surprising that, by the eleventh century—when neo-Confucian rectitude was coming into full swing—, the genre should have become well-nigh extinct.

A final literary reference to transformations is to be found under the year 694 of the *Unified Chronology of the Buddhist Patriarchate* 佛祖統記, ch. 39,[50] where there occurs a note that includes a most important citation from the *Orthodox Line of Śākyamuni's School* 釋門正統.[51] The latter text was initially published in the first quarter of the thirteenth century by Wu K'o-chi 吳克己 and completed in 1237 or soon thereafter by a monk named Tsung-chien 宗鑑 of Liang-chu 良渚. The note in question was prompted by the mention of the arrival at Wu Tse-t'ien's 武則天 (Empress Wu, 624–705) court of a Persian bishop (*Pi̯uət-tâ-d'ân* 拂多誕, Sogdian [*A*]*ftādān*)[52] named Mihr-Ormuzd 密烏沒其[53] who brought with him the apocryphal (read "Manichaean") sūtra called *Scripture of the Two Principles* 二宗經. The scripture was obviously uncanonical to the editor of the *Unified Chronology*, Chih-p'an 志磐, a T'ien-t'ai monk. Tsung-chien, the author of the note under discussion, here and elsewhere[54] displays an acute awareness of what he believes properly within Buddhism and what not. The note is rather difficult to understand[55] in all its details, but the general import should be comprehensible from the following crude translation:[56]

> [The monk from] Liang-chu said: "In accordance with the laws of our dynasty, 'all those who propagate and practice the *Scripture of the Two Principles* and other baseless scriptures not included in the *Tripiṭaka* in order to confuse the people shall be convicted of heresy.' That which is called the *Two Principles*[57] [is the scripture of Manichaeism, according to which] men and women need not marry, one does not speak during mutual undertakings, one does not take medicine when ill, the dead should be buried naked, and so forth. By 'baseless scriptures' is meant *Buddha, Master of the Heart; [The Scripture of] Crying and Tears Spoken by the Buddha*; *Scripture of the Appearance of the Greater and Lesser Kings of Light*[58] *in the World upon the Opening of the Origin* 開元; *Transformation Text on the Embracement of the Earth*[59] 括地變文; *Discussion on Equivalence with Heaven; Canto on the Fifth Envoy* [*of Light*],[60] and the like....

The note continues with an exposition of the confusing similarities in both doctrine and practice that debased Manichaeism holds with Buddhism. On the basis of this note, we may observe that, around the year 1237, transformation texts (such as were known at that time) were identified as heretically (to the Buddhists) Manichaean. What is worse, this was Buddhicized Manichaeism and, hence, the distinction between it and Buddhism was insufficiently marked for the comfort of purists such as Tsung-chien. It also was a source of trouble for the Buddhists, since the lack of a clear-cut distinction between the two religions caused proscriptions and persecutions of Manichaeism to spill over into the Buddhist camp.[61] It was, therefore, in the vital self-interest of orthodox Buddhists to delineate as sharply as possible the dividing line between themselves and Manichaeans. For this very reason, a sūtra lecturer (T464.10 and 12) criticizes Persians (that is Nestorianism), Manichaeism, and Zoroastrianism. He is at pains to make explicit the distinction between Buddhism and other religions that entered China from the West. This mention of the "Transformation Text on the Embracement of the Earth" in the *Orthodox Line of Śākyamuni's School* is the last known textual reference to *pien-wen* until the twentieth century, when transformation texts were rediscovered and written about.

The perceived (to the Confucians and establishment Buddhists) cultic associations of the "Transformation Text on the Embracement of the Earth" and related scriptures is evident from a remarkable memorandum submitted by Wang Chih 王質 (Advanced Scholar 1160, d. 1188). It is entitled "Notes for a Discussion on the Suppression of Bandits" 論鎮盜疏[62] and proposes strategies for the arrest of a group known as "Vegetarian Servants of the Devil" 喫菜事魔[63] This was a so-called heretical cult that has usually been identified as a branch of Manichaeism. Like other underground sects of Manichaeism that came into existence after the severe suppression of 842, it borrowed heavily from popular Buddhist concepts, ritual, and terminology. With minor variations, it gives the identical list of unauthorized scriptures as that supplied by Tsung-chien in the *Orthodox Line of Śākyamuni's School*. The most likely explanation for this agreement is that Tsung-chien relied on Wang Chih's memorandum as source material for his own work. Be that as it may, there can be little doubt that, by the end of the Northern Sung, *pien-wen* (at least one in particular) were well beyond the pale of acceptability to the arbiters of culture. To those in positions of authority, the milieu of *pien-wen* bespoke subversion, heresy, and banditry. While from our vantage point we may view the matter otherwise, such power politics of the post-T'ang period doubtlessly goes a long way to explain the swift disappearance of *pien-wen* (if only in name) from the scene at that time. While T'ang society was much more open, repressive trends directed against popular culture existed even then. Put simply, had it not been for the nearly miraculous preservation of the Tun-huang manuscripts, *pien-wen*—like so much of popular culture—would virtually have "disappeared" from the T'ang historical record as well as from that of the Sung and later periods.

It is, however, curious that the term *pien-wen* appears to have survived in the realm of oral entertainment even into the beginning of the twentieth century. In old Peking, there was an entertainment center called the Nan-fang chi-yuan 南方妓院 that supposedly featured performers from the southern part of China. To judge from the center's name (it means "Southern Brothel"), the social status of the performers was low and it is probable that—like some of the Kumano *bikuni*[64]—they performed other services than singing. What is most interesting about their performance of "treasure scrolls" (*pao-chüan* 寶卷) is that it was called "proclaiming scrolls" (*hsuan chüan* 宣卷) in the south and "singing transformation texts" (*ch'ang pien-wen* 唱變文) in the north.[65] How this latter name survived from the Five Dynasties to the twentieth century remains a mystery, since it is mentioned—so far as I know—only twice[66] in texts produced during the interim. This demonstrates that written records are inadequate in their description of popular culture for pre-modern times. The connection between *pien-wen* and *pao-chüan* is also noteworthy. It is, furthermore, significant that early twentieth-century "treasure scrolls," whose Ming and Ch'ing origins we know to have been popular Buddhist in nature, were sometimes situated in the demimonde. This was true even when they were referred to in the north as "sūtras of ['monks' who sponsor] vegetarian feasts" or, more literally, "sūtras of [monks] on call" (*ying-fu* [*-seng*] *ching* 應赴[僧]經).

Recently another alleged T'ang reference to *pien-wen* has been uncovered[67] in the 9th fascicle of the biography of the famous pilgrim to India, Hsuan-tsang, and much has been made of it. There are, however, a number of dubious aspects concerning this reference that deserve the most serious and careful scrutiny. It is the Korean wood-block edition of 1245[68] that forms the basis of the text cited from *T*50(2053).272b and reads as follows: "On 26 December 656 . . . , the Master of the Dharma (that is, Hsuan-tsang) . . . memorialized [the Throne], saying: 'With all deference, I present a gold-lettered copy of the *Prajñā*[*-pāramitā*]*-hṛdaya sūtra* in one fascicle together with its case and a "Transformation on the *Sūtra of Recompense for Kindness*, One Set" ' " 顯慶元年...十二月五日...法師...表曰:輒敢進金字般若心經一卷并函, 報恩經變一部.[69] Hui-li, who composed the first five fascicles of the biography, died around 670 or shortly thereafter, while Yen-ts'ung, who was responsible for the final five fascicles, did not complete them until 688, more than twenty years after Hsuan-tsang's death.[70]

Upon examination of the manuscript of the earliest extant edition of the biography, dated 1021 and preserved in the Nanto (Nara) Kōfukuji 南都興福寺, we discover that *pien* is missing from the text,[71] hence "and one copy of the *Sūtra of Recompense for Kindness*." A Uighur translation of Hsuan-tsang's biography was made during the first quarter of the tenth century. Unfortunately, due to the greed of an unscrupulous Chinese manuscript dealer in Urumchi, the only copy that appears to have survived to this century was torn apart and sold off in bits and pieces to maximize profits. Hence we are unable at the present time to locate the precise page on which the disputed title occurs.[72]

Even assuming that the *pien* was really in Hui-li's and Yen-ts'ung's original biography (which we have now seen to be somewhat doubtful), there are still problems surrounding its occurrence in this context. In the first place, the numerary adjunct (measure word or classifier) *pu* 部 is a normal usage when referring to sūtras, but I have never seen it connected to *pien*. The only measure word regularly applied to *pien* in the sense of a written text is *chüan* 卷 (hence XX *pien*[*-wen*] *i chüan*—"such-and-such a transformation [text] in one scroll"). The usual measure word applied to *pien* in the sense of a picture or sculpture is *p'u* 鋪 (hence XX *pien*

[*-hsiang*] *i p'u*—"such-and-such a transformation [tableau] in one layout").

Another irregularity of the title given in the *T* version of Hsuan-tsang's biography is the appearance together of *ching* and *pien*. Nowhere else does this juxtaposition occur with reference to a written text, only as a designation for a work of art, such as several wall-paintings at Tun-huang. Because the expression XX *ching-pien i pu* is so unusual, our skepticism over the interlinear *no hen* (see note 71) on the Kōfukuji version deepens.

The question then arises whether the putative "(Transformation on the) *Sūtra of Recompense for Kindness*, One Set" might possibly bear some relationship to F96 ("Inventory" 440), the "Record of a Pair of Kindnesses" (*Shuang en chi* 雙恩記) preserved in Leningrad. This text is clearly based, at least partially, on the *Sūtra of Recompense for Kindness* (for example, T[a]62.8a and 64.7). Although not typical in all respects, the "Record of a Pair of Kindnesses" is easily identifiable, both by its form and its contents, as a type of sūtra lecture text (*chiang-ching-wen*). Any attempt to identify it as a transformation text is hazardous, and efforts to equate it with the problematic title in Hsuan-tsang's biography are sheer speculation.

Since there are so many questions surrounding this highly atypical appearance of *pien* in Hsuan-tsang's biography, it would seem that the wisest course of action would be to refrain from constructing any elaborate theories based upon it. Until further evidence of a more definite kind can be adduced either to corroborate or disqualify it, all that we can do is simply record—albeit with a healthy dose of skepticism—this lone occurrence of *pien* in connection with an elite monk. If it were not for the anomalous *i pu* as a numerary adjunct, we might simply identify the *Pao-en ching pien* as a work of art, in which case this occurrence would not be altogether unusual, since *pien*[*-hsiang*] ("transformation [tableaux]") were indeed mentioned in a variety of T'ang texts.[73] Finally, since the *Pao-en ching pien i pu* occurs in the overall context of "implements of the faith" 道具 presented to the Throne, which included such things as a gold-lettered sūtra, a monk's robe, and other fine objects, it seems highly improbable that a vernacular lecture for laymen would have been a part of the gift. All of the extant transformation and sūtra lecture texts are of a much inferior quality (in terms of paper, calligraphy, language usage, and style) when compared with the sort of scriptures and commentaries suitable for formal presentation to the Throne. What is more, transformation texts and sūtra lecture texts are nowhere else recorded as constituting "implements of the faith," whereas transformation tableaux were common fixtures for even highly placed monks and officials with Buddhist inclinations. Regardless, we certainly do not now have sufficient data to draw any meaningful conclusions concerning either transformation texts (*pien-wen*) or sūtra lectures (*chiang-ching-wen*) from the unusual title "(Transformation on the) *Sūtra of Recompense for Kindness*, One Set."

The unfortunate paucity of references to transformation texts in pre-modern sources has led occasionally, perhaps out of wishful thinking, to scholars' finding them where they do not actually exist. An example of such a spurious reference is Yang Yin-shen's quotation[74] of the Ming writer Tsang Mou-hsun's 臧懋循 (Advanced Scholar 1580) preface (c. 1619) to his edition of *Records of Transcendent Wandering and Dream Wandering* (*Hsien-yu mong yu erh lu* 仙遊夢遊二錄) attributed to the late Yuan author Yang Wei-chen 楊維楨 (1296–1370). The quotation is taken out of context so as to make it appear that Tsang is identifying "strum lyrics" (*t'an-tz'u* 彈詞) as a type of *pien-wen*: "As for strum-lyricists, they are mostly blind men who beat the rhythm with a small drum as they recite and sing 說唱 at the Nine Crossroads and the Three Markets. There are also women with stringed instruments. It is likely that this is the last [representative of] *pien*." But Tsang was discussing a series of linked *changes* in literary form. *Pien* ought here to be interpreted as "change," not "transformation" in the sense of the name of a genre. Thus Tsang meant to say that strum lyrics were the "most recent" or "latest" development in a long line of evolution passing through the odes (*feng* 風 and *ya* 雅) to the ballads (*yueh-fu* 樂府), lyrics (*tz'u* 詞), and cantos (*ch'ü* 曲). The statement[75] has no bearing on the history of transformation texts.

Another example of a spurious contemporaneous reference to *pien-wen* was made by Ch'iu Chen-ching when he cited[76] a "Flood *pien*" 大水變 by Huang-fu Sung 皇甫松 supposedly mentioned in ch. 10 of *T'ang Gleanings* 唐摭言. None of the half-dozen editions of the work that I have checked, however, have this title. The piece by Huang-fu Sung was, rather, a "Critique of [the Handling of] the Flood" 大水辨.

In spite of the fact that there are only a mere handful of references to transformations in contemporaneous literature (the paucity is attributable to the low social status of the genre), we have learned a great deal from them. We know that transformations were performed in secular settings by professional entertainers, some of whom were women. Picture scrolls were an important part of the performance. Distinguished poets were familiar with transformations and referred to them to make fun of each other. High-ranking officials and even emperors enjoyed transformation performances, in spite of the fact that they were not "proper literature." Transformations had tremendous crowd-drawing power in spite of the fact that they were denounced by righteous monks. This may be due in part to the perceived cultic, risqué, and magical or illusionary qualities of some performances and derivative texts.

All of these findings and others presented in this chapter are in basic conformity with what we know about transformations from internal examination[77] and by comparative study of parallel and related traditions elsewhere.[78] In sum, transformations were a form of Buddhist-influenced prosimetric storytelling (normally associated with pictures) that enjoyed broad currency, particularly among the lower strata of society, from the middle of the T'ang period to its end.[79]

Abbreviations Used in the Notes and Bibliography

AKPAW	*Abhandlungen der Königlich Preussischen Akademie der Wissenschaften.*
AM	*Asia Major.*
ArchOr	*Archiv Orientální.*
BBK	*Bukkyō bungaku kenkyū* [Studies on Buddhist Literature] 佛教文學研究. For publication information on individual volumes, see under Bukkyō bungaku kenkyū kai.
BCL	*Fo-chiao yü Chung-kuo wen-hsueh* [Buddhism and Chinese literature] 佛教與中國文學. Hsien-tai Fo-chiao hsueh-shu ts'ung-k'an [Modern studies of Buddhism] 現代佛教學術叢刊, 19 (Series 2, no. 9). Taipei: Ta-ch'eng wen-hua ch'u-pan-she, 1978.
BEFEO	*Bulletin de l'École Française d'Extrême-Orient.*
BHS	Buddhist Hybrid Sanskrit. See under Edgerton.
BK	*Bijutsu kenkyū* (Journal of Art Studies) 美術研究.
BMFEA	*Bulletin of the Museum of Far Eastern Antiquities.*
BS	*Bukkyō shigaku* (The Journal of the History of Buddhism) 佛教史學.
BSOAS	*Bulletin of the School of Oriental and African Studies.*
BSOS	*Bulletin of the School of Oriental Studies.*
BSS	Kuo-hsueh chi-pen ts'ung-shu (Basic Sinological series) 國學基本叢書. Chinese texts published by the Commercial Press of Shanghai.

CBH	*Chūgoku bungaku hō* (Journal of Chinese literature) 中國文學報.
CH	Chung-hua shu-chü typeset and punctuated edition of the standard, dynastic histories.
CKYW	*Chung-kuo yü-wen* [Chinese language] 中國語文.
CTW	Tung Kao 董誥 (1740–1818), et al., ed. *Ch'in-ting ch'üan T'ang wen* [Imperially commissioned complete prose of the T'ang] 欽定全唐文. Taipei: Hui-wen shu-chü, 1961. Photocopy of 1814 ed.
CYYY	*Chung-yang yen-chiu-yuan li-shih yü-yen yen-chiu-so chi-k'an* (Bulletin of the Institute of History and Philology, Academia Sinica) 中央研究院歷史語言研究所集刋.
D	Numbered manuscripts in the Dun'-khuanskogo Fonda at the Instituta Narodov Azii, Leningrad.
F	Numbered Flug manuscripts at the Instituta Narodov Azii, Leningrad.
GSR	Karlgren Bernhard. *Grammata Serica Recensa*. Reprinted in 1972 from *Bulletin of the Museum of Far Eastern Antiquities* 29. Stockholm, 1957.
HJAS	*Harvard Journal of Asiatic Studies*.
HSYP	*Hsiao-shuo yueh-pao* (The Short Story Magazine) 小說月報.
HT	Hsiang Ta 向達. *T'ang-tai Ch'ang-an yü Hsi-yü wen-ming* [Ch'ang-an during the T'ang period and the civilization of the western regions] 唐代長安與西域文明. Peking: Sheng-huo, tu-shu, hsin-chih san-lien shu-tien, 1957. This is a greatly expanded and revised version of Hsiang's work of the same title which appeared as No. 2 in the *Yen-ching hsueh-pao* chuan-hao [Special issues of the learned journal of Yenching University] 燕京學報專號 series. Peiping: Harvard-Yenching Institute at Yenching University, 1933.
HTFH	*Hsien-tai Fo-hsueh* (Modern Buddhism) 現代佛學.
"Inventory"	Victor H. Mair. "Lay Students and the Making of Written Vernacular Narrative: An Inventory of Tun-huang Manuscripts." *CHINOPERL Papers* 10:5–96 (1981).

JA	*Journal Asiatique.*
JAOS	*Journal of the American Oriental Society.*
JAS	*Journal of Asian Studies.*
JRAS	*Journal of the Royal Asiatic Society of Great Britain and Ireland.*
KDHR	*Kanazawa daigaku hōbungakubu ronshū, bungaku hen* (Studies and Essays by the Faculty of Law and Literature, Kanazawa University, Literature) 金澤大學法文學部論集, 文學篇.
KITLV	Koninklijk Instituut voor Taal-, Land- en Volkenkunde.
KKK	*Kokubungaku: Kaishaku to Kanshō* [Japanese literature: Interpretation and appreciation] 國文學解釋と鑑賞 47.11 (October 1982). Special edition on "Etoki: Ima kokubungaku no chikei o terasu" [Painting recitation: Now shedding light on the horizons of Japanese literature] 繪解き—いま國文學の地形を照らす.
KM	K'ai-ming shu-tien reduced format edition of the standard, dynastic histories.
LitHer	*Wen-hsueh i-ch'an* [Literary heritage] 文學遺產. Section of the *Kuang-ming jih-pao* (Kuang-ming Daily) 光明日報.
LitHer, Suppl.	*Wen-hsueh i-ch'an tseng-k'an* [Literary heritage, supplements] 文學遺產增刊.
LWL	Chou Shao-liang 周紹良 and Pai Hua-wen 白化文, eds. *Tun-huang pien wen lun-wen lu* [Papers on Tun-huang *pien-wen*] 敦煌變文論文錄. 2 vols. Shanghai: Ku-chi ch'u-pan-she, 1982.
MSI	*Saiiki bunka kenkyū* (Monumenta Serindica) [Studies on the culture of the western regions] 西域文化研究. 6 vols. Kyoto: Hōzōkan, 1958–1963.
NT	Naba Toshisada 那波利貞. *Tōdai shakai bunka shi kenkyū* (Historical Studies on the Society and Culture of T'ang China) 唐代社會文化史研究. Tōyōgaku sōsho (Oriental Studies Library) 東洋學叢書 8. Tokyo: Sōbunsha, 1974.
P	Numbered Pelliot manuscripts from Tun-huang in the Bibliothèque Nationale, Paris.

PekCat	Shang-wu yin-shu-kuan (Commercial Press) 商務印書館, ed. *Tun-huang i-shu tsung-mu so-yin* [Index and general catalog of preserved manuscripts from Tun-huang] 敦煌遺書總目索引. Peking: Commercial Press, 1962. Revised ed., Peking: Chung-hua shu-chü, 1983.
PK	Numbered manuscripts from Tun-huang in the Peking National Library.
RK	*Rekishi Chiri* [History and geography] 歷史地理.
S	Numbered Stein manuscripts from Tun-huang in the British Library, London.
SCD	*Shanghai Chung-yang jih-pao* (Shanghai Central Daily News) 上海中央日報.
SCWK	*Shih-chieh wen-k'u* [World library] 世界文庫.
SH	William Edward Soothill and Lewis Hodous. *A Dictionary of Chinese Buddhist Terms with Sanskrit and English Equivalents and a Sanskrit-Pali Index*. London: Kegan Paul, Trench, Trübner & Co., 1937.
Shi	*Shirin* (Journal of History) 史林.
Shina	*Shinagaku* [Sinology] 支那學.
SPPY	*Ssu-pu pei-yao* [Essential works of the four categories of literature] 四部備要. Elegant, Sung-style typeset editions of Chinese classics published by Chung-hua shu-chü in Shanghai, 1927–1937. Taipei rpt., 1966.
SPTK	*Ssu-pu ts'ung-k'an* [Collection of republished works from the four categories of literature] 四部叢刊. Facsimile reproductions of Chinese classics published by the Commercial Press in Shanghai, 1919–1936.
SWH	*Su-wen-hsueh* [Popular literature] 俗文學.
T	Wang Chung-min 王重民, Wang Ch'ing-shu 王慶菽, Hsiang Ta 向達, Chou I-liang 周一良, Ch'i-kung 啓功, and Tseng I-kung 曾毅公, eds. *Tun-huang pien-wen chi* [Collection of *pien-wen* from Tun-huang] 敦煌變文集. 2 vols. Peking: Jen-min wen-hsueh ch'u-pan-she, 1957. The form of citation for this collection is T page. line, e.g. T365.7.

T[a] — Pan Chung-kwei [P'an Ch'ung-kuei] 潘重規, ed. *Tun-huang pien-wen chi hsin shu* [New collection of Tun-huang *pien-wen*] 敦煌變文集新書, Tun-huang-hsueh ts'ung-shu (Tunhuangology series) 敦煌學叢書 6. 2 vols. Taipei: Chung-kuo wen-hua ta-hsueh Chung-wen yen-chiu-so, 1983–1984.

T — Takakusu Junjirō 高楠順次郎 and Watanabe Kaigyoku 渡邊海旭, eds. *Taishō shinshū Daizōkyō* (The *Tripitaka* in Chinese) 大正新修大藏經. 100 vols. Tokyo: The Taisho Issai-kyo Kanko Kwai, 1922–1934. Individual works from this collection are not listed separately in the bibliography. The form of citation is *T* (number of work) volume of *Taishō shinshū Daizōkyō*. page and section of page from same, e.g. *T*(9)4.433c.

TCC — Sun K'ai-ti 孫楷第. *Ts'ang-chou chi* [The collected works of Ts'ang-chou]. Peking. Chung-hua shu-chü, 1965.

TCTC — Ssu-ma Kuang 司馬光 (1019–1086). *Tzu-chih t'ung-chien* [Comprehensive mirror for aid in government] 資治通鑑, annot. Hu San-hsing 胡三省 (1230–1287). 4 vols. Peking: Ku-chi ch'u-pan-she, 1957, second printing. 1956, first printing in 10 vols.

TCTKP — *T'ien-chin ta-kung pao* (Tientsin l'Impartial) 天津大公報.

TGK — *Tōhō gakuhō* (Kyoto) (Journal of Oriental Studies) 東方學報

Tiger — Kawaguchi Hisao 川口久雄. *Saiiki no tora* [Tiger of the western regions] 西域の虎. Tokyo: Yoshikawa Kōbunkan, 1974.

TLTC — *Ta-lu tsa-chih* (The Continent Magazine) 大陸雜誌.

TP — *T'oung Pao.*

TSCK — *T'u-shu chou-k'an* [Book weekly] 圖書周刊.

TsSCC — *Ts'ung-shu chi-ch'eng ch'u-pien* [Compilation of collectanea, first series] 叢書集成初編. Wang Yun-wu 王雲五, chief ed. Shanghai: Commercial Press, 1935–1940. Typeset and photo-reproduced editions of Chinese texts in 3,464 *ts'e*; not finished.

TTTS — Ch'en Lien-t'ang 陳蓮塘 (Ch'ing), ed. *T'ang-tai ts'ung-shu* [T'ang dynasty collectanea] 唐代叢書. Shanghai: Chin-chang t'u-shu-chü, 1921 [?]), lithograph.

Wen-hsuan Hsiao T'ung 蕭統 (501–531), ed. *Wen-hsuan* [Literary selections] 文選. Taipei: I-wen yin-shu-kuan rpt. of the 1809 recutting of the Sung Ch'un-hsi (1174–1189) wood-block edition.

WFC Wang Fu-ch'üan 汪馥泉. *Chung-kuo wen-hsueh yen-chiu i-ts'ung* [Collection of translations of studies on Chinese literature] 中國文學研究譯叢. Shanghai: Pei-hsin shu-chü, 1930.

WW-TH *Wen-wu ts'an-k'ao tzu-liao* [Materials for the study of cultural artifacts] 文物參考資料 2.4 and 5 (1951). Tun-huang wen-wu chan-lan t'e-k'an [Special number for the exhibition of cultural artifacts from Tun-huang] 敦煌文物展覽特刊 A, B.

WWTKL *Wen-wu ts'an-k'ao tzu-liao* [Research material on cultural artifacts] 文物參考資料.

Z Nakano Tatsuei 中野達慧, et al., comps. *Dai Nippon zoku zōkyō* [Great Japanese continuation of the Tripiṭaka] 大日本續藏經. 750 vols. Kyoto: Kyōto zōkyō shoin, 1905–1912. Individual works from this collection are not listed in the bibliography. The form of citation is *Z* division 輯. case 套. fascicle 册. page, e.g. *Z*1.87.4.302b.

ZDMG *Zeitschrift der Deutschen Morgenländischen Gesellschaft.*

Notes

CHAPTER ONE

1. Also referred to in English as Whistling or Whispering Sands Hill.

2. For a rough count of the extant manuscripts, see the first appendix to my "Lay Students and the Making of Written Vernacular Narrative: An Inventory of Tun-huang Manuscripts," hereafter referred to as "Inventory." When I visited Tun-huang for the first time in the summer of 1981, the director of the research institute at the Grottoes of Unsurpassed Height, Ch'ang Shu-hung 常書鴻, told me that, during construction in 1945, some new manuscripts came to light. There are in this group approximately 300 items, of which 86 are scrolls. These newly discovered manuscripts, which are all sūtras, are kept in the research institute at the Grottoes of Unsurpassed Height. They had been sealed in the belly of an earth god (*t'u-ti p'u-sa* 土地菩薩) by the Taoist caretaker of the caves *before his discovery of the major cache of manuscripts* in cave 17 (Tun-huang Institute number). According to Ch'ang, this proves that manuscripts were preserved at Tun-huang in more than one location.

3. For a summary of the discovery, disposition, and significance of the Tun-huang manuscripts, see Denis Twitchett, "Chinese Social History from the Seventh to Tenth Centuries."

4. See Paolo Daffinà, "L'ltinerario di Hui Shêng," Appendix 1 (pp. 259–260), especially p. 260n4, which cites the extensive scholarship on this name. Also see H. W. Bailey, "Ttaugara," p. 893, who suggests a possible Tocharian origin, and Ikeda On, "Tonkō," p. 194. In her *Einführung in die Zentralasienkunde*, von Gabain gives *Droana* as the name for Tun-huang.

5. Harold Bailey, *The Culture of the Sakas*, p. 20n46. Attempts by Chinese commentators, such as Ying Shao 應劭 (second century), to explicate Tun-huang literally as "Great Splendor" (*Han History* 28B.425c) or the like should be dismissed as folk etymologies similar to explanations of *Fo* (short for *Fo-t'o* 佛陀 [ancient *b'i̯uət-d'â*], i.e. "Buddha") as "perverse, contrary." The latter interpretation of *Fo* was advocated by the sixth-century anti-Buddhist polemicist, Hsun Chi 荀濟 (see *T*52[2031].129b). More recently, Feng Ch'eng-chün (*Hsi-yü ti-ming*, p. 23), has suggested that Daxata "from an old Greek geography" may refer to Tun-huang. I have been able to find this name in Ptolemy (6.16.8), but its location, 174°/39°40′ by the Greek geographer's reckoning, puts it much farther south

than Throana, which Ptolemy gives as located at 174°40′/47°40′, precisely where we would expect to find Tun-huang on his map. What is more, the last syllable of the name makes it seem rather improbable as a source for the transcription of Tun-huang (if that is what Feng had in mind).

6. John Brough, "Nugae Indo-Sericae," p. 82, however, has "r" devolving into "n" of the Chinese name.

7. For example, some Tun-huang manuscripts that refer to Khotan include the following: S5659, S6551v, P2022 *et seq.*, P2647, P2812, P2826, P2889, P3151, P3184v, P3397, P5535, F191, D1502b, D1265 and 1457, D2143, D2149v, and D1074. Manuscripts that mention Uighurs, to name only a few, include P2992v, P3016v, P3028, and P3077v. Uighur, Khotanese, and Tibetan writing occurs separately on Tun-huang manuscripts and in combination with Chinese.

8. There are many evidences in the Tun-huang manuscripts of frequent contact with other parts of China. PK6836 (copied in the year 630), S523, and S3870 are sūtras from Ch'ang-an; S996 is a sūtra copied in the year 479 in Lo-yang; S2140 is a list of Buddhist works from Ch'ang-an; S8101 is a calendar from Ch'ang-an; P3629 is a letter from the Fukien area; and so forth.

9. Demiéville, tr., *Le concile*, p. 308n. For a sketch of the geography and history of Tun-huang, see Kanaoka Shōkō, *Tonkō no bungaku*, Ch. 1 (pp. 3–23). Also cf. L. I. Čuguevskiĭ, "Touen-houang du VIIIe au Xe siècle," for the history of Tun-huang during the period when the *pien-wen* were written.

10. *Science and Civilisation* I, 126.

11. Tun-huang was occupied by the Tibetans in 781 and freed from their control by Chang I-ch'ao 張義潮 in 848. See Fujieda Akira, "Toban shihai-ki no Tonkō," p. 199. For a detailed chronology of the history of Tun-huang, see "Tonkō Bukkyōshi nenpyō," by Yoshimura Shūki, et al. Convenient and accessible chronological information concerning Tun-huang is available in Kanaoka Shōkō, *Tonkō no minshū*, pp. 359–365. Also see A. Róna-tas, "A Brief Note on the Chronology of the Tun-huang collections."

12. His will is given on S4427. For information on Yun-pien, see Kanaoka Shōkō, *Tonkō no minshū*, p. 167.

13. Pañcaśirsa or Pañcaśikha.

14. See Su Pai, "Tun-huang Mo-kao-k'u chung te 'Wu-t'ai-shan t'u,'" especially pp. 53ff.

15. See Richard Aldrich, "Tun-huang: The Rise of the Kansu Port."

16. The *History of the Northern Dynasties*, which also records (CH, 1389) this same passage, has here "the Kingdom of An" (安 instead of 女).

17. CH, 1579–1580; KM, 67.2507b.

18. *Chinese Art and Culture*, p. 221.

19. See, for example, Kanaoka Shōkō, *Tonkō no minshū*, p. 29; Nakano Miyoko, *Tonkō monogatari*; and numerous articles by Kawaguchi Hisao.

20. See Fu Chen-lun, "Tun-huang Ch'ien-fo-tung wen-wu fa-hsien te ching-kuo."

21. Many of the relevant materials regarding the discovery of the manuscripts have been conveniently assembled in a chronological narrative by Eugene

Eoyang in "The Historical Context for the Tun-huang *pien-wen*." The first-hand description of Stein may be found in *Serindia* II, xxi–xxii, and *Ruins of Desert Cathay* I, 166–194, 211–219, especially 217–218. Pelliot's account may be found in his "Une bibliothèque médiévale." See also, for the discovery of the manuscripts, the accounts given in Kanaoka Shōkō, *Tonko no bungaku*, Chapter 2 (pp. 24–45); Kanaoka Shōkō, *Tonkō no minshū*, pp. 23–24, 56–63; and Kanda Kiichiro, *Tonkō-gaku gojū nen*, *passim*.

22. *Tonkō no bungaku*, p. 67.

23. *On Ancient Central Asian Tracks*, pp. 203, 205, 206.

24. Pelliot, "Une bibliothèque médiévale," p. 506; Su Ying-hui, "Pa Hei-ch'eng so ch'u Hsi-hsia shih hsieh-pen"; Saeki, *Nestorian Documents*, p. 253; Weng T'ung-wen, "Tun-huang shih-shih feng-pi nien-tai chih mi." An alternative explanation, which minimizes the role of the Tanguts, is that the handwritten scrolls were discarded upon development of wood-block printing and thread-bound book format. The latter two developments, according to this explanation which is common among Japanese authorities, would have made manuscript scrolls obsolete because such innovations afforded greater reliability and ease of usage.

25. Lionel Giles in Stein, *Serindia* II, 821n2a.

26. Grousset, *Chinese Art and Culture*, p. 222, gives the year 366 for the digging of the first cave. Most scholars hold that the caves were begun in 353.

27. Introduction to *Opisanie Kitaiskikh Rukopisei*, Dun'-khuanskogo fonda II, 5, and "Izuchenie Drevnekitaiskikh Pis'mennykh Pamyatnikov," p. 59.

28. When I visited Leningrad in the summer of 1981, the authorities of the Library of the Institute of Asian Peoples (Academy of Sciences) kindly granted me access to their collection of Tun-huang manuscripts. While there, I examined several hundred items and wish to express publicly my deep gratitude for this rare opportunity afforded me. Professor Lev Men'shikov generously allowed me to use a draft catalog for 3,000 entries not included in *Opisanie kitaiskikh rukopisei* and a preliminary index of an additional 4,000 manuscripts, both of which were prepared by him and his colleagues.

29. During my visit to China in the summer of 1981, the authorities of Peking National Library informed me that there are plans to make a descriptive catalog of the Tun-huang manuscripts in the rare-book collection. I was told the same at the library of Peking University for the manuscripts that are kept there. I was privileged at both libraries to see all of the manuscripts that I requested.

30. For a good general introduction to the manuscripts, see Fujieda Akira, "The Tun-huang Manuscripts" in *Zinbun* and "The Tun-huang Manuscripts" in *Essays on the Sources for Chinese History*.

31. "Shina zokubungaku shi kenkyū no zairyō."

32. See Chen Tsu-lung, "Chung-shih Tun-huang yü Ch'eng-tu chih chien te chiao-t'ung lu-hsien," pp. 80–83, and Hsiang Ta, "Lun T'ang-tai Fo-ch'ü," p. 1587b. My impression is that some Indian influence passed directly to Tun-huang from Szechwan without first going through Central Asia. See Chang Yi, "West Szechwan and East India," pp. 8–9, who documents travel between Szechwan and Kansu, and Chen Chien, "Preliminary Research on the Ancient

Passage to India," who documents early intercourse with India through Burma, Yunnan, Szechwan, and thence to Shensi. This route flourished particularly during the T'ang. On popular Buddhism in the Szechwan area during the T'ang period, see Fujii Kiyoshi, "Tōdai Shoku chihō ni okeru shomin to Bukkyō." On the general cultural history of the city of Ch'eng-tu in Szechwan, see Naba Toshisada, "Bunka-shijō yori kansatsu suru Shisenshō Seito."

33. See my discussion of the colophons of this manuscript on p. 133. The crucial issue is that, where the T editors (T618.12) and the T[a] editor (T[a]335.15) read Hsi-ch'uan 西川 (in modern Szechwan), Kanaoka Shōkō (*Tonkō no bungaku*, p. 181) gives Hsi-chou 西州 (in modern Sinkiang). My own reading ("Inventory," item 15) agrees with that of the T and T[a] editors. Cf. T420.3, where there is a parallel reference to Tung-ch'uan 東川 and Hsi-shu 西蜀 which surely must indicate the eastern and western parts of Szechwan. Other Tun-huang manuscripts that originated in the Szechwan area or have some connection with it include S5444 (colophon dated 905), S4540.1 (905), S5534 (905), S5451 (906), S5544.1, S5669 (906), S5965 (905), and S6726 (926) (all the preceding are handwritten copies of the printed editions of the *Vajracchedikā-prajñāpāramitā-sūtra* in 32 sections that had been made in West Szechwan [Hsi-ch'uan 西川] by the Kuo family 過家) and printed document number 10 of the Stein collection, a calendar printed by the family of Fan Shang 樊賞 of Ch'eng-tu 成都 in Hsi-ch'uan 西川, province of Chien-nan 劍南. Also see PK6499, PK2062v, S6836, S8100, P2003, P2094, P2249v, P2292, P2816, P2876 (943), P3398.1 (943), P3493 (943), P3649 (names three rivers in Szechwan), P3761, D700, D2776, San 262, and D11051Bv(?).

34. See Naba Toshisada, "Tō shōhon zasshō kō," p. 226.

35. This is not to deny that the inhabitants of Tun-huang were in direct contact with other, more easterly, places such as Five Terraces Mountain (Wu-t'ai shan 五臺山), Ch'ang-an, and Korea. It is interesting to note that there even seems to have been some sort of contact between Tun-huang and the distant Wenchow 溫州 (in Chekiang). S4487 is "An Account of Repentence and Elimination of Sin through the *Suvarṇa-prabhāsa-sūtrā*" 懺悔滅罪金光明經傳. It relates to an official of Wen-chou named Chang Chü-tao 張居道. This is most suggestive, for Wen-chou is known for being perhaps the most important coastal point of entry for Indian influence that came to China by way of the sea.

36. For someone newly or partially literate, the fascination with and necessity to practice characters is readily understandable. On the first page inside the front cover of a handwritten shadow-play script owned by Harvard University, there is a series of practice characters (る る, etc.) reminiscent of similar exercises on many Tun-huang manuscripts. Harvard-Yenching Library catalog number T5722/4622, *ts'e* 23, *Borrowing the Barbarian Coiffure* (*Chieh ti chi* 借狄髻).

CHAPTER TWO

1. Kaji Tetsujō, "Zoku-bungaku," pp. 102–103.
2. Yu Tien-ts'ung, "Su-chiang yü pien-wen," p. 12. Ch'en Kuo-ning, *Tun-*

huang pi-hua Fo-hsiang t'u yen-chiu, p. 29, also posits *yuan-ch'i*, "seat-settling texts" (*ya-tso-wen*), etc., as types of *pien-wen*.

3. For a full account of *pien-hsiang*, see my article entitled "Records of Transformation Tableaux."

4. Jen Pan-t'ang, *T'ang hsi-nung*, p. 51.

5. For both these opinions, see Kanaoka, "Mokuren henbun," pp. 133, 139n2.

6. In spite of this minimal caution excercised by the T editors, Tochio Takeshi, "Tonkō henbun . . . no hikaku," p. 91, persisted in referring to a mysterious **Pien-wen sou-shen chi* 變文搜神記.

7. Leong Weng Kee, "Pien-hsiang yü ch'a-t'u hua-pen," p. 8.

8. "Hen to henbun."

9. In his "T'an T'ang-tai min-chien wen-hsueh."

10. Ibid. p. 77.

11. "Some Questions," p. 212.

12. "Ts'ung pien-wen tao ta-ku, pao-chüan, yü t'an-tz'u" [From *pien-wen* to *ta-ku*, *pao-chüan*, and *t'an-tz'u*] 從變文到大鼓寶卷與彈詞, in *Hsiao-shuo yü hsi-chü*, pp. 90–97 (p. 91).

13. T196–206.

14. This appears to say "There have been no omissions in copying" or "There has been no plundering," but I have interpreted it as given in the translation because the manuscript itself is obviously not illustrated (i.e., it must be referring to a separate scroll or booklet) and because I think 略 *lịak* may be a mistake for 錄 *lịwok*.

15. See Chapter 4 near the end (at notes 109 ff).

16. By "documents" I mean deeds, loans, contracts, registers, lists of names of property, etc.

17. As, for example, the narrative verses on Tung Yung (S2204; T109–113), the story in verse about Chi Pu (P3697 and other manuscripts; T51–71), etc.

18. *Tun-huang ch'ü ch'u-t'an*, p. 300.

19. See also Jen's preface, p. 3.

20. Approximately 180 texts, if we count individual manuscripts rather than separate titles. Jen's ready acceptance of numerous verse forms would raise this number to at least two or three times higher.

21. The number varies depending on whether one is willing to count multiple copies of the same text as separate transformations. A listing of the manuscripts in the "narrow" corpus will be given in the middle of this chapter.

22. For a list, see Kanaoka, "On the Word '*Pien*'" and my translation of Pai Hua-wen, "What Is '*pien-wen*'?" I touch on all of these titled *pien* or *pien-wen* in this chapter and in "Inventory." Attempts to discern a consistent distinction in T'ang usage of these two designations (*pien* and *pien-wen*), with regard to specific written texts from Tun-huang, are doomed to failure. It is obvious, however, that the first designation may also be used in reference to oral performances, artistic representations, and the epiphanies that serve as their inspiration, while the second designation can be used only in reference to a written text.

23. For a discussion of this title, see below, pp. 100ff.

24. Fully discussed in Chapter 4 below and in *Tun-huang Popular Narratives*, "Appendix."

25. For a discussion of these texts, see pp. 25–26.

26. The character 物 ends one line and 成 begins the next. It is possible (though highly unlikely) that 成 is not part of the man's name as indicated by the T editors and my translation but that it refers to the completion of the copies.

27. Naturally, we would not expect that the antecedent oral performances could have been called *pien-wen*.

28. *Catalogue*, p. 248.

29. For a discussion of this concept, see pp. 120–121.

30. I have summarized this transformation text at greater length than the others because it is less well known.

31. *Nidāna* or *hetupratyaya*.

32. In the text (T768.15, T769.2) 后 (= 後) is missing. At T765.6, before the start of the story proper, there is reference to an "inner palace" 內宮.

33. *Nidāna* or *pratyaya*.

34. It is noteworthy that both appear verbatim in the Tun-huang manuscript collections of stories on filial piety (T902.6–10).

35. See Pai Hua-wen, "What Is '*pien-wen*'?" pp. 512–513.

36. But compare the so-called "Tale of the Bombast of the Teacher of Teachers (?)" 師師謾語話 (on S4327–337) which does include some verse. The title, however, has been taken from within the text and does not stand at the beginning or end of the piece. See "Inventory," item 337.

37. A less plausible explanation is that the term *pien* in the title of the Shun-tzu piece is being used in the sense of "wonder, miracle." According to this explanation, *pien* could then be taken as referring to the miraculous ways in which the boy Shun is rescued from the nefarious machinations of his stepmother (T131.7–8; 132.5 [note the use of the word *hua* 化]; 133.1 [note the use of the word *pien*]; 133.6–7) and the wondrous manner in which he cures his father of blindness (T134.1).

38. See "Inventory," item 150.

39. On these anecdotes and their presumed relationship to the main story, see Eoyang's extensive discussion in "Word of Mouth," pp. 91–114.

40. The manuscript itself, however, does not stop here.

41. Like the *pien* about Shun-tzu, this brief story is replete with miraculous happenings (T160.7–8, 161.6, 161.7–10, and 161.12). Similarly, these may account for the seemingly anomalous generic designation as *pien*.

42. SH, p. 38.

43. See my discussion of one such title for the Wu Tzu-hsu story in "Inventory," item 241.

44. See Chiang Li-hung, *Tun-huang pien-wen tzu-i t'ung-shih*, pp. 177–178.

45. It is not certain whether this is meant to be construed as a title.

46. Three months?

47. Discussed in the introductory section of "Inventory."

48. The T editors (T344.2 and 355n1) incorrectly insert the character 神 after 變.

49. See the discussion of this opening section in "Inventory," item 11.

50. Again, it is possible that the word *pien* in the titles of both these works (the "Eight Aspects" and the "Destruction of Demons") refers less to a literary classification than to the supernatural happenings recorded therein. Such occurrences are particularly prominent in the latter text (e.g., T349.2ff, 352.14ff, and 353.7ff) but are also found in the former (e.g., T333.9ff) and, indeed, Buddhist doctrine holds the worldly existence of all Buddhas to be a series of "transformations."

It is conceivable, then, to think of the *pien* in the titles of the special group of texts under discussion as referring generally to the "unusual" or "strange" incidents that occur in the stories themselves rather than as a formal, generic designation. This is certainly possible in the case of the story of Shun as a boy and the Crown Prince of the Liu house during the Former Han dynasty. As for the title of the tale of the maiden in the women's palace of King Bimbisara, it is plausible to explain *pien* as referring to the actual transformations of the young lady that take place therein. Admittedly, there is no hard and fast line between *pien* in the sense of "unusual or strange incident" and in the generic sense of "transformation," for both usages ultimately derive from the same Buddhistic notions (to be discussed in detail in the next chapter).

51. The connection between transformations and pictures will be documented fully in Chapters 4 and 6.

52. Note that Tu Ying-t'ao's 杜穎陶 edition of the text in *Tung Yung ch'en hsiang ho-chi* 董永沉香合集 (Shanghai, 1957), pp. 5–7, has 採將下 for 揲將 (T111.13).

53. The authors of a recent history of Chinese fiction published in the People's Republic also deny that the Wu Tzu-hsu story is a *pien-wen*. They refer to it, rather, as being in form "closer to the early *hua-pen*" 話本 (story roots). See Pei-ching ta-hsueh chung-wen hsi, *Chung-kuo hsiao-shuo shih*, p. 57.

54. Except T69.14; but see T83n168.

55. It is instructive to compare these mislabeled "*pien-wen*" with P2999–75 which bears the title "Sūtra of the Crown Prince's Attainment of the Way, One Scroll" 太子成道經壹卷 (T296.11). The related text on S4626–351 is actually a seat-settling text (see T287.13, 301n1, 823, and 830).

56. In the Russian catalog of Tun-huang manuscripts, there is not a single text among the 25 placed in the category of *pien-wen* that, according to a narrow definition of the genre, can legitimately be called by that name. See Men'shikov, et al., *Opisanie Kitaiskikh* I, 579–585 (nos. 1470–1482) and II, 499–506 (nos. 2861–2872). There may, however, be other genuine *pien-wen* in Russia, in China, or in private collections elsewhere that have not been publicly described adequately and of which I am, therefore, unaware. All of the extant *pien-wen* that I know of have been listed in this chapter. For a recent addition to the corpus, see "Inventory," item 599, and Mair, "A Newly Identified Fragment." It is also not impossible that future archeological discoveries might yield additional manuscripts. More Buddhist texts were recently found in a tomb in Chiang-yin 江陰 county

(near the Yangtze River), Kiangsu province. Preliminary reports (*China Daily*, 1.54 [13 August 1981]) indicate, however, that these are mostly scriptures and date from the Northern Sung.

57. E.g. "Inventory," p. 5; "Oral and Written Aspects of Chinese Sutra Lectures"; and Chapter 5 below.

58. *Tun-huang hsueh kai-yao*, p. 55.

59. The causal matrix which gives rise to events and things. See Shoson Miyamoto, "A Reappraisal of Pratītya-samutpāda," in *Yamaguchi [Susumu] Hakushi kanreki kinen*. From as early as the sixth century, prefaces to Buddhist treatises were called *yuan-ch'i* or *yin-yuan* 因緣 (reason for writing). As a literary genre, it comes to mean approximately "legend (of a founder or saint, etc.)."

60. T712.13.

61. T816.2.

62. T824.11.

63. See P3375v and two manuscripts in the Shanghai Museum, one of which has marginal notations written in red.

64. See T813n1 and "Inventory," item 144.

65. Such references also often occur in T'ang poems.

66. See Naba Toshisada, "Shidda taishi shudō innen kaisėtsu." Also see *MSI* I, 240c.

67. This same note occurs near the beginning of S3711v–320. I have also consulted this manuscript in making the translation.

68. Cf. T697.5.

69. T481.4–5; cf. T484.4. For other evidence of music in sūtra lectures, see T485.11, 15, and 16; 482.2 ("intone" 吟); 484.5 ("What follows is the singing of the sūtra" 此下唱經) and, by contrast, 483.6 ("What follows is to be spoken" 此下白道).

70. This is true, as well, to a lesser degree, of pentasyllabic, decasyllabic, and other lengths of verse. There is also the technique of intoning verse described by John Bishop in his "Prosodic Elements in T'ang Poetry," pp. 52–53: ". . . the prominence of the tonal pattern seems to have led to a technique by which lyric poems were chanted, the emphasizing of the tone of each word producing a definite, though limited melodic line."

71. In the *Sūtra of the Wise and the Foolish* 賢愚經, the story is called "Vajrā, the Daughter of King Prasenajit" 波斯匿王女金剛. All these references are from T801n1. Also see Lo Tsung-t'ao, *Tun-huang chiang-ching pien-wen yen-chiu*, pp. 322–332.

72. My translation of this term is an attempt to render the content of its meaning as explained by Hsiang Ta, "T'ang-tai su-chiang k'ao," p. 305. I do not, however, agree with Hsiang that a *ya-tso-wen* was meant to "adumbrate an entire scripture." See also Sun K'ai-ti, "T'ang-tai su-chiang kuei-fan," p. 52, who explains the term as meaning to settle (literally "press") in their seats all those in attendance. 押者即是鎮壓之壓, 座即四座之座. Cf. Kanaoka Shōkō, "Ōza kō," and Kaji Tetsujō, "Zoku-bungaku," p. 119, who cites S4417–340 (an order of

service for a popular lecture 俗講儀式): "Having spoken [the part] which settled them in their seats" 說押座了. Note the use of the quasi-perfective ending.

73. See my "Introduction" to *Tun-huang Popular Narratives* and cf. Kenneth Ch'en, *Buddhism in China*, p. 289.

74. *Chiang-shih-hsing chih pien-wen yen-chiu*, pp. 2, 34.

75. See the "Introduction" to my *Tun-huang Popular Narratives*.

76. For a detailed study of the sources of the Tun-huang Wu Tzu-hsu story, see Hsieh Hai-p'ing, *Chiang-shih-hsing chih pien-wen yen-chiu*, pp. 19–34.

77. In Wang Chung-min, *Tun-huang ku-chi hsu-lu*, p. 336; also see Liu's original article on the subject in *T'ien-chin ta-kung pao*.

78. Hsieh Hai-p'ing dates the Chang I-ch'ao transformation text to sometime between the years 856–873. *Chiang-shih hsing chih pien-wen yen-chiu*, p. 3. For a study of the historical materials related in the Chang I-ch'ao transformation text, see ibid., pp. 81–88.

79. For some evidence concerning the dating of the Chang Huai-shen transformation text, see T128n1.

80. See *History of the Han Dynasty* (CH), p. 3803.

81. Cf. Nemoto Makoto, "Ō Shō-kun henbun no seiritsu nendai ko."

82. *Śāriputra et les six maîtres*, p. 1.

CHAPTER THREE

1. "On the Word '*Pien*.'"

2. "Some Questions Connected with Tun-huang pien-wen."

3. "Alcune osservazioni terminologiche sui *bianwen*."

4. This notion is propounded in almost identical language ([它是]從散文變化而來[的]所以就稱為變文) by Lao Kan, "Tun-huang chi Tun-huang te hsin shih-liao," p. 52, and Su Ying-hui, *Tun-huang lun-chi*, pp. 46–47. The fallacy of Lao's reasoning is clinched by the fact that, in his previous sentence, he had declared that *pien-wen* are called what they are because they have been *transformed* from canonical or classical literature into something more accessible to the common people. It is inconceivable that *pien* could stand for two such different ideas at one and the same time.

5. Yang Chia-lo, *Hsiao-shuo yü chiang-ch'ang wen-hsueh* I, 7.

6. Eugene Eoyang, "Word of Mouth," p. 50, and cf. pp. 167, 212.

7. Chou Shao-liang, "T'an T'ang-tai min-chien wen-hsueh," p. 75.

8. Kuan Te-tung, "T'an 'pien-wen'," pp. 199, 201.

9. *Ch'a-t'u pen Chung-kuo wen-hsueh shih*, p. 449. Cf. Jaworski, "Notes sur l'ancienne littérature populaire en Chine," p. 184.

10. *Chung-kuo su-wen-hsueh shih* I, 190.

11. *Ch'a-t'u pen Chung-kuo wen-hsueh shih*, p. 451.

12. For example, Fujino Iwatomo, *Chūgoku no bungaku to reizoku*, p. 164; Yang Yin-shen, *Chung-kuo su-wen-hsueh*, p. 93. A typical formulation of this view is that

given by Ch'iu Chen-ching in his *Tun-huang pien-wen shu-lun*, p. 19 (copied almost verbatim from *Tz'u-hai* [Sea of Phrases] 辭海, yu 63 [p. 2709]): "'*Pien-wen*' means to alter 更易 the original text 文 of a Buddhist sūtra or an indigenous Chinese story and, furthermore, to expand and elaborate upon it, causing it to be changed 變 into a popular, vivid lay lecture."

13. Shih Wei-liang, *Yin-yueh hsiang li-shih ch'iu cheng*, p. 18. Meng Yao (Yang Tsung-chen), *Chung-kuo hsiao-shuo shih* I, 110 offers a similar explanation.

14. Wang P'ei-lun, *Hsi-ch'ü tz'u-tien*, p. 641.

15. Ku Huai, "Ta-chung wen-i yü k'ou-yü-shih," p. 13.

16. Werner Eichhorn, *Chinese Civilization* (New York: Praeger, 1969), p. 224.

17. Kaji Tetsujō, "Zoku-bungaku," p. 105.

18. Hattori Katsuhiko, who made a very careful study of the relevant Chinese sources, mentions singing, music, acrobatics, dancing, all sorts of conjuring, and magic during the Northern Wei, particularly as they reveal foreign influence. But nowhere does he mention storytelling with pictures or *pien*. See his *Hokugi Rakuyō no shakai to bunka*, especially Chapter 1 (pp. 143–187) of the second section ("Culture" [*Bunka hen* 文化編]), entitled "Court Plays and Entertainments in Loyang during the Northern Wei" (Hokugi Rakuyō ni okeru kyūtei hyakugi to sono geinō 北魏洛陽における宮庭百戲とその藝能) and Chapter 5 (pp. 232–283) of the third section ("Buddhism and Culture in Loyang during the Northern Wei" [Hokugi Rakuyō no Bukkyō to bunka 北魏洛陽の佛教と文化]), entitled "Buddhism in Loyang during the Northern Wei and Amusements and Entertainments" (Hokugi Rakuyō ni okeru Bukkyō to goraku geinō 北魏洛陽における佛教と娯樂藝能). See also Hattori's *Zoku Hokugi Rakuyō no shakai to bunka*.

19. Ch'en Shou-yi, *Chinese Literature*, p. 323. Brown, "From Sutra to *Pien-wen*," p. 71, subscribes to a similar view.

20. Ch'en Shou-yi, p. 182.

21. Gerty Kallgren, "Studies in Sung Time Colloquial," p. 6.

22. "Pien-ko, pien-hsiang, yü pien-wen," p. 75.

23. Rulan Pian, in conversation, informed me that *pien* occurs in musical usage (一變) with a meaning that might be translated as "realization" or "rendering." Adele Rickett has called to my attention the use of *pien* in criticism of the *Book of Poetry* to contrast with *cheng* 正 (poems supposedly dealing with periods of good governance). Cf. James Liu, *Chinese Theories of Literature*, pp. 64–65, 120. It is intriguing that *pien* had not taken on this pejorative sense until the later Han period. See Maureen Robertson, "Periodization in the Arts," p. 8. There is only a remotely conceivable connection between *pien* as found in musical usage or in literary criticism and the Buddhist world of *pien-wen* and *pien-hsiang*.

The two characters for *pien-wen* occur next to each other at the beginning of the 29th chapter of Liu Hsieh's 劉勰 (465–522) *Wen-hsin tiao-lung* [The literary mind and ornate rhetoric] 文心雕龍. This chapter, the title of which is "T'ung-pien" [The unvarying and the varying] 通變, has been studied exhaustively by Ferenc Tökei, *Genre Theory in China*, pp. 135–163. Liu Hsieh was himself a Buddhist, and a great deal of Buddhist ontology worked its way into the *Literary Mind*. He explicitly mentions *prajñā* ("transcendental wisdom") in Chapter 18, and there are many other evidences of Buddhist philosophical underpinnings, as has been demonstrated by Leei Shih, *Wen-hsin tiao-lung yuan-tao yü Fo-tao shu-cheng* (A comparative study). But Liu's understanding of *pien* is strictly classical and is founded squarely on its usage in the "Appended Explanations" of the *Book of Change*. Hence, when he speaks of *pien-wen chih shu* 變文之數 ("the art/technique by which a literary work is rendered an [individual] variant [of the genre, *t'i* 體]"), there is no question of wholly new transformational creation in the Indian sense but only of modification of a pre-existent entity. This is in conformity with our expectations of the general level of understanding of Buddhist notions of transformation in China even so late as this period. It would seem that other Buddhist concepts, such as "emptiness" (*śūnyatā*), "extinction" (*nirvāṇa*), and so on, were more easily comprehended because there were similar Taoist concepts (*wu* 無, absorption into the Tao 道, etc.). This also helps to account for the persistent Chinese interpretation of Buddhist *pien* as "strange" until well into the T'ang period and, in many cases, even after that time.

In a letter to Hui-sheng 與惠生書, the T'ang literary critic Ssu-k'ung T'u 司空圖 (837–908) also juxtaposed the graphs *pien* and *wen*. Read in context, however, we see that he was actually discussing a "change in the quality of writing" 變文質 since the time of the sages. He was not referring to transformation texts. *Ch'in-ting ch'üan T'ang wen*, Vol. 163, 807.6a. Called to my attention by Andrew Jones.

24. "Tu T'ang-tai su-chiang k'ao," p. 381

25. "Kuan-yü pien-wen te t'i-ming," pp. 196–197, 214–215.

26. "T'ang-tai su-chiang k'ao," pp. 310–312.

27. A. N. Zhelokhovtsev and Yu L. Krol', "Ob Etimologii i Znachenii Termina Byanven'," especially pp. 141–142.

28. "The K'uai-t'i," pp. 113–114.

29. *Jigoku-hen*, p. 150.

30. H. C. Chang, *Chinese Literature*, p. 23.

31. Shao Hung, *Tun-huang shih-shih chiang-ching-wen yen-chiu*, p. 1 of the English summary.

32. E.g. Chen Tsu-lung, *La vie et les oeuvres*, p. 57; Li-li Ch'en, "Pien-wen Chantefable."

33. As cited by Průšek, "Researches into the Beginning of the Popular Chinese Novel," p. 104n1.

34. *Ballads and Stories*, p. 246.

35. *Ancient Buddhism in Japan* I, 328.

36. "Dans en écran de radar," pp. 482ff.

37. *Li-tai ming-hua chi*, p. 60.

38. *Some T'ang and Pre-T'ang Texts on Chinese Painting* I, 257n3.

39. Chou I-liang, "Tu T'ang-tai su-chiang k'ao," pp. 380–381. Those who would agree with Chou include Tanaka Ichimatsu, *Emakimono*, p. 3, and Kuan Te-tung, "Lueh shuo 'pien' tzu te lai-yuan," p. 2.

40. "Tun-huang Texts," p. 186. The French equivalents may be found in "Les débuts," p. 569: "les 'scènes,'" "les 'scènes' littéraires," and "les 'scènes'

figurées." Demiéville's remarks on this subject in his review article "Manuscrits chinois de Touen-houang à Leningrad," p. 373n1, are also helpful: "Men'šikov ([*Byan'ven' o Veimotsze,*] p. 28, n. 50) incline à adopter l'interprétation de Souen K'ai-ti: *pien*, '[événement] insolite, miraculeux,' qui me paraît très discutable; mes propres recherches sur l'emploi de ce terme dans un certain nombre de contextes variés m'ont conduit à le traduire simplement par 'scene.' Je suis par contre d'accord pour reconnaître avec Men'šikov (pp. 23–24) que la forme de chantefable (prose et verse), qui devait connaître une telle fortune en Chine, est un emprunt à l'Inde à travers les traductions de textes bouddhiques." Demiéville's fullest remarks on the meaning of *pien*, probably the most perceptive statements on the subject to date, may be found in his review of Men'shikov and Zograf, *Bjan'ven' o vozdaijanii*, pp. 166–169. Knechtges shows his usual good sense by endorsing them in his review of Jenner, *Memories of Loyang*, p. 348.

41. *Einführung*, p. 76.

42. *Bukkyō no bijutsu oyobi rekishi*, pp. 866ff.

43. "Zokkō to henbun," pp. 427, 429.

44. "Hen to henbun," p. 224.

45. Cited in Hsiang Ta, "Kuan-yü 'Su-chiang k'ao' tsai shuo chi chü hua fu-chi."

46. Chou I-liang, "Tun-huang pi-hua yü Fo-ching," p. 105.

47. See my "Records of Transformation Tableaux."

48. *Bukkyō daijiten*, 5.4534c–4535a.

49. Or "characteristic mark or distinguishing sign (*nimittam* or *lakṣaṇa*) made apparent through transformation." There are good grounds for this assertion in the earliest available textual references to *pien* as pictorial representation of Buddhist subjects. See my "Records of Transformation Tableaux."

50. The Sanskrit equivalent of *rnam pa(r)* by itself is *ākāra* ("outward appearance" "shape," "form"). Cf. Tibetan *č̆ós-skui rnám-par ̥gyúr-ba* ("to appear in a misty form"). See Jäschke, *Dictionary*, p. 313b, no. 5.

51. "Tu pien-wen tsa-chih," *TCC*, pp. 61–64.

52. *The Chinese Knight-Errant*, pp. 100, 210–211.

53. *Chung-kuo wen-hsueh fa-chan shih*, Vol. II, "Pien-wen te lai-yuan [The origins of *pien-wen*]" 變文的來源, p. 395.

54. "Urban Centers," p. 262. Průšek may be relying here on the interpretation of Sun K'ai-ti, for which see above at note 51. Earlier, however, Průšek followed Pelliot closely when he referred to *pien-wen* as "changed texts." See "The Narrators of Buddhist Scriptures," p. 378.

55. See *T*(2122) 53.530a–533a and 769a.

56. Sun erroneously cites a passage from the biography of Fan Sui 范雎傳 in the 79th fascicle of the *Records of the Grand Historian.* As Sun himself admits, 關東有何變? means no more than "What is going on (i.e., What change is there) east of the passes?" There need be no mention of "strangeness" in this case. It is doubtful whether *pien* in such late first-century productions as Pan Ku's (32–92) *Universal Discussions at White Tiger Lodge* (*Pai-hu t'ung-i* 白虎通義 A.D. 79,

BSS, 6.221) and Chang Heng's 張衡 (78–139) "Rhapsody on the Western Capital" (Hsi-ching fu 西京賦, A.D. 107, *Wen-hsuan*, 2.5b) really meant *ch'i* 奇 ("strange"), although T'ang commentators occasionally offered such an interpretation. At this early period in the Buddhist-influenced evolution of the word, it is unlikely that *pien* meant much more than "unusual."

57. See Mair, "Ontological Presuppositions."

58. *T*(2060) 50.658a; cf. *T*(2064) 50.974c.

59. See, for example, the vocabularies in the backs of the individual volumes of James Legge's *The Chinese Classics*. The *Great Chung Hwa Dictionary of Single Characters* lists 28 meanings for *pien*, only 2 of which (numbers 8 and 13) may show some Buddhist influence and none of which are suitable as explanations for the *pien* of *pien-wen* or *pien-hsiang*. See *Chung-hua ta tzu-tien*, p. 2375.3–2376.1 (shen 213.3–214.1).

60. Joseph Needham, *Science and Civilisation* II, 220n7.

61. Peking: Chung Hwa Book Co., 1954.

62. *Candid Questions in the Inner Classic of the Yellow Sovereign* in *I-pu ch'üan-lu* [Complete corpus of medical texts] 醫部全錄 ed. (Peking: People's Hygiene Press, 1956).

63. *The Theoretical Foundations of Chinese Medicine*, pp. 15–16.

64. *Science and Civilisation* II, 74ff. The quotation is from p. 74.

65. James Legge, tr., Z. D. Sung, ed., *The Text of Yi King*, p. 345.

66. P'ang P'u, ed., *Kung-sun lung-tzu*, pp. 26ff.

67. *Han shu*, 61.510b.

68. *China in Central Asia*, p. 225 and note 852.

69. Watson, pp. 195–196; Chinese text in *A Concordance to Chuang Tzu*, pp. 47–48 (18.41–46). Isabelle Robinet, "Metamorphosis and Deliverance," thoroughly documents my contention that the early Taoist concept of *pien-hua* presented no ontological discontinuities. Jing Wang, "The Mythology of Stone," section 2 ("Nü-kua and Stone") collects passages from several early texts that refer to the ability of the goddess Nü-wa to create through metamorphosis (*hua* 化). All of the texts cited are products of Han redaction and none are entirely free of probable or at least possible Indian contamination. Even if they are free of such influence, the metamorphoses described are not the *nirmāṇa*-type transformations from nothing or from mind specified by Buddhist *pien*.

70. See, for example, *Chu-tzu yü-lei*, 75.9b (p. 3078): "To evolve is to begin gradually to change; the point at which there is division [i.e., when the evolving thing becomes something else—note Chu Hsi's use of *ch'u* as a sequence marker] is transformation." 化是漸漸移將去;截斷處便是變. Cf. P2940, a commentary on an unspecified Buddhist text by an unknown author, where the term *pien-i* 變易 is explained as follows: "*pien* means 'change', *i* means 'vary'" 變者改變, 易者移易. D48, an original Chinese Buddhist text on supreme *bodhi* or enlightenment (*ta-chueh* 大覺), defines *pien-hua* as "the constant of heaven and earth" 變化者天地之常.

71. *Wang Yu-ch'eng chi chien-chu* II, 375–378. First cited by Jao Tsung-i in "Ts'ung 'Shan pien' lun pien-wen," p. 635. Wang also has a "Eulogy on a Transformation Painting of a Western Paradise, with Preface" 西方變畫讚并序. *Wang Yu-ch'eng chi chien-chu*, pp. 367–372.

72. Modified slightly from Legge, *The Text of Yi King*, p. 278. Wang cites only the four Chinese graphs I have given. There is no point in referring to T'ang or other commentators of the *Book of Change* on this passage for they were not, like Wang Wei, engaged in a discussion of *pien* as it occurs in the expressions *pien-hsiang* or *pien-wen*.

73. 楚元王傳, *Han shu*, p. 452c. This in turn may be traced back to the *Records of Ritual:* "The flesh and bones revert to the soil—that is one's allotted span. As for the vital energy of the soul, it reaches everywhere, it reaches everywhere." *Li chi*, in *Shih-san ching chu-shu*, 10.19b (p. 195a).

74. *Paunar-bhaviki.*

75. 道 *mārga.*

76. Cf. 妙身體 *mūrtimat* (incarnate).

77. *Āśraya-parivṛtti.*

78. The six conditions of sentient existence which one must transcend to achieve holy rebirth. They are existence in one of the hells, as a hungry ghost, as an animal, as a malevolent native spirit, as a human, or as a deva (celestial).

79. For an elaborate demonstration of this meaning of *pien* in titles of paintings, see my "Records of Transformation Tableaux." It is not surprising that Wang Wei would be unable to deal with Sanskrit terminology directly. As van Gulik has forcefully demonstrated in *Siddham*, even learned Chinese Buddhist monks (except for a very few rare individuals who had been to India) were not conversant with Indic languages. Translations from Sanskrit and Pāli were done almost exclusively by Indian or Central Asian monks, often working with Chinese collaborators who were responsible for the final product.

80. *Chinese Popular Fiction in Two London Libraries*, p. 20. Other scholars, including Nomura Yosho, "Tonkō henbun ni miru Daiba-bon no keitai," p. 308, have accepted *pien* as meaning essentially *shen-pien*; no one, to the best of my knowledge, has demonstrated this identification by reference to specific texts.

81. *Transformation of Buddhism*, pp. 25, 252; *Buddhism in China*, pp. 287–290; "Filial Piety in Chinese Buddhism," p. 91. H. G. Quaritch Wales gives the same rendering in his *The Indianization of China*, p. 83.

82. "*Pien-wen* Chantefable," p. 256n5.

83. Preface to Basil Gray, *Buddhist Cave Paintings*, p. 14.

84. *Tun-huang pien-wen hui-lu*, p. x.

85. "Tu T'ang-tai su-chiang k'ao," pp. 381–383. In one of his later statements on the subject, Sun K'ai-ti also seems to have accepted that the *pien* of *pien-wen* derived from *shen-pien* Cf. "Tu pien-wen erh tse," in *LWL*, pp. 239ff.

86. *Tun-huang pien-wen hui-lu*, preface, pp. x–xi.

87. "Kuan-yü p'o-mo pien-wen," p. 13.

88. *BHS*, p. 392b. Nakamura, *Bukkyōgo daijiten*, p. 1215b, says that *prātihārya*

(also written as 變化 or 變現 in Chinese) are transformational appearances. They are the miracles by which the Buddha ravishes the spirits of men in order to convert them.

89. *BHS*, p. 151.

90. Nakamura, p. 795bc, and Mochizuki, pp. 2090b–2091a.

91. We should also bear in mind, when we discuss later the *rapprochement* of Buddhism and Manichaeism during the T'ang period and the possible effect this had on storytelling with pictures, that the Manichaeans borrowed heavily from Buddhist notions of transformational manifestation. See, for example, Chavannes and Pelliot, "Un traité manichéen," pp. 608, col. 3–11, and p. 553: "grâce à sa pénétration surnaturelle, produit par transformation la liberté d'être invisible ou visible." 神通 [*abhijñā*] 變化隱現自在.

92. Tr. Saṅghavara (?). *T*(2043) 50.134b.

93. *Ṛddhy* (*-abhisaṃskāra*); *anubhāva*; *prabhāva*; *abhijñāna*.

94. *Rāja-haṃsa*.

95. "A Study of the Svāgata Story," *HJAS*, pp. 298–299n233. Cf. Unrai Wogihara, *Bodhisattvabhūmi*, pp. 58–63 and *T*(1579) 30.491c–493.

96. *T*(176) 3.443c.

97. Cowell and Neil, ed., p. 192, 1.8, p. 313, 1.15: "*ācu prithagjanasya riddhir āvarjanakarī*;" p. 133, 1.9: "*ācu prithagjanāvarjanakarī riddhir*. Quoted by Ch'en, *Chinese Transformation*, p. 272.

98. *T*(262) 9.60a.

99. *T*(2088) 51.954c–955a.

100. Blofeld, *Bodhisattva of Compassion*, pp. 139–140. Blofeld's transcriptions of Chinese and Sanskrit have not been normalized.

101. Wang Chi-lan, *Chung-kuo min-chien i-shu*, pp. 196ff.

102. *T*(2040) 50.65b. This text was written by Seng-yu 僧佑 (fl. 482–518). The same passage also speaks of "manifesting" (*hsien* 現) a "transformation" (*pien*) and Raudrākṣa is said to be good at "illusionism" (*huan-shu* 幻術). Another passage in the same text (*T* 50.81c) says of a blind musician who played a stringed instrument that he possessed extraordinary ability as an entertainer 備六十四伎變弄殊絕. The mention of "sixty-four entertainers' transformations" indicates that, by the time of Seng-yu, *pien* had already acquired the meaning of "technique" or "trick."

103. T383.13 and 15, 386.16, 388.5, etc.

104. *T*(2122) 53.592a.

105. This is a precise rendering of Sanskrit *nir-* $\sqrt{m\bar{a}}$, "to make [manifest through] transformation." Nakamura, p. 1215c.

106. *Prātihārya*, "to [make] manifest through transformation." The entire complex of Buddhist technical terms dealing with transformational manifestation (*pien* 變, *hsiang* 相, *hsien* 現, *pien-hsien* 變現, and so forth) may be found in an unidentified manuscript of the collection of Robert Hatfield Ellsworth (New York), said to date from the T'ang period. See *An Exhibition of Chinese and Korean Sūtra Manuscripts from the Collection of Robert Hatfield Ellsworth* (Hong Kong: Fine Arts Department, University of Hong Kong, 1987), no. 33 on p. 46.

107. Cave numbers (Pelliot system) 8, 138, 74, 63, 118, 52, 167, and 149. See J. Leroy Davidson, *The Lotus Sutra in Chinese Art*, p. 91 and plates 36–37.

108. *MSI*, Vol. III, fig. 245 (cave 2).

109. See Grousset, *Chinese Art and Culture*, p. 230. Altogether, Chin Wei-no ("Tun-huang pi-hua Ch'i-yuan chi-t'u k'ao," p. 13) lists 19 different cave-walls at Tun-huang and in the surrounding area that depict these scenes.

110. S4257.2 is a list of happenings that were regularly included in depictions of the scenes where Śāriputra causes the wind to blow down Raudrākṣa's canopy. There are several errors in this list as it is printed by the editors of *PekCat*, p. 196: in the 2nd, 4th, and 6th lines, 時 should come before the commas; in the 4th line, after 道, the two characters 仙人 (*ṛṣi*) are missing; in the 6th line, the missing character is 風; and in the last line 入 ([cause] to enter) should be added after 水.

111. *T*(191)3.968a.

112. *Dhārāni* or *mantra*.

113. *Sapta ratna*.

114. *Vajra*.

115. The *garuḍa*.

116. That is, with the knees, elbows, and head touching the ground.

117. 攝→躡. 神足 stands for *ṛddhipāda* or *ṛddhi-sākṣāt-kriyā*.

118. *Hsien-yü ching*, *T*(202)4.420b.

119. Pp. 174–177 in the Gilgit ms. text as edited by Raniero Gnoli. Compare with the passage from the *Sūtra of the Wise and the Foolish* translated above on pp. 53–55, which describes the same contest.

120. Cf. Edgerton, *BHS*, p. 302b.

121. See Mair, "Ontological Presuppositions."

122. Kern and Nanjio, eds., p. 8. A line from Yuan Chen's (*Collected Works*, 13.6b) "Poem on Great Cloud Monastery" 大雲寺詩 reveals the close relationship between exposition of the sūtras and spiritual manifestation: "While listening to the sūtras, spirits appear;/ While reciting the gāthās, birds gather in great profusion."

123. *T*(263)9.63c.

124. Katō et al., trs., *The Threefold Lotus Sutra*, p. 34. Hurvitz's rendering (*Scripture of the Lotus Blossom of the Fine Dharma*, p. 4) of Kumārajīva is "Now . . . the World-Honored One has shown these extraordinary signs. . . ."

125. *T*(262)9.2b.

126. *T*(264)9.135c.

127. Kern, tr., *Saddharma-Puṇḍarīka*, p. 263.

128. Kern and Nanjio, eds., p. 276, line 6.

129. See Monier-Williams, *Sanskrit-English Dictionary*, pp. 525bc, 568bc.

130. *T*(262)9.37a. The translation of Dharmagupta and Jñānagupta, *T*(264)9.171c, follows Kumārajīva verbatim. Dharmarakṣa's earlier paraphrase, *T*(263)9.107b, is "Do not gather in the same place with singers and actors" 不與歌樂遊戲衆會同處.

131. There is some question about the relationship between the first group of 3 characters and the second of 6. I take it to be essentially genitive.

132. *BHS*, p. 289a.

133. Bendall, ed., *Çikshāsamuccaya*, p. 126, lines 3–4; Bendall and Rouse, trs., *Śikshā-samuccaya*, p. 125.

134. See Mair, "The Buddhist Tradition of Prosimetric Oral Narrative in Chinese Literature."

135. Yang Hsuan-chih, *Lo-yang ch'ieh-lan chi chiao-chu*, p. 271; *Ch'ung-k'an Lo-yang ch'ieh-lan chi*, 5.39b–40a; Iriya, tr., *Rakuyō garan ki*, p. 97ab; Jenner, tr., *Memoirs of Loyang*, p. 257.

136. The so-called "Demon of Havoc."

137. Wu Ch'eng-en, *Hsi-yu chi*, Vol. I, Chapter 2, p. 22; Waley, tr., p. 30 (cited); Anthony Yu, tr., I, 97. Cf. also Wu, Chapter 4, p. 43; Waley, p. 49; Yu, p. 128 and Wu, Chapter 7, p. 71; Waley, p. 73; Yu, p. 169.

138. See Mair, "The Buddhist Tradition of Prosimetric Oral Narrative in Chinese Literature."

139. "Some Questions Connected with Tun-huang pien-wen," p. 222. Kanaoka, "On the Word '*Pien*,'" p. 21, also seems to accept this identification. But his explanation that this has to do with something "changing itself" or being "transitory" is not convincing.

140. Ingalls, "Sanskrit Poetry," p. 11.

141. "Lueh shuo 'pien' tzu te lai-yuạn," pp. 2–3.

142. *A History of Chinese Darma*, p. 11.

143. "Gakujutsu to bungaku," pp. 246b–247a.

144. *Shina bungaku gairon*, p. 357.

145. It will be noticed that I have not spoken against Kuan's assertion of an exchange between the two labials *p* and *m*.

146. Such as I carry out in my article "Records of Transformation Tableaux (*pien-hsiang*)." In Chapters 4 and 6, below, I shall justify my assertion that *pien* may refer to pictorial representation and that *pien-hsiang* may legitimately be rendered as "transformation tableau."

147. See Chapters 4 and 5 of Mair, *Painting and Performance*.

148. *Bhadramayākāravyākaraṇa*, p. 11.

149. See *K'ai-yuan lu* [Catalogue of Buddhist texts from the Epochal Beginning reign period] 開元錄, *T*(2154) 55.567c.

150. *T*(1451, ch. 17) 24.283ab.

151. 神通 usually translates Sanskrit *ṛddhi*[*-sampad*]; Tib. *rdsu ḥphrul*. See Nakamura, *Bukkyōgo daijiten*, p. 794b. For a most detailed explanation of what *ta shen-pien* is, see the section of the *Ratnakūta* which deals with its various types and subdivisions, *T*(310) 11.492b–501b. Cf. also *mahānimittaṃ-prātihāryaṃ* 神變相. Nakamura, *Bukkyōgo daijiten*, p. 795c.

152. See the volumes of the Gilgit manuscripts edited by Nalinaksha Dutt.

153. Yuyama, *Systematische Übersicht*, pp. 24–28.

154. *'Dul-ba phran-tshegs-kyi gźi*, tr. by Vidyākaraprabha, Dharmaśrīprabha, Dhar-'byor (*Derge* text no. 6).

155. Dutt, *Gilgit Manuscripts*, Vol. III, part 2, p. iii, and Vogel, *The Teachings of the Six Heretics*, p. 4. Vogel states that the *terminus ante quem* for the Gilgit manu-

scripts of the *Mūlasarvāstivādavinaya* is based on the certain palaeographical evidence of their being written in Gupta characters of the sixth century. The *terminus post quem* is to be found on fol. 342a (see Dutt, *Gilgit Manuscripts*, Vol. III, part 1, p. 2.3) where the Kuṣāna King Kaniṣka (fl. 78–103?) is mentioned. Cf. Basham, *Papers on the Date of Kaniṣka*, pp. 432–435.

156. Vol. *tha*, p. 225b.3.

157. See Das, *Tibetan-English Dictionary*, p. 426b: *ṛdsu-ḥphrul-gyi cho-ḥphrul* [*ṛddhiprātihārya*] "magical and miraculous exhibitions," and Jäschke, *Tibetan-English Dictionary*, p. 161b: "magical trick, jugglery." Cf. my discussion of *śaubhika* in Chapter 1 of *Painting and Performance*.

158. Derge, text no. 6, Vol. *tha*, p. 225b.5. See Das, p. 1169b, and Jäschke, pp. 524b–525a. Masatoshi Nagatomi (conversation of 22 April 1982) appreciably sharpened my understanding of the key word *rabs* by explaining that it can mean "succession, development, generation; membership in a family or category." Hence we may interpret *dmyal-baḥai-rabs* as "that which belongs to the hell category" or "that which belongs to the tradition of/about hell." Probably the most natural approximation in English would be "Account of Hell" (Cf. a hypothetical Chinese 地獄傳).

159. "Tu T'ang-tai su-chiang k'ao," p. 382.

160. Monier-Williams, pp. 396–397, and Wogihara, pp. 472–473.

161. "Kuan-yü 'Su-chiang k'ao'."

162. "Tu T'ang-tai su-chiang k'ao," p. 382.

163. See especially Chapter 4.

164. Horner's note 3 says that "*koṭṭhaka* is a word of unsettled meaning." She cites the *Cūḷavaggavaṇṇanā* to the effect that this is a long house of seven stories with a porch (or storehouse) at the gateway. See *Samantapāsādikā*, ed. Takakusu and Nagai, VI, 1221. In Tamil, *koṭṭhaka* means a "porch" or "canopy-like construction."

165. Horner, tr., *Book of Discipline* V, 223; Oldenburg, ed., *The Vinaya Piṭakaṃ* II, 159. Cf. the less elaborate description in *The Jātaka*, ed. Fausbøll I, 92–93; T. W. Rhys Davids, tr., *Buddhist Birth Stories* I, 131–132.

166. *Barhut* I, 92–93.

167. *T*(1442)23.811ab.

168. Cowell and Neil, eds., pp. 300–301.

169. See Chapter 1 of Mair, *Painting and Performance*.

170. Ibid., Chapter 2.

171. *Essence and Development*, p. 18b.

172. Régamey, p. 12.

173. P. 7.

174. *T*(324)12.31a–37a.

175. *T*(310[21])11.486b–492b.

176. See Leumann, *Das nordarische Lehrgedicht*, Chapter 2, and Emmerick, *The Book of Zambasta*, Chapter 2.

177. Régamey, pp. 70–71, § 18. In the Chinese versions 1 and 2, these words for magic are all rendered as various types of illusion 幻.

178. Régamey, p. 100. I here list several lines of the *Bhadramāyākāravyākaraṇa*, together with the corresponding Chinese versions, where they exist, that have a bearing on our present study.

A description of the Buddha says that he was "possessed of supernatural faculties (p. 55 §1, line 4)." Chinese 2 得大神通變現自在.

A list of the various types of miraculous powers (*prātihārya*) with which the Buddha is endowed (p. 57 §3, lines 12–13). Ch. 1 refers to them as 變化; Ch. 2 as 神變.

Buddha speaks of "the essence of [his] magic"; Tib. *sgyu-ma'i chos-ñid* = *Skt. māyādharmatā* (p. 65 §9, line 19). Cf. 1 幻法; Ch. 2 幻術之法.

The Bodhisattva Prabhāvyūha says: "[All is] void like the magic of the mind (p. 72 §25, line 3)." Ch. 1 所有幻亦空; Ch. 2 皆幻心所爲.

"This arrangement" *vyūha* (p. 72 §24, lines 2–3). Ch. 1 (312c) unexpectedly has 此化 instead of 莊嚴. Bhadra asks how one who has seen the "magical transformations" of the Buddha can avoid thinking of Enlightenment (p. 77 §41); Tib. *rnam par 'phrul-ba 'di-'dra* (p. 33); Ch. 2 神變.

"Had created such an arrangement (p. 66 §12, line 1)"; Tib. *bkod-pa* [*vyūha*] *de-lta-bur sprul* (p. 25). Ch. 1 作是化已; Ch. 2 化作是已.

"Created (p. 67 §12, line 7)"; Tib. *mnan-par sprul-to* (p. 26). Ch. 1 化作; Ch. 2 變現. Words for "create" occur several other times in the following Tibetan passage (§13). They are rendered in Chinese by expressions such as those already indicated. It is clear that Buddhist Chinese 變 and 化 imply creativity.

179. Bhikku Ñāṇananda, *Magic of the Mind.*

180. Conze, tr., *Buddhist Scriptures*, pp. 122–129. Cf. Lamotte, *La traité de la grand vertu de sagesse* IV, 1982–1984.

181. *Buddhism: Its Essence and Development*, p. 172.

182. For further discussion of these and related terms, see my "Ontological Presuppositions" and cf. above in this chapter at pp. 49ff.

183. A temple was built at this spot near Wenchow 溫州 in the province of Chekiang sometime between 860 and 873.

184. Literally, "five-colors," Skt. *pañca-varṇa*, *pañca kāma*, *pañca rūpa*, etc. The five colors have various symbolic meanings in Buddhism (SH p. 125b).

185. Literally, "seven jewels," Skt. *sapta ratna* (SH, pp. 11b–12a).

186. In Ch'en Yuan-lung, comp., *Yü-ting li-tai fu hui* II, 1481a (106.29a–30b).

187. "Two Final Consonant Clusters in Archaic Tibetan," p. 88. The cognation between the two words is obscured by the peculiar spelling habits of Tibetan.

188. "Ensemble sémantique," especially pp. 418, note 21 on that page, and 421–422.

189. Stein compares this expression to Chinese *tsao-hua* 造化 (make-transform) which connotes magic, supernatural, illusory creation. For full entries on *rju-'phrul*, see Das, *Tibetan-English Dictionary*, pp. 1058b–1059a, and Jäschke, *Tibetan-English Dictionary*, pp. 360ab, 468b–469a.

190. In Emmerick's *Tibetan Texts Concerning Khotan*, we often encounter *cho-'phrul* (e.g. p. 6) and *rju-'phrul* (e.g. p. 52) in the sense of "miracle." But even more interesting for our purposes is the occurrence of *sprul-pahi* (p. 87 [thrice], Sanskrit *nirmita*, cf. *sprul-ba* ["to be transformed (into)," "appear miraculously (as)," see Emmerick, p. 138] and *sprul-pa* "an apparition, transformation").

191. P. 417n21. As an addendum to this note, I should like to draw attention to another Tibetan word that may have some bearing on *pien-wen* and *pien-hsiang*. On P(Tib.) 1293v, there are scenes from the Śāriputra transformation. Three times the word *'vyen* (following the transliteration of Imaeda Yoshirō 今枝由郎 in Jao, et al., *Peintures monochromes*, p. 38) occurs in the Tibetan inscription. Though its meaning has not been determined, it is supposedly a transcription from Chinese. Could this perhaps be meant as a medieval transcription of *pien*?

192. Ku Yeh-wang, [*Ta-kuang i-hui*] *yü-p'ien*, 5.6a; Hsing-chün, *Lung-k'an shou-chien*, 1.64b; Han Tao-chao, *Wu-yin lei-chü ssu-sheng p'ien-hai*, 10.2ab. Also see *K'ang-hsi tzu-tien* and Morohashi, *Dai Kan-Wa jiten*. It should be noted that the second-named work, written by a monk of the Liao period, is particularly valuable for explaining unusual Buddhist words. Cf. my discussion of the historical relationship between *pien* and optical phenomena in the introduction to *Painting and Performance* and in the various notes given there.

193. Information culled from D. N. MacKenzie, *Buddhist Sogdian Texts*, pp. 119 and 147; Henning, *Sogdica*, pp. 17 and 21; D. N. MacKenzie, *The 'Sūtra of the Causes and Effects*,' pp. 28–29 (11.500 and 502) and 64; Ilya Gershevitch, *A Grammar of Manichaean Sogdian*, p. 86 (no. 549); studies by Benveniste and Weller; and my own examination of Chinese texts against their Sogdian equivalents.

194. Lane, *Lexicon*, Book I, part 4, p. 1559a.

195. Jacob, "Zur Geschichte des Schattenspiels," p. 234, citing a footnote from Quatremière's translation of al-Maqrīzī, *Histoire* I, 152–153. Cf. Lane, *Lexicon*, Book I, part 2, p. 835c, and Metin And, *Karagöz*, p. 22.

196. See Mair, *Painting and Performance*, beginning pages of Chapter 3.

197. Among other places where I touch on the frequent linkage between *pien* and optics, see the discussion of shadow-plays in "Contributions" and *Painting and Performance*, passim, but especially the chapter on Indonesia.

198. In Hopei.

199. Also in Hopei.

200. "Buddha" images were also worshiped later by various Manichaean sects.

201. 彌勒出世, Skt. *Maitreya-utpāda* (the appearance of Maitreya).

202. Skt. *paunar-bhaviki* or Pāli *pubbenivāsa*.

203. *Sui shu*, 23.2417c.

CHAPTER FOUR

1. For this part of the formula, see T90.4, 373.4, etc.

2. For the T'ang colloquial interrogative use of *jo-wei*, cf. Nakamura, *Bukkyōgo daijiten*, p. 1055a.

3. The bracketed parts of the question in Chinese, though not always supplied, are usually implied. I have given the known variations of the formula in the appendix to my *Tun-huang Popular Narratives*.

4. This finding is of such importance that a full and detailed exposition of the Indological evidence is provided in the 5th chapter of my *Painting and Performance*. A summary of the more important points may be found in the "Note on the Indian Hypothesis" to be found at the end of this chapter.

5. "Kegon engi no setsuwa," p. 20a. Kawaguchi refers to the wall-painting as a transformation tableau on the eight aspects of achieving the Way 八相成道變相, but I did not see this title during my visits.

6. Kwang-chih Chang reported to me several years earlier that he had seen the same inscription.

7. On the north wall of the same cave, at the bottom of a panel showing events in the Buddha's life, there is an inscription that only superficially resembles the formulaic usage I have been describing: "In those foothills, [he] hunted for a level place." 於彼山麓間求平正處. Beyond it, there is another similar inscription: "Wishing to seek quiet, he suddenly saw a place." 欲求寂静忽見處. In neither of these instances does *ch'u* function in the formulaic sense under discussion. It means, rather, quite literally a topographical location.

8. Recorded and discussed in Sun Hsiu-shen, "Bakukokutsu no engi setsuwaga," p. 236.

9. Kuo Wei-ch'ü, *Chung-kuo pan-hua shih-lueh*, p. 25.

10. In the collection of Baron Iwasaki Koyata 岩崎小彌太. See Matsumoto Yeiichi, "Hokekyō bijutsu—Hokekyō hensōhen," *Kokka* 428:175–184 (July 1926).

11. Kadokawa shoten, ed., *Kegon engi*, pp. 48–59.

12. This use of the word *tokoro* in the *Kegon engi emaki* was first pointed out for students of popular literature by Kawaguchi Hisao, "Tonkō henbun no seikaku," p. 33. Barbara Ruch referred me to Kawaguchi's article.

13. This scroll has been studied by Miya Tsugio, "Mokuren kyūbo setsuwa to sono eiga." My remarks here are based on a reading of his article and observation of the photographs that accompany it.

14. I have also noticed on the scroll mention of the 5th month of 1304.

15. In the introduction to *Painting and Performance* and elsewhere, I posit an evolutionary connection between *pien-wen* and *p'ing-hua*.

16. In *Kindai Nihon bungaku taikei* [Outline of modern Japanese literature] 近代日本文學大系 (Tokyo: Kokumin tosho, 1928) I, 171–226.

17. I am indebted to Margaret Childs for this information. For other evidence that this story of the seven nuns was derived from an *etoki* performance, see her "Religious Awakening Stories," Chapter 3, part 1.

18. Suzuki Kei and Akiyama Terukazu., *Chūgoku bijitsu*, Vol. I, pl. 12.

19. S5600, a booklet of explanatory notes on Buddhist terms, comments on *pien*, *hua* 化, and *ch'u* together.

20. See "Inventory," item 147.

21. Nihon daijiten kankō-kai, ed., *Nihon kokugo daijiten* XIV, 624d.

22. Gabelentz, *Elemens de la grammaire Mandchoue*, pp. 128ff, esp. section 261.

23. *Chu-tzu yü-lei*. For a discussion of related usages, see Gerty Kallgren, "Studies in Sung Time Colloquial Chinese," p. 43. Kallgren mentions that "Chu Hsi often uses *ch'u* in the sense of «passage» (in a book or a demonstration . . .)."

24. This is documented through a wealth of citations by Wang Ying, *Shih tz'u ch'ü yü-tz'u li-shih*, pp. 23–24. Among the early poets cited are Tu Fu 杜甫 (712–770), Liu Ch'ang-ch'ing 劉長卿 (709–785?), Ku K'uang 顧況 (725–820?), Yuan Chen 元稹 (779–831), and Li Shang-yin 李商隱 (813–858).

25. The latest possible *terminus ad quem* is A.D. 800; the *terminus a quo* is about the middle of the seventh century. See Bendall, pp. v–vi.

26. Both cited by Edgerton, *BHS*, p. 486b.

27. Bendall and Rouse, pp. 176.11, 221.30–31; Bendall, pp. 180.4, 236.2–3; *T*(1636)32.110c.25f., 122b.7ff.

28. See *T*(1590)31.74ff; also Clarence Hamilton, *Wei shih er shih lun* and Lévi, *Vijñaptimātratāsiddhi*, passim. *Shih* ("time") is also prominent in this short text. I am indebted to an anonymous reviewer for this reference.

29. *Chuan* is particularly noteworthy, since it may refer to the style of delivery of the verse portion. For a discussion of this term in the context of *pien* storytelling, see notes 35 and 40 to Chapter 6.

30. For a fuller analysis and translations, see the appendix to my *Tun-huang Popular Narratives*.

31. Hirano Kenshō, "Beppon taishi jōdō henbun ni tsuite."

32. Ibid., pp. 44, 54.

33. In cave 92 (Tun-huang Institute no. 85; dating from the late T'ang), I saw many cartouches ending in *shih* and, interspersed among them, a few ending in *ch'u*.

34. See my paper entitled "India and China: Observations on Cultural Borrowing."

35. SH, p. 408b.

36. Hsieh Chih-liu, *Tun-huang i-shu hsu-lu*, p. 431b.

37. Other inscriptions ending in *shih* on Tun-huang wall-paintings listed by Hsieh Chih-liu, *Tun-huang i-shu hsu-lu* are: p. 103b, cave 47 east side, 6th inscription, T'ang period during the Tibetan occupation; p. 105a, same cave, west side, 13th inscription; p. 105b, same cave, north side, 7th inscription. I have seen hundreds of this type of inscription during my visits to Tun-huang. Michel Soymié, in his "Un recueil d'inscriptions sur peintures," has published and translated (pp. 194–203) an interesting text (P3304v) that consists of 60 cartouche-length inscriptions of the Śāriputra story (cf. the first text in my *Tun-huang Popular Narratives*), all of which end with *shih* 時. He interprets this marker as "moment"

or "episode" and explains that it clearly links the text to illustrations (pp. 177–179). Also see my discussion of S4527 on p. 83.

38. See Akiyama, "Tonkō ni okeru henbun to kaiga," p. 439.

39. Ibid., pp. 444–445; also see Chin Wei-no, "Ch'i-yuan chi-t'u," pp. 34–35.

40. This is transposed to the beginning of the translations.

41. That is, an image of the Buddha. See Morohashi, Vol. XI, 40152.624, which gives references to similar stories that are recorded in the dynastic histories.

42. Reading 大 [宛] [國]. Other possible reconstructions are *ta* [*Yueh-huo* ... ...] 大 [月] [氏] (Indoscythia) and *ta* [*Hsia-kuo* ... ...] 大 [夏] [國] (Bactriana).

43. Recorded in Hsieh Chih-liu, *Tun-huang i-shu hsu-lu*, p. 188b.

44. Recorded in Shih Yai, *Tun-huang shih-shih hua-hsiang t'i-chih*, p. 73ab.

45. This has been reproduced many times, most recently as pl. 61 in the *Ts'ai-se Chung-hua ming-hua chi-lan*. One of the earliest reproductions is Matsumoto, *Tonkō-ga no kenkyū*, LXXVIa. It is beautifully presented in Suzuki Kei and Akiyama Terukazu, *Chūgoku bijutsu*, pl. 70. See also ibid, pl. 71, for a ninth-century banner with four scenes and empty cartouches. Cf. Aurel Stein, *The Thousand Buddhas*, plates XII, XXVI, and XXX.

46. Cf. *tasyāṃ velāyām*.

47. *Kumārarāja*, the Buddha-to-be.

48. *Hetupratyaya*.

49. Visited in August 1985.

50. Ōtani Kōzui, *Saiiki kōko zufu*, Vol. I, pl. 45.3. Yūki Somei, *Saiiki ga*, Vol. XIII, no. 4, shows a Central Asian painting of an elephant that is most probably the one conjured up by Śāriputra in the "Transformation on the Subduing of Demons." The cartouches that describe the action thereon end with the temporal narrative sequence marker *shih*.

51. See also Paul Pelliot, *Grottes de Touen-houang: Carnet de notes*, p. 15, fig. 22.

52. Cf. T301.7–8.

53. See Jao Tsong-yi and Paul Demiéville, *Airs de Touen-houang*, pp. 29–30 (edited), 37 (comment), 128–132 (translated).

54. See the edition published by Chung-kuo ku-tien wen-hsueh ch'u-pan-she in 1954.

55. Barua, *Barhut* I, 47.

56. Ibid. II, 27, Jātaka scene 45; pls. XXVIII.3 and LVIII in Vol. III.

57. Ibid., p. 82, Jātaka scene 87; pl. XLVIII.2 in Vol. III.

58. Ibid., p. 135, Jātaka scene 125; pl. XXVII.12 in Vol. III.

59. In the illustrated *Siwarātrikalpa* of Mpu Tanakuṅ, ed. A. Teeuw, et al., there are 20 scenes (Plate V, Series 1646, 49—formerly in the possession of Mr. L. van der Wilk of Haarlem). Five of the accompanying superscriptions include the Balinese word for "place" (*gnah* [*ipune*]?). This usage is not exactly the same as that of *ch'u* in Tun-huang *pien-wen* because it does not come at the end of a formula and also because it refers to an actual place in the scene depicted. Nevertheless, it does merit our consideration, since the poem has an Indian source and also for the more general reason that it shows the tendency for serial narrative pictures

to use the word "place" (i.e., "locus") in inscriptions. Burmese narrative wall-paintings often bear inscriptions and legends beginning with the word *wo* (this [place]), cf. *Kubyaukkyi* 210: "Here, the dragon king Kāla creates a likeness of the Buddha and shows it to King Dhammāsoka." *Wo smiṅ kālanāgarāj nimit rup kyek tabaḥ smiṅ dhammāsoka.* (Shorto, *Dictionary of Mon*, pp. 214–215.) Note the use of *nimit* (= Pāli *nimmita*, Sanskrit *nirmita*) meaning "conjure up, cause to appear, call into being, create, assume [shape], etc." This usage of *wo* brings to mind *eṣa* (this) as used to designate sequential episodes in the picture storytelling scene of *Dūtavākyaṃ*, for which see Chapter 1 of my *Painting and Performance*.

60. Number TK–119 in Men'shikov, ed., *Opisanie Kitaiskoi Chasti Kolletsii iz Khara-khoto*, pp. 255–256.

61. In my "Oral and Written Aspects of Chinese Sūtra Lectures."

62. This is the actual title on the manuscript, S2073.

63. Cf. Mair, "Chinese Sūtra Lectures."

64. Li-li Ch'en, "*Pien-wen* Chantefable," p. 255n2, and *Master Tung's Western Chamber Romance*, p. ix.

65. Quoted in *The Compact Edition of the Oxford English Dictionary*, p. 1491.

66. Monier-Williams, p. 818a; Böhtlingk and Roth, *Sanskrit-Wörterbuch* V, 786a.

67. Cf. Das, *Dictionary*, p. 801.

68. Although this famous Sanskrit-Tibetan lexicon existed from approximately the ninth century, the Chinese equivalents were added at a much later period (eighteenth century?). Furthermore, they were based on the Tibetan rather than the Sanskrit and thus have no authenticity whatsoever for Chinese-Sanskrit Buddhist terminology. See Sakaki, introduction to the 1916 edition, and Demiéville, p. 23, of Jao, *Airs*.

69. Sushilkumar De, *History of Sanskrit Literature*, p. 433.

70. *Pai-hua wen-hsueh shih*, pp. 150–153, 178. Both of Hu's two chapters entitled "Fo-chiao te fan-i wen-hsueh" [Translated literature of Buddhism (A and B)]" 佛教的翻譯文學 make worthwhile reading.

71. "P'i-p'an Hu Shih te *Pai-hua wen-hsueh shih*."

72. Is Lu thinking of *tz'u* and/or *fu*? On the writing of *fu*? Or the nebulous literary genre *tz'u-fu*? Or still *tsa-fu* 雜賦 (miscellaneous *fu*)?

73. See note 44 of Chapter 5 for a discussion of this troublesome graph.

74. "Kuan-yü pien-wen te chi-tien t'an-so." Many of Ch'eng's same basic points are repeated in Chang Hsi-hou's recent *Tun-huang Literature*, pp. 66, 83.

75. Ibid., p. 82.

76. Ibid., p. 83. Liao Fu-shu, *Chung-kuo ku-tai yin-yueh shih*, p. 61, duplicates much of the same argumentation. Of the specific "native sources" of the prosimetric form that he mentions, "Southeastward Flies the Peacock" 孔雀東南飛 (which itself can by no means be certified to be free from foreign influence) has a prose preface while the remainder is verse; Han and Wei stele inscriptions do not even remotely resemble extended fictional narrative; and the "Ch'eng-hsiang" 成相 chapter of Hsun-tzu as well as several *fu* written by him are even less deserving of serious consideration in this connection.

77. "Kuan-yü pien-wen te chi-tien t'an-so," p. 86.

78. Ibid., p. 85.

79. *Tun-huang-hsueh kai-yao*, p. 53.

80. *Chung-kuo su-wen-hsueh kai-lun*, p. 94.

81. "Tun-huang chiang-ch'ang wen-hsueh," p. 82.

82. Liu Hsiang 劉向 (77–76 B.C.), *Lieh-nü chuan* 列女傳 (*SPPY*, Vol. 1338), 1.4ab.

83. Pei-ching shih-fan ta-hsueh Chung-wen-hsi wu-shih-wu chi hsueh-sheng, *Chung-kuo min-chien wen-hsueh shih*, p. 313.

84. Ibid., pp. 313–314.

85. *Ch'a-t'u pen Chung-kuo wen-hsueh shih*, p. 448

86. *Chung-kuo su-wen-hsueh shih*, I, 191.

87. *Ch'a-t'u pen Chung-kuo wen-hsueh shih*, p. 579.

88. Section 4 (pp. 275–293) of the title essay in HT.

89. *Tun-huang pi-hua Fo-hsiang t'u yen-chiu*, p. 29.

90. "The First Translations of Buddhist Sūtras in Chinese Literature," p. 114; also see p. 133.

91. See also her article written with Zdeněk Hrdlička, "On the Origins of 'Narration Combined with Song,'" and Milena Velingerová, "The Art of Chinese Storytelling."

92. "Indian Literature in China," p. 125. Chi's simplified Sanskrit transcription has not been regularized.

93. *The Home of the Puppet Play*, pp. 14–15.

94. That poetry was more important in the early periods and that prose was added later has been posited by von Bradke, "Uebur das Mānava-Gṛhya-Sūtra," pp. 474ff. See also Oldenberg's two important studies, "Die altindischen Âkhyâna" and "Âkhyâna-Hymnen in Ṛigveda." It is remarkable that a similar situation seems to have obtained with regard to the early Greek epics. See Stephen Kelly's paper "Homeric Metrics and the Nature of Greek Proto-Epic," epitome: "The Higher levels of correption (a so-called license of Greek metrics) found in the speeches of the *Iliad* and the *Odyssey* reveal that the speeches in the Homeric poems are of greater antiquity than the narrative, and that Greek proto-epic consisted of versified speeches and an interstitial prose narrative." The prosimetric form is also to be found in other literatures, for which see H. M. and N. K. Chadwick, *The Growth of Literature* III, 716. But nowhere in the world has it been so pervasive or typical as in the Indian Buddhist tradition.

95. "Original Nature of Jātakas." The groundwork for De's study was laid by Oldenberg in his "The Prose-and-Verse Type of Narrative and the Jātakas."

96. *Pre-Buddhist India*, p. xxi. This sequence of development is borne out by the Sinhalese tradition, which "asserts that during the process of translation into the Old Sinhalese language and retranslation into Pāli of the *Jātakaṭṭhakathā*, it was only the prose that was open to this process; the *Gāthās* were preserved unchanged in Pāli." These canonical texts were transmitted orally until the time of the Sinhalese king Vaṭṭagāmaṇī (first century B.C.) when they were first written down.

97. Ibid., p. xxii.

98. Blader, "'Yan Chasan,'" p. 87.

99. See, for example, the annotations to my *Tun-huang Popular Narratives*, M223.2 and "Inventory," items 147, 296, and especially 555.

100. *Tonkō no bungaku*, p. 196. A large number of the manuscripts found at Tun-huang consist of or include drawings, and many of these have strong narrative characteristics. See, for example, P2002, 2003, 2010, 4513, 2013, 2544v, 2564v, 2598v, 2671v, 2682, 2683, 2695, 2702v, 2723v, 2868v, 2869v, 2870, 2993v, 2998, 3059, 3614, 3652v, 3666, 3882v, 3951, 4100, 4513, 4514a, 4517, 4518b, 4518.4, 4523, 4524, 4757, 4886, 5019, 6001, PTib.1293v, S259v, 705, 1360v, 1586v, 1918v, 3961, 5407v, 5429v, 5638, 5655, 6983, 5642, S-Uighur frag. OR 12452.3 [Kao 0111], PK5883v, 3905, 1863, 883, 6110v, 685v, San621v, and D1277.

101. For a lengthy discussion of a very important inscription on this manuscript, see "Inventory," item 207.

102. For a discussion of this contest, see Watters, *On Yuan Chwang's Travels* I, 394–395.

103. Granoff, "Scholars and Wonder-Workers."

104. In the favorite shadow-play called "Story of the White Snake" 白蛇傳, the White (Snake) Lady 白娘子 and the priest "Dharma-Sea" 法海 fight each other with magically produced demons and dragons. Some of the most delightful episodes from the beginning of *Journey to the West* center around Monkey's magic battles of transformational appearances with various heroes sent down from heaven to subdue him. The same is true again later when Tripiṭaka faces off against his Taoist enemies in Cart-Slow Country 車遲國.

105. These illustrations are described in full detail by Vandier-Nicolas, *Śāriputra*, pp. 17–32.

106. See Akiyama Terukazu, "Miroku Kashōkyōhen hakubyō funbon," p. 70. The cartouches in cave 92 (Tun-huang Institute no. 85) are similar. Pelliot Tibetan manuscript 1293 (cf. Lalou, *Inventaire*) includes several sketches for scenes from the Śāriputra story. Even though they are sketches, one gets the impression that they are by a more accomplished artist than the individual responsible for P4524. It would seem that the sketches on Tib. 1293 were for a projected wall-painting of the Śāriputra story (there are many examples at Tun-huang).

107. See my translation in *Tun-huang Popular Narratives*.

108. *Mu-lien chiu-mu ch'üan-shan hsi-wen* by Cheng Chih-chen.

109. An attendant.

110. Nakanokimi's sister-in-law.

111. Nakanokimi's dead sister.

112. Murasaki Shikibu, tr. Seidensticker, p. 958.

113. For detailed photographs of this scene, see Kadokawa shoten hensūbu, ed., *Genji monogatari emaki*, last color plate and pl. 37 (enlarged); Akiyama Terukazu, ed., ibid.; Akiyama Terukazu, *Heian jidai seizokuga no kenkyū*, pl. 44r and pl. 51; Hideo Okudaira, *Narrative Picture Scrolls*, fig. 9 (p. 26).

114. Minamoto Tamenori, *Sanbōe shūsei*, pp. 3–6.

115. The meaning of 寶 (*pâu:*) 護 is not certain. The PK catalog editors,

p. 279, indicate that it may be the name of the copyist. The back of the scroll, however, would be an unusual place to find such a notation. My impression is that it means something like what is given in the translation or, perhaps, → 保 (*pâu:*) 護 "protect/take care [of this]." It is also possible that it might be the name of the owner of the scroll.

116. See "Inventory," item 555, for a description and analysis of these spaces.

117. Also see other reasons adduced above on p. 27.

118. Strassberg's recent analysis ("Buddhist Storytelling Texts from Tun-huang," pp. 59–60) tends to confirm my suppositions. In their catalogs, both Giles (p. 198) and Kanaoka, *Classified Catalogue* (p. 14) suggest that the standing figure at the beginning of S5511 (the opening section of the Śāriputra *pien-wen*) is a warrior with a sword and that this ink-sketch may be an illustration for the text.

119. As was done in medieval Italy (see Chapter 5 of *Painting and Performance*).

120. Pelliot, *Les grottes*, pl. CXXI There are a number of other interesting features in this cave relating to sūtra lectures and so forth. On the left wall at the front are several platforms 高座 on which men are sitting and lecturing (pl. CXVIII). On the left part of the left wall a man is seated reading from a scroll which he is holding up. At the top right, just below the ceiling, is a multiple-sided structure. Does the front panel of this structure represent a picture of a man or does it represent the man himself? (pl. CXIX). And what is the object held by the strange man at the bottom right of the second section of the left wall? (pl. CXX).

121. On all of my first three trips to Tun-huang (summers of 1981, 1983, and 1985), officials of the Research Institute for Tun-huang Antiquities informed me that such a project was under way.

CHAPTER FIVE

1. See Chapters 3, 4, and 5 of Mair, *Painting and Performance*. While it is not my intention to equate the skills and social level of *pien* storytellers with performers of any other tradition, at the same time I do not wish to ignore analogical evidence altogether.

2. "Medieval Jongleurs," p. 286.

3. *Analects*, p. 51.

4. "Professional Training of Storytellers," p. 226.

5. [Original note] Karim stated that occasionally, for the benefit of illiterate pupils, he draws sketches of various incidents in the repertoire to which the pupils may refer. Hussein (Pedu, Kedah) possesses a book of similar sketches but in his case the drawings are explained with captions in Thai.

6. [Original note] Hamzah copied part of Awang Lah's repertoire from my transcript of the latter's narration, but this is not the usual practice!

7. *The Ramayana and the Malay Shadow-Play*, pp. 52–53; italics mine.

8. Hinzler, *Bima Swarga*, p. 84 (other information drawn primarily from pp. 83, 85).

9. "Puppet Play," p. 189.

10. Kuan Chün-che, *Pei-ching p'i-ying-hsi*, p. 14.

11. Information in this paragraph gleaned from a lecture given before the Oriental Club of Philadelphia on 30 April 1982 by Wolfram Eberhard, who has carried out extensive field work on this subject in Taiwan.

12. The various categories of Indonesian drama (including picture storytelling, shadow-plays, and puppet plays) are discussed in Chapter 3 of Mair, *Painting and Performance*.

13. *Literature of Java* I, 248.

14. Ensink, "On the Old-Javanese Cantakaparwa," section 16, has also written on the reluctance of *dalangs* to commit their texts to writing. He, too, mentions the instigative role of Western scholars in causing this to happen in some cases.

15. "Shuo-shu yu-wu chiao-pen?"

16. Ibid.

17. *The Way of the Storyteller*, p. 59. Amin Sweeney, in his "Professional Malay Story-telling," points out the qualitative difference between storytelling (folk or oral literature) and the literary texts that derive from it. The scribe nearly always adapts what he records.

18. In "Inventory" I have tried to show some of the reasons why they were recorded. See also the latter part of this chapter. The introduction to *Painting and Performance* discusses some of the probable causes of their disappearance.

19. "Peking Drumsinging," pp. 23, 250n11.

20. I am not, of course, necessarily making the case that the transcribers of transformation texts were entrepreneurs. My point is only that, where there was a demand for transcription, it could be done without the permission of performers.

21. *The Home of the Puppet-Play*, pp. 15–16.

22. Joshi, *Painted Folklore*, p. 16.

23. "Medieval Jongleurs," p. 304. For the meaning of *etoki* and Kumano *bikuni*, see Chapter 5 of Mair, *Painting and Performance*.

24. "Vorgeschichte."

25. *Bazaar Paintings of Calcutta*. For the meaning of *Bänkelsänger* and *paṭuā*, see Chapters 4 and 5 of *Painting and Performance*.

26. Published by Lo Chen-yü, 1.1; 1.2,3; and Chapter 3, last page (p. 72).

27. See also C. T. Lo, "Clues Leading to the Discovery of *Hsi Yu Chi p'ing-hua*," pp. 180–181, especially 180n9.

28. "New Studies," pp. 454–455.

29. *Shui-tung jih-chi*, 21.11b–12a.

30. I have relied chiefly on Marshall Pihl, "The Tale of Sim Ch'ŏng," for the information in this paragraph.

31. Salmen, *Fahrende Musiker*, pp. 136ff.

32. Blindness among *biwa* singers is well-known. Documentation for blindness in Chinese fiddle singers may be found in *Pei-ching min-chien feng-su pai-t'u*, no. 65.

33. Personal communication from Masato Nishimura, 8 December 1978; old film shown by Holmes Welch at Harvard University, 6 December 1978. Blind-

ness has been a traditional characteristic of performers of many other oral genres throughout Asia.

34. By the same token, Jen Erh-pei (*Tun-huang ch'ü ch'u-t'an*, p. 121) concluded that the Tun-huang cantos must have been transcribed from oral presentation. Cf. note 41.

35. This is not the same as taking down a text from dictation 筆授 (see *T*50[2061].813c, 1.3). Here the reader or speaker will go as slowly as the transcriber requires. It is also not the same as the transcription of a ritualistic oral text where the utterance of a single word may be drawn out to enormous lengths and repeated many times.

36. "Sung and Yüan Vernacular Fiction," *The Chinese Short Story*, etc.

37. E.g., "The Early Chinese Short Story: A Critical Theory in Outline," p. 171.

38. "The Nature of Ling Meng-ch'u's Fiction," p. 87.

39. Eoyang has attempted to demonstrate this in his recent article entitled "Oral Narration in the Pien and Pien-wen." By "spoken literature," I mean texts that had their origins in the oral realm; by "written literature," I intend texts that were initially consigned to paper.

40. See Chapter 5 of Mair, *Painting and Performance*.

41. But see my discussion in "Chinese Sutra Lectures" on the possibility of phonetic error apart from any actual oral setting. The likelihood of affinity with oral performance becomes a question of the prominence and frequency of such error.

42. Dissatisfaction with T on other grounds has been mounting during the past few years. Cf. the reviews by Chang Chin-ch'üan, Lü Shu-hsiang, and Kuo Tsai-i, and the reworking of P'an Ch'ung-kuei in T[a].

43. Eoyang, "Word of Mouth," p. 52.

44. *Kăm*. This is the reading suggested by the editors of the Paris catalogue, pp. 198–199. It is interchangeable with 椷, which is another conceivable reading. Both these characters might be construed in the sense of "one letter." But it is difficult to understand either character in the sense of "one unit of verse." Ōta, *Kōgobun*, p. 139, suggests 減 and Kanaoka, *Tonkō . . . bungaku . . . mokuroku*, p. 21, suggests 械, but I cannot make sense of either of these readings. The character as written on the manuscript appears thus: [illegible]. In any event, the syntax demands some such numerary adjunct as 件 which was already in use before the period when *pien-wen* were written down. It is not likely, however, that 件 itself could have been exchanged for the difficult character, because it is not in the same rhyme group as either of the proposed readings that seem plausible.

45. For a part of the text that has been well annotated, see Ōta, *Kōgobun*, pp. 138–149. P2319 has been translated by Eugene Eoyang in Ma and Lau, eds., *Traditional Chinese Stories*, pp. 443–455.

46. See "Inventory," items 207 and 307, for evidence concerning the procurement of one such illustrated scroll. The question of the relationship of written *pien-wen* to pictures is also discussed in Chapter 4.

47. See "Inventory," item 18.

48. *Catalogue*, pp. 212–213.

49. I.e., the four *varga: Bhikṣu* and *bhikṣuṇī*, *upāsaka* and *upāsikā*, monks and nuns, male and female devotees; i.e., all the Buddhist faithful.

50. *PekCat*, p. 254. Cf. Bibliothèque Nationale, *Catalogue des manuscrits chinois de Touen-houang*, p. 39, and Jen Erh-pei, *Tun-huang ch'ü chiao-lu*, pp. 140–162. See "Inventory," item 4, for an alternative interpretation of the last sentence.

51. Hsu Kuo-lin, *Tun-huang shih-shih hsieh-ching t'i-chi*, AA.19a. This manuscript was not available for examination when I visited Peking in the summer of 1981.

52. See "Inventory," item 590, and, for a very close study of the writing of one manuscript, my "A Newly Identified Fragment of the 'Transformation on Wang Ling.'" The "Inventory" provides much evidence about the copying activities of lay students at Tun-huang.

53. The intercalary month in the designated year fell after the *7th* month. The Western equivalent is computed on the assumption that this was the month intended and not the 6th month as written.

54. Kanaoka (*Tonkō bungaku mokuroku*, p. 250n7) reads this quite differently: . . . 楊顯, 受一人思, 微發 . . . Hence, "Yang Hsien, the thought having been suggested by (received from?) someone, secretly (?) made. . . ." Admittedly, this colophon presents problems, but Kanaoka's reading seems to complicate them. 發願作福 reads smoothly as a unit and resists being connected to the 微. As for 顯 rather than 願 in the man's name, the manuscript has [illegible], which speaks for itself. The copyist's name is therefore either Yang Yuan or Yang Yuan-shou, depending on how one punctuates the colophon. The problem is somewhat exacerbated by the fact that, for 微, the manuscript has 㣲. If this character was meant to stand for 徽 *xjwei̯*, perhaps we should read 恩惠, *ɣiwei*—in which case the translation would be "Yang Yuan, receiving the favor of a certain person. . . ." However, my preference is as given in the translation, particularly since I have a suspicion that, by 思微 (*i̯wi*), the copyist must have meant 思惟 (*mjwei̯*) which is a very common Buddhist expression (Skt. *cetanā*) for "reflection," "thought," and so on). See "Inventory," items 385 and 555 for positive identification of Yang Yuan-shou.

55. The manuscript has 佛.

56. Where T755.6 has 生作, Hsu Kuo-lin, *Tun-huang tsa-lu*, 40a.12, inexplicably gives 王. Neither reading is satisfactory, but I have been unable to come up with a better one.

57. The manuscript has 壹. The translation of this sentence is not certain.

58. The future Buddha.

59. Literally, "living beings" (*sattva*).

60. 信心 *adhyāśaya*.

61. 願力 *praṇidhāna-balika* (or *bala*).

62. *Tsa-lu* 40b.1 inexplicably has 之 for 三.

63. *Gati*.

64. Giles, *Catalogue*, p. 259.

65. The transcriber or copyist of the story in verse (S5441) about Chi Pu 季布

railing in front of the troops, who has the striking name Yin Nu-er ("Slaveboy Yin," showing possible Uighur influence) 陰奴兒, is designated by a similar title, "Lay Student of Recording Officer Fan" 氾孔目學仕郎. A recording officer with this surname is mentioned on P3757 and P2633.2. See Giles, *Catalogue*, p. 234b. The inscription at the end of S5441 is dated in accordance with 19 May 978.

66. For a fuller description of this manuscript and its inscriptions, see "Inventory," item 590.

67. Des Rotours, *Fonctionnaires*, pp. 198, 567.

68. Cf. Kanaoka, *Tonkō no minshū*, p. 173.

69. The translation is from Giles, *Catalogue*, p. 234. Also see his "A Chinese Geographical Text," and Naba, "Zokkō to henbun," p. 451.

70. There are other conceivable interpretations of this brief inscription, but most are compatible with the notion that a monk was responsible for the making of this copy.

71. Translation by Giles, *Catalogue*, p. 138. Also see T314–315n205.

72. 賜紫. Cf. Reischauer, *Ennin's Diary*, p. 298n1131. The manuscript has space for two characters which, it may be surmised, would most likely be 沙門 *śramaṇa*. The last three characters (雲辯述 "narrated by Yun-pien"), however, appear to have been added in a different hand, using lighter ink.

73. Cf. Reischauer, *Ennin's Diary*, p. 75 ("Archbishop") and n317 on that page.

74. See S4472.3, which is his will. The exact date, given by a certain Li Yuan 李琬 in a note of 954, is in accordance with 24 July 951.

75. See T839.4. Yun-pien is not to be confused with the "Yuan-chien of Great Virtue, Commissioned by the Emperor to Oversee the Inner Circle of Truth (*Bodhimaṇḍala*) of the Ch'ien-fu ('Thousand Blessings') Monastery on the Right Side of the Thoroughfare," who is mentioned in fascicle 1 of P3886 as the author of a pentasyllabic poem. The latter Yuan-chien would have lived approximately one hundred years before Yun-pien. See Reischauer, *Ennin's Diary*, pp. 289, 311.

76. The one and one-quarter lines of prose that the T editors have printed on page 840 have no necessary relationship to the seat-settling text. On the manuscript, the title is placed just before the seat-settling text, which consists of 27 lines of verse. This is directly followed on the same scroll by the "Seat-Settling Text on the Twenty-four Exemplars of Filiality." These two exhortations are separated by a heavy, crudely drawn line which stands out clearly as a later addition to the manuscript.

77. Fuller coverage may be found in "Inventory."

78. Other manuscripts of popular literature from Tun-huang that were transcribed or bear inscriptions by such lay students include the "Rhapsody on Swallows" 鷰子賦 (S214, dated in accordance with 29 January 924) by Tu Yu-sui of Eternal Tranquillity Monastery 永安寺學士郎杜友遂.

79. There are, however, isolated instances in which the authors of other, slightly more elegant types of Tun-huang popular literature are known, such as Wang Fu, a graduate in the Third Provincial Examination 鄉貢進士王敷, who was responsible for the clever "Discussion between Tea and Wine" 茶酒論

(P2718, dated in accordance with 1 February 972; K'ai-pao ["Opening of Treasures"] 3 is undoubtedly a mistake for K'ai-pao 5 because the latter year has the cyclical designation *jen-shen* given in the colophon). The copyist, Yen Hai-chen, was enrolled in an academy 知術院弟子閻海眞.

80. Other inscribed manuscripts taken into account include P3210, P3757, P2633.2, S610, S548, S2491, S1156v, and a lecture on the *Vimalakīrtī Sūtra* in the Russian holdings.

81. A number of lists (S2614, S2669, S6542) have been published in Chung-kuo k'o-hsueh-yuan, *Tun-huang tzu-liao* I, 225–282. An important study of these registers may be found in Fujieda Akira, "Tonkō no sōniseki."

82. *Māra-bhañjaka* or *māra-pratyarthika*.

83. The description of blowing upon a frozen brush to soften and warm its bristles is reminiscent of the scene in Liu E's 劉鶚 *The Travels of Old Derelict* (*Lao-ts'an yu-chi* 老殘遊記), where we find the following: "Ts'ui-huan, afraid that the ink on the slab would freeze, blew without stopping, but the brush still picked up bits of ice, and, the more Lao Ts'an wrote, the thicker the tip became." See Liu T'ieh-yun, *The Travels of Lao Ts'an*, tr. Shadick, p. 140.

84. T355.10–11. *Fa-lü* (Dharma and Vinaya) identifies Yuan-jung as an ecclesiastical official under the regional *saṅgha* administrator 僧政.

85. On the manuscript it would appear that there has been an effort to blot out these two graphs, which in itself might lead to several interesting speculations.

86. T446. 14–15.

87. T389.10.

88. Parts of the Wu Tzu-hsu story indicate that the author(s) or scribe(s) made reference to encyclopedic accounts of the hero. One such source discovered at Tun-huang is S2072.

89. Kanaoka, *Tonkō no bungaku*, p. 181, indicates that there are 4 missing characters after *nien* 年, undoubtedly a cyclical designation of the year.

90. Kanaoka, ibid., has Hsi-chou 州 instead of Hsi-ch'uan 西川. If we accept the former reading as the correct one, the area referred to would be that of Turfan in modern Sinkiang.

91. This graph (㤘) is somewhat difficult to decipher but well within the range of Tun-huang orthographical variants for *ying* 應 ("responsive"). Kanaoka (*Mokuroku*, p. 4) holds that we should read *su* 宿 (past). Strassberg, "Buddhist Storytelling Texts from Tun-huang," p. 47, states that both colophons are in the same calligraphic hand as the main text but that the second is in a lighter, more watery ink on a succeeding sheet of paper. Cf. "Inventory," item 15.

92. T618.12–14.

93. 因緣 *hetupratyaya* or *nidāna*. This title is actually on S3491.

94. The story is not original with the author of this particular version since it occurs in the *Chuan-chi pai yüan ching* [Compilation of the Sūtra of the Hundred Occasions] 撰集百緣經, fascicle 6 (*T*[200]4.229c–230b).

95. I.e., Buddhists.

96. By 論典 "corpus of discussions," Pao-hsuan probably meant 論藏, that is, the *Abhidharma-piṭaka*.

97. 緝 in the sense of 輯.

98. 緣 *pratyata*.

99. 三界 *trailokya* or *triloka*.

100. Another manuscript of the same piece, formerly owned by Lo Chen-yü and entrusted to the Shanghai Committee for the Preservation of Cultural Artifacts, has "6th" which would yield a date equivalent to 28 June 955 (?).

101. This is a practice that has its roots in early Indian educational systems. See Radhakumud Mookerji, "Hindu Educational Systems," *The Cultural Heritage of India* III, 247. See also R. K. Mookerji, *Ancient Indian Education: Brahmanical and Buddhist*, and S. Dutt, *Buddhist Monks and Monasteries*.

102. Takakusu, tr., *A Record of the Buddhist Religion*, p. 106.

103. *The Buddhist Conquest* I, 9.

104. Yen Keng-wang, "T'ang-jen hsi-yeh shan-lin ssu-yuan chih feng-shang," p. 414.

105. Ibid., pp. 374–375, and Yen Keng-wang, *T'ang-shih yen-chiu ts'ung-kao*, preface, p. 3.

106. See, for example, the colophons and signatures on P2609v, P2621, P2633v, P2712, P3189, P3381, P3393, P3466v, P3649, P3691v, and P3698v. Culled from Naba, "Tō shōhon zasshō kō."

107. At some point in his career, however, Chang I-ch'ao did become a declared adherent of the Buddhist faith. S5835 is a short explanation of the *Śālistambhaka-sūtra* 佛說大乘稻芉經, which was "copied by the Buddhist disciple of pure faith (*upāsaka*) Chang I-ch'ao." 淸信佛弟子張義朝書. It is Giles's opinion (*Catalogue*, p. 173) that, at this time, he was probably a lay pupil in the monastery. I suspect that he became an *upāsaka* when he ceased being a lay student.

108. He is mentioned in fascicle 216B of the *New T'ang History* (KM 4139.2) and in fascicle 490 of the *Sung History* (KM 5719.1). See also *TCTC*, Vol. IV, 249.8048–8049.

109. "(Pu *T'ang-shu*) Chang I-ch'ao chuan."

110. "Lo Shu-yen 'Pu *T'ang-shu* Chang I-ch'ao chuan' pu-cheng." See also James Hamilton, *Ouighours*, pp. 12–15, 38n1, and the lengthy note on pp. 47–49.

111. For descriptions of this manuscript, see Giles, *Catalogue*, pp. 233–234, and Kanaoka, *Tonkō mokuroku*, p. 22.

112. Demiéville, *Concile*, p. 168.

113. The fullest and best account of this army and its governors may be found in A. Huzieda, "Sashū kigigun setsudoshi shimatsu."

114. Demiéville, *Concile*, p. 168n.

115. The title is taken from an inscription in cave 281 (Pelliot no. 80) by his nephew, Chang Huai-shen (d. 890), to whom he had entrusted the administration of the Ho-hsi region when he went to Ch'ang-an. Though Chang I-ch'ao's fiefdom was of the rank of 10,000 households, it was nominally composed of 2,000 households and in actuality consisted only of 200 households 食邑二千戶實封二百戶. See Hiang Ta. "Amendements ('Pu T'ang-shu'), pp. 7, 16.

116. *T*(2061)50.743b.

117. Only the preface survives (on P3554v). For the text, translation, and

notes, see Chen Tsu-lung, *La vie et les oeuvres*, pp. 101–109. For other references to Chang I-ch'ao on Tun-huang manuscripts that attest to his strong advocacy of Buddhism, see NT, pp. 38–39, and Men'shikov, *Opisanie* I, 319–320 (no. 823, D566).

118. A helpful study of this subject is Ogawa Kan'ichi's "Tonkō butsuji no gakushirō," which is based both on Tun-huang manuscripts and standard historical sources.

119. B. A. Litvinsky, "Outline History of Buddhism in Central Asia," *Kushan Studies in U.S.S.R.*, pp. 128–130.

120. Naba Toshisada, "Tō shōhon zasshō ko."

121. Hui-shan Monastery is in Kiangsu province, 5 *li* west of Wu-hsi 無錫 district town.

122. From the preface by Li Chih to the poem that he inscribed at Hui-shan Monastery ("Li Chih t'i Hui-shan ssu shih hsu" 李騭題惠山寺詩序) in *CTW*, 724.11b (p. 9438a).

123. Monks, nuns, nun-candidates, together with male and female novices.

124. *Anitya.*

125. *Kṣama.*

126. Note that here and at the beginning of each succeeding sentence the conjunction in Chinese is 若爲 which, in the pre-verse formula of the transformation texts, has an interrogative function.

127. *Gṛhapati*, "householder."

128. *T*(2059)50.417c. For a discussion of the social and educational significance of the evangelistic activities of Buddhist monks and preachers during the T'ang period, see Michihata, *Tōdai Bukkyō shi no kenkyū*, pp. 210–270.

129. *PekCat*, p. 161. Punctuated texts are not uncommon in the Tun-huang manuscripts. For another, see S4510v.

130. Note the use of the personal pronoun 余.

131. This is not a completely literal translation. I have had to rely on examination of the manuscript to make some sense of this rather garbled sentence.

132. By?

133. See "Inventory," items 251 and 590.

134. The recto of this scroll is a portion of fascicle 233 of the *Mahāprajñāpāramitā sūtra.*

135. Wang Fan-chih's dates are c. 590–660.

136. Ma Shih-ch'ang, "Kuan-yü Tun-huang ts'ang ching tung," plate 4.2.

137. Translated from Jean Sauvaget's French version, *Relation de la Chine et de l'Inde*, p. 17 §36 and p. 21 §48. See also p. 58n36. Evelyn Rawski has shown (*Education and Popular Literacy in Ch'ing China*) that, during the eighteenth and nineteenth centuries, there was surprisingly widespread "functional" literacy (*though of varying degrees*) among the male populace, both in the cities and in the countryside.

138. Among many others, scholars who subscribe to this view include: Ogawa Tamaki, "Henbun to kōshi," p. 128; Kanda Kiichiro, *Tonkō-gaku gojūnen*, p. 69; Hsu Chia-ling, "Wo tui pien-wen te chi-tien ch'u-pu jen-shih"; Li Hui-ying (fol-

lowing Hsiang Ta in the preface to T [pp. 1 and 3]), *Chung-kuo hsiao-shuo shih*, p. 117; Shao Hung, *Tun-huang shih-shih chiang-ching-wen yen-chiu*, p. 8; Pei-ching ta-hsueh chung-wen hsi (1955), *Chung-kuo wen-hsueh shih*, p. 217; Ch'iu Chen-ching. *Tun-huang pien-wen shu-lun*, p. 9; Hu Shih-ying, "T'ang-tai te shuo-hua"; and Ch'eng I-chung, "Lueh-t'an Sung Yuan chiang-shih te yuan-yuan." Kenneth Ch'en (*Chinese Transformation*, p. 252) even goes so far as to declare: "All agree that the *pien-wen* was composed primarily to serve as texts for the popular lectures." I, for one, do not.

139. See Schipper's important article entitled "Vernacular and Classical Ritual in Taoism." On p. 35, he makes the telling observation that, whereas the *tao-shih* were classically oriented, generally read their ritual which was transmitted through manuscripts, emphasized meditation, employed elaborate music, used texts that were mainly in prose, were members of an organized profession, belonged to higher classes, and were recognized by the state, the *fa-shih*, on the other hand, were vernacularly oriented, recited their orally transmitted narratives by heart, would fall into trances, employed monotonous chanting of texts that were mainly in heptasyllabic rhymed verse, were loosely linked to cults, belonged to the lower classes, and were not recognized by the state. He also lists a number of other contrasts between the two types of priests, virtually all of which parallel the differences between ordained Buddhist monks and lay transformation performers.

140. *Ho-shang* 和尙 ("monk").

141. The music schools, that is.

142. *Yin-hua lu*, Chapter 4, pp. 94–95.

143. *Yueh-fu tsa-lu*, no. 1, p. 40. Consult also the annotated translation of the 35th chapter by Gimm, pp. 500–507.

144. Paintings of figures with eyes that seemed to follow the beholder were not at all uncommon. At the Great Cloud Temple 大雲寺 in Ch'ang-an, there was "an averter of evil [demon-quelling deity, probably Chung K'uei 鍾馗], the two eyes of which turn and glare at one wherever one moves" 雙目隨人轉盼 (Acker, pp. 299–300). And, at the Prospect Publican Temple 景公寺, there were "paintings of circumambulating monks who turn their eyes to look at people" 畫行僧轉目視人 (Acker, p. 270).

145. Acker, p. 268.

146. See Mair, "Records of Transformation Tableaux," p. 34.

147. Quoted by Acker, p. 268n3.

148. Reischauer, pp. 298–299. See also the very full annotations on this passage given by Ono Katsutoshi, in his *Nittō guhō junrei gyōki no kenkyū* III, 343–345n4, 348n14.

149. Li Fang, comp., *T'ai-p'ing kuang-chi*, ch. 204, p. 1546; Wang Cho, *Pi-chi man-chih*, Chapter 5, p. 91. There are a few minor differences between the two accounts, but they are essentially the same.

150. Tuan An-chieh, *Yueh-fu tsa-lu*, ch. 35 (also note 143 above).

151. For other views on the subject, see Ono Katsutoshi, "Bunjo to Bunshuku," and Kanaoka Shōkō, "Sairon Bunjo hōshi." Perhaps Wen-shu, who

relied on audiences for a living, modeled his name after Wen-hsu's because of the latter's popularity and prestige (suggested by Andrew Jones).

152. Kanaoka Shōkō, *Tonkō no minshū*, p. 99, offers a combined chronological sketch covering the years c. 820–841.

153. *TCTC*, ch. 243, p. 7850.

154. *T*(2035)49.384c. Cf. Jan Yun-hua, tr. and annot., *Fo-tsu t'ung-chi*, p. 89. In note 15 of pp. 89–90, Jan states that there is no biography of Wen-hsu in the *Sung Biographies of Eminent Monks* or other historical records. He also follows Hsiang Ta, "T'ang-tai su-chiang k'ao," in claiming that Wen-hsu was important for the development of *pien-wen*.

155. "Chū Tō jidai zokkō sō Bunjo hōshi."

156. In the introduction to Nagendra Nath Vasu, *The Modern Buddhism*, p. 17.

157. Yang Pin-kuei, "Praying for Rain."

158. The majority of contemporaneous literary references to transformation performers that I cite in Chapter 6 describe them as entertainers rather than as monks.

159. "Notes sur l'ancienne littérature," p. 192. See "Inventory," item 559, for a very different interpretation of PK2496v.

160. For more possible evidence of the lay status of transformation performers, see also Mair, "The Origins of an Iconographical Form."

161. "Obiter Dicta," p. 66.

162. "Funerals in North China," p. 50 of pre-publication version.

163. Information supplied by Harvey Molé in a letter of 6 May 1981, by C. K. Wang in a letter of 20 June 1984, John Lagerwey in a letter of 25 June 1984, and by Susan Naquin in a conversation of 26 June 1984. Their sources included personal observation in Taiwan, nineteenth-century reports of Westerners, and late-Ch'ing gazetteers. See also van der Loon, "Les origines rituelles," pp. 158, 160, who refers to the performance by professional actors of the Maudgalyāyana story in K'ai-feng at the beginning of the twelfth century and to later professional and semi-professional troupes putting on the same play in Chekiang. On p. 141 of the same article, van der Loon offers cogent justification for using recent and contemporaneous sources to understand the origins and evolution of the theater.

In the following discussion, I consistently use the word *professional* to mean "[one who is] customarily engaged in a specific activity for the purpose of earning a livelihood." Thus there are both "funeral professionals" (viz. drama troupes who undertake to perform at funerals for monetary compensation or payment-in-kind) and "professional religious" or "religious professionals" (i.e. ordained monks, nuns, priests, etc., who normally live in monasteries or temples and derive their income from the resources of these institutions).

164. "Sexual Politics," p. 388.

165. "Magic and Religion in Sinhalese Society," p. 98.

166. For some of Seaman's articles, see the bibliography. The pertinent films are "Chinese Funeral Ritual" and "Breaking the Blood Bowl." The information in the following paragraphs was graciously supplied to me by Seaman in a very long letter of 5 August 1984.

167. In his "Spirit Money," p. 90, Seaman refers to the *sai-kong* as a "funeral professional . . . of scornfully low status."

168. *T*(2060) 50.602c. See Fukui Fumimasa (Bunga), "Tōdai zokkō gishiki."

169. Translated by Chen Tsu-lung, *La vie et les oeuvres*, pp. 58–60.

170. Translated by Chen Tsu-lung, ibid., pp. 61–65.

171. See Bush and Mair, "Some Buddhist Portraits and Images," pp. 33–34, 49n1–10.

172. *T*(1805) 40.403c–409b.

173. See Michihata Ryōshū, "Dōkyō no zokkō ni tsuite" [On Taoist popular lectures] 道教の俗講に就いて, in *Chūgoku Bukkyō to shakai*, pp. 192–200.

174. "Tōdai zokkō gishiki no seiritsu o meguru sho mondai," "Zokkō no imi ni tsuite," and "Some Problems about the Origin of the Religious Lectures for Laymen, *su-chiang*." The last-named paper gives bibliographical references to other articles on *su-chiang*. The secondary literature on this subject is extensive: Hsiang Ta, "T'ang-tai su-chiang k'ao"; Sun K'ai-ti, "T'ang-tai su-chiang kuei-fan"; Naba Toshisada, "Zokkō to henbun"; Sawada Mizuho, "Shina Bukkyō shōdō bungaku"; Yamazaki Hiroshi, *Shina chūsei Bukkyō no tenkai*, part 3; Michihata Ryōshū, *Tōdai Bukkyō shi no kenkyū*, part 2, pp. 228–270; Chou I-liang, "Tu 'T'ang-tai su-chiang k'ao' "; [Hsiang] Chueh-ming (i.e., Ta), "Pu shuo T'ang-tai su-chiang"; Kuan Te-tung, "T'ang-tai su-chiang k'ao te shang-ch'ueh"; Hsiang Ta, "Kuan-yü su-chiang k'ao tsai shuo chi chü hua"; etc. One of the chief reasons for the popularity of this subject is its presumed relationship to *pien-wen*.

175. Ennin's diary is an invaluable source for anyone investigating popular lectures. See Reischauer's translation, pp. 298–299, 310–311, 316. Sun K'ai-ti's "T'ang-tai su-chiang kuei-fan," which relies heavily on the various collections of biographies of eminent monks, is also essential reading. Lo Tsung-t'ao, *Tun-huang chiang-ching pien-wen yen-chiu*, pp. 872–978, gathers in one place much information on the performance features of popular lectures.

176. Ch'ing and earlier versions. *T* incorporates Tun-huang materials. The single exception known to me, from a historiographical work that denies that *pien-wen* is a Buddhist phenomenon, is discussed at length in Chapter 6. Another highly problematic occurrence of *pien* is examined in detail at the end of the same chapter. It is possible that I have missed an occasional reference to *pien-wen* as a genre in the tens of thousands of pages that constitute the *Tripiṭaka*. Even assuming that there were one or two mentions of the term in this vast canon, it would not negate my contention that *pien-wen* is an extreme rarity in the context of establishment Buddhism.

177. See Chapter 6.

CHAPTER SIX

1. 轉. See below, note 35.

2. An important river in Szechwan.

3. Cf. the famous Yuan drama on the theme of Wang Chao-chün by Ma Chih-yuan 馬致遠 (c. 1270–1330) entitled *Autumn in the Han Palace* 漢宮秋.

4. *Ch'üan T'ang shih* XI, 8771; *Ts'ai-tiao chi*, 8.18a.
5. T98–107.
6. T105.13, which states that, after 800 years, Chao-chün's grave still exists.
7. Demiéville, "Quelques traits," p. 72.
8. Ō Shō-kun henbun no seiritsu nendai kō."
9. *Ch'üan T'ang shih* V, 3434.
10. Chang Ping-lin, *Hsin fang-yen* III, 88a. Cf. Sawada, "Shina Bukkyō shōdō bungaku no seisei," p. 45 and T'an Ts'ui, *Shuo man*. My translation of *man* as "Szechwanese [maid]," while plausible in this context, is, of course, not mandated.
11. *The Poems of Li Ho (791–817)*, p. 245.
12. Saitō Shō, *Ri Ga*, pp. 343–344, and Suzuki Torao II, 253.
13. *Li Ch'ang-chi ko-shih*, 4.25b.
14. *Li Ch'ang-chi ko-shih*, 4.29b.
15. *San chia p'ing-chu Li Ch'ang-chi ko-shih*, p. 277.
16. In Ch'en Hung-chih, *Li Ch'ang-chi ko-shih chiao-shih*, p. 558. Also cited by Wang Ch'i.
17. In ibid. Also cited by Wang.
18. Note especially the expression "Shu (i.e., Szechwan) paper."
19. More literally, "Lengthily, [she] turns over [the] Shu paper, [un]rolling [the story in pictures of] Ming-chün." It is possible that *chüan* has been used for *chuan* 轉 or 囀, for which see notes 1 above and 35 below. Wang Ch'i states that he feels *chüan* is most likely an incorrect usage. Perhaps *chuan* was avoided because it occurs in the succeeding line. Rather than suggest an emendation, however, I have simply read *chüan* in the rising (third) tone and have understood it somewhat in the sense of *chüan-shu* 卷舒. Iriya, rev. of Kanaoka Shōkō, *Tonkō shutsudo bungaku*, p. 97, interprets *chüan Ming-chün* as referring to the story of Chao-chün portrayed on an illustrated scroll, an interpretation with which I am in basic agreement.
20. Wang Ting-pao, *T'ang chih-yen*, ch. 13, p. 148 (under "Contradictions"); Meng Ch'i, *Pen-shih shih*, p. 23 (under "Jests"); Li Fang, comp., *T'ai-p'ing kuang-chi*, ch. 251, p. 1949, citing *T'ang chih-yen*.
21. Hirano Kenshō, *Tōdai bungaku to Bukkyō*, pp. 4–8.
22. See below, note 28.
23. Note the colloquial use of 阿誰.
24. See Chang's poem entitled "Thoughts on the Death of General Wang's 'Silkworm Thorn' Songstress" 感王將軍柘枝妓歿 in Li Fang et al., comps., *Wen-yuan ying-hua*, 305.10b (p. 1911b).
25. See Po's famous "Song of Lasting Sorrow" 長恨歌, *Po shih Ch'ang-ch'ing chi*, 12.64a (reduced format pagination); *Po Hsiang-shan chi* 白香山集 (*SPPY*), 12.8b.
26. These precise lines do not occur in the Maudgalyāyana transformation texts that are extant but may be said to encapsulate the first portion of the story.
27. 柘枝. This may be a transliteration of the Persian name Chaj (Tashkent). Another interpretation holds that it is a corruption of 拓跋 Toba or, more properly, Tabgatch, the name of the founder of the Northern Wei.

28. 問頭, in Zen Buddhist parlance, is a T'ang colloquial expression meaning "conundrum for meditation." See *Tsu-t'ang chi* (Record of the Hall of Patriarchs) 祖堂集 (bibliographical information in my *Tun-huang Popular Narratives*), I-180.10, III-47.1, and V-85.10, 103.13, and 111.1. In the Sung, this was usually referred to as a "topic" 話頭. It is the same device now best known as a *kōan* 公案 (public case). But 問頭 is also T'ang colloquial for 訊問, which is the basis for my translation. See T213.4, 5, 6, 7, 8, 10, 15, and 252.9. The *T'ai-p'ing kuang chi* and *Pen-shih shih* versions both have 款頭.

29. *Ts'e* 34, 13.4b.

30. *Ts'e* 14, 13.5a.

31. In *ts'e* 159–160, 13.4b–5a.

32. *Goblet Words from the Garden of Art*, 4.7a. But perhaps I am giving Wang too much credit. It is possible that he was simply using *pien* in its established (since the Six Dynasties period) literary critical sense of "defective." See above, Chapter 3, note 23.

33. *Kao Li-shih wai-chuan* 高力士外傳 (*TTTS*), *ts'e* 8, 7b.

34. *Upadeśa*, "dogmatic treatises, sermon, preaching." Here, however, the expression most likely refers to a type of T'ang Buddhist humorous dialogue (*hsiang-sheng* 相聲). See Chang Hung-hsun, "Tun-huang chiang-ch'ang wen-hsueh," p. 78.

35. Literally "to turn" or "to revolve," which might well refer to the actual manipulation of the scrolls. The parallel expressions *chuan-ching* 轉經 and *chuan-tu* 轉讀 both mean to hold a sūtra in one's hands and recite it while *turning* the scroll. See Ryūkoku daigaku, comp., *Bukkyō daijii* VI, 3385, and Nakamura Hajime, *Bukkyō daijiten*, pp. 988.2 and 989.2. Sun K'ai-ti ("Chung-kuo tuan-p'ien pai-hua hsiao-shuo te fa-chan," *TCC*, p. 72), however, understands *chuan* in the expression *chuan pien* as meaning 囀 "warble" (i.e., 囀喉發調 "to trill out a tune"). Cf. Sawada, *Bukkyō to Chūgoku bungaku*, p. 44, who says that it means "to recite with rhythm." Tseng Yung-i, "Kuan-yü pien-wen te t'i-ming," p. 218, holds that it means simply "recite" 轉讀. James Liu, *The Chinese Knight-Errant*, pp. 100, 210, renders *chuan-pien* as "chanting about the unusual." Cf. note 40 below.

36. In the *Works of Yuan Chen*, there is a poem entitled "In Response to the Han-lin Academician Po's Poem of One Hundred Rhymes in Lieu of a Letter" 酬翰林白學士代書一百韻 (written around the year 800). The reference is to "A Poem of One Hundred Rhymes Sent to Yuan Chen in Lieu of a Letter" 代書詩一百韻寄微之 in the *Collected Works of Po Chü-i*, 13.1a–4b. Yuan (10.4b–5a) has a very interesting note to his own poem which reads as follows: "Every time Chü-i and I were out wandering, we always would write our names on the walls of houses. We also once [had?] someone tell the story 說話 of Li Wa 李娃 in the house at Hsin-ch'ang. It went on from 3 in the morning to 11 o'clock and still it was not finished." This note is frequently cited as evidence that there was a tradition of professional storytelling for the T'ang classical tale. Y[au] W[oon] Ma's careful critique no longer allows us to make this assumption. See his "The Beginnings of Professional Storytelling in China," pp. 232–233, 238. Cf. also Dudbridge's close analysis in *The Tale of Li Wa*, pp. 20–25, esp. pp. 23–24. Still, the

fact that both Kuo Shih and Yuan Chen casually mention "storytelling" indicates that there was at least an informal tradition that went by this name.

37. Li Fang, comp., *T'ai-p'ing kuang-chi*, ch. 269, p. 2109, citing *T'an pin lu* [Records of talks about guests] 譚賓錄. This passage also affords definite proof that oral transformation performances were already very well established by the middle of the eighth century in Szechwan.

38. An administrative circuit in what is now Chengtu, Szechwan.

39. An administrative district established by the T'ang government in what is now Yunnan.

40. This might possibly be understood as 轉→囀 "warble," i.e., "chanted" or "sang." But the totality of evidence regarding the form of transformations available from T'ang sources indicates that "unroll [their] transformation [scrolls]," hence "perform transformations," is not incorrect here. See note 35 above.

41. It is impossible to say for certain whether the syntactical force of "order" implies that the "monks" also were made to "perform transformations." My translation tries to be as ambiguous as the original. The second clause might also be rendered with an indeterminate agent as "or [ordered] transformations to be performed along important roads" or even "[had] transformations performed along important roads." In any case, *seng* 僧 has wide applications in non-Buddhist texts and does not necessarily refer to formally ordained monks. Thus, even if the sentence is construed to have the "monks" performing the transformations, they might still be entertainers masquerading as monks (cf. Chapter 5). The performance, it should be noted, takes place in a secular setting. Furthermore, the word *cha* renders suspect as genuine manifestations of the Buddhist religion per se all that follows it in this sentence.

42. *Huan-ying chuan, ts'e* 11.22a. This story is also recorded in Tuan Ch'eng-shih's *Miscellany of Rarities*, First Collection, 5.4a.10.

43. See T670.9.

44. *Yu-yang tsa-tsu*, 5.2b–3a, under the heading "Strange Technique" 怪術.

45. See my translation of the Maudgalyāyana transformation text in *Tun-huang Popular Narratives* at note 315 on p. 235.

46. Huang Hsiu-fu, *Mao-t'ing k'o-hua, ts'e* 13, 4.7ab. Cited (with two minor errors) in Yeh Te-chün, *Hsi-ch'ü hsiao-shuo ts'ung-k'ao* II, 689. On the following page, Yeh also cites (in abridged form) the texts mentioned in notes 47 and 49.

47. Ho Yuan, *Ch'un-chu chi-wen, ts'e* 209, 2.3ab.

48. See Li Fang, comp., *T'ai-p'ing kuang-chi*, ch. 299, "Spirits" 神類, no. 9 (Wei An-tao), quoting *I-wen lu* (Record of extraordinary hearsay) 異聞錄.

49. Yen Yu-i 嚴有翼 (Sung), *I-yuan tz'u-huang* [Criticism from the garden of art] 藝苑雌黃, cited in Hu Tzu, *T'iao-hsi yü-yin ts'ung-hua, ts'e* 2567, 18.539.

50. *T*(2035)49.370a.

51. *Z*(2).a3.650.412ab–ba. This text is to be found in Vol. CXXX (p. 412) of the 1967 Hong Kong reprint of *Z*.

52. Henning, "Neue Materialen," pp. 13–14n6 and "Bet- und Beichtbuch," p. 119.

53. Pelliot, "Les traditions," p. 203n6.

54. Cf. *T*(2035)49.475a.

55. Chavannes and Pelliot, "Un traité manichéen," pp. 353–362, have performed an inestimable service with their translation and annotations of this note. But even these two vastly learned savants complain at one point (p. 356n2) that "toute cette série de titres est d'une obscurité désespérante." See also Devéria, "Musulmans," pp. 458–463. Readers who wish to gain a fuller understanding of Tsung-chien's note are urged to consult these studies. I have provided only minimal commentary.

56. There is some discrepancy among the available texts. I have followed what I consider to be the best readings from the *Unified Chronology*, the *Orthodox Line*, and *Snow Mountain Collection* (see note 62). The last text named, being primary, is generally the most reliable and the next to the last text is next in reliability.

57. This surely refers to the Chinese translation of the Middle Persian Manichaean scripture entitled *Šābuhragān*. The page headings of this Manichaean scripture include such phrases as *dō bun wazarg* (the two great foundations) and *dō bun šābuhragān* (the two foundations of the *Šābuhragān*). Chinese *tsung* 宗 (principle) corresponds to Middle Persian *bun* (base or foundation). See David Utz's unpublished paper, "Two Parthian Words in the Chinese Manichaean Tradition," p. 11. Piet van der Loon's contention (*Taoist Books*, pp. 44–45 and nn62–63) that *erh tsung ching* refers to the scriptures of Buddhism and Taoism cannot be sustained.

58. In Buddhism, 明王 means *vidyā-rāja*, spirit-king of the pure word who invokes the wrath of Vairocana against evil beings.

59. The binomes (*k'ai-yuan* and *kua-ti*) are, respectively, ancient Chinese cosmogonic and astrological terms. Devéria, "Musulmans," p. 459, gives as his translation "Dissertations sur le commencement du Ciel et de la Terre."

60. Māni?

61. This confusion in the highest official circles between the two doctrines occurs as early as 732 when, in the 7th month, Hsuan-tsung issued a rescript in which he stated that Manichaeism "fraudulently declares itself to be Buddhism" 妄稱佛教. See Tu Yu, *T'ung tien*, 40.229c.

62. In Wang's *Snow Mountain Collection*, 3.24–27.

63. This group has been carefully studied by Chikusa Masaaki in *Studies in the Social History of Chinese Buddhism*. The document under discussion is cited on p. 220. I am indebted to Piet van der Loon for this reference (16 March 1984). For a long discussion in English of the "Vegetarian Demon Worshipers," see Lieu, "Diffusion and Persecution of Manichaeism," pp. 102ff.

64. See *Painting and Performance*, Chapter 5.

65. Information gained during a conversation with Wu Hsiao-ling and Li Shih-yü in Peking 3 August 1981. I have also seen references in written sources to a "Southern Group Brothel" (Nan-pang chi-yuan 南幫妓院) and suspect that it may be the same center as the Nan-fang chi-yuan mentioned by Li and Wu. Cf. Li Chia-jui, *Pei-p'ing feng-su*, pp. 385–386.

66. See the paragraphs preceding this one. The term *pien-wen* may also be

found in several Ming and Ch'ing texts where the author or editor is citing a T'ang period source. In no case that I am aware of does a source written after the Five Dynasties but before this century fully comprehend the meaning of the term.

67. By P'an Ch'ung-kuei. See his "New Discussion on Tun-huang *pien-wen* [Tun-huang pien-wen hsin lun] 敦煌變文新論, pp. 1297–1322, esp. pp. 1303–1304 in T[a].

68. *Tripiṭaka Koreana* facsimile (1975) XXXII, 721b.

69. Julien, who states (p. vii) that he is relying on the Nanking and "imperial" editions, totally ignores the *pien* in his translation (p. 328). Li Yung-hsi skips the thorny sentence altogether in his translation of Hui-li's *Life of Hsuan-tsang*, p. 253, lines 11–12. Waley. *The Real Tripitaka*, p. 120, renders *pien* as "legends."

70. See Utsunomiya's article in *Shirin.*

71. Tsukishima, *Kokugogakuteki kenkyū*, Vol. I, and Utsunomiya, ed., *Kōi* II, 187 (9.94a). An early Japanese editor of the text has added interlineally *no hen* ノ變 which indicates that the accretion of *pien* to the text may be due to non-Chinese redaction. The earliest manuscript versions of Hsuan-tsang's collected memorials, as recorded in *T*52(2119).825a, probably originated in the Nara or Heian periods (one is ostensibly dated 765), also include the character *pien* after *Sūtra of Recompense for Kindness*.

72. I am grateful to Kahar Barat, who is preparing the most thorough study of the Uighur fragments of Hsuan-tsang's biography, for checking this.

73. See Mair, "Records."

74. *Chung-kuo su-wen-hsueh kai-lun*, p. 108. Several examples of spurious references to *pien-hsiang* are given in my "Records of Transformation Tableaux."

75. For the whole passage in context, see Tsang's *Fu-pao t'ang chi*, ch. 3, p. 57. Meng Yao's citation of the same passage in *Chung-kuo hsiao-shuo shih* IV, 604–605, is liable to misinterpretation for its lack of context as well.

76. *Tun-huang pien-wen shu-lun*, p. 18.

77. See especially Chapters 4 and 5.

78. See Mair, *Painting and Performance.*

79. For a study of the survival of the *pien* tradition after the demise of the name itself, see my "The Contributions of Transformation Texts (*pien-wen*) to Later Chinese Popular Literature."

Bibliography

While this bibliography is extensive, it is by no means intended to be exhaustive for Tun-huang literature in general, nor even for Tun-huang transformation texts in particular. It consists chiefly of works that have been cited herein and in certain related publications of the author or useful works consulted during the period of research for this study. I have tried to be reasonably thorough in bringing together all significant works known to me that deal with general, theoretical, and historical aspects of *pien-wen*. Articles and monographs dealing with individual *pien-wen* as well as those treating solely of linguistic, religious, philosophical, and other such matters relating to *pien-wen* have not always been included. (It should be noted that most important articles on *pien-wen* in Chinese have been collected in the two volumes of *LWL* [q.v.]). Additional references for all languages may be found in the section that lists catalogs and bibliographies. Many other works that are relevant for the study of *pien-wen* may also be found in the references and bibliographies to other books and articles by the author. The author's "A Partial Bibliography for the Study of the Influence of India on Chinese Popular Literature" (215 pages), available on request, may be consulted as well. In a few instances, works that I have not been able to examine but that would appear to be particularly relevant for someone who wishes to continue these investigations have been included. Such works are listed in the last section of the bibliography. Please note that not all items cited in the main body of the text and in the notes have been entered in the bibliography.

All Chinese, Japanese, and Korean titles have been given in English as well as in romanization and characters. The translations in square brackets are my own. Those in parentheses are either established equivalents or have been provided by the authors and editors of the works concerned. Occasionally I have made minor, cosmetic changes in these latter renderings to bring them into agreement with acceptable English grammar and usage. In the majority of cases, the translations of East Asian titles that I have provided are not at all elegant; they are meant to serve primarily as identifying tags for readers unfamiliar with morphographic East Asian written languages.

In the Chinese entries of the bibliography, basic information about the listed texts has been noted. Many of the pre-twentieth-century works have been described more fully in the following: Gimm (especially pp. 583–620), des Rotours (especially pp. 72–118), Pian (especially pp. 235–237), Teng and Biggerstaff, and

Edwards. For works of consequence not covered by these authors, where necessary I have discussed in greater detail problems of authenticity, dating, filiation, and so on, at appropriate places in the text itself or in the notes. For all pre-twentieth-century works, I have tried to provide some indication of the time when the author, compiler, translator, or editor(s) lived. Failing this, the date of original publication or date of the preface is usually given.

Citations in the notes are to author and abbreviated forms of titles listed in the bibliography. Since these are sufficiently differentiable, it has not been felt necessary to provide an additional list of shortened titles.

N.B. Works from the Chinese and Tibetan Buddhist canons are not listed individually in the bibliography: Specific references to such works occur only in the notes. The same is true of the standard dynastic histories of China and Tun-huang manuscripts. For the latter, where in the notes I do not refer specifically to the published source of a manuscript, the reference is either to the original in London, Paris, Leningrad, Taipei, and Peking or to microfilms, photographs, and photocopies in my private collection, in the Harvard-Yenching Library, the Van Pelt Library of the University of Pennsylvania, and in Olin Library of Cornell University.

CATALOGUES OF TUN-HUANG MANUSCRIPTS AND BIBLIOGRAPHIES OF STUDIES (also see Works Referred to in Abbreviated Fashion)

Bibliothèque Nationale, Département des Manuscrits. *Catalogue des manuscrits chinois de Touen-houang* (Fonds Pelliot chinois). I: Paris: Bibliothèque Nationale, 1970. III: Paris: Foundation Singer-Polignac, 1983.

Chen Yuan (Ch'en Yuan) 陳垣. *Tun-huang chieh-yü lu* (An Analytical List of the Tun-huang Manuscripts in the National Library of Peiping) [Catalogue of Tun-huang manuscripts remaining after the theft] 敦煌劫餘錄. *CYYY* chuan-k'an [Special issue] 專刊 4. Peiping: The National Research Institute of History and Philology of *Academia Sinica*, 1931.

Cheng A-ts'ai 鄭阿財, comp. "Chin wu-nien lai T'ai-wan ti-ch'ü Tun-huang-hsueh yen-chiu lun-chu hsuan-chieh (shang)" [A selection and introduction to research on Tun-huang studies carried out in Taiwan during the past five years (Part One)] 近五年來臺灣地區敦煌學研究論著選介(上), *Han-hsueh yen-chiu t'ung-hsun* (Newsletter for Research in Chinese Studies) 漢學研究通訊 5.1:1–8 [cumulative no. 17] (March 1986), Hsia (Part Two) 下, ibid. 5.2:53–57 [18] (June 1986).

——, comp. "Tun-huang-hsueh yen-chiu lun-wen chu-tso mu-lu ch'u-kao" [A preliminary draft for a catalogue of monographs and articles on research in Tunhuangology] 敦煌學研究論文著作目錄初稿, *Hua-kang wen-k'o hsueh-pao* (Hua-kang Journal of the Humanities) 華岡文科學報 14:1–81 (1982); 15:1–16 (1983).

——, comp. "Tun-huang-hsueh yen-chiu lun-wen chu-tso mu-lu kao (chung-wen p'ien) (hsu)" [Draft for a catalogue of monographs and articles on research in Tunhuangology (Chinese section) (with continuations)] 敦煌學研究論文著作目錄稿(中文篇), *Tun-huang hsueh* (Studies on Tun-huang) 敦煌學 5:71–120 (1982); 6:116–121 (1983); 7:123–130 (1984); 8:65–70 (1984).

Cheng A-ts'ai 鄭阿財 and Chu Feng-yü 朱鳳玉, comps. *Tun-huang-hsueh yen-chiu lun-chu mu-lu* (Bibliography of Tun-huang Studies) 敦煌學研究論著目錄. Han-hsueh yen-chiu tzu-liao chi fu-wu chung-hsin ts'ung-k'an, mu-lu lei, ti 4 chung (Resource & Information Center for Chinese Studies Series, Catalogues 4) 漢學研究資料及服務中心叢刊目錄類第 4 種. Taipei: Han-hsueh yen-chiu tzu-liao chi fu-wu chung-hsin, 1987.

Chou P'ei-hsien 周丕顯. "Tun-huang i-shu mu-lu tsai t'an" [A re-examination of the catalogue of preserved manuscripts from Tun-huang] 敦煌遺書目錄再探. Mimeograph, 1985 (?).

Chung-hua hsueh-shu-yuan Fo-chiao wen-hua yen-chiu-so [The Buddhist Cultural Research Institute of China Academy] 中華學術院佛教文化研究所, ed. *Erh shih nien-lai Fo-chiao ching-shu lun-wen so-yin* (Catalogue of Chinese Buddhist Articles and Books Published in Taiwan During the Last 20 Years) 二十年來佛教經書論文索引. Yang-ming-shan; Chung-hua ta-tien pien-yin-hui, 1972.

Demiéville, Paul. "Récents travaux sur Touen-houang; aperçu bibliographique et notes critiques," *TP* 56.1–3:1–95 (1970). Reprinted separately Leiden. Brill, 1970.

Dohi Yoshikazu 土肥義和. *Saiiki shutsudo Kanbun bunken bunrui mokuroku shokō—hi-Bukkyō bunken no bu, jiin bunsho rui*, II [Preliminary draft of a classified catalogue of Chinese documents recovered from the western regions—part dealing with non-Buddhist documents, temple papers, II] 西域出土漢文文献分類目錄初稿 II — 非佛教文献之部, 寺院文書類. Tokyo: Tōyō bunko Tonkō bunken kenkyū iinkai, 1964.

Giles, Lionel. *Descriptive Catalogue of the Chinese Manuscripts from Tunhuang in the British Museum*. London: The Trustees of the British Museum, 1957.

Huang Yung-wu 黃永武, ed. *Tun-huang i-shu tsui-hsin mu-lu* [Newest catalogue of preserved manuscripts from Tun-huang] 敦煌遺書最新目錄. Taipei: Hsin-wen-feng ch'u-pan-she, 1986.

Ishihama Juntarō 石濱純太郎, Sanada Ariyoshi 眞田有美, and Inokuchi Taijun 井ノ口泰淳. "Bibliography of Central Asiatic Studies," *MSI*, Vol. I, (Western languages section).

Kanaoka Shōkō 金岡照光. "Tonkō henbun kenkyū no dōkō (1)—Shiryō kenkyū o chūshin ni" (Recent Studies on Tunhuang *Pien-wen* [1]) 敦煌變文研究の動向(一)資料研究を中心に, *Tōyō gakuhō* (Reports of the Oriental Society) 東洋學報 46.3:118–125 (December 1963).

——. "Tonkō henbun kenkyū no dōkō (2)—Henbun no honshitsu, sōron ni kansuru kenkyū" (Recent Studies on Tunhuang *Pien-wen* [2]) 敦煌變文研究の動向(二)變文の本質．総論に関する研究, *Tōyō gakuhō* (Reports of the Oriental Society) 東洋學報 46.4: 106–116 (March 1964).

——. *Tonkō no bungaku*, pp. 1–10 ("Sankō bunken" [Reference materials] 參考文獻.

——. *Tonkō no minshū*, pp. 349–357 ("Shuyō sankō bunken" [Main reference materials] 主要參考文獻).

——. *Tonkō shutsudo kanbun bungaku bunken bunrui mokuroku fu kaisetsu* (Classified Catalogue of Literary and Popular Works in Chinese in Tun-huang Documents—From Stein and Pelliot Collections—) 敦煌出土漢文文學文獻分類目錄附解說. Saiiki shutsudo kanbun bunken bunrui mokuroku (Classified Catalogues of Chinese Manuscripts from Chinese Turkestan) 西域出土漢文文獻分類目錄, Vol. IV. Tokyo: Tōyō bunko Tonkō bunken kenkyū iinkai, 1971.

K'uang Shih-yuan 鄺士元. *Tun-huang-hsueh yen-chiu lun-chu mu-lu* (A Review of Tun-huang Studies in the Past Century) 敦煌學研究論著目錄. Taipei: Hsin-wen-feng ch'u-pan-she, 1987.

Lalou, M. *Inventaire des manuscrits tibétains de Touen-houang conservés à la Bibliothèque Nationale* (Fonds Pelliot tibétain), 3 parts. Paris: Librairie d'Amérique et d'Orient, Adrien-Maisonneuve, and Bibliothèque Nationale, 1939–1961.

de LaVallée Poussin, Louis. *Catalogue of the Tibetan Manuscripts from Tun-huang in the India Office Library*, with an Appendix on the Chinese Manuscripts by Kazuo Enoki. London: Oxford University Press for the Commonwealth Relations Office 1962.

Li Ping-ch'eng 李幷成. "Tun-huang, T'u-lu-fan hsueh kung-chü shu-mu" (A Catalogue of Research References of Dunhuangology and Turfanology) 敦煌・吐魯番學工具書目, *Tun-huang-hsueh chi-k'an* (Collection of Articles on Dunhuangology) 敦煌學輯刊 7: 158–166 (first issue of 1985).

Lo Tsung-t'ao. *Tun-huang chiang-ching pien-wen yen-chiu*. Pp. 1182–1226.

Lou Tzu-k'uang 婁子匡 and Chu Chieh-fan 朱介凡. *Wu-shih nien lai te Chung-kuo su-wen-hsueh* [Chinese popular literature in the past fifty years] 五十年來的中國俗文學. Taipei: Cheng-chung shu-chü, 1963. Pp. 32–40.

Lu Shan-huan 盧善煥 and Shih Ch'in 師勤. *Chung-kuo Tun-huang T'u-lu-fan hsueh shu-chu tzu-liao* (1909–1984) [Written materials on Chinese Tun-huang studies] 中國敦煌吐魯番學著述資料. Chung-kuo Tun-huang T'u-lu-fan hsueh tzu-liao ts'ung-shu [Series of materials on Chinese Tun-huang and Turfan studies] 中國敦煌吐魯番學料叢書. Sian: Shensi sheng she-hui k'e-hsueh-yuan ch'u-pan-she fa-hsing-shih, 1985.

Mair, Victor H. "Inventory." *See* under abbreviations.

——, comp. "A Partial Bibliography for the Study of Indian Influence on Chinese Popular Literature." In *Sino-Platonic Papers* 3 (March 1987).

Men'shikov, L. N., ed. *Opisanie Kitaiskoi Chasti Kollektsii iz Khara-khoto (Fond P. K. Kozlova)*. Moscow: Glavnaya Redaktsiya Vostochnoi Literatur'i, 1984.

Men'shikov, Lev Nikolaevich, with M. I. Vorob'eva-Desyatovskaya, I. S. Gurevich, V. S. Spirin, and S. A. Shkolyar (Vol. I); with M. I. Vorob'eva-Desyatovskaya, I. T. Zograf, A. S. Martinov, and B. L. Smirnov (Vol. II). *Opisanie Kitaiskikh Rukopisei*. 2 vols. Dun'-khuanskogo Fonda Instituta Narodov Azii, Akademiya nauk SSSR. Moscow: Izdatel'stvo Vostochnoi Literatury and Nauka, 1963–1967.

Ōta Tatsuo 太田辰夫. "Tonkō bungaku kenkyū shomoku" (A Bibliography of the Tun-Huang Manuscripts Concerning Chinese Literature) 敦煌文學研究書目. *Kōbe gaidai ronsō* (The Kobe City University Journal) 神戸外大論叢 5.2 (July 1954), 119–130.

PekCat. See under abbreviations.

Tachibana Zuichō 橘瑞超. Catalogue of 429 Tun-huang manuscripts. Published in Vol. X of Lo Chen-yü's *Hsueh-t'ang ts'ung-k'e*.

Tonkō bunken kenkyū renraku iinkai (Committee for the Study of Tunhuang Materials) 敦煌文獻研究連絡委員會. *Tonkō bunken kenkyū ronbun mokuroku* (A Classified Catalogue of Japanese Books and Articles Concerning Tunhuang Documents) 敦煌文獻研究論文目錄. Tokyo: Tōyō Bunko, 1959.

Wang Chung-min, et al., eds. *Tun-huang pien-wen chi* (*see* T), Pp. 915–922.

Wang Yung-hsing 王永興. "Ch'i-shih nien lai wo-kuo Tun-huang yen-chiu wen-hsien mu-lu" [Catalogue of publications on Tun-huang research in China during the past seventy years] 七十年來我國敦煌研究文獻目錄. In Ssu-ch'ou chih lu k'ao-ch'a-tui [Silk Road Investigation Group] 絲綢之路考察隊, ed., *Ssu-lu fang ku* [Visits to ancient sites along the Silk Road] 絲路訪古. Lanchow: Kansu jen-min ch'u-pan-she, 1982.

Yoshioka Yoshitoyo (Gihō) 吉岡義豊. *Tonkō bunken bunrui mokuroku, Dōkyō no bu* [Classified catalogue of Tun-huang documents: Taoism] 敦煌文獻分類目錄道教之部. Saiiki shutsudo Kanbun bunken bunrui mokuroku [Classified catalogs of Chinese documents recovered from the western regions] 西域出土漢文文獻分類目錄, Vol. III. Tokyo: Tōyō bunko Tonkō bunken kenkyū iinkai, 1969.

MAIN ENTRIES

Acker, William Reynolds, tr. and annot. *Some T'ang and Pre-T'ang Texts on Chinese Painting*. Vol. I. Leiden: E. J. Brill, 1954. Vol. II, parts 1 and 2. Leiden: E. J. Brill, 1974.

'Ahbār aṣ-Ṣīn wa l-Hind. Relation de la Chine et de l'Inde, rédigée en 851. Ed. and tr. Jean Sauvaget. Paris: Société d'Edition "Les Belles Lettres," 1948.

Akiyama Terukazu 秋山光和, ed. *Genji monogatari emaki* [Picture scroll of *The Tale of Genji*] 源氏物語繪卷. Heibonsha Gallery 平凡社ギャラリー 29. Tokyo: Heibonsha, 1974.

——. *Heian jidai seizokuga no kenkyū* (Secular Painting in Early Mediaeval Japan) 平安時代世俗畫の研究. Tokyo: Yoshikawa kōbunkan, 1964.

——. "Miroku Kashōkyōhen hakubyō funbon (S259) to Tonkō hekiga no seisaku" (Les dessins illustrant des passages du "Mi-lo hia-cheng king" [Maitreyavyâkaraṇa] au verso d'un sûtra de Touen-houang [Stein 259] et leurs rapports avec les peintures murales de la même région) 彌勒下生經變白描粉本(S二五九V)と敦煌壁畫の製作. In *MSI*, Vol. VI. French summary, plus 2 plates and numerous figures.

——. "Tonkō-bon gōma-hen (Rōtakusha tōsei hen) gakan ni tsuite" (A Scroll-painting, Illustrating the Pien-wen, about the Magic Competition between Śāriputra and Raudrākṣa; Brought back by Paul Pelliot from Tun-huang) 敦煌本降魔變(牢度叉闘聖變)畫巻について, *BK* 187:1–35(43–77) (July 1956), with one plate and twelve illustrations. English summary.

——. "Tonkō ni okeru henbun to kaiga—Futatabi Rōtakusha tōsei-hen (gōma-hen) o chūshin ni—" (Pien-wen and Paintings at Tun-huang.... again with special reference to the "Magic competition between Śāriputra and Raudrākṣa" [Chiang-mo-pien]) 敦煌における變文と繪畫—再び牢度叉闘聖變(降魔變)を中心に—, *BK* 211:1–28 (July 1960), with 16 photographs. English summary.

Aldrich, Richard Lewis. "Tun-huang: The Rise of the Kansu Port in the T'ang Dynasty." PhD dissertation, University of Michigan, 1942.

And, Metin. *Karagöz: Turkish Shadow Theatre*. Ankara: Dost Yayinlarli, 1975.

Aoki Masaru 青木正兒. "Kuan-yü Tun-huang i-shu 'Mu-lien yuan-ch'i,' 'Ta-mu-ch'ien-lien ming-chien chiu-mu pien-wen' chi 'Hsiang-mo pien ya-tso-wen'" [Concerning the texts preserved at Tun-huang: "Maudgalyāyana *yuan-ch'i*," "*Pien-wen* on Mahāmaudgalyāyana rescuing his mother from the nether world," and "*Ya-tso-wen* for the *pien* on the subduing of demons"] 關於敦煌遺書「目連緣起」「大目乾連冥間救母變文」及「降魔變押座文」. Tr. Wang Fu-ch'üan 汪馥泉. In WFC.

——. *Shina bungaku geijutsu kō* [A study of Chinese literary arts] 支那文學藝術考. Tokyo: Kōbun-do, 1949, 5th ed. 1st ed., 1942.

——. "Tonkō isho 'Mokuren engi' 'Daimokkenren meikan kyūbo henbun' oyobi 'Gōma hen ōzabun' ni tsuite" [On "Maudgalyāyana *yuan-ch'i*," "*Pien-wen* on Mahāmaudgalyāyana rescuing his mother from the nether world," and "*Ya-tso-wen* for the *pien* on the subduing of demons" among the texts preserved at Tun-huang] 燉煌遺書「目蓮緣起」「大目乾連冥間救母變文」及び「降魔變押座文」に就いて. *Shina* 4.3:123–130 (October 1927); reprinted in the author's *Shina bungaku geijutsu kō* with some additions.

Archer, W. G. *Bazaar Paintings of Calcutta*. London: Her Majesty's Stationery Office for the Victoria and Albert Museum, 1953.

Bailey, H. W. *The Culture of the Sakas in Ancient Iranian Khotan*. Columbia Lectures on Iranian Studies 1. Delmar, New York: Caravan, 1982.

——. "Ttaugara," *BSOS* 8.4:883–921 (1937).

Barat, Kahar. "Hui-he-wen liang-chien" [Two old Uighur fragments] 回鶻文兩件. Unpublished paper presented at the International Conference on Tunhuang and Turfan Studies, Urumchi, Sinkiang, August 1985.

——. Letters of 4 October and 14 November 1986.

Barua, Benimadhab. *Barhut. Book 1, Stone as a Story-Teller* and *Book 2, Jātaka-Scenes*. Indian Research Institute Publications, Fine Arts Series—1 and 2. Calcutta: Satis Chandra Seal, 1934.

Basham, A. L., ed. *Papers on the Date of Kaniṣka*. Submitted to the Conference on the Date of Kaniṣka, London, 20–22 April 1960. Australian National University Centre of Oriental Studies, Oriental Monograph Series 4. Leiden: E. J. Brill, 1968.

Bendall, Cecil, ed. *Çikshāsamuccaya*. Bibliotheca Buddhica 1. Osnabrück: Biblio Verlag, 1970. Originally published 1897–1902 by the Imperial Academy of Sciences, St. Petersburg. Also reprinted by the Editorial Board of the *Indo-Iranian Journal* ('s-Gravenhage: Mouton, 1957).

—— and W. H. D. Rouse, trs. *Śikshā samuccaya: A Compendium of Buddhist Doctrine, compiled by Śāntideva, Chiefly from Earlier Mahāyāna Sūtras*. London: John Murray, 1922.

Benveniste, Émile. *Études sogdiennes*. Beiträge zur Iranistik 9. Wiesbaden: Ludwig Reichert, 1979.

Bhikkhu Ñāṇananda. *The Magic of the Mind in Buddhist Perspective: An Exposition of the Kālakārāma Sutta*. Kandy: Buddhist Publication Society, 1974.

Birch, Cyril, ed. *Studies in Chinese Literary Genres*. Berkeley: University of California Press, 1974.

Bishop, John L. "Prosodic Elements in T'ang Poetry." In Horst Frenz, ed., *Indiana Conference*.

Blader, Susan. "'Yan Chasan Thrice Tested': Printed Novel to Oral Tale," *Chinoperl Papers* 12:84–111 (1983).

Blofeld, John. *Bodhisattva of Compassion: the Mystical Tradition of Kuan Yin*. Boulder: Shambala, 1978.

Böhtlingk, Otto and Rudolph Roth. *Sanskrit-Wörterbuch*. 7 vols. St. Petersburg: Buchdruckerei der Kaiserlichen Akademie der Wissenschaften, 1855–1875.

von Bradke, Peter. "Ueber das Mānava-Gṛhya-Sūtra," *ZDMG* 36.3–4:417–477 (1882).

Brednich, Rolf Wilh. "Zur Vorgeschichte des Bänkelsangs," *Jahrbuch des Österreichischen Volksliederwerkes* 21:78–92 (Vienna, 1972), plus four plates.

Brough, John. "The Chinese Pseudo-Translation of Árya-Śūra's *Jātaka-mālā*," *AM*, n.s. 11.1:27–53 (1964).

——. "Nugae Indo-Sericae." In *W. B. Henning Memorial Volume*. Ed. Mary Boyce and Ilya Gershevitch. London: Lund Humphries, 1970.

Brown, William Ira. "The Distinction between *Pien-wen* and *Chiang-ching-wen*: An Analysis of the Literary Forms and Preaching Methods of the *Overcoming*

Demons Story and *Exposition of the Diamond Sutra*." PhD dissertation, University of Wisconsin, 1981.

——. "From Sutra to *Pien-wen*: A Study of 'Sudatta Erects a Monastery' and the *Hsiang-mo Pien-wen*," *Tamkang Review* 9.1 : 67–101 (Fall 1978).

Bukkyō bungaku kenkyū kai [Association for studies on Buddhist literature] 佛教文學研究會. *BBK* 2, 5, and 6. Kyoto: Hōzōkan, 1964, 1967, and 1968.

Bush, Susan H. and Victor H. Mair. "Some Buddhist Portraits and Images of the Lü and Ch'an Sects in Twelfth- and Thirteenth-Century China," *Archives of Asian Art* 31 : 32–51 (1977–1978).

Cadonna, Alfredo. *Il Taoista di Sua Maestà*: *Dodici episodi da un manoscritto cinese di Dunhuang*. Venice: Cafoscarina, 1984.

Chadwick, Hector Munro and Nora Kershaw Chadwick. *The Growth of Literature*. 3 vols. Cambridge: Cambridge University Press, 1932–1940. Reprint 1968.

Chang Chin-ch'üan 張金泉. "Ch'ung-pan *Tun-huang pien-wen chi* shih i" [A tentative discussion of the reissue of *Tun-huang pien-wen chi*] 重版《敦煌變文集》試議, *Hang-chou ta-hsueh hsueh-pao* (Journal of Hangzhou University) 杭州大學學報 12.4 : 51–57 (December 1982).

Chang, H[sin]-c[hang]. *Chinese Literature: Popular Fiction and Drama*. Edinburgh: Edinburgh University Press, 1973.

Chang Hsi-hou 張錫厚. *Tun-huang wen-hsueh* [Tun-huang literature] 敦煌文學. Chung-kuo ku-tien wen-hsueh chi-pen chih-shih ts'ung-shu [Library of basic knowledge about classical Chinese literature] 中國古典文學基本知識叢書. Shanghai: Shanghai ku-chi ch'u-pan-she, 1980.

Chang Hung-hsun 張鴻勛. "Tun-huang chiang-ch'ang wen-hsueh te t'i-chih chi ch'i lei-hsing ch'u-t'an: chien lun chi-chung 'Chung-kuo wen-hsueh shih' yu-kuan t'i-fa te wen-t'i" [A preliminary investigation of the system of organization and types of Tun-huang prosimetric literature, together with a discussion of several questions regarding the formulation of "The history of Chinese literature"] 敦煌講唱文學的體制及其類型初探—兼論幾種『中國文學史』有關提法的問題. Lan-chou ta-hsueh Tun-huang-hsueh yen-chiou-tsu [Lanchow University Tunhuangology Research Unit] 蘭州大學敦煌研究組, ed., *Tun-huang hsueh chi-k'an* [Journal of Tunhuangology] 敦煌學輯刊 2 : 73–86 (1982). Also in *LitHer* 2 : 62–73 (1982).

Chang Kwang-chih. Private communication after his trip to Tun-huang in late 1978.

Chang Ping-lin 章炳麟 (*tzu* T'ai-yen 太炎 1868–1936). *Hsin fang-yen* [New topolectology] 新方言. In *Chang-shih ts'ung-shu* [Collected works of Mr. Chang] 章氏叢書. N. P.: Chekiang t'u-shu-kuan, 1917–1919.

Chang Shou-lin 張壽林. "Wang Chao-chün ku-shih yen-pien chih tien-tien ti-ti" [The step-by-step evolution of the Wang Chao-chün tale] 王昭君故事演變之點點滴滴, *Wen-hsueh nien-pao* (Chinese Literature) 文學年報 1 (July 1932) unnumbered, 25 pages. Rpt. *LWL*, Vol. II.

Chang Yen-yuan 張彥遠 (fl. 847–874). *Li-tai ming-hua chi* [A record of famous painters of successive dynasties] 歷代名畫記 (847). References to the Chinese text are to the pages in Acker where it is reprinted. I have also consulted the Chung-kuo mei-shu lun-chu ts'ung-k'an [Writings on Chinese art series] 中國美術論著叢刊 edition published in Peking by Jen-min mei-shu ch'u-pan-she, 1963, the annotated edition of Yü Chien-hua, *q.v.*, and the annotated translation of Nagahiro Toshio, *q.v.* I have not been able to locate Ono Katsutoshi's 2-volume annotated translation.

Chang Yi. "West Szechwan and East India: Studies in Early Sino-Indian Relations." N.p., 1980 (?), mimeograph.

Chang Yung-yen 張永言. "Tu Tun-huang pien-wen tzu-i t'ung-shih ou-chi" [Random notes on reading the *Comprehensive explanations of the meaning of characters in Tun-huang* pien-wen] 讀《敦煌變文字義通釋》偶記, *CKYW* 3 (cumulative 130): 200–230 (22 June 1964).

Chao Chin-ming. See Zhao Jinming.

Chao Ching-shen 趙景深. "Mu-lien chiu-mu te yen-pien" [The evolution of the tale "Maudgalyāyana rescues his mother"] 目連救母的演變. In his *Tu ch'ü hsiao chi* [Brief notes on readings of drama] 讀曲小記. Shanghai: Chung-hua shu-chü, 1959. This is an adaptation of the following entry.

——. "Mu-lien ku-shih te yen-pien" [The evolution of the Maudgalyāyana story] 目連故事的演變. In his *Yin-tzu chi* [Collected works of "Silver"] 銀子集. Shanghai: Yung-hsiang yin-shu-kuan, 1946.

Chao Lin 趙璘 (fl. 836–846). *Yin-hua lu* [Record of tales of causation] 因話錄. Chung-kuo wen-hsueh ts'an-k'ao tzu-liao hsiao ts'ung-shu [Small collectanea of reference materials for Chinese literature] 中國文學參考資料小叢書, series 1, number 3. Shanghai: Ku-tien wen-hsueh ch'u-pan-she, 1957.

Chavannes, Éd. and P. Pelliot, trs. and annots. "Un traité manichéen retrouvé en Chine" *JA* 2: 499–617 (November–December 1911); second part, series 11, 1: 99–199 (January–February 1913) and 261–394 (March–April 1913), plus two plates.

Chen Chien. "Preliminary Research on the Ancient Passage to India from Szechwan via Yunnan and Burma." The History Research Institute of Yunnan, May 1980. Mimeograph.

Chen Tsu-lung [Ch'en Tso-lung] 陳祚龍. "Chung-shih Tun-huang yü Ch'eng-tu chih chien te chiao-t'ung lu-hsien—Tun-huang-hsueh san-ts'e chih i" (Les voies de communication entre Tch'eng-tou et Touen-houang au Moyen âge). 中世敦煌與成都之間的交通路線—敦煌散策之一—, *Tun-huang-hsueh* (*Études sur Touen-houang*) 敦煌學 1: 79–86 (1974). Also in the author's *Tun-huang tzu-liao k'ao hsieh*, Vol. II.

——. *La vie et les oeuvres de Wou-tchen (816–895): Contribution à l'histoire culturelle de Touen-houang*. Publications de l'école française d'Extrême-Orient 60. Paris: Ecole française d'Extrême-Orient, 1966.

Ch'en Hung-chih 陳弘治. *Li Ch'ang-chi ko-shih chiao-shih* [Li Ho's poems and songs, collated and explained] 李長吉歌詩校釋. Kuo-wen yen-chiu-so chi-k'an 12. Taipei (?): Kuo-wen yen-chiu-so (?), 1967 (?).

Ch'en Kenneth K. S. *Buddhism in China: A Historical Survey*. Princeton: Princeton University Press, 1964.

——. *The Chinese Transformation of Buddhism*. Princeton: Princeton University Press, 1973.

——. "Filial Piety in Chinese Buddhism," *HJAS* 28:81–97 (1968).

——. "A Study of the Svāgata Story in the *Divyāvadāna* in its Sanskrit, Pāli, Tibetan, and Chinese Versions," *HJAS* 9.3–4:207–314 (February 1947).

Ch'en Kuo-ning 陳國寧. *Tun-huang pi-hua Fo-hsiang t'u yen-chiu* [Studies on Tun-huang wall-paintings and pictures of Buddha images] 敦煌壁畫佛像圖研究. Taipei: Chia-hsin shui-ni kung-ssu wen-hua chi-chin-hui, 1973.

Ch'en Li-li, tr. and intro. *Master Tung's Western Chamber Romance* (Tung Hsi-hsiang chu-kung-tiao): *A Chinese Chantefable*. Cambridge and London: Cambridge University Press, 1976.

——. "Outer and Inner Forms of *Chu-kung-tiao*, with Reference to *pien-wen*, *tz'u* and Vernacular Fiction," *HJAS* 32:124–149 (1972).

——. "*Pien-wen* Chantefable and *Aucassin et Nicolette*," *Comparative Literature* 23.3: 255–261 (1971).

Ch'en Shih-fu 陳世福. *Tun-huang fu yen-chiu* [Studies on Tun-huang rhapsodies] 敦煌賦研究. Taipei: T'ien-i ch'u-pan-she, 1978.

Ch'en Shou-yi. *Chinese Literature: A Historical Introduction*. New York: Ronald Press, 1961.

Ch'en T'ieh-fan 陳鐵凡. *Tun-huang pen Hsiao-ching lei-tsuan* [Categorical compilation of manuscripts of the Classic of Filial Piety from Tun-huang] 敦煌本孝經類纂. Taipei: Yenching wen-hua shih-yeh, 1977.

Ch'en Tso-lung 陳祚龍 (see also Chen Tsu-lung). *Tun-huang tzu-liao k'ao hsieh*. [Investigations of details relating to Tun-huang materials] 敦煌資料考屑. 2 vols. Taipei: Taiwan Commercial Press, 1979.

Ch'en Yin-k'o 陳寅恪. "Hsu-ta ch'i ching-she in-yuan ch'ü pa" [Colophon to the canto on the causes for Sudatta's building of the Jetavana Monastery] 須達起精舍因緣曲跋, *Kuo-hsueh lun-ts'ung* (Chinese Classical Review) 國學論叢 4:189–191 (October 1928).

Ch'en Yuan-lung 陳元龍 (1652–1736), et al., comp. *Yü-ting li-tai fu hui* [Imperially commissioned compendium of rhapsodies] 御定歷代賦彙. 4 vols. Kyoto: Chūbun shuppansha, 1974. Photoreprint of 1706 ed.

Cheng Chen-to 鄭振鐸 (see also Hsi-ti). *Ch'a-t'u pen Chung-kuo wen-hsueh shih* [Illustrated history of Chinese literature] 插圖本中國文學史. 4 vols., continuous pagination. Peking: Tso-chia ch'u-pan-she, 1957. Originally 1932.

——. *Chung-kuo su-wen-hsueh shih* [History of Chinese popular literature] 中國俗文學史. 2 vols. Chung-kuo wen-hua-shih ts'ung-shu [Collected works on Chinese cultural history] 中國文化史叢書, series 2. Changsha: Commercial Press, 1938. Republished Peking: Tso-chia ch'u-pan-she, 1957.

——. "Pa-hsiang pien-wen" [*Pien-wen* on the eight aspects of the Buddha's life] 八相變文. *SCWK* [World library] 9. Shanghai: Sheng-huo shu-tien, 1936.

——. "Pien-wen" [*Pien-wen*] 變文. In his *History of Popular Chinese Literature*.

——. "Pien-wen te ch'u-hsien" [The emergence of *pien-wen*] 變文的出現. Chapter 33 of his *Illustrated History of Chinese Literature*, Vol. II.

——. "Shen-mo chiao-tso 'pien-wen'? Ho hou-lai te 'pao-chüan', 'chu-kung-tiao', 't'an-tz'u', 'ku-tz'u' teng wen-t'i yu tsen-yang te kuan-hsi?" [What is referred to by the term *pien-wen*? And what kind of relation does it bear upon such later literary genres as *pao-chüan*, *chu-kung-tiao*, *t'an-tz'u*, and *ku-tz'u*?] 什麼叫做「變文」? 和後來的「寶卷」「諸宮調」,「彈詞」,「鼓詞」 等文體有怎樣的關係? In Fu Tung-hua 傅東華, ed. *Wen-hsueh pai t'i* [A hundred topics concerning literature] 文學百題. Shanghai: Sheng-huo shu-tien, 1949, reprint.

——. ed. "Shun-tzu chih-hsiao pien-wen" [*Pien-wen* on the utmost filiality of Shun as a boy] 舜子至孝變文. *SCWK* 12. Shanghai: Sheng-huo shu-tien, 1936.

——. ed., "Ta-mu-chien-lien ming-chien chiu-mu pien-wen" [*Pien-wen* on Mahāmaudgalyāyana rescuing his mother from hell] . *SCWK* 10. Shanghai: Sheng-huo shu-tien, 1936. Includes preface and appendices, the latter containing variant texts.

——. "T'ang-tai te min-chien ko-fu" [Folk songs and poetic compositions during the T'ang dynasty] 唐代的民間歌賦. In this *History of Popular Chinese Literature*.

——. "Ts'ung pien-wen tao t'an-tz'u" [From *pien-wen* to *t'an-tz'u*] 從變文到彈詞. In his *Chung-kuo wen-hsueh yen-chiu* [Researches into Chinese literature] Vol. III. 中國文學研究. Peking: Tso-chia ch'u-pan-she, 1957. First given as a lecture at Peking University, 14 October 1932, notes taken by Wang Wei 汪偉. Also reprinted in *Chü-lou chi* [Collected works of the hunchback] 痀僂集. Ch'uang-tso wen-k'u [Creation library] 創作文庫. Shanghai: Sheng-huo shu-tien, 1934. Includes diagram.

——. "Tun-huang te su-wen-hsueh" [Popular literature from Tun-huang] 敦煌的俗文學, *Hsiao-shuo yueh-pao* (The Short Story Magazine) 小說月報 20.3: 475–496 (10 March 1929).

——, ed. "Wang Chao-chün pien-wen" [The Wang Chao-chün *pien-wen*] 王昭君變文. *SCWK* 12. Shanghai: Sheng-huo shu-tien, 1936.

——, ed. "*Wei-mo-chieh-ching* pien-wen ti-erh-shih chüan" [The *Vimalakīrti-sūtra pien-wen*, Fascicle 20] 維摩詰經變文第二十卷. *SCWK* 11. Shanghai: Sheng-huo shu-tien, 1936. Also included in this volume are two other selections from the so-called *Vimalakīrti-sūtra pien-wen* on pp. 4886–4895 and 4896–4901.

Cheng Chih-chen 鄭之珍 (fl. 1582). *Hsin-pien Mu-lien chiu-mu ch'üan-shan hsi-wen* [A new compilation of the text to the play about Maudgalyāyana rescuing his mother and exhorting her to goodness] 新編目連救母勸善戲文. Ku-pen shi-ch'ü ts'ung-k'an [Ancient editions of drama] 古本戲曲叢刊, Series 1, 67. Shanghai: Commercial Press, 1954. Vols. 80–82.

——. *Hsiu-hsiang yin-chu Mu-lien chiu-mu ch'üan-shan chi* [Phonetically glossed and annotated tale of Mahāmaudgalyāyana rescuing his mother and exhorting her to do good] 繡像音註目連救母勸善記. Chin-ling: Fu-ch'un t'ang, n.d.

Cheng Te-k'un. *Tun-huang Studies in China*. Chengtu: West China Union University, 1947.

Ch'eng I-chung 程毅中. "Kuan-yü pien-wen te chi-tien t'an-so" [Several investigations concerning *pien-wen*] 關於變文的幾點探索. *LitHer*, *Suppl*. 10. Peking: Chung-hua shu-chü, 1962.

——. "Lueh-t'an Sung Yuan chiang-shih te yuan-yuan [A brief discussion on the origins of history-telling during the Sung and Yuan dynasties] 略談宋元講史的淵源, *LitHer* 211 (1 June 1958).

Cheung, Hung-nin Samuel. "The Language of the Tun-huang *Pien-wen*." PhD dissertation, University of California, Berkeley, 1974.

——. "Perfective Particles in the *bian-wen* Language," *Journal of Chinese Linguistics* 5:55–74 (1977).

——. "The Use of Verse in the Dun-huang Bian-wen," *Journal of Chinese Linguistics* 8.1:149–162 (1980) with Chinese and English summaries.

Chi Hsien-lin. "Indian Literature in China," *Chinese Literature* 4:123–130 (July–August 1958).

Chiang Fu 蔣斧 and Lo Fu-ch'ang 羅福萇. *Sha-chou wen-lu* [A record of writings from Sha-chou] 沙州文錄. Printed 1924 by Lo Chen-yü.

Chiang Li-hung 蔣禮鴻. *Tun-huang pien-wen tzu-i t'ung-shih* [Comprehensive explanations of the meanings of characters in Tun-huang *pien-wen*] 敦煌變文字義通釋. Peking: Chung-hua shu-chü, 1962, rev. and enlgd. ed. First published 1959. Also available in Taiwan reprint. Further revised and enlarged edition published by Shanghai ku-chi ch'u-pan-she, 1981.

Chiang Liang-fu 姜亮夫. "Tun-huang ching-chüan tsai Chung-kuo hsueh-shu wen-hua shang chih chia-chih" [The value of Tun-huang manuscripts for Chinese science and culture] 敦煌經卷在中國學術文化上之價值, *Shuo-wen yueh-k'an* [Etymology monthly] 說文月刊 3.10:73–81 (15 May 1943).

——. *Tun-huang, wei-ta te wen-hua pao-tsang* [Tun-huang—a great treasury of culture] 敦煌—偉大的文化寶藏. Shanghai: Ku-tien wen-hsueh ch'u-pan-she, 1956.

Chiang Po-ch'ien 蔣伯潛. *Hsiao-shuo yü hsi-chü* [Fiction and drama] 小說與戲劇. Shih-chieh wen-k'u shih-chieh ch'ing-nien ts'ung-shu kuo-wen tzu-hsueh fu-tao ts'ung-shu [World library: Study aids for self-study of the national language series in the world youth series] 世界文庫·世界青年叢書·國文自學輔導叢書. Taipei: Shih-chieh shu-chü, 1956.

Chih I 摯誼. "Kuan-yü T'ang-tai min-chien wen-hsueh yen-chiu te chi-tien i-chien" [Several opinions on studies of T'ang period folk literature] 關於唐代民間文學研究的幾點意見. In *LWL*, Vol. I.

Chikusa Masaaki 竺沙雅章. *Chūgoku Bukkyō shakai-shi kenkyū* (Studies in the Social History of Chinese Buddhism) 中國佛教社會史研究. Tōyōshi kenkyū sōkan (Oriental Research Series) 東洋史研究叢刊 34. Kyoto: Dōhōsha, 1982.

——. "Tonkō no jiko ni tsuite" (On the *Ssu hu*, Individuals who Belonged to Buddhist Temples in Tun-huang) 敦煌の寺戶について, *Shi* 44.5:40–73 (September 1961), with two photographs and an English summary.

——. "Tonkō no sokan seido" (The Clergy in Tun-huang in Late T'ang) 敦煌の僧官制度 *TGK* 31:117–198 (March 1961), with one illustration.

——. "Tonkō shutsudo 'sha' bunsho no kenkyū" (A Study of Documents from Tunhuang Concerning "Club") 敦煌出土「社」文書の研究, *TGK* 35:215–288 (March 1964), with 16 illustrations.

Childs, Margaret Helen. "Religious Awakening Stories in Late Medieval Japan: The Dynamics of Didacticism." PhD dissertation, University of Pennsylvania, 1983.

Chin Ch'i-tsung 金啓綜. "T'ang mo Sha-chou (Tun-huang) Chang I-ch'ao te ch'i-i—Tun-huang hsieh-pen Chang I-ch'ao pien-wen" [Chang I-ch'ao's righteous rebellion at Sha-chou (Tun-huang) at the end of the T'ang—The Tun-huang manuscript "Chang I-ch'ao *pien-wen*"] 唐末沙州(敦煌)張義潮的起義—敦煌寫本張義潮變文—, *Li-shih chiao-hsueh* [Historical pedagogy] 歷史教學 38:31–35 (February 1954).

Chin Jung-hua 金榮華, comp. *Tun-huang su-tzu so-yin* [An index of vernacular forms of tetragraphs from Tun-huang] 敦煌俗字索引. Taipei: Shih-men t'u-shu kung-ssu, 1980.

Chin (sic)-lo (Ch'iu-le) 秋樂. "Pien-wen yü Chung-kuo wen-hsueh" (*Pien-wen* and Chinese Literature) 變文與中國文學, *HTFH* 11 (cumulative 99):17–21 (3 November 1958). Reprinted *BCL*.

Chin Wei-no 金維諾. "Ch'i-yuan chi-t'u yü pien-wen" [The pictorial records of the Jetavana Park and *pien-wen*] 祇園記圖與變文, *WWTKL* 11 (cumulative 99); 32–35. (November 1958).

——. "Tun-huang pi hua Ch'i-yuan chi-t'u k'ao" [A study of the pictorial records of the Jetavana Park in Tun-huang cave-drawings] 敦煌壁畫祇園記圖考 *WWTKL* 10:8–13. (cumulative 98) (8 October 1958). Includes two pages of plates.

Ch'in-ting ch'üan T'ang wen [Imperially commissioned complete prose of the T'ang period] 欽定全唐文. Kuang-ya shu-chü woodblock ed. of 1901.

Ching-an 靜庵 (pseud. Wang Kuo-wei 王國維). "Tun-huang fa-hsien T'ang-ch'ao chih t'ung-su shih chi t'ung-su hsiao-shuo" [Popular poetry and popular fiction of the T'ang dynasty discovered at Tun-huang] 敦煌發見唐朝之通俗詩及通俗小說, *Tung-fang tsa-chih* (The Eastern Miscellany) 東方雜誌 17.8: 95–100. (April 25, 1920).

Ch'iu Chen-ching 邱鎮京. "Tun-huang Fo-ching pien-wen shu-lun" [An account of the Buddhist sūtras and *pien-wen* from Tun-huang] 敦煌佛經變文述論, parts 1 and 2, *Shih-tzu hou* (The Lion's Roar Monthly) 獅子吼 6.7–8:24–27 (August 1967) and 6.9:19–23 (September 1967).

——. *Tun-huang pien-wen shu-lun* [An account of Tun-huang *pien-wen*] 敦煌變文述論 Jen-jen wen-k'u [Everyman's library] 人人文庫 1325–1326. Taipei: Commercial Press, 1970.

——. "Tun-huang pien-wen yen-chiu" [Studies on Tun-huang *pien-wen*] 敦煌變文研究. Taipei: Chinese Cultural Academy thesis, 1965.

Ch'iu-le. *See* Chin-lo

Choe Sang-su. "Puppet Play." In *Survey of Korean Arts: Folk Arts*. Seoul: National Academy of Arts, 1974.

Chou I-liang 周一[乙]良. "Kuan-yü Su-chiang k'ao tsai shuo chi chü hua" [A few more words concerning "An examination of popular lectures during the T'ang period"] 關於俗講考再說幾句話, *TSCK* 21. *TCTKP*, 20 June 1947.

——. "Tu T'ang-tai su-chiang k'ao" [On reading the article "An examination of popular lectures during the T'ang period"] 讀唐代俗講考. In his *Wei Chin nan-pei-ch'ao shih lun-chi* [Collected essays on the history of the Wei, Chin, and Northern and Southern dynasties] 魏晉南北朝史論集. Peking: Chung-hua shu-chü, 1963. Reprints the two articles by Chou I-liang from the *Tientsin l'Impartial* listed in this bibliography.

——. "Tu T'ang-tai su-chiang k'ao" [On reading the article "An examination of popular lectures during the T'ang period"] 讀唐代俗講考 *TSCK* 6. *TCTKP*, 8 February 1947.

——. "Tun-huang pi-hua yü Fo-ching" [Tun-huang wall-paintings and Buddhist sūtras] 敦煌壁畫與佛經. *WW-TH*(A).

Chou Shao-liang 周紹良. "T'an T'ang-tai min-chien wen-hsueh" [On the folk literature of the T'ang period] 談唐代民間文學, *Hsin chien-she* [Reconstruction] 新建設 169:75–81 (January 1963). Reprinted in *LWL*.

——. *Tun-huang pien-wen hui-lu* [A collection of Tun-huang *pien-wen*] 敦煌變文彙錄. Chung-kuo wen-i yen-chiu ts'ung-shu [Collection of studies on Chinese literature] 中國文藝研究叢書. Shanghai: Shang-hai ch'u-pan kung-ssu, 1955. This revised and expanded version first published in 1954.

——. "Tun-huang so-ch'u T'ang pien-wen hui-lu" [Registrar of T'ang period *pien-wen* which came from Tun-huang] 敦煌所出唐變文彙錄, *HTFH* 1.10:7–10 (June 1951).

Chou Shu-chia 周叔迦. "Man-t'an pien-wen te ch'i-yuan" [An informal talk on the origins of *pien-wen*] 漫談變文的起源, *HTFH* 2:13–15 (February 1954). Reprinted *BCL*.

Chu Chieh-fan 朱介凡. "Tun-huang pien-wen mu-lu chi K'ung-tzu Hsiang T'o hsiang-wen shu chih ch'uan-ch'eng" [A table of titles of Tun-huang manuscripts and the transmission of the story "Confucius and Hsiang T'o ask each other scholarly questions"] 敦煌變文目錄及「孔子項託相問書」之傳承, *TLTC* 22.7:10–15 (15 April 1961).

Chu Hsi 朱熹. *Chu-tzu yü-lei* [Classified conversations of Chu Hsi (1130–1200)] 朱子語類, issued 1270. Taipei: Cheng-chung shu-chü, 1973, 3rd ed. 1962, 1st ed. Based on a Ming edition of 1473 which is a reprint of the Sung edition of 1269.

Ch'uan T'ang shih. *See* P'eng Ting-ch'iu.

Chueh-hsien 覺先. "Ts'ung pien-wen te ch'an-sheng shuo-tao Fo-chiao wen-hsueh tsai she-hui shang chih ti-wei" [A discussion of the position of Buddhist literature in society judged from the emergence of *pien-wen*] 從變文的產生說到佛教文學在社會上之地位, *BCL*. Originally appeared in *Jen hai teng* [A lantern for the ocean of mankind] 人海燈 4.1 (1937).

Chueh-ming 覺明 (pseudonym of Hsiang Ta). "Lun T'ang-tai Fo-ch'ü" [A discussion of Buddhist cantos in the T'ang dynasty] 論唐代佛曲, *HSYP* 20.10: 1579–1588 (10 October 1929).

Chung-hua ta tzu-tien [Great Chung Hwa dictionary of single characters] 中華大字典. Reduced format edition in 2 vols. Taipei: Chung Hwa, 1974. 4th Taiwan printing.

Chung-kuo k'o-hsueh-yuan li-shih yen-chiu-so tzu-liao shih [Office of Reference Materials in the Historical Research Institute of Academia Sinica] 中國科學院歷史研究所資料室, ed. *Tun-huang tzu-liao* [Reference matter from Tun-huang] 敦煌資料. Vol. I. Peking: Chung-hua shu-chü, 1961. Rpt. Tokyo: Kobayashi Sanihisa, 1963.

A Concordance to Chuang Tzu. Harvard-Yenching Institute Sinological Index Series, Supplement No. 20. Cambridge: Harvard University Press, 1956.

Conze, Edward. *Buddhism: Its Essence and Development*. New York: Harper Torchbooks, 1965.

——, tr. *Buddhist Scriptures*. Baltimore: Penguin Books, 1959.

Coomaraswamy, Ananda K. "Nirmaṇa-kāya," *JRAS* (January 1938), pp. 81–84.

——. "On Translation: Māyā, Deva, Tapas," *Isis* 19.1 (55): 74–91 (April 1933).

Cowell, E. B. and R. A. Neil, eds. *The Divyâvadâna*. Cambridge: Cambridge University Press, 1886.

Crump, J. I. "Dans un écran de radar: un thème de la littérature vulgaire du Moyen Âge chinois," *JA* 249.4: 477–485 (1961).

——. Review of *Ballads and Stories from Tun-huang, An Anthology*, by Arthur Waley, *JAS* 21.3: 389–391 (May 1962).

Čuguevskiĭ, L. I. "Touen-houang du VIIIe au Xe siècle." In Michel Soymié, ed., *Nouvelles contributions*.

Daffinà, Paolo. "L'Itinerario di Hui Shêng," *Rivista degli Studi Orientali* 38.3: 235–267 (1963).

Das, Sarat Chandra. *A Tibetan-English Dictionary with Sanskrit Synonyms*. Calcutta: Bengal Secretariat Book Depot, 1902.

Davidson, J. Leroy. *The Lotus Sutra in Chinese Art—A Study in Buddhist Art to the Year 1000*. Yale Studies in the History of Art. New Haven: Yale University Press, 1954.

De, Gokuldas. "Original Nature of the Jātakas," *Calcutta Review*, 3rd series, 34: 78–97 (January–March 1930).

De, Sushilkumar. *History of Sanskrit Literature*. Calcutta: University of Calcutta, 1957.

Demiéville, Paul. *Le concile de Lhasa—Une controverse sur le quiétisme entre Bouddhistes de l'Inde et de la Chine au VIIIe siècle de l'ère chrétienne*, Vol. I. Bibliothèque de l'Institut des Hautes Etudes Chinoises, Vol. VII. Paris: Imprimerie Nationale de France, 1952.

——. "Les débuts de la littérature en Chinois vulgaire." *Académie des Inscriptions et Belles-Lettres, Comptes Rendus* (November–December 1952).

——. "L'Introduction au Tibet du Bouddhism sinisé d'après les manuscrits de Touen-houang: Analyse de récents travaux japonais." In Michel Soymié, ed., *Contributions aux études sur Touen-houang*, pp. 1–16.

——. "Langue et littérature chinoises," *Annuaire du College de France* 53: 218–223 (1953); 54 (1954), not seen; 55 (1955), not seen; 56: 284–290 (1956); 57: 349–

357 (1957); 58:381–391 (1958); 59:435–438 (1959); 60:317–320 (1960); 61:289–301 (1961); 62:329–335 (1962); 63:325–336 (1963).

——. "Manuscrits chinois de Touen-houang à Leningrad," *TP* 51.4–5:355–376 (1964).

——. "Quelques traits de moeurs barbares dans une chantefable chinoise des T'ang," *Acta Orientalia* 15.1–3:71–85 (1962).

——. Review of L. N. Men'shikov and I. T. Zograf, *Bjan'ven'o vozdajanii za milosti* (q.v.), *TP* 61.1–3:161–169 (1975).

——. "Tun-huang Texts." In *Dictionary of Oriental Literatures*, Vol. I: *East Asia*, ed. Zbigniew Słupski, under the general editorship of Jaroslav Průšek. New York: Basic Books, 1974.

van der Loon, Piet. "Les origines rituelles du théâtre chinois," *JA* 265.1–2:141–168 (1977), with English summary.

——. *Taoist Books in the Libraries of the Sung Period: A Critical Study and Index*. Oxford Oriental Institute Monographs 7. London: Ithaca Press, 1984.

Devéria, M. G. "Musulmans et manichéens chinois," *JA* n.s. 10:445–484 (November–December 1897).

de Visser. *See under* "V".

Dolby, William. *A History of Chinese Drama*. New York: Barnes and Noble Import Division of Harper and Row, 1976.

Drège, Jean-Pierre. "Clefs des songes de Touen-houang." In Michel Soymié, ed., *Nouvelles contributions*, plus plates 24–38.

Dudbridge, Glen. *The Tale of Li Wa: Study and critical edition of a Chinese story from the ninth century*. Oxford Oriental Monographs 4. London: Ithaca Press for the Board of the Faculty of Oriental Studies, 1983.

Dunn, Robert. Letter of 22 May 1978.

Dutt, Nalinaksha, ed., with the assistance of Vidyavaridhi Pandit Shiv Nath Shastri Sahityacharya. *Gilgit Manuscripts*, Vol. III, part 1. Srinagar, Kashmir: J. C. Sarkhel, 1941 (?). Vol. III, part 2. Srinagar, Kashmir: J. C. Sarkhel, 1942. Vol. III, part 3. Srinagar, Kashmir: J. C. Sarkhel, 1943. Vol. III, part 4. Calcutta: Oriental Press, 1950.

Dutt, Sukumar. *Buddhist Monks and Monasteries of India: Their History and Their Contribution to Indian Culture*. London: Allen and Unwin, 1962.

——. "The Origin of the Commoners in Ancient Tun-huang," *Sinologica* 4.3: 141–155 (1955).

——. *Studies in Chinese Folklore and Related Essays*. Indiana University Folklore Institute Monograph Series 23. Bloomington and the Hague: Indiana University Research Center for the Language Sciences and Mouton, 1970.

Eberhard, Wolfram. Lecture on Chinese theatre delivered to the Oriental Club of Philadelphia, 30 April 1982.

Edgerton, Franklin. *Buddhist Hybrid Sanskrit Grammar and Dictionary*. 2 vols. New Haven: Yale University Press, 1953,

Edwards, E. D. *Chinese Prose Literature of the T'ang Period (A.D. 618–906)*. 2 vols. London: Arthur Probsthain, 1937–1938. Reprint New York: AMS Press, 1974.

Egami, Namio. "The K'uai-t'i 駃騠, the T'ao-yü 騊駼, and the Tan-hsi 驒騱, the Strange Domestic Animals of the Hsiung-nu 匈奴," *Memoirs of the Research Department of the Toyo Bunko* 13:87–123 (1951).

Emmerick, R. E., ed. and tr. *The Book of Zambasta: A Khotanese Poem on Buddhism*. London Oriental Series 21. London: Oxford University Press, 1968.

——, ed. and tr. *Tibetan Texts Concerning Khotan*. London Oriental Series 19. London: Oxford University Press, 1967.

Ensink, J. "On the Old-Javanese Cantakaparwa and Its Tale of Sutasoma." *Verhandelingen van het KITLV*, 54. 's-Gravenhage: Martinus Nijhoff, 1967.

Euyang, Eugene. "The Historical Context for the Tun-huang *pien-wen*," *Literature East and West* 15.3:339–357 (1971).

——. "Oral Narration in the Pien and Pien-wen," *ArchOr* 46.3:232–252 (1978).

——. "The Wang Chao-chün Legend: Configurations of the Classic," *CLEAR* 4.1:3–22 (January 1982).

——. "Word of Mouth: Oral Storytelling in the *Pien-wen*." PhD dissertation, Indiana University, 1971.

Evers, Hans-Dieter. "Magic and Religion in Sinhalese Society," *American Anthropologist* 67.1:97–99 (February 1965).

Fang Hui 方回 (pseud. Hsiang Ta 向達). "Chi Lun-tun te Tun-huang su-wen-hsueh" [Notes on popular literature from Tun-huang in London] 記倫敦的敦煌俗文學, *Hsin Chung-hua* (New China Magazine) 新中華 5.13:123–128 (10 July 1937).

Fausbøll, V., ed. *The Jātaka*. 7 vols. London: Kegan, Paul, Trench, and Trübner, 1875–1897.

Feng Ch'eng-chün 馮承鈞, comp., Lu Chün-ling 陸峻嶺 rev. *Hsi-yü ti-ming* [Place names of the western regions] 西域地名. Peking: Chung-hua shu-chü, 1980, 1982. First ed. 1930.

Feng Yü 馮宇. "Man t'an 'pien-wen' te ming-ch'eng, hsing-shih, yuan-yuan chi ying-hsiang" [Desultory remarks on the name, form, origin, and influence of *pien-wen*] 漫談「變文」的名稱, 形式, 淵源及影響. Originally appeared in *Ha-erh-pin shih-fan hsüeh-yüan hsüeh-pao* [Journal of Harbin Normal College] 哈爾濱師範學院學報 (Jen-wen k'e-hsueh [Humanistic sciences] 人文科學) 1 (1960). Rpt. *LWL*, Vol. I.

Frenz, Horst and G. L. Anderson, eds. *Conference on Oriental-Western Literary Relations, Indiana University*, First. University of North Carolina Studies in Comparative Literature 13. Chapel Hill: North Carolina University Press, 1955.

Frodsham, J. D., tr. and intro. *The Poems of Li Ho (791–817)*. Oxford: Clarendon Press, 1970.

Fu Chen-lun 傅振倫. "Tun-huang Ch'ien-fo-tung wen-wu fa-hsien te ching-kuo" [The sequence of events in the discovery of the artifacts in the Caves of the Thousand Buddhas at Tun-huang] 敦煌千佛洞文物發現的經過. *WW-TH* (A).

Fu Yun-tzu 傅芸子. "Ch'ou-nü yuan-ch'i yü *Hsien-yü ching* chin-kang p'in" [The legend of the ugly girl and the Vajra section in the *Sūtra of the Wise and the Foolish*] 醜女緣起與賢愚經金剛品, *I-wen tsa-chih* [Literature magazine] 藝文雜誌 3.3:8–11 (1 March 1945).

——. "Kuan-yü p'o-mo pien-wen—Lun-tun tsu-pen chih fa-hsien" [Concerning the *pien-wen* on the destruction of demons—the discovery of the integral London text] 關於破魔變文—倫敦足本之發見, *I-wen tsa-chih* [Literature magazine] 藝文雜誌 1.3:13–16 (September 1943).

——. "Su-chiang hsin-k'ao" [A new examination of "Popular lectures"] 俗講新考 *Hsin ssu-ch'ao* [New tide of thought magazine] 新思朝 1.2:39–41 (1 September 1946). Rpt. *LWL*, Vol. I.

——. "Tun-huang su-wen-hsueh chih fa-hsien chi ch'i chan-k'ai" [The discovery of Tun-huang popular literature and its development] 敦煌俗文學之發見及其展開. In his *Pai-ch'uan chi* [Collected works of Fu Yun-tzu] 白川集. Tokyo: Bunkyūdō, 1943. Originally appeared in *Chung-yang Ya-hsi-ya* [Central Asia] 中央亞細亞 1.2:36–42 (October 1942).

Fujieda Akira 藤枝晃 (*see also* Huzieda, A). "Oashisu Tonkō" [Oasis Tun-huang] オアシス敦煌. In *Zusetsu sekai bunka-shi taikei, Chugoku II* [Illustrated history of world cultures, China II] 圖說世界文化史大系, 中國 II. Vol. XVI. Tokyo: Kadokawa shoten, 1959. With 26 illustrations.

——. "Toban shihai-ki no Tonkō" (Tun-huang under the Tibetans) 吐蕃支配期の敦煌 *TGK* 31:199–292 (March 1961), with 2 illustrations and 8 charts.

——. "Tonkō no sōniseki" (Lists of Buddhist Monks and Nuns in the Tun-huang Manuscripts) 敦煌の僧尼籍, *TGK* 29:285–338 (March 1959), with 4 photographs.

——. "The Tun-huang Manuscripts." In Leslie, Mackerras, and Wang.

——. "The Tunhuang Manuscripts—A General Description," parts 1 and 2, *Zinbun*, Memoirs of the Research Institute for Humanistic Studies 9:1–32 (1966), and 10:17–39 (1969).

Fujii Kiyoshi 藤井清. "Tōdai Shoku chihō ni okeru shomin to Bukkyō" (The People and Buddhism in Shu District in the T'ang Period) 唐代蜀地方に於ける庶民と佛教, *BS* 3.4:13–26 (December 1953).

Fujino Iwatomo 藤野岩友. *Chūgoku no bungaku to reizoku* [Literature and ritual customs of China] 中國の文學と禮俗. Tokyo: Kadokawa shoten, 1976. Especially pp. 152–184: "Chūgoku no minzoku bungei" [Folk literature of China] 中國の民俗文藝. Originally appeared in *Kokugakuin zasshi* [Journal of Kokugakuin University] 國學院雜誌 54.1 (April 1953).

Fukui, Fumimasa-Bunga. "Some Problems about the Origin of the Religious Lectures for Laymen, *su-chiang*." In *The Proceedings of the 27th International Congress of Orientalists* (1967). Ed. Denis Sinor. Wiesbaden: Otto Harrassowitz, 1971.

Fukui Fumimasa (Bunga) 福井文雅. "Tōdai zokkō gishiki no seiritsu o meguru sho mondai" (On the Structure and Times of Formation of Su-chiang [Lecture Ceremony Held by or for Laymen] in T'ang China) 唐代俗講儀式の成立をめぐる諸問題, *Taishō daigaku kenkyū kiyō; Bungaku-bu, Bukkyōgakubu* (Memoirs of Taisho University, The Departments of Literature and Buddhism) 大正大學研究紀要, 文學部·佛教學部54. 1968.

——. "Zokkō no imi ni tsuite" (Essential Meaning of the *su-chiang* in T'ang China) 俗講の意味について, *Firosofia* (*Philosophia*) フィロソフィア 53:51–64 (20 March 1968), with a postscript for M. Demiéville.

von Gabain, Annemarie. *Einführung in die Zentralasienkunde*. Darmstadt: Wissenschaftliche Buchgesellschaft, 1979.

Gabelentz, H. Conon de la. *Elémens de la grammaire Mandchoue*. Altenbourg: Comptoir de la littérature, 1832.

Gershevitch, Ilya. *A Grammar of Manichean Sogdian*. Publications of the Philological Society. Oxford: Basil Blackwell, 1954.

Giles, Lionel. "A Chinese Geographical Text of the Ninth Century," *BSOS* 6.4: 825–846 (1932), plus 4 plates.

——. "Dated Chinese Manuscripts in the Stein Collection." *BSOAS* 7.4:809–836 (1933–1935), plus 1 plate; 8.1:1–26 (1935–1937), plus 1 plate; 9.1:1–26 (1937–1939), plus 1 plate; 10.1:317–344 (1939–1942), plus 1 plate; and 11.1:148–173 (1943–1946).

——. *Six Centuries at Tunhuang*. A Short Account of the Stein Collection of Chinese Mss. in the British Museum. In W. Perceval Yetts, ed., China Society Sinological Series 2. London: The China Society, 1944.

——. "A Topographical Fragment from Tunhuang," *BSOS* 7.3:545–573 (1933–1935), plus 2 plates.

——. "Tun Huang Lu: Notes on the District of Tun-huang," *JRAS* 703–728 (July 1914), plus 3 plates.

Gimm, Martin, tr. *Das Yüeh-fu tsa-lu des Tuan An-chieh* [fl. 894–898]: *Studien zur Geschichte von Musik, Schauspiel und Tanz in der T'ang-Dynastie*. Wiesbaden: Harrassowitz, 1966.

Gnoli, Raniero, ed., with the assistance of T. Venkatacharya. *The Gilgit Manuscript of the Saṅghabhedavastu: Being the 17th and Last Section of the Vinaya of the Mūlasarvāstivādin*. Serie Orientale Roma, Vols. XLIX.1 and 2. Rome: Istituto Italiano per il Medio ed Estremo Oriente, 1977 and 1978.

Graham, Thomas E. "The Reconstruction of Popular Buddhism in Medieval China: Using Selected Pien-wen from Tun-huang." PhD dissertation, University of Iowa. Ann Arbor: Xerox University Microfilms, 1975.

Granoff, Phyllis. "Scholars and Wonder-Workers: Some Remarks on the Role of the Supernatural in Philosophical Contests in Vedānta Hagiographies," *JAOS* 105.3:459–467 (July–September 1985).

Gray, Basil. *Buddhist Cave Paintings at Tun-huang*. Photographs by J. B. Vincent. Chicago: University of Chicago Press, 1959.

Grousset, René. *Chinese Art and Culture*. Tr. Haakon Chevalier. New York: Orion, 1959. Originally published as *La Chine et son art*. Paris: Plon, 1951.

van Gulik, R. H. *Siddham: An Essay on the History of Sanskrit Studies in China and Japan*. Nagpur: International Academy of Indian Culture, 1956.

Gurevich, I. S. "Fragment Byan'ven' iz tsikla 'O Zhizni Budd'i'" *Kratkie Soobshcheniya* (Instituta Narodov Azii) 69:99–115 (1965), plus three plates.

——. "K Voprosu o Zhanre Nebuddiiskikh byan'ven' (na Materiale byan'ven' ob U Tsz'i-syue)." In *Dal'nii Vostok*. Moscow: Vostochnoi Literatur'i. 1961.

Hamilton, Clarence H. *Wei shih er shih lun* 唯識二十論 *or The Treatise in Twenty Stanzas on Representation-Only* by Vasubandhu 世親. Translated from the Chinese Version of Hsuan Tsang (玄奘), Tripiṭaka Master of the T'ang dynasty. American Oriental Series 13. New Haven: American Oriental Society, 1938.

Hamilton, James Russell, ed. and tr. *Le conte bouddhique du bon et du mauvais prince en version ouïgoure*. Mission Paul Pelliot, Documents conservés a la Bibliothèque nationale, III. Manuscrits ouïgours de Touen-Houang. Paris: Klincksieck, 1971.

——. *Les Ouighours à l'époque des Cinq Dynasties*. Paris: Presses Universitaires de France, 1955.

Han Tao-chao 韓道昭 (Chin 金). *Wu-yin lei-chü ssu-sheng p'ien-hai* [A compendium of the five sounds grouped according to classes and the four tones] 五音類聚四聲篇海. Published between 1575 and 1589.

Hanan, Patrick. *The Chinese Short Story: Studies in Dating, Authorship, and Composition*. Harvard-Yenching Institute Monograph Series 21. Cambridge: Harvard University Press, 1973.

——. *The Chinese Vernacular Story*. Cambridge: Harvard University Press, 1981.

——. "The Early Chinese Short Story: A Critical Theory in Outline," *HJAS* 27:168–207 (1967). Reprinted in Birch, *Genres*.

——. Letter of 28 September 1982.

——. "The Nature of Ling Meng-ch'u's Fiction." In Andrew Plaks, ed., *Chinese Narrative: Critical and Theoretical Essays*. Princeton: Princeton University Press, 1977.

——. "Sung and Yüan Vernacular Fiction: A Critique of Modern Methods of Dating," *HJAS*, 30:159–184 (1970).

Haneda Toru 羽田亨 and Paul Pelliot, eds. *Tonkō isho* [Lost works preserved at Tun-huang] 敦煌遺書. Shanghai: Tōa kōkyū-kai, 1926.

Hattori Katsuhiko 服部克彥. *Hokugi Rakuyō no shakai to bunka* [Society and culture of Lo-yang during the Northern Wei] 北魏洛陽の社會と文化. Kyoto: Minerva shobō, 1965.

——. *Zoku Hokugi Rakuyō no shakai to bunka* [Society and culture of Lo-yang during the Northern Wei, continued] 續北魏洛陽の社會と文化. Kyoto: Minerva shobō, 1968.

Hayakawa Mitsusaburō 早川光三郎. "Henbun ni tsunagaru Nihon shoden Chūgoku setsuwa" (Pien-wen and Chinese Legends as Told in Japan) 變文に繫がる日本所傳中國說話, *Tōkyō shinagaku hō* (Bulletin of Tokyo Sinological Society) 東京支那學報 6:53–68 (June 1960).

Henning, W. B. "Ein manichäisches Bet- und Beichtbuch." In his *Selected Papers*. 2 vols. Acta Iranica, series 2, Vols. V and VI. Teheran-Liège: Bibliothèque Pahlavi, 1977. Vol. I, pp. 417–557 (3–143). Originally appeared as *AKPAW* 10 (1936).

——. "Neue Materialen zur Geschichte des Manichäismus," *ZDMG* 90:1–18 (1936).

——. *Sogdica*. James G. Forlong Fund, Vol. XXI. London, 1940. As reprinted in the author's *Selected Papers*, II (see second entry above), with errata and addenda.

Hiang Ta. "Amendements au Pou T'ang-chou Tchang Yi-tch'ao tchouan de Lo Tchen-yu." In *Mélanges sinologiques*. Peking, 1951. For the Chinese version of this article, see HT.

——, ed. and intro. "Tun-huang ts'ung-ch'ao" (A Selection of Tun-huang Mss. Preserved in the National Library of Peiping) 敦煌叢抄, parts 1 and 2, *Kuo-li Pei-p'ing t'u-shu-kuan kuan k'an* (Bulletin of the National Library of Peking) 國立北平圖書館館刊 5.6:53–79 (November–December 1931) and 6.2:21–56 (March–April 1932).

Hinzler, H. I. R. *Bima Swarga in Balinese Wayang*. Verhandelingen van het Koninklijk Instituut voor Taal-, Land- en Volkenkunde 90. The Hague: Martinus Nijhoff, 1981.

Hirano Kenshō 平野顯照. "Beppon taishi jōdō henbun ni tsuite" (Another Text of the Tai tzu Cheng dao Pien wen) 別本太子成道變文について, *BBK*. plus English summary.

——. *Tōdai bungaku to Bukkyō no kenkyū* (Study on Literature and Buddhism in the T'ang Dynasty) 唐代文學と佛教の研究. Kyoto: Hōyū shoten, 1978

——. "Tonkō-bon kōkyōbun to Bukkyō kyōso to no kankei" ("Scripture-Lectures" in Tun-huang Mss. and Buddhist Sutra Commentaries)" 敦煌木講經文と佛教經疏との關係, *Ōtani gakuhō* (The Journal of Buddhology and Cultural Science) 大谷學報 40.2:21–32 (September 1960).

Ho Yuan 何薳 (Sung). *Ch'un-chu chi-wen* [Records of things heard by water's edge in spring] 春渚紀聞. In *Hsueh-chin t'ao yuan* [Seek the source of the Ford of Learning] 學津討源.

Horner, I. B., tr. *The Book of the Discipline* [*Vinayapiṭaka*]. 6 vols. London: H. Milford for Oxford University Press and L. Luzac, 1938–1966. Especially Vol. III (*Suttavibhaṅga*). Sacred Books of the Buddhists, Vol. XIII 1942; Vol. V (*Cullavagga*), 1952; and Vol. VI (*Parivāra*). Sacred Books of the Buddhists, Vol. XXV, 1966.

Hrdlička, Vera and Zdeněk. "On the Origins of 'Narrations Combined with Song,'" *New Orient* 3.4:116–119 (August 1962).

Hrdličková, Věra. "The First Translations of Buddhist Sūtras in Chinese Literature and Their Place in the Development of Storytelling," *ArchOr* 26.1:114–144 (1958).

——. "The Professional Training of Chinese Storytellers and the Storytellers' Guilds," *ArchOr* 33.2:225–248 (1965).

——. "Some Questions Connected with Tun-huang pien-wen," *ArchOr* 30.2:211–230 (1962).

——. *Tun-chuangské pien-weny o "Oddaném synovi Mu-lienovi"*. Prague: Universita Karlova, 1958. Summary in Russian and in English.

Hsi-ti 西諦 (pseud. of Cheng Chen-to 鄭振鐸). "Fo-ch'ü hsu-lu" [Catalog of

Buddhist cantos] 佛曲叙錄. *Chung-kuo wen-hsueh yen-chiu* [Studies of Chinese literature] 中國文學研究, ed. Cheng Chen-to. Special issue (13) of *HSYP* 17. Shanghai: Commercial Press, 1927.

Hsiang Ta 向達. *See also* Chueh-ming, Fang Hui, Hiang Ta, and abbreviated entries under HT.

——. "Chi Lun-tun so ts'ang te Tun-huang su-wen-hsueh" [Notes on popular literature from Tun-huang kept in London] 記倫敦所藏的敦煌俗文學. In HT.

——. "Kuan-yü 'Su-chiang k'ao' tsai shuo chi-chü hua fu-chi" [A few more words on "Examination of popular lectures" as an appendix] 關於俗講考再說幾句話附記, *TSCK* 21. *TCTKP* (June [?] 1947). Cited in Wu Hsiao-ling's article of the same year.

——. "Lo Shu-yen 'Pu T'ang-shu Chang I-ch'ao chuan' pu-cheng" [Additions and corrections to Lo Chen-yü's "Additions to the biography of Chang I-ch'ao in the T'ang history"] 羅叔言「補唐書張議潮傳」補正. In HT. Also see Hiang Ta. "Amendements au Pou T'ang-chou Tchang Yi-tch'ao tchouan de Lo Tchen-yu." In *Mélanges Sinologiques*. Peking, 1951.

——. "Lun T'ang-tai Fo-ch'ü" [On Buddhist cantos of the T'ang period] 論唐代佛曲. In HT. Originally appeared in *HSYP* 20.10:1579–1588 (10 October 1929).

——. "Lun-tun so ts'ang Tun-huang chüan-tzu ching-yen mu-lu" [Catalog of Tun-huang scrolls I have seen that are preserved in London] 倫敦所藏敦煌卷子經眼目錄. In HT.

——. "Pu-shuo T'ang-tai su-chiang erh-san shih chien ta Chou I-liang Kuan Te-tung liang hsien-sheng" [Two or three additional matters concerning the "Popular lectures" of the T'ang dynasty as well as a reply to Mssrs. Chou I-liang and Kuan Te-tung] 補說唐代俗講二三事兼答周一良關德棟兩先生, *TSCK* 18. *TCTKP* (14 May 1947).

——. "T'ang-tai su-chiang k'ao" [An examination of the popular lectures of the T'ang dynasty] 唐代俗講考. In HT, plus 3 plates. Originally appeared in *Wen-shih tsa-chih* [Literature and history magazine] 文史雜誌, special issue devoted to T'ang culture 3.9–10:40–60 (May 1944). This is a greatly expanded and revised version of the article by the same title that appeared in *Yen-ching hsueh-pao* (Yenching Journal of Chinese Studies) 燕京學報 16:119–132 (December 1934) (English title given as "Story-telling in the Tang Dynasty").

——. "Tun-huang so-ch'u su-chiang wen-hsueh tso-p'in mu-lu" [Catalog of the literature of popular lectures which came from Tun-huang] 敦煌所出俗講文學作品目錄. Appendix 2 in "T'ang-tai su-chiang k'ao" [An examination of popular lectures of the T'ang dynasty] 唐代俗講考, *Wen-shih tsa-chih* [Literature and history magazine] 文史雜誌 3.9–10:59–60 (May 1944).

Hsieh Chih-liu 謝稚柳. *Tun-huang i-shu hsu-lu* [Catalog of art at Tun-huang] 敦煌藝術叙錄. Shanghai. Shanghai ch'u-pan kung-ssu, 1955.

Hsieh Ch'un-p'in 謝春聘. *Tun-huang chiang-ching pien-wen chien* [Notes on Tun-huang *chiang-ching* and *pien-wen*] 敦煌講經變文箋. Taipei: T'ien-i ch'u-pan-she, 1975.

Hsieh Hai-p'ing 謝海平. *Chiang-shih hsing chih pien-wen yen-chiu* [Research on historical *pien-wen*] 講史性之變文研究. Taipei: T'ien-i ch'u-pan-she, 1970. Also Taipei: Chia-hsin shui-ni kung-ssu wen-hua chi-chin-hui, 1973.

Hsing-chün 行均 (fl. 997). *Lung-k'an shou-chien* [Dragon niche handbook] 龍龕手鑑 *SPTK*.

Hsu, Winnifred Wang-hua W. Tung. "A Study of Four Historical *pien-wen* Stories." PhD dissertation, Ohio State University, 1984.

Hsu Chia-jui 徐嘉瑞. *Chin-ku wen-hsueh kai-lun* [Outline of literature since the Middle Ages] 近古文學概論. Shanghai: Pei-hsin shu-chü, 1947.

——. "Tun-huang Fo-ch'ü" [Buddhist cantos from Tun-huang] 敦煌佛曲. In his *Chin-ku wen-hsueh kai-lun*.

Hsu Chia-ling 徐嘉齡. "Wo tui pien-wen te chi-tien ch'u-pu jen-shih" [My preliminary views on several points regarding *pien-wen*] 我對變文的幾點初步認識. In *Wen-hsueh i-ch'an hsuan-chi* [Literary heritage anthology] 文學遺產選集 3. Peking: Chung-hua shu-chü, 1960. Originally appeared in *LitHer* 122 (16 September 1956).

Hsu Fu 徐復. "P'ing Tun-huang pien-wen tzu-i t'ung-shih, tseng-ting pen" [A review of the expanded and revised edition of *Comprehensive Explanations of the Meanings of Characters in Tun-huang pien-wen*] 評《敦煌變文字義通釋》(增訂本), *CKYW*, 10–11 (cumulative 109): 88–90 (22 November 1961).

——. "Tun-huang pien-wen tz'u-yü yen-chiu" [Research into the language of Tun-huang *pien-wen*] 敦煌變文詞語研究, *CKYW*, 8 (cumulative 107): 29–34 (22 August 1961).

Hsu Kuo-lin 許國霖. *Tun-huang shih-shih hsieh-ching t'i-chi yü Tun-huang tsa-lu* [Inscriptions and colophons of manuscript scriptures from the Tun-huang stone chamber and register of assorted subjects related to Tun-huang] 敦煌石室寫經題記與敦煌雜錄. Shanghai: Commercial Press, 1937.

Hsu T'iao-fu 徐調孚. "Chiang-ch'ang wen-hsueh te yuan-tsu—'pa hsiang pien-wen' chi ch'i-t'a" [The distant ancestor of prosimetric literature, 'The eight aspects *pien-wen*,' and so forth] 講唱文學的遠祖—「八相變文」及其他, *Chung hsueh-sheng* [The high-school student magazine] 中學生 189: 55–60 (1 July 1947). Subtitled "Chung-kuo wen-hsueh ming-chu chiang-hua chih liu" [Lectures on famous works of Chinese literature 6] 中國文學名著講話之六.

Hsueh Chao-yun 薛昭蘊 (T'ang). *Huan-ying chuan* [Biographies of illusionists] 幻影傳. In. *TTTS*.

Hu Chu-an 胡竹安. "Tun-huang pien-wen chung te shuang-yin lien-tz'u" [Paired rhyming conjunctions in the *pien-wen* from Tun-huang] 敦煌變文中的雙音連詞, *CKYW*, 10–11 (cumulative 109): 41–46 (October–November 1961).

Hu Shih 胡適. *Pai-hua wen-hsueh shih* [A history of Chinese vernacular literature] 白話文學史. Vol. I. 2nd ed. Shanghai: Commercial Press, 1934. 1st ed., 1928.

Hu Shih-ying 胡士瑩. "T'ang-tai min-chien, kung-t'ing, ssu-yüan chung te shuo-hua" [Storytelling among the people, in the palaces, and in the monasteries during the T'ang period] 唐代民間, 宮廷, 寺院中的說話, *LitHer* 456 (24 March 1963).

Hu Tzu 胡仔 (Sung). *T'iao-hsi yü-yin ts'ung-hua* [Collected tale of the fisherman hermit from Trumpet Creeper Creek] 苕溪漁隱叢話. In TsSCC.

Huang Hsiu-fu 黃休復 (fl. 1001–1006). *Mao-t'ing k'o-hua* [Guest talks from the Thatched Pavilion] 茅亭客話. In *Lin-lang mi-shih ts'ung-shu* [Collectanea from the secret room of gems] 琳瑯秘室叢書.

Hui-li. *The Life of Hsuan-tsang, The Tripiṭaka-Master of the Great Tzun En Monastery*. Tr. Li Yung-hsi. Peking: The Chinese Buddhist Association, 1959.

Hui-li 慧立 and Yen-ts'ung 彥悰. *Ta tz'u-en ssu san-tsang fa-shih chuan* [Biography of Tripiṭaka, Dharma Master of the Temple of Great Compassion and Grace] 大慈恩寺三藏法師傳. Chung-wai chiao-t'ung shih-chi ts'ung-k'an [Historical materials for the study of communication between China and foreign countries] 中外交通史籍叢刊. Peking: Chung-hua shu-chü, 1983.

Hulsewé, A. F. P., with an introduction by M. A. N. Loewe. *China in Central Asia: The Early Stage: 125 B.C.–A.D. 23.* An Annotated Translation of Chapters 61 and 96 of the History of the Former Han Dynasty. Sinica Leidensia, Institutum Sinologicum Lugduno Batavum 14. Leiden: E. J. Brill, 1979.

Hung Ch'eng 洪誠. "P'ing Chiang Li-hung *Tun-huang pien-wen tzu-i t'ung-shih*" [A review of Chiang Li-hung's comprehensive explanations of the meanings of characters in Tun-huang *pien-wen*] 評蔣禮鴻《敦煌變文字義通釋》, *LitHer* 282 (11 October 1959).

Huo Shih-hsiu 霍世休. "Wang Chao-chün te ku-shih tsai Chung-kuo wen-hsueh shang te yen-pien" [The evolution of the story of Wang Chao-chün in Chinese literature] 王昭君的故事在中國文學上的演變, *Ch'ing-hua Chung-kuo wen-hsueh hui yueh-k'an* [The Tsing Hua University Chinese Literature Association monthly] 清華中國文學會月刊 1.4:13–29 (15 August 1931).

Hurvitz, Leon, tr. *Scripture of the Lotus Blossom of the Fine Dharma*. New York: Columbia University Press, 1976.

Huzieda, A. (Fujieda Akira) 藤枝晃. "Sashū kigigun setsudoshi shimatsu" (A History of the Régime of the *Kuei-i-chün* at Tun-huang, 851-c. 1050 A.D.) 沙州歸義軍節度使始末, Parts 1–4, *TGK* (1) 12.3:58–98 (December 1941); (2) 12.4:42–75 (March 1942); (3) 13.1:63–95 (June 1942), with one photograph; (4) 13.2:46–98 (January 1943).

Ienaga Saburō 家永三郎. "Jigoku-hen ni tsuite" [On hell transformations] 地獄變に就いて, *RK* 76.5:1–16 (November 1940), with one illustration.

——. "Jigoku-hen to rikudō-e" [Hell transformations and pictures of the six paths] 地獄變と六道繪. In *Jōdai Bukkyō shisōshi kenkyū* [Studies on the history of ancient Buddhist philosophy] 上代佛教思想史研究. Kyoto: Hōzōkan, 1966. With 3 illustrations. Originally appeared in *BK* 150 (October 1948).

Ikeda On 池田溫. "Tonkō" [Tun-huang] 敦煌, *Tō Ajia sekai no henbō* [The changing face of the world of East Asia] 東アジア世界の變貌. Sekai no rekishi (Historia Mundi) 世界の歷史 6. Tokyo: Chikuma shobō, 1961.

Ingalls, Daniel H. H. "Sanskrit Poetry and Sanskrit Poetics." In Frenz and Anderson, eds., *Indiana Conference*.

Inoue Yasushi. *Tun-huang: A Novel*. Tr. Jean Oda Moy. Tokyo, New York, and San Francisco: Kodansha, 1978.

Iriya Yoshitaka 入矢義高. Assisted by Furuta Kazuhiro 古田和弘 and Andō Tomonobu 安藤智信. *Bukkyō bungaku shū* [A collection of Buddhist literature] 佛教文學集. Chūgoku koten bungaku taikei [Chinese classical literature series] 中國古典文學大系 60. Tokyo: Heibonsha, 1975.

——. "Henbun nisoku" (Two Materials of *Bien Wen*) 變文二則. In *Torii Hisayasu sensei kakō kinen ronshū—Chūgoku no gengo to bungaku* (Studies in Chinese Literature and Language Dedicated to Professor Torii Hisayasu on His Sixty-First Birthday) 鳥居久靖先生華甲記念論集(中國の言語と文學). Nara: Tenri daigaku, 1972.

——, et al., trs. and annots. *Rakuyō garan ki·Suikei chū* (*shō*) [Notes on monasteries of Loyang; Notes on the *Water Classic*] 洛陽伽藍記·水經注(抄). Chūgoku koten bungaku taikei [Chinese classical literature series] 中國古典文學大系 21. Tokyo: Heibonsha, 1974.

——. Review of Arthur Waley: *Tonkō no kayō to setsuwa* (Ballads and Stories from Tun-huang)「ウェーリー・譯注敦煌の歌謠と說話」, *CBH* 16:115–125 (April 1962).

——. Review of Chiang Li-hung 蔣禮鴻, *Tun-huang pien-wen tzu-i t'ung-shih* [Comprehensive explanations of the meanings of characters in Tun-huang *pien-wen*]「敦煌變文字義通釋」, *CBH* 11:175–180 (October 1959).

——. Review of Chou Shao-liang 周紹良, *Tun-huang pien-wen hui-lu* (A Collective Anthology of "Popularizations" from Tun-huang)「敦煌變文彙錄」, *CBH* 5:122–145 (October 1956).

——. Review of Kanaoka Shōkō, *Tonkō shutsudo bungaku bunken bunrui mokuruku* and *Tonkō no bungaku*, *CBH* 23:93–98 (October 1972).

——, comp. "*Tonkō henbun shū*" *kōgo goi sakuin* [Index of colloquial expressions in Tun-huang *pien-wen chi*]「敦煌變文集」口語語彙索引. Privately printed, 1961. Greatly expanded and revised, 1987.

Iwamoto Yutaka 岩本裕. *Bukkyō setsuwa kenkyū* [Studies of Buddhist narratives] 佛教說話研究. Vol. II. Tokyo: Kaimei shoin, 1978.

——. "Engi no bungaku" (On "*Engi* Literature") 緣起の文學, *Tōhōgaku* (Eastern Studies) 東方學 30:92–101 (July 1965), plus English summary.

——. *Jigoku meguri no bungaku* [Literature of journeys through hell] 地獄めぐりの文學. Bukkyō setsuwa kenkyū [Studies of Buddhist narratives] 佛教說話研究. Vol. IV. Tokyo: Kaimei shoin, 1979.

——. *Mokuren densetsu to urabon* [The story of Maudgalyāyana and the festival for hungry ghosts] 目連傳說と盂蘭盆. Kyoto: Hōzōkan, 1968.

——. "Mokuren 'jigoku meguri' setsuwa no genryū (Die Quelle der Legende von Maudgalyāyana's Wanderung in Hades)" [On the origins of the legend of Maudgalyāyana's tour of hell] 目連「地獄めぐり」說話の源流, *BBK* 5, plus German summary.

——. "Mokuren kyūbo densetsu kō" [A study on the legend of Maudgalyāyana's rescue of his mother] 目蓮救母傳說攷. *Kokugo·kokubun* [Japanese language and literature] 國語國文 35.9:1–22 (September 1966).

Jacob, Georg. "Zur Geschichte des Schattenspiels," *Keleti Szemle* 1:233–236 (1900).

Jan Yun-hua, ed., tr., annot., and intro. *A Chronicle of Buddhism in China—581–960 A.D.* Translations from Monk Chih-p'an's *Fo-tsu t'ung-chi*. Santiniketan: Visva-Bharati, 1966.

Jao Tsung-i 饒宗頤. "Ts'ung 'Shan pien' lun pien-wen yü t'u-hui chih kuan-hsi" (On the Relationship between the Pien-wên and the Painting, According to the Sāma-jataka Pien) 從"睒變"論變文與圖繪之關係. *Ikeda Suetoshi hakushi koki kinen Tōyōgaku ronshū* (Oriental Studies: Essays and Studies Presented to Dr. Ikeda Suetoshi in Honor of His Seventieth Birthday) 池田末利博士古稀記念東洋學論集, ed. Ikeda Suetoshi hakushi koki kinen jigyōkai jikkō iin [Executive Board of the Committee for the Commemoration of the Seventieh Birthday of Dr. Ikeda Suetoshi] 池田末利博士古稀記念事業會實行委員. Hiroshima: Ikeda Suetoshi hakushi koki kinen jigyōkai, 1980.

Jao Tsong-yi and Paul Demiéville. *Airs de Touen-houang: Touen-houang k'iu. Textes a chanter des VIIIe–Xe siècles*. Mission Paul Pelliot. Documents conservés a la Bibliothèque Nationale 2. Paris: Editions du Centre National de la recherche scientifique, 1971.

Jao Tsong-yi, Pierre Ryckmans, and Paul Demiéville. *Peintures monochromes de Dunhuang* (*Dunhuang Baihua*). École française d'Extrême-Orient, Mémoire archéologique 13. Paris: École française d'Extrême-Orient, 1978.

Jäschke, H. A. *A Tibetan-English Dictionary*. London: Kegan, Paul, Trench, and Trübner, 1934.

Jaworski, Jan. "Notes sur l'ancienne littérature populaire en Chine," *Rocznik Orjentalistyczny* 12:181–193 (1936).

Jen Erh-pei 任二北. *Tun-huang ch'ü chiao-lu* [Tun-huang cantos collated] 敦煌曲校錄. Shanghai: Shanghai wen-i lien-ho ch'u-pan-she, 1955.

——. *Tun-huang ch'ü ch'u-t'an* [Initial investigation of Tun-huang cantos] 敦煌曲初探. Shanghai: Shanghai wen-i lien-ho ch'u-pan-she, 1954.

Jen Pan-t'ang 任半塘 (same person as Jen Erh-pei). *T'ang hsi-nung* [T'ang theatricals] 唐戲弄. Peking: Tso-chia ch'u-pan-she, 1958.

Jenner, W. J. G., tr. and intro. *Memories of Loyang: Yang Hsüan-chih and the Lost Capital (493–534)*. Oxford: Clarendon, 1981.

Johnson, David. "The Wu Tzu-hsü *pien-wen* and Its Sources," *HJAS* 40.1:93–156 (June 1980) and 40.2:465–505 (December 1980).

Joshi, Om Prakash. *Painted Folklore and Folklore Painters of India* (*A Study with Reference to Rajasthan*). Delhi: Concept Publishing Company, 1976.

Julien, Stanislas, tr. *Histoire de la Vie de Hiouen-thsang*. Paris: L'Imprimerie Impériale, 1853.

Kadokawa shoten henshūbu [Editorial office of Kadokawa bookstore] 角川書店編集部. *Genji monogatari emaki* [Illustrated scroll of *The Tale of Genji*] 源氏物語繪卷. Nihon emakimono zenshū [Japanese picture scrolls] 日本繪卷物全集, Vol. I. Tokyo: Kadokawa shoten, 1958.

——. *Kegon engi* (Legends Concerning the Origin of Kegon Buddhism) 華嚴縁起. Nihon emakimono zenshū [Japanese picture scrolls] 日本繪卷物全集. Vol. VII. Tokyo: Kadokawa shoten, 1959.

Kaji Tetsujō 加地哲定. *Chūgoku Bukkyō bungaku kenkyū* [Studies on Chinese Buddhist literature] 中國佛教文學研究. Kyoto: Kōyasan daigaku bungaku-bu Chūgoku tetsugaku kenkyū-shitsu, 1965. Rev. ed. Tokyo: Dōhō sha, 1979.

——. "Zoku-bungaku to shite no Bukkyō bungaku" [Buddhist literature as popular literature] 俗文學としての佛教文學. In *Chūgoku Bukkyō bungaku kenkyū*.

Kallgren, Gerty. "Studies in Sung Time Colloquial Chinese as Revealed in Chu Hsi's Ts'üanshu," *BMFEA* 30:1–165 (1958).

Kameta Tsutomu 龜田孜. *Bukkyō setsuwa kai no kenkyū* [Studies on Buddhist narrative paintings] 佛教說話繪の研究. Tokyo: Tokyo bijutsu, 1979.

——, comp. List of identifying inscriptions of scenes on the *Kegon engi* scrolls. Kadokawa shoten, ed., *Kegon engi*.

Kanaoka Shōkō 金岡照光. "Chūgoku minkan ni okeru Mokuren setsuwa no seikaku" (The Folklore on Mu Lien in China) 中國民間における目連說話の性格, *Bukkyō shigaku* (The Journal of the History of Buddhism) 佛教史學 7.4:16–37 (224–245) (February 1959).

——. "Henbun" [*Pien-wen*] 變文. In *Chūgoku bunka sōsho, bungaku shi* [Chinese culture collectanea, history of literature] 中國文化叢書 Vol. V. Tokyo: Daishūkan shoten, 1968.

——. "Hen, hensō, henbun satsuki" (Some Notes on *Pien*, *Pien-Hsiang*, and *Pien-Wên*) 變·變相·變文札記. *Tōyō daigaku bungaku bu kiyō* 30, Bukkyōgaku ka, Chūgoku tetsugaku bungaku ka hen II, *Tōyōgaku ronsō* (Bulletin of the Faculty of Letters, Toyo University, Buddhology Section, Vol. III on Chinese Philosophy and Literature, *Bulletin of Orientology*) 東洋大學文學部紀要 30:1–33 佛教學科,中國哲學文學科篇 II,東洋學論叢 (March 1977).

——. "Hen to henbun: Tonkō no etoki" [*Pien* and *pien-wen*: Painting recitation of Tun-huang] 變と變文:敦煌の繪解き. In *KKK*.

——. "Mokuren henbun" [Maudgalyāyana *pien-wen*] 目連變文. In *Chūgoku no meicho* [Famous works of Chinese literature] 中國の名著. Tokyo: Keisō shobō, 1961.

——. "On the Word '*Pien*,'" *Tōyō University Asian Studies* 1:15–23 (1961).

——. "Ōza kō" (A Study on Ya-tso) 押座考, *Tōyō daigaku kiyō bungakubu hen* (Bulletin of Toyo University) 東洋大學紀要文學部篇 18:41–69 (September 1964).

——. "Sairon Bunjo hōshi—zokkō no sho yōsō—" [Another discussion of the Dharma Master Wen-hsu—Aspects of popular lectures] 再論文漵法師—俗講の諸樣相—, *Tōyō-gaku kenkyū* [Oriental studies] 東洋學硏究 3:69–84 (March 1969).

——. "Tonkō-bon 'Hassō ōzabun' kōshaku" (Critical Interpretation on "*Pa-hsiang Ya-tso-wen*" excavated in Tun-huang) 敦煌本八相押座文校釋, *Tōhō shūkyō* (The Journal of Eastern Religions) 東方宗教 32:1–27 (November 1968), plus English summary.

——. *Tonkō no bungaku* [Literature of Tun-huang] 敦煌の文學. Tokyo: Ōkura shuppan, 1971.

——. *Tonkō no emonogatari* [Illustrated tales from Tun-huang] 敦煌の繪物語. Tokyo: Tōhō shoten, 1981.

——. *Tonkō no minshū—sono seikatsu to shisō—* [The people of Tun-huang—Their lives and ideas] 敦煌の民衆—その生活と思想. Tōyōjin no kōdō to shisō [Behavior and thought of Orientals] 東洋人の行動と思想, Vol. VIII. Tokyo: Hyōronsha, 1972.

Kanda Kiichirō 神田喜一郎, ed. *Tonkō-bon monzen chū* [Tun-huang edition of the annotated literary selections] 敦煌本文選注, by Hsiao T'ung 蕭統 (501–531). Tokyo: Eisei bundo, 1965.

——. *Tonkō-gaku gojū nen* [Fifty years of Tun-huang studies] 敦煌學五十年. Tokyo: Nigensha, 1960.

K'ang-hsi tzu-tien [K'ang-hsi dictionary of single characters] 康熙字典, pref. 1716. N.p.: Chung-hua shu-chü, 1958. Photoreprint of T'ung-wen shu-chü ed.

Kanō Naoki 狩野直喜. "Chung-kuo su-wen-hsueh shih yen-chiu te ts'ai-liao" [Materials for research on the history of Chinese popular literature] 中國俗文學史研究底材料. Tr. Wang Fu-ch'üan. In WFC.

——. "Shina zokubungaku shi kenkyū no zairyō" [Materials for the history of Chinese popular literature] 支那俗文學史の材料, parts 1 and 2, *Geibun* [Literature] 藝文 7.1:104–109 (January 1916) and 7.3:95–102 (March 1916). Also in *Shinagaku bunsō* [Collection of essays on Chinese studies] 支那學文藪. Tokyo: Kōbundō shobō, 1930.

Katō, Bunnō, Yoshirō Tamura, and Kōjirō Miyasaka, trs.; W. E. Soothill, Wilhelm Schiffer, and Pier P. Del Campana, revs. *The Threefold Lotus Sutra*. New York and Tokyo: Weatherhill/Kosei, 1975. 2nd printing, 1975.

Kawaguchi Hisao 川口久雄. "Arthur Waley no shōgai o tsuranuku Tonkō kenkyū" [Tun-huang studies, a lifelong interest of Arthur Waley] アーサー・ウェイリーの生涯を貫く敦煌研究. In *Tiger*. With 3 photographs.

——. "Etoki no rutsu Tonkō" [The roots of picture explanations—Tun-huang] 繪解きのルーツ敦煌, parts 1 and 2, *Asahi shinbun* [Morning sun news] 朝日新聞, evening ed. (20 February 1978), p. 5 and (21 February 1978), p. 5.

——. *Etoki no sekai—Tonko kara no kage* [The world of picture storytelling: Reflections from Tun-huang] 繪解きの世界—敦煌からの影—. Tokyo: Meiji shoin, 1981.

——. "Hasshō jōdo henbun to *Konjaku monogatari shū* butsuden setsuwa—wagakuni setsuwa bungaku no enhen to Tonkō shiryō—(The "Touen-Houang Pien-Wen" and their influence on the Japanese Literature with special reference to "Pahsiang-Chengtao Pien-Wên," the tales of Gautama's biography in the "Konzyaku-Monogatari-Syū" and the variations of their musical and dramatic performance) 八相成道變文と今昔物語集佛傳說話—我が國說話文學の演變と敦煌資料—. *KDHR* 4:1–36 (1956) plus 7 figures on 2 plates.

——. "Kegon engi no setsuwa" [Storytelling aspects of the legends concerning the origin of Kegon Buddhism] 華嚴緣起の說話. Kadokawa shoten, *Kegon Engi*.

——. "Setsuwa yori gigaku e—Tonkō henbun no seikaku to Nihon bungaku—(From Narrative to Drama—On the Relationship between the Character of Tun-huang *Pien-wen* and Japanese Literature—) 說話より戲劇へ—敦煌變文の性格と日本文學—. *KDHR* 12:1–11 (1964).

——. "Soviet ni aru Tonkō shiryō—Nippon bungaku to no kankei—" [Tun-huang materials in USSR—Their relationship to Japanese literature] ソヴェートにある敦煌資料—日本文學との關係—. *Bungaku* [Literature] 文學 38.12:113–118 (December 1970).

——. "Tonkō-bon Shunshi henbun, Tōei henbun to wagakuni setsuwa bungaku" (A Study on the Traditional Legends of the Shun Tzu *Pien-wen* and the Tung Yung *Pien-wen* from Tun-huang and the Relevant Materials Quoted in Japanese Popular Literature) 敦煌本舜子變文·董永變文と我が國說話文學. *Tōhōgaku* (Eastern Studies) 東方學 40:64–81 (September 1970), with 4 photographs.

——. "Tonkō henbun no seikaku to Nihon bungaku—etoki no sekai—[The nature of Tun-huang *pien-wen* and Japanese literature—the world of picture explanations—]. 敦煌變文の性格と日本文學—繪解きの世界—, *Nihon bungaku* [Japanese literature] 日本文學 12.10:27–41 (761–765) (October 1963), with one photograph.

——. "Tonkō henbun no sozai to Nihon bungaku—Mokuren henbun, Gōma henbun—" (The "*Tun huang pien-wên*" and Their Influence on Japanese Literature, with Special Reference to "*Mu-lien pien-wên*" and "*Hsiang-mo pien-wên*") 敦煌變文の素材と日本文學—目蓮變文,降魔變文—, *Nippon-chūgoku-gakkai-hō* (Bulletin of the Sinological Society of Japan) 日本中國學會報 8: 116–133 (October 1956), with three photographs.

——. "Tonkō henbun no sozai to Nihon bungaku—Mo Kyōnyo setsuwa to kigi shinwa—" (The Materials of Tun-huang *Pien-wen* and Japanese Literature.—On the Relationship between the Chinese Tales of Mêng Chiang-nü and the Japanese Mythologies of Kojiki and Nihonshoki—) 敦煌變文の素材と日本文學—孟姜女說話と記紀神話—, *KDHR* 13:1–11 (1965).

——. "Tonkō henbun no sozai to Nihon bungaku—So metsu Kan kō O Ryō hen, So Bu Ri Ryo shitsubetsushi to waga senki bungaku—" (The Materials of Pien-wen Discovered in the Touen-houang Cave in China and their Influence on Japanese Literature) 敦煌變文の素材と日本文學—楚滅漢興王陵變;蘇武李陵執別詞とわが戰記文學—. *KDHR* 3:16–31 (1955).

——. "Tonkō henbun no sozai to Nihon bungaku—Tō Taisō nyūmeiki to Kitano tenjin engi—" (Tun-huang Narrative Story and Japanese Narrative Literature—The Story of the T'ang Emperor T'ai Tsung in Hell and the Story of Sugawara Michizane's Deified Spirit—) 敦煌變文の素材と日本文學—唐太宗入冥記と北野天神緣起—. *BBK*, Vol. V, plus English summary.

——. "Tonkō henbun no seikaku to Nihon bungaku—Tonkō henbun no gainen—" [The nature of Tun-huang *pien-wen* and Japanese literature—the concept of Tun-huang *pien-wen*—] 敦煌變文の性格と日本文學—敦煌變文の概念—. *Kanbun kyoshitsu* [The Chinese literature classroom] 漢文教室 50: 1–8 (September 1960).

Kelly, Stephen T. "Homeric Metrics and the Nature of Greek Proto-Epic." Bowdoin Graduate Prize Essay at Harvard University, 1975.

Kern, H., tr. *Saddharma-Puṇḍarīka or the Lotus of the True Law*. New York: Dover, 1963. Republication of Vol. XXI of The Sacred Books of the East. Oxford: Clarendon Press, 1884.

—— and Bunyiu Nanjio, eds. *Saddharmapuṇḍarīka*. Bibliotheca Buddhica 10. St. Petersburg: Imprimerie de l'Académie Impériale des Sciences, 1912.

Knechtges, David R. Review of W. J. G. Jenner, *Memories of Loyang*, *JAOS* 104.2:347–349 (1984).

——. "Whither the Asper?" *CLEAR* 1.2:271–272 (July 1979).

Kōza Tonkō [Lectures on Tun-huang] 講座敦煌. A series of collections of scholarly essays by eminent Japanese Tun-huang specialists in 13 vols. Tokyo: Daitō shuppansha, 1980 and continuing.

I. Enoki Kazuo 榎一雄, ed. *Tonkō no shizen to genjō* [Tun-huang's natural surroundings and present state of affairs] 敦煌の自然と現狀.

II. Enoki Kazuo, ed. *Tonkō no rekishi* [History of Tun-huang] 敦煌の歷史.

III. Ikeda On 池田溫, ed. *Tonkō no shakai* [Tun-huang society] 敦煌の社會.

IV. Akiyama Terukazu 秋山光和, ed. *Tonkō no bijutsu* [Tun-huang art] 敦煌の美術.

V. Ikeda On, ed. *Tonkō kanbun bunken* [Tun-huang documents in Chinese] 敦煌漢文文獻.

VI. Yamaguchi Zuihō 山口瑞鳳, ed. *Tonkō kogo bunken* [Tun-huang documents in Tibetan and Altaic languages] 敦煌胡語文獻.

VII. Makita Tairyō 牧田諦亮, ed. *Tonkō butten to Chūgoku Bukkyō* [Tun-huang Buddhist texts and Chinese Buddhism] 敦煌佛典と中國佛教.

VIII. Shinohara Hisao 篠原壽雄 and Tanaka Ryōshō 田中良昭, eds. *Tonkō butten to zen* [Tun-huang Buddhist texts and Zen] 敦煌佛典と禪.

IX. Fukui Fumimasa (Bunga) 福井文雅, ed. *Tonkō Bukkyō to Chūgoku bunka* [Tun-huang Buddhism and Chinese culture] 敦煌佛教と中國文化.

X. Yoshioka Yoshitoyo (Gihō) 吉岡義豊, ed. *Tonkō to Chūgoku Dokyō* [Tun-huang and Chinese Taoism] 敦煌と中國道教.

XI. Kanaoka Shōkō 金岡照光, ed. *Tonkō no bungaku to gengo* [Tun-huang literature and language] 敦煌の文學と言語.

XII. Editorial Committee, ed. *Tonkōgaku no genjō to tenbō* [Present state of affairs of and outlook for Tun-huang studies] 敦煌學の現狀と展望.

XIII. Kanaoka Shōkō, ed. *Tonkō handobukku* [Tun-huang handbook] 敦煌ハンドブック.

Ku Huai 谷懷. "Ta-chung wen-i yü k'ou-yü-shih—ts'ung 'pien-wen' t'an tao shuo-pu" [Mass literature and oral poetry—A talk on the popular novel from the point of departure of *pien-wen*] 大衆文藝與口語詩—從「變文」談到說部. In his *K'ou-yü wen-i ts'ung-t'an* [Collected talks on oral literature] 口語文藝叢談. Taipei: Bodhi wen-i ch'u-pan-she, 1960.

Ku Yeh-wang 顧野王 (519–581). *Yü-p'ien* [Jade leaves] 玉篇. 1604 recutting in Japan of 1366 Nan-shan shu-yuan ed.

Kuan Chün-che 關俊哲. *Pei-ching p'i-ying-hsi* [Peking shadow-plays] 北京皮影戲. Peking (?): Peking ch'u-pan-she, 1959.

Kuan Te-tung 關德棟. "Ch'ou-nü yuan-ch'i ku-shih te ken-chü [The source of the story on karmic affinities of the ugly girl] 醜女緣起故事的根據. In his *Ch'ü-i lun-chi*, *q.v.* Originally appeared in *SWH* 9. *SCD* (19 December 1947).

——. *Ch'ü-i lun-chi* [Collected essays on song arts] 曲藝論集. Peking: Chung hua shu-chü, 1960, 2nd printing. 1st ed. 1958.

——. Letter of March 14, 1985.

——. "Lueh shuo 'pien' tzu te lai-yuan" [A brief discussion of the origin of the word *pien*] 略說"變"字的來源. In his *Ch'ü-i lun-chi*. Originally appeared in *T'ung-su wen-hsueh* [Popular literature] 通俗文學 25. *Shanghai ta wan-pao* [Shanghai evening news] 上海大晚報 (14 April 1947).

——. "Pien-wen mu" [*Pien-wen* catalog] 變文目. In his *Ch'ü-i lun-chi*. Originally appeared in *SWH* 64. *SCD* (date uncertain, probably around 23 April 1948).

——. "T'an 'pien-wen' " [Discussion on *pien-wen*] 談「變文」. In *BCL*. Originally appeared in *Chüeh-ch'ün chou-k'an* [Wake the masses weekly] 覺羣周刊 1.1 and 9.11 (1964 [?] (These publication data not verified). Rpt in *LWL*, Vol. I.

——. "Tu T'ang-tai su-chiang k'ao te shang-ch'ueh" [A consideration of the notice "On reading the article 'An examination of popular lectures during the T'ang period' "] 讀唐代俗講考的商榷, *TSCK* 15. *TCTKP* (20 April 1947).

Kuo Tsai-i 郭在貽. "Tun-huang pien-wen chiao-k'an shih-i hsu pu" [A continuation of supplements to the collations and remedying of deficiencies in Tun-huang *pien-wen*] 敦煌變文校勘拾遺續補, *Hang-chou ta-hsueh hsueh-pao* (Journal of Hangzhou University) 杭州大學學報 13.3:41–47 (September 1983).

Kuo Wei-ch'ü 郭味蕖. *Chung-kuo pan-hua shih-lueh* [A concise history of wood-block engravings in China] 中國版畫史略. Peking: Chao-hua mei-shu ch'u-pan-she, 1962.

Kuraishi Takeshiro 倉石武四郎. "Hsieh tsai 'Mu-lien pien-wen' chieh-shao chih hou" [Written after an introduction to the Maudgalyāyana *pien-wen*] 寫在「目連變文」介紹之後. Tr. Wang Fu-ch'üan 汪馥泉. In WFC.

——. " 'Mokuren henbun' shōkai no ato ni" [After the introduction of the Maudgalyāyana *pien-wen*] 「目連變文」紹介の後に, *Shina* 4.3:130–138 (432–440) (October 1927).

Lai Ming. *A History of Chinese Literature*. New York: John Day, 1964.

Lamotte, Etienne, tr. *Le traité de la grande vertu de sagesse de Nāgārjuna* (*Mahāprajñāpāramitāśāstra*) *avec une étude sur la vacuité*. Vols. II and IV. Bibliothèque du Muséon, 18 and Publications de l'Institut Orientaliste de Louvain, 2 and 12.

Louvain: Bureaux du Muséon, 1944, and Université de Louvain, Institut Orientaliste, 1976.

Lanciotti, Lionello. "Alcune osservazioni terminologiche sui *bianwen* 變文." In *Studi di Cinese classico*. Ed. Manurizio Scarpari. Venice: Cafoscarina, 1983.

——. Review of Arthur Waley, *Ballads and Stories from Tun-huang: An Anthology*. London: George Allen and Unwin, 1960. In *East and West*, n.s. 12.2–3:213 (June–September 1961).

Lane, Edward William. *An Arabic-English Lexicon*, in 8 parts. Beirut: Librairie du Liban, 1968. Reprint of London: Williams and Norgate, 1872.

Lao Kan 勞榦. "Tun-huang chi Tun-huang te hsin shih-liao" [Tun-huang and the new historical materials from Tun-huang] 敦煌及敦煌的新史料, *TLTC* 1.3:6–9 (15 August 1950).

Legge, James, tr. and annot. *The Chinese Classics*. 5 vols. Hong Kong: Hong Kong University Press, 1960 reprint.

——, tr. Z. D. Sung, ed. *The Text of Yi King (and Its Appendixes): Chinese Original with English Translation*. Shanghai: The China Modern Education Company, 1935, Rpt. Taipei: Wen-hua t'u-shu kung-ssu, 1975.

Leong Weng Kee [Liang Jung-chi] 梁榮基. "Pien-hsiang yü ch'a-t'u hua-pen" (On the Relationship between Pictorial Illustrations in Buddhist Texts and Illustrations in Traditional *pai-hua* Novels) 變相與插圖話本, *Hsin-she hsueh-pao* (Journal of the Island Society) 新社學報 1 (December 1967), 7th article. Reprinted *BCL*.

Leslie, Donald, Colin Mackerras and Wang Gungwu, eds. *Essays on the Sources for Chinese History*. Columbia: University of South Carolina Press, 1973.

Leumann, Ernst, ed. and tr. *Das nordarische (sakische) Lehrgedicht des Buddhismus*. Abhandlungen für die Kunde des Morgenlandes Vol. XX, nos. 1, 3. Leipzig: F. A. Brockhaus for Deutsche Morgenländische Gesellschaft, 1933–1936.

Li Chia-jui 李家瑞, comp. *Pei-p'ing feng-su lei-cheng* [Classified references to the customs of Peking] 北平風俗類徵. 2 vols. *CYYY*. Chuan-k'an [Special issue] 專刊 14. Shanghai: Commercial Press, 1937.

Li Fang 李昉 (925–996) et al., comps. *T'ai-p'ing kuang-chi* [Extensive register of great tranquility] 太平廣記 (977–988). 5 vols. Peking: Jen-min wen-hsueh ch'u-pan-she, 1959.

——, comp. *Wen-yuan ying-hua* [Beauty and adornment of the garden of literature] 文苑英華. Taipei: Hua-wen shu-chü, 1965. Rpt. of 1567 ed.

Li Ho 李賀. *Li Ho ko-shih pien* [The songs and poems of Li Ho] 李賀歌詩編. *SPTK* ed.

Li Hui-ying 李輝英. *Chung-kuo hsiao-shuo shih* [A history of Chinese fiction] 中國小說史. Hong Kong: Tung-ya shu-chü, 1970.

Liao Fu-shu 廖輔叔. *Chung-kuo ku-tai yin-yueh shih* [A history of ancient Chinese music] 中國古代音樂史. Peking: Yin-yueh ch'u-pan-she, 1964.

Lieu, Samuel Nan Chiang. "The Diffusion and Persecution of Manichaeism in Rome and China—A Comparative Study." DPhil dissertation, Oxford University, 1981. Revised as *Manichaeism in the Later Roman Empire and Medieval*

China: A Historical Survey. Foreword by Mary Boyce. Manchester: Manchester University Press, 1985.

Lin Mei-i 林玫儀. *Tun-huang ch'ü yen-chiu* [Studies on Tun-huang cantos] 敦煌曲研究. Taipei: 1976 [?].

Lin Ts'ung-ming 林聰明. *Tun-huang su-wen-hsueh yen-chiu* [Studies on Tun-huang popular literature] 敦煌俗文學研究. Taipei: Soochow University and Chung-kuo hsueh-shu chu-tso chiang-chu wei-yuan-hui, 1984.

Litvinsky, B. A. "Outline History of Buddhism in Central Asia." In *Kushan Studies in U.S.S.R.* Calcutta: Indian Studies, Past and Present, 1970.

Liu Fu 劉復, ed. *Tun-huang to-so* [Assembled fragments of Tun-huang texts] 燉煌掇瑣. Nanking: Kuo-li chung-yang yen-chiu yuan li-shih yü-yen yen-chiu-so (Institute of History and Philology, Academia Sinica) 國立中央研究院歷史語言研究所, special publication 2, 1925. In 3 cases.

Liu Hsiang 劉向 (77-6 B.C.). *Lieh-nü chuan* [Biographies of illustrious women] 列女傳. *SPPY* ed.

Liu Hsiu-yeh 劉修業. "Tun-huang pen Wu Tzu-hsu pien-wen chih yen-chiu" [A study of the Tun-huang Wu Tzu-hsu *pien-wen* manuscript] 敦煌本伍子胥變文之研究. *T'u-shu fu-k'an* (Bookman) 圖書副刊 184. *TCTKP* (3 June 1937).

Liu, James J. Y. *The Chinese Knight-Errant*. London: Routledge and Kegan Paul, 1967.

——. *Chinese Theories of Literature*. Chicago: The University of Chicago Press, 1975.

Liu K'ai-jung 劉開榮. '"Yu-hsien k'u' yü pien-wen te kuan-hsi" [The relation between the "Grotto of Transcendant Maidens" and *pien-wen*] 遊仙窟與「變文」的關係. In his *T'ang-tai hsiao-shuo yen-chiu* [Studies of T'ang dynasty fiction] 唐代小說研究. Shanghai: Commercial Press, 1946. Rpt. in Jen-jen wen-k'u [Everyman's library] 人人文庫. Taipei: Commercial Press, 1966. N.B. The coverage of *pien-wen* in the revised edition, of which I have seen the 3rd printing (Shanghai: Commercial Press, 1955) is vastly inferior to that of the original 1946 edition.

Liu Ta-chieh 劉大杰. *Chung-kuo wen-hsueh fa-chan shih* [A history of the development of Chinese literature] 中國文學發展史. Shanghai: Chung-hua shu-chü, 1962.

Liu T'ieh-yun (Liu E). *The Travels of Lao Ts'an*. Tr. and annot. Harold Shadick. Ithaca: Cornell University Press, 1952. Reissued 1966.

Liu Ts'un-yan. *Chinese Popular Fiction in Two London Libraries*. Hong Kong: Lung Men Bookstore, 1967.

Liu Wu-chi. *An Introduction to Chinese Literature*. Bloomington and London: University of Indiana Press, 1966.

Lo, C. T. [Chin-t'ang]. "Clues Leading to the Discovery of *Hsi Yu Chi p'ing-hua*," *Journal of Oriental Studies* 7.2: 176–194 (July 1969).

Lo Chen-yü 羅振玉, comp. *Chen-sung t'ang ts'ang hsi-ch'ui pi-chi ts'ung-ts'an* [Collected fragments of secret manuscripts from the western frontierland preserved in unwavering Pine Hall] 貞松堂藏西陲祕籍叢殘. Photographic reproduction by the compiler, 1933.

——, comp. *Chi-shih an ts'ung-shu,* ti-i chi [Collectanea from Lucky Stone Cottage, first series] 吉石盦叢書, 第 1 集. 6 vols. By the authors, 1914–1917.

——. "Fo-ch'ü san-chung pa" [Colophons to three Buddhist cantos] 佛曲三種跋. In his *Sung-weng chin-kao* [Recent manuscripts of Old Pine] 松翁近稿. Published by the author.

——, comp. *Ming-sha shih-shih i-shu* [Writings preserved in the Howling Sands Stone Chamber] 鳴沙石室佚書. Photoreproduced by Tung-fang hsueh-hui, 1928.

——, comp. *Ming-sha shih-shih ku-chi ts'ung-ts'an* [Collected fragments of ancient manuscripts from the Howling Sands Stone Chamber] 鳴沙石室古籍叢殘. Photoreproduced by the compiler, n.d.

——, comp. "Mo-kao k'u shih-shih mi-lu" [Secret catalog of the stone chamber at the caves of unsuppassed height] 莫高窟石室祕錄. *Tung-fang wen-k'u* [Oriental library] 東方文庫 71. *K'ao-ku-hsueh ling-chien* (Essays on Paleography) 考古學零簡. Shanghai: Commercial Press, December 1923. 3rd ed. July 1925.

——. "(Pu *T'ang-shu*) Chang I-ch'ao chuan" [(A supplement to the *T'ang history*) "Biography of Chang I-ch'ao"] (補唐書)張義潮傳. In his *Hsueh-t'ang ts'ung-k'e* [Snowy Hall collection] 雪堂叢刻. By the author, 1914 (?). Also in his *Ping-yin kao* [Manuscripts of 1926] 丙寅稿. By the author, 1926.

——, comp. *Tun-huang ling-shih* [A gathering of assorted texts from Tun-huang] 敦煌零拾. By the compiler, 1924 (?).

——, comp. *Tun-huang shih-shih i-shu* [Manuscripts preserved in the *stone* chamber at Tun-huang] 敦煌石室遺書. By the compiler (?), 1909.

Lo Fu-ch'ang 羅福萇, ed. *Sha-chou wen-lu i-chüan. Pu-i i-chüan. Fu-lu i-chüan* [Register of writings from Sha-chou. Supplementary writings. Additional items.] 沙州文錄一卷. 補遺一卷. 附錄一卷. Printed by Lo Chen-yü, 1924.

Lo Tsung-t'ao 羅宗濤. "Pien-ko pien-hsiang yü pien-wen (Discussion and Research on the Versified Vernacular in the Tun-huang Stone Cave) 變歌變相與變文, Cheng-ta Chung-kuo wen-hsueh yen-chiu-so, *Chung-hua hsueh-yuan* (Journal of Chinese Arts) 政大中國文學研究所中華學苑 7:73–99 (March 1971).

——. *Tun-huang chiang-ching pien-wen yen-chiu* [Studies on Tun-huang *chiang-ching* and *pien-wen*] 敦煌講經變文研究. Taipei: Wen shih che ch'u-pan-she, 1972.

——. *Tun-huang pien-wen she-hui feng-su shih-wu k'ao* [An examination of social customs and objects as reflected in Tun-huang *pien-wen*] 敦煌變文社會風俗事物考. Taipei: Wen-she-che ch'u-pan-she, 1974.

Lo Tzung-t'ao. "Au sujet du terme *bian* 變: Les procédés d'adaptation des textes bouddhiques aux *bianwen*," *JA*, 269.1–2:151–157 (1981).

Lu K'an-ju 陸侃如. "P'i-p'an Hu Shih te *Pai-hua wen-hsueh shih*" [Criticism of Hu Shih's *History of vernacular literature*] 批判胡適的白話文學史. *LitHer* 54 (15 May 1955).

Lu Kung 路工. "T'ang-tai te shuo-hua yü pien-wen" [T'ang dynasty storytelling and *pien-wen*] 唐代的說話與變文, *Min-chien wen-hsüeh* [Folk literature] 民間文學 6 (cumulative 87): 106–111 (4 December 1962).

Lü Shu-hsiang 呂叔湘. "Hsin pan *Tun-huang pien-wen tzu-i t'ung-shih* tu hou" [After reading the new edition of Chiang Li-hung's *Comprehensive explanations of the meanings of characters in Tun-huang pien-wen*] 新版《敦煌變文字義通釋》讀後, *CKYW* 168:233–236 (3rd issue, 1982).

Ma Shih-ch'ang 馬世長. "Kuan-yü Tun-huang ts'ang ching tung te chi-ko wen-t'i" (Some Questions Concerning the Old Hidden Monastery Library in Tun-huang) 關於敦煌藏經洞的幾個問題, *Wen Wu* (Cultural Relics) 文物 12:21–30, 20 (1978).

Ma T'ai-lai 馬泰來. "Shih li-p'u" [An explanation of the phrase *li-p'u*] 釋「立鋪」. In Jao Tsung-i chiao-shou nan-yu tseng-pieh lun-wen chi pien-chi wei-yuan-hui [Committee on editing a collection of essays as a parting present for Professor Jao Tsung-i on the occasion of his southern voyage] 饒宗頤教授南遊贈別論文集編輯委員會, ed. *Jao Tsung-i chiao-shou nan-yu tseng-pieh lun-wen chi* (Essays in Chinese Studies Dedicated to Professor Jao Tsung-i) 饒宗頤教授南遊贈別論文集. Hong Kong: Jao Tsung-i chiao-shou nan yu tseng-pieh lun-wen chi pien-chi wei-yuan-hui, 1970.

Ma Yaw-Woon. "Traditional Chinese Fiction in Modern Scholarship, 1920–1980." A large, unpublished annotated bibliography.

——. "The Beginnings of Professional Storytelling in China: A Critique of Current Theories and Evidence." In *Etudes d'histoire et de littérature chinoises offertes au Professeur Jaroslav Průšek*. Bibliothèque de l'Institut des Hautes Etudes chinoises, Vol. XXIV. Paris: Presses Universitaires de France, 1976.

—— and Joseph S. M. Lau, eds. *Traditional Chinese Stories*. New York: Columbia University Press, 1978.

MacKenzie, D. N., ed. and tr. *The Buddhist Sogdian Texts of the British Library*. Acta Iranica, series 3, Vol. III. Teheran-Liège: Bibliothèque Pahlavi, 1977.

——. "Buddhist Terminology in Sogdian: a Glossary" *AM*, n.s. 17.1:28–89 (1971).

——, ed. and tr. *The 'Sūtra of the Causes and Effects of Actions' in Sogdian*. London Oriental Series 22. London: Oxford University Press, 1970.

Mair, Victor H. "The Buddhist Tradition of Prosimetric Oral Narrative in Chinese Literature." Forthcoming in *Oral Tradition*.

——. "The Contributions of Transformation Texts (*pien-wen*) to Later Chinese Popular Literature." Forthcoming.

——. "India and China: Observations on Cultural Borrowing." Forthcoming.

——. "Inventory." Listed as such under abbreviated references.

——. "The Narrative Revolution in Chinese Literature: Ontological Presuppositions," with a symposium based on the article, *CLEAR* 5.1: 1–27 (July 1983).

——. "A Newly Identified Fragment of the 'Transformation on Wang Ling,'" *Chinoperl Papers* 12:130–142 (1983).

——. "Notes on the Maudgalyāyana Legend in East Asia." *Monumenta Serica* (in press).

——. "Oral and Written Aspects of Chinese Sutra Lectures (*chiang-ching-wen*)," *Han-hsueh yen-chiu* (Chinese Studies) 漢學研究 4.2 (cumulative 8):311–334 (December 1986).

——. "The Origins of an Iconographical Form of the Pilgrim, Hsüan-tsang," *T'ang Studies* 4:29–41 (1986), plus 7 plates.

——. *Painting and Performance: Chinese Picture Recitation, Its Indian Genesis, and Analogues Elsewhere*. Honolulu: University of Hawaii Press, 1988.

——. "Popular Narratives from Tun-huang." Cambridge, Massachusetts: PhD dissertation, Harvard University, 1976.

——. "Records of Transformation Tableaux (*pien-hsiang*)," *TP* 72:3–43 (1986).

——. "Scroll Presentation in the T'ang Dynasty," *HJAS* 38.1:35–60 (June 1978).

——, tr., annot., and intro. *Tun-huang Popular Narratives*. Cambridge: Cambridge University Press, 1983.

—— and Marsha Wagner. "Tun-huang wen-hsüeh [Literature]." In William H. Nienhauser, ed., *The Indiana Companion to Traditional Chinese Literature*. Bloomington: Indiana University Press, 1986.

—— and Maxine Belmont Weinstein. "Folk Literature." In Nienhauser, ed., *Companion* (see previous entry).

al-Maqrīzī, Aḥmad ibn 'Alī (1364–1442). *Histoire des Sultans Mamlouks, de l'Égypte*. Tr. and ed., Étienne Marc Quatremère. 2 vols. Paris: The Oriental Translation Fund of Great Britain and Ireland, 1845.

Matsumoto Yeiichi [Eiichi] 松本榮一. "Hokekyō bijutsu—Hokekyō hensōhen" (Fine Art in Relation to the *Hokke* Sūtra) 法華經美術—法華經變相篇, 1–3, *Kokka* [Essence of the nation] 國華 427:155–160 (June 1926); 428:175–184 (July 1926), with 4 illustrations; and 433:340–344 (December 1926). All with English summaries.

——. "Rōtakusha tōsei hensō no ichi-danpen" [A fragment of the *pien-hsiang* of Raudrākṣa having a magic competition] 牢度叉闘聖變相の一斷片, *Kenchikushi* [The history of architecture] 建築史 2.5:32–37 (September 1940), with 2 illustrations.

——. "Tonkō chihō ni ryūko seshi Rōtakusha tosei hensō" (Paintings representing the overcoming of Raudrâksa, chief of the heretics, by Sâriputta, Abounding in Touen-houang District) 燉煌地方に流行せし牢度叉闘聖變相, *The Bukkyo bijutsu* (Quarterly Journal of Buddhist Art) 佛教美術 19:2–11 (October 1933).

——. *Tonkō-ga no kenkyū* [A study of Tun-huang paintings] 敦煌畫の研究. 2 vols. Tokyo: Tōhō bunka gakuin Tōkyō kenkyūjo, 1937.

Mehta, Ratilal N. *Pre-Buddhist India; Being a Comprehensive, Critical and Scientific Survey of Ancient India Based on the Jātaka Stories*. Bombay: Examiner Press, 1939.

Meng Ch'i 孟棨 (fl. 886). *Pen-shih shih* [Topical poetry] 本事詩. Shanghai: Ku-tien wen-hsueh ch'u-pan-she, 1957.

Meng Yao 孟瑤, pseud. Yang Tsung-chen 楊宗珍. *Chung-kuo hsiao-shuo shih* [History of Chinese fiction] 中國小說史. 4 vols., continuous pagination. Wen-hsing ts'ung-k'an [Star of Literary Geniuses series] 文星叢刊 145 (1–4). Taipei: Wen-hsing shu-tien, 1966. Also in Wen-shih hsin-k'an [New series on literature and history] 文史新刊 33–36. Taipei: Chuan-chi wen-hsueh ch'u-pan-she, 1969.

Men'shikov, L. N., ed. and tr. *Byan'ven' o Veimotsze. Byan'ven' Desyat' blagikh znamenii*. Neizvestnye rukopisi byan'ven' iz Dun'khuanskogo fonda Instituta Narodov Azii. Moscow: Izdatel'stvo Vostochnoi Literatury, 1963.

——, ed. and tr. *Byan'ven' o Vozdayanii za Milosti*. Rukopis' iz Dun'-khuanskogo fonda. With a grammatical sketch by I. T Zograf in Vol. II. Instituta Vostokovedeniya. 2 vols. Moscow: Nauka, 1972.

——, tr. and annot. *Byan'ven' po Lotesovoi Sutre*. Moscow: Nauka, Glavnaya Redaktsiya Vostochnoi Literatur'i, 1984. English summary pages 526–534.

——. "Fragment neizvestnoi Leishu iz Dun'xuana," *Kratkie soobscheniya* (Instituta Narodov Azii) 69. Moscow, 1965.

——. "Izuchenie Drevnekitaĭskikh Pis'menn'ikh Pamyatnikov," *Vestnik Akademii Nauk SSSR* 5:59–62 (May 1967).

——, ed. *Kitaiskie rukopisi iz Dun'khuanu. Pamyatniki buddiskoi literatury suven'siue*. Akademiya nauk SSSR. Institut Narodov Azii, Dun'khuanskii Fond. Moscow: Izdatel'stvo Vostochnoi Literatury, 1963.

——. "Problem'i Izucheniya Okruzheniya byan'ven'," *Teoreticheskie problem'i vostochn'ikh literatur*. Moscow: Nauka, 1969.

Michihata Ryōshū 道端良秀. *Chūgoku Bukkyō to shakai to no kōshō* [Chinese Buddhism and its relationship to society] 中國佛教と社會との交渉. Kyoto: Heirakuji shoten, 1980.

——. "Shina ni okeru Bukkyō no minshū kyōka" [Education of the masses by Buddhists in China] 支那に於ける佛教の民衆教化, *Nihon bukkyōgaku kyōkai nenpō* [Annual report of the Association of Japanese Buddhist Scholars] 日本佛教學教會年報 12:47–89 (December 1940).

——. *Tōdai Bukkyō shi no kenkyū* [Study of the history of Buddhism in the T'ang period] 唐代佛教史の研究. Kyoto: Hōzōkan, 1957.

Minamoto[no] Tamenori 源為憲 (d. 1011). *Sanbōe shūsei* [Variorum edition of the (Notes on the) pictures of the three jewels (i.e. *triratna*)] 三寶繪集成. Ed. Koizumi Hiroshi 小泉弘 and Takahashi Nobuyuki 高橋伸幸. Tokyo: Kasama shoin, 1980.

Miya Tsugio 宮次男. "Mokuren kyūbo setsuwa to sono eiga—Mokuren kyūbo kyoei no shutsugen ni tsukite—" (Illustrated Scripture of the Story of Mokuren's Salvation of His Mother) 目連救母說とその繪畫—目連救母經繪の出現に就きて—, *BK* 255:1–24 (January 1968), with 3 plates.

Mizutani Shinjō 水谷眞成. "'Ippo' no igi ni tsuite—henbun enshutso hō ni kansuru ichi shiron" [On the meaning of "*i-p'u*"—a preliminary discussion regarding the method of performance of *pien-wen*] 『一鋪』の意義について—變文演出法に關する—試論, *Shina gakuhō* (Ōtani University) [China journal] 支那學報 2:29–32 (1957).

Mochizuki Shinkyō 望月信亨 et al. *Bukkyō daijiten* [Great Buddhist dictionary] 佛教大辭典. 10 vols. Tokyo: *Bukkyō daijiten* hakkōsho and Seikai seiten kankō kyōkai, 1931–1963.

Monier-Williams, Monier. *A Sanskrit-English Dictionary*. Oxford: Clarendon Press, 1899.

Mookerji, Radhakumud. *Ancient Indian Education: Brahmanical and Buddhist*. 2nd ed. London: Macmillan, 1951.

——. "Hindu Educational Systems." In *The Cultural Heritage of India*. 3 vols. Calcutta: Sri Ramakrishna Centenary Committee, 1936–1944. Vol. III.

Morohashi Tetsuji 諸橋轍次. *Dai Kan-Wa jiten* [Great Chinese-Japanese dictionary] 大漢和辭典. 13 vols. Tokyo: Taishūkan shoten, 1955–1960.

Murasaki Shikibu (b. 978?). *The Tale of Genji*. Tr. Edward Seidensticker. 2 vols. New York: Knopf, 1976.

Naba Toshisada 那波利貞. "Bantō jidai no senjutsu to kōsatsu seraruru cha ni kansuru tsūzokuteki kokkei bungaku sakuhin" [A comical, popular work of literature concerning tea regarded to be of the late T'ang period] 晩唐時代の撰述と考察せらるる茶に關する通俗的滑稽文學作品, *Shi* 30.3:60–90 (March 1946), plus plate of the manuscript.

——. "Bukkyō shinkō ni motozukite soshiki seraretaru Chū-ban Tō Godai jidai no shayū ni tsukite" (On "Shayu," an intimate Union of Buddhists, in the days of T'ang and the Five-Dynasties) 佛教信仰に基きて組織せられたる中晩唐五代時代の社邑に就きて, parts 1 and 2, *Shi* 24.3:1–72 (July 1939) and 24.4:81–122 (October 1939). Pages cited are to the republished version in NT, pp. 575–673, English title "On the Shê-i (Organized by Buddhism) in the T'ang and the Five Dynasties Periods."

——. "Bunka-shijō yori kansatsu suru Shisenshō Seito" [Chengtu, Szechwan seen from the point of view of cultural history] 文化史上より觀察する四川省成都, 1–2, *RK* 12.5:28–44 (November 1923) and 12.6:15–40 (December 1923).

——, tr. "Cha shu mondō" [Questions and answers between tea and wine] 茶酒問答, translation of "Ch'a-chiu lun" [Debate between tea and wine] 茶酒論 *Sadō koten zenshū* [Collected classics of the tea ceremony] 茶道古典全集 2:271–280 (July 1958).

——. "Chū-ban Tō Godai no Bukkyō jiin no zokkō no za ni okeru henbun no enshutsu hōhō ni tsukite" (On the Performance of "Hembun" on the Stage of Popular Buddhistic Preaching in T'ang and Five Dynasties) 中晩唐五代の佛教寺院の俗講の座に於ける變文の演出方法に就きて, *Kōnan daigaku bungaku kai ronshū* (Journal of the Literary Society of Kōnan University) 甲南大學文學會論集 2:1–74 (February 1955).

——. "Chū-ban Tō jidai ni okeru giran sō ni kansuru ichi-konpon-shiryō no kenkyū" [Studies of a basic source relating to spurious monks in the middle and late T'ang periods] 中晩唐時代に於ける偽濫僧に關する一根本史料の研究. In *Ryūkoku daigaku Bukkyō shigaku ronsō* [Ryukoku University studies in Buddhist history] 龍谷大學佛教史學論叢. Tokyo: Fuzanbō, December 1939.

——. "Chū Tō jidai zokkō sō Bunjo hōshi shakugi" (Etudes sur le prêcheur *Wen-Hsiu* des moyens *Tangs*) 中唐時代俗講僧文溆法師釋疑, *Tōyōshi kenkyū* (Revue des études d'histoire de l'Extrême Orient) 東洋史研究 4.6:1–24 (July–August 1939).
——. "Henbun tangen" (Searching for the Beginning of Pien-wen) 變文探源, *The Ritsumeikan bungaku* (The Ritsumeikan Journal of Cultural Sciences) 立命館文學 180:130–154 (496–520) (June 1960). This volume also published as *Hashimoto hakushi koki kinen tōyōgaku ronsō* (Oriental Studies Presented to Jun Hashimoto in Honor of His Seventieth Birthday) 橋本博士古稀記念東洋學論叢. Kyoto: Ritsumeikan daigaku jinbun gakkai, 1960.
——. "Kanpō-fu kō" [An examination of the rhymeprose of Han P'eng] 韓朋賦攷, *RK* 34.4–5:170–199 (November 1934)
——. "Senbutsu-gan Bakkōkutsu to Tonkō bunsho" (Chinese Manuscripts from Tunhuang Cave Temples) 千佛巖莫高窟と敦煌文書. In *MSI*, Vol. II, with English summary.
——. "Shidda taishi shudō innen kaisetsu" (A Complete Manuscript of the *Hsi ta t'ai tzŭ hsiu tao yin yuan*) 悉達太子修道因緣解說. In *MSI*, Vol. I, with English summary and a photograph of the manuscript.
——. "Tōdai no shayū ni tsukite" (On "Shayū," an Intimate Union of Masses, in the days of T'ang Dynasty) 唐代の社邑に就きて, 1–3, *Shi* 23.2:15–57 (April 1938); 23.3:71–110 (July 1938), plus 2 plates; 23.4:93–157 (October 1938), plus 2 plates. Pages cited are to the republished version in NT. English title "On the Shê-i (Voluntary Associations) in the T'ang Periods."
——. "Tō no kyōkō shinshi Ō Fu sen no chashu-ron no kenkyū" (Studies on the Battle of Tea and Wine by Hsiang-kung-chin-shih Wang Fu: Copy Manuscript of the T'ang Dynasty Discovered at Tun-Huang) 唐の鄉貢進士王敷撰の茶酒論の研究, *Kōnan daigaku bungaku kai ronshū* (Journal of the Literary Society of Kōnan University) 甲南大學文學會論集 8:1–62 (November 1958), plus two plates.
——. "Tō shōhon zasshō kō" (On the *Tsa-Ch'ao* [Textbooks for children] among the Tun-huang Manuscripts) 唐鈔本雜抄攷. In NT. Originally appeared in *Shina*, special number (April 1942).
——. "Zokkō to henbun" (Popularised Lectures and Peculiar Style) 俗講と變文, 1–3, *BS* 1.2:61–72 (January 1950); 1.3:73–91 (June 1950); and 1.4:39–65 (October 1950). Citations are to the republished version in NT. English title "Vulgarized Stories and Ballads from Buddhist Texts."
Nagahiro Toshio 長廣敏雄, tr. *Rekidai meigaki* [A record of famous painters of successive dynasties] 歷代名畫記. Tokyo: Heibonsha, 1977.
Nagasawa Kikuya 長澤規矩也. "Gakujutsu to bungaku" [Scholarship and learning] 學術と文學. In Ishida Mikinosuke 石田幹之助, ed., *Zui Tō no sei-sei* [The flourishing age of the Sui and T'ang] 隋唐の盛世, Vol. III of Tōyō bunkashi taikei [History of oriental culture series] 東洋文化史大系. Tokyo: Seibundō shinkōsha, 1938.
Nakamura Hajime 中村元. *Bukkyōgo daijiten* [Dictionary of Buddhist terms] 佛教語大辭典. 3 vols. Tokyo: Tōkyō shoseki kabushiki kaisha, 1975.

Nakano Miyoko 中野美代子. *Tonkō monogatari* [Tun-huang tales] 敦煌物語. *Chūgoku no tojō* [Cities of China] 中國の都城. Vol. III. Tokyo: Shūeisha, 1987.

Ñāṇananda. *See* Bhikku.

Naquin, Susan. "Funerals in North China: Uniformity and Variation." In James L. Watson and Evelyn S. Rawski, eds. *Death Ritual in Late Imperial and Modern China*. Berkeley: University of California Press, 1988.

Needham, Joseph. *Science and Civilisation in China*. Vol. I, *Introductory Orientations*, with the assistance of Wang Ling. Cambridge: Cambridge University Press, 1954. Vol. II, *History of Scientific Thought*, with the assistance of Wang Ling. Cambridge: Cambridge University Press, 1956; reprint 1975. Vol. IV, *Physics and Physical Technology*, pt. 1, *Physics*, with the collaboration of Wang Ling and the special cooperation of Kenneth Girdwood Robinson. Cambridge: Cambridge University Press, 1962; reprint 1977.

Nelson, Howard. Letter of 1 June 1978.

Nemoto Makoto 根本誠. "Chūgoku bungaku no ittokuchō (jō)—Go Shisho henbun no jinbutsu byōsha no genkaisei" [A special feature of Chinese literature, part 1—The limited nature of character description in the Wu Tzu-hsu *pien-wen*] 中國文學の一特徵(上)—伍子胥變文の人物描寫の限界性, *Tōyō bungaku kenkyū* [Studies of Oriental literature] 東洋文學研究 14:7–16 (March 1966) and its sequel in 15:38–49 (March 1967).

——. "Ō Shō-kun henbun no seiritsu nendai kō" [A study of the date of the composition of the Wang Chao-chün *pien-wen*] 王昭君變文の成立年代考, *Tōyō bungaku kenkyū* [Studies of Oriental literature] 東洋文學研究 9:57–80 (March 1961).

Nihon daijiten kankō-kai [Publications committee for the great Japanese dictionary] 日本大辭典刋行會, ed. *Nihon kokugo daijiten* [Great dictionary of the Japanese national language] 日本國語大辭典. 20 vols. Tokyo: Shōgakukan, 1972–1976.

Nishino Teiji 西野貞治. "Tō Ei densetsu ni tsuite" (On the Legend of Tung-yung) 董永傳說について, *Jimbun kenkyū* (Studies in the Humanities) 人文研究 6.6:67–81 (July 1955).

——. "Tonkō zoku-bungaku no sozai to sono tenkai" (The Original Materials for Tunhuang Popular Literature and Their Use in Later Periods) 敦煌俗文學の素材とその展開, *Jimbun Kenkyū* (Studies in the Humanities—The Journal of the Literary Association of Osaka City University) 人文研究 10.11:57–73 (1148–1164) (November 1959), with 5 photographs.

Nomura Yosho 野村耀昌, ed. *Hokekyō shinkō no shokeitai* (The *Lotus Sutra* and Religious Realities) 法華經信仰の諸形態. Hokekyō kenkyū [Studies on the *Lotus Sūtra*] 法華經研究, Vol. VI. Kyoto: Heirakuji shoten, 1976.

——. "Tonkō henbun ni miru Daiba-bon no keitai" (A Popularized Edition of the Daiba-hon) 敦煌變文に見る提婆品の形態. Pp. 303–345 of previous entry. English summary, pp. 8–9.

Ogawa Kan'ichi 小川貫弌. *Bukkyō bunka-shi kenkyū* [Studies on Buddhist cultural history] 佛教文化史研究. Kyoto: Nagata bunshōdō, 1973. Especially Section

II: "Bukkyō bunka no Chūgoku taishūka" [The popularization in China of Buddhist culture] 佛教文化の中國大衆化.

——. "Mokuren kyūbo henbun no genryū" [On the origins of the *pien-wen* on Maudgalyāyana rescuing his mother] 目蓮救母變文の源流. In *BBK* Vol. II. Also in the author's *Bukkyō bunka-shi kenkyū.*

——. "Tonkō butsuji no gakushirō" (The *Gakushiro* [scholar] of Temple at *Tun-huang*) 敦煌佛寺の學士郎, *Ryūkokudaigaku Ronshū* (The Journal of Ryūkoku University) 龍谷大學論集, combined issue of nos. 400–401:488–506 (March 1973).

Ogawa Tamaki 小川環樹. "Henbun to kōshi—Chūgoku hakuwa shōsetsu no keishiki no kigen" (From *Pien-Wen* to the Historical Romance—The Earlier Stage of the Chinese Colloquial Novels) 變文と講史—中國白話小說の形式の起源—, *The Nippon Chūgokugakkai hō* (Bulletin of the Sinological Society of Japan) 日本中國學會報 6:72–82 (October 1954). Reprinted in the author's *Chūgoku shōsetsu shi no kenkyū* [Studies on the history of fiction in China] 中國小說史の硏究. Tokyo: Iwanami shoten, 1968.

Ogawa Yoichi 小川陽一. "Bukkyō to katarimono ('henbun' no sekai)" [Buddhism and narrative tales—the world of *pien-wen*] 佛教と語り物(「變文」の世界). In Uchida Michio, ed., *Chūgoku shōsetsu no sekai.*

——. "Henbun no kōzō—kōshi dan ni mirareru 'kurikaeshi' o chūshin ni—" (A View on the Structure of the *Pien-Wen*) 變文の構造—孝子談に見られる「くりかえし」を中心に—. *Shukan Tōyōgaku* (Chinese and Oriental Studies) 集刊東洋學 3:38–51 (May 1960).

——. "Henbun no shūhen—Fubo onchō kyōmon·zasshō no sozaironteki kōsatsu" (*Pien-wen* and Didactic Literature) 變文の週邊—父母恩重經文·雜抄の素材論的考察, *Shūkan Tōyōgaku* (Chinese and Oriental Studies) 集刊東洋學 7:58–70 (May 1962).

——. "Mō Kyōnyo henbun no seiritsu ni tsuite" (Mêng Chiang-nü Pien-wên, Its Sources and Character) 孟姜女變文の成立について, *Bunka* (Culture) 文化 25:16–49 (Spring 1961).

Okudaira, Hideo. *Narrative Picture Scrolls*. Tr. and adapted by Elizabeth ten Grotenhuis. Arts of Japan, 5. New York: Weatherhill, 1973.

Oldenburg, Hermann. "Âkhyâna-Hymnen im Ṛigveda," *ZDMG* 39.1:52–90 (1885).

——. "Die altindischen Âkhyâna, mit besondrer Rücksicht auf das Suparṇâkyâna," *ZDMG* 37.1:54–86 (1883).

——. "The Prose-and-Verse Type of Narrative and the Jātakas," *Journal of the Pāli Text Society* (1910–1912), pp. 19–50.

——, ed. *The Vinaya Piṭakaṃ*. Vol. II, *The Cullavagga*. London: Williams and Norgate, 1880.

Ono Genmyo 小野玄妙. *Bukkyō no bijutsu oyobi rekishi* [The art and history of Buddhism] 佛教の美術及び歷史. Tokyo: Bussho kenkyū-kai, 1916.

Ono Katsutoshi 小野勝年. "Bunjo to Bunshuku" [Wen-hsu and Wen-shu] 文漵と文淑, *Tōyōshi kenkyū* (Revue des études d'histoire de l'Extrême Orient) 東洋史研究 5.1:59 (September–October 1939).

——. *Nittō guhō junrei gyōki no kenkyū* ([Studies on] The Record of a Pilgrimage to T'ang in Search of the Law) 入唐求法巡禮行記の研究. 4 vols. Tokyo: Suzuki gakujutsu zaidan, 1964–1969.

Ōta Tatsuo 太田辰夫. *Chūgoku rekidai kōgobun/ Zhongguo lidai kouywen* [Colloquial Chinese texts from successive periods] 中國歷代口語文. Tokyo: Kōnan sho-in, 1957.

Ōtani Kōzui 大谷光瑞, ed. *Saiiki kōko zufu* [Archeological album of the western regions] 西域考古圖譜. 2 vols. Tokyo: Kokkasha, 1915.

Pachow, W. [Pa Chou] 巴宙, ed. and annot. *Tun-huang yun-wen chi* (An Anthology of Poetical Compositions from Tun-huang) 敦煌韻文集. Kaoh Siung [Kao-hsiung], Taiwan: Buddhist Culture Service, 1965.

Pai Hua-wen 白化文. "Shen-me shih pien-wen" (What Is "*pien-wen*"?) 甚麼是變文? In *LWL*, Vol. I. English translation by Victor H. Mair, *HJAS* 44.2:493–514 (December 1984).

Pan Chung-kwei [P'an Ch'ung-kuei] 潘重規. "Kuo-li chung-yang t'u-shu-kuan so ts'ang Tun-huang chüan-tzu t'i-chi" (An Annotated List of the Scrolls of Tun-huang Conserved in the National Central Library at Taipei) 國立中央圖書館所藏敦煌卷子題記, *Tun-huang hsueh* (*Studies on Tun-huang*) 敦煌學 2: 1–55 (1975).

——. "Kuo-li chung-yang t'u-shu-kuan so ts'ang Tun-huang chüan-tzu t'i-chi" (A Survey of the Tun-huang Manuscripts in the Taiwan National Library) 國立中央圖書館所藏燉煌卷子題記, *Hsin-ya hsueh-pao* [New Asia journal] 新亞學報, 抽印本, offprint, 8.2:321–373 (1 August 1968), plus 16 pages of plates and English symmary.

——, comp. *Tun-huang su-tzu p'u* [Charts of colloquial graphs from Tun-huang] 敦煌俗字譜. Taipei: Shih-men t'u-shu, 1978.

P'ang P'u 龐樸, ed. *Kung-sun lung-tzu yen-chiu* [Studies on Kung-sun lung-tzu] 公孫龍子研究. Peking: Chung-hua shu-chü, 1979.

Pei-ching min-chien feng-su pai-t'u [One hundred drawings of popular customs in Peking] 北京民間風俗百圖, originally entitled *Pei-ching min-chien sheng-huo ts'ai t'u* [Colored drawings of folk life in Peking] 北京民間生活彩圖. A facsimile reproduction of a Ch'ing-period album preserved in the Peking National Library. Peking: Shu-mu wen-hsien ch'u-pan-she, 1983.

Pei-ching shih-fan ta-hsueh Chung-wen-hsi wu-shih-wu chi hsueh-sheng chi-t'i pien-hsieh [Collectively written and edited by students in the Chinese Department of Peking Normal University, Class of 1955] 北京師范大學中文系55級學生集體編寫. *Chung-kuo min-chien wen-hsueh shih* [A history of Chinese folk literature] 中國民間文學史, Vol. I. Peking: Jen-min wen-hsueh ch'u-pan-she, 1959, 2nd printing.

Pei-ching ta-hsueh chung-wen hsi [Chinese Department of Peking University] 北京大學中文系. *Chung-kuo hsiao-shuo shih* [History of Chinese fiction] 中國小說史. Peking: Jen-min wen-hsueh ch'u-pan-she, 1978.

Pei-ching ta-hsueh chung-wen-hsi wen-hsueh chuan-men-hua i-chiu wu-shih-wu chi chi-t'i pien-chu [Collectively written and edited by specialists in literature in the Chinese Department of Peking University, Class of 1955] 北京大學中文系文學專門化1955級集體編著. *Chung-kuo wen-hsueh shih* [A history of Chinese literature] 中國文學史, Vols. I and II. Peking: Jen-min wen-hsueh ch'u-pan-she, 1959.

Pelliot, Paul (*see also* Po Hsi-ho). *Les grottes de Touen-houang: peintures et sculptures bouddhiques des époques des Wei, des T'ang et des Song*. 6 vols. Série In-Quarto, 1. Paris: Paul Geuthner, 1914–1924.

——. "Les traditions manichéennes au Fou-kien," *TP* 22:192–208 (1923).

——. "Une bibliothèque médiévale retrouvée au Kan-Sou," *BEFEO* 8:501–529 (1908).

P'eng Ting-ch'iu 彭定求 (1645–1719), et al., eds. *Ch'üan T'ang shih* [Complete T'ang poetry] 全唐詩. 12 vols. Peking: Chung-hua shu-chü, 1960.

P'i-ying hsi chü-pen [Shadow play scripts] 皮影戲劇本. Manuscripts preserved in the Treasure Room of Harvard-Yenching Library. Cat. no. T5722/4622 (1–24).

Pian, Rulan Chao. *Sonq Dynasty Musical Sources and Their Interpretation.* Harvard-Yenching Institute Monograph Series 16. Cambridge: Harvard University Press, 1967.

Pigeaud, Th. G. Th. *Literature of Java.* Catalogue Raisonné of Javanese Manuscripts in the Library of the University of Leiden and Other Public Collections in the Netherlands. 3 vols. KITLV, Leiden. The Hague: Martinus Nijhoff, 1967–1970.

Pihl, Marshall R. "Korea in the Bardic Tradition: *P'ansori* as an Oral Art," *Korean Studies Forum* 2:1–105 (Spring–Summer, 1977).

——. "The Tale of Sim Ch'ŏng: A Korean Oral Narrative." PhD dissertation, Harvard University, 1974.

Pischel, Richard. *Die Heimat des Puppenspiels.* Address to Friedrichs-universität. Halle a.S.: M. Niemayer, 1900. Translated by Mildred C. Tawney as *The Home of the Puppet Play*. London: Luzac, 1902.

Po Chü-i 白居易 (772–846). *Po shih Ch'ang-ch'ing chi* [Collected works of Po Chü-i] 白氏長慶集 *SPTK* ed.

Po Hsi-ho [Paul Pelliot] 伯希和 and Haneda Toru 羽田亨, eds. *Tun-huang i-shu ti-i chi* (Manuscrits de Touen-houang) 敦煌遺書第一集. 2 vols. Kyoto: Tōa-kōkyūkwai (Shanghai), 1926.

Porkert, Manfred. *The Theoretical Foundations of Chinese Medicine: Systems of Correspondence.* M. I. T. East Asian Science Series 3. Cambridge and London: The MIT Press, 1974.

Průšek, Jaroslav. "The Beginnings of Popular Chinese Literature: Urban Centres—The Cradle of Popular Fiction," *ArchOr* 36.1:67–121 (1968). Reprinted in Birch, *Genres.*

——. "The Narrators of Buddhist Scriptures and Religious Tales in the Sung Period," *ArchOr* 10.3:375–389 (December 1938), plus 5 plates.

——. "New Studies on the Chinese Colloquial Short Story," *ArchOr* 25.2:452–499 (1957).

——. "Researches into the Beginnings of the Popular Chinese Novel," *ArchOr* 11.1:91–132 (1939), and 23.4:620–662 (1955).
——. Review of Arthur Waley, *Ballads and Stories from Tun-huang, an Anthology, ArchOr* 31.3:488–491 (1963).
Pulsŏl Amita-gyŏng [*Amitābha-sūtra* spoken by the Buddha] 佛說阿彌陁經. Ch'ungch'ŏng-do, Ch'ungju-ji, Wŏrak-san: Dŏkchu-sa, 1572.

Quaritch Wales, H. G. *The Indianization of China and of South-East Asia*. London: Bernard Quaritch, 1967.

Rawski, Evelyn Sakakida. *Education and Popular Literacy in Ch'ing China*. Ann Arbor: The University of Michigan Press, 1979.
Régamey, Konstanty, ed. and tr. *The Bhadramāyākāravyākaraṇa*. The Warsaw Society of Sciences and Letters, Publications of the Oriental Commission 3. Warsaw: Nakładem Towarzystwa naukowego warszawskiego, 1938. A simultaneous reference to Ch. 1 is to the translation attributed to Dhramarakṣa (fl. 266–317) entitled *Fo-shuo huan-shih jen-hsien ching* 佛說幻士仁賢經, *T* (324) 12.31a–37a. A reference to Ch. 2 is to the translation by Bodhiruci done between 693 and 713 entitled *Shou huan-shih Po-t'u-lo chi hui* 授幻師跋陀羅記會, *T*(310, sect. 21) 11.486b–492b.
Reischauer, Edwin O., tr. *Ennin's Diary: The Record of a Pilgrimage to China in Search of the Law*. New York: The Ronald Press, 1955.
Rhys Davids and Thomas William, trs. *Buddhist Birth Stories: or, Jātaka Tales*. Vol. I. London: Trübner, 1880.
Robertson, Maureen. "Periodization in the Arts and Patterns of Change in Traditional Chinese Literary History." In Susan Bush and Christian Murck, eds., *Theories of the Arts in China*. Princeton: Princeton University Press, 1983.
Robinet, Isabelle. "Metamorphosis and Deliverance from the Corpse in Taoism," *History of Religions* 19.1:37–70 (August 1976).
Róna-tas, A. "A Brief Note on the Chronology of the Tunhuang Collections," *Acta Orientalia, Academiae Scientiarum Hungaricae* 21.3:313–316 (1968).
des Rotours, Robert. *Traité fonctionnaires et traité de l'armée*. Traduits de la Nouvelle Histoire des T'ang (Chap. XLVI-L). 2 vols. Bibliothèque de l'Institut des Hautes Etudes Chinoises, 6. Leiden: E. J. Brill, 1947–1948.
Ruch, Barbara. "Medieval Jongleurs and the Making of a National Literature." In John W. Hall and Toyoda Takeshi, eds., *Japan in the Muromachi Age*. Berkeley: University of California Press, 1977.
Ryūkoku daigaku 龍谷大學, comp. *Bukkyō daijii* [Great Buddhist encyclopedic glossary] 佛教大辭彙. 7 vols. Tokyo: Fuzanbō, 1975.

Saeki, P. Y. *The Nestorian Documents and Relics in China*. Tokyo: The Maruzen Company, 1951.
Saiiki bunka kenkyū kai (The Research Society of Central Asian Culture) 西域文化研究會. *Chūō Asia kodaigo bunken* (Buddhist Manuscripts and Secular Docu-

ments of the Ancient Languages in Central Asia) 中央アジア古代語文獻. In *MSI*, Vol. IV (supplement).
——. *Tonkō Bukkyō shiryō* (Chinese Buddhist Texts from Tunhuang) 敦煌佛教資料. In *MSI*, Vol. I.
Saitō Shō 齊藤晌. *Ri Ga* [Li Ho] 李賀. Kanshi taikei [Chinese poetry series] 漢詩大系 13. Tokyo: Shūeisha, 1967.
Sakai Kenichi 坂井健一. "Tonkō henbun no ōinji ni mirareru oninjō to tokushoku" [The phonetic characteristics found in rhyme characters of Tun-huang *pien-wen*] 敦煌變文の押韻字にみられる音韻上の特色, *Chūgoku bunka kenkyū* [Studies on Chinese culture] 中國文化研究 1:1–11 (August 1958).
Sakaki Ryōzaburō 榊亮三郎, comp. *Honyaku meigi taishū* [A compendium of Buddhist terms in Sanskrit, Tibetan, Chinese, and Japanese: *Mahāvyutpatti*] 飜譯名義大集. 2 vols. Kyōto teikoku daigaku bunka daigaku sōsho [Kyōto Imperial University College of Literature series] 京都帝國大學文科大學叢書 3. Kyoto: Shingon-shū Kyōto daigaku, 1916–1925. Also in Fukkan sōsho [Reprint series] 複刊叢書. Tokyo: Suzuki gakujutsu zaidan, 1965, 3rd ed. (reprint).
——. *Honyaku meigi taishū bon zō sakuin* (*Maha Vyutpatti* Index) 飜譯名義大集梵藏索引. Fukkan sosho [Reprint series] 複刊叢書 1. Tokyo: Suzuki gakujutsu zaidan, 1965, 3rd ed. (reprint).
Salmen, Walter. *Der fahrende Musiker in europäischer Mittelalter*. Kassel: Johann Philipp Hinnenthal, 1960.
Śāntideva (seventh century), compl. *Śikshū-samuccaya: A Compendium of Buddhist Doctrine*. See Bendall and Rouse.
Sawada Mizuho 澤田瑞穗. *Jigoku-hen* [Hell transformations] 地獄變. Kyoto: Hōzōkan, 1968.
——. "Shina Bukkyō shōdō bungaku no seisei" [The formation of Chinese Buddhist literature of preaching] 支那佛教唱導文學の生成. In his *Bukkyō to Chūgoku bungaku* [Buddhism and Chinese literature] 佛教と中國文學. Tokyo: Kokusho kankō-kai, 1975. Originally appeared in *Chizan gakuhō* [Journal of Chizan College] 智山學報, n.s. 13–14 (December 1939 and December 1940).
Sawyer, Ruth. *The Way of the Storyteller*. New York: The Viking Press, 1962. Originally published 1942.
Schipper, Kristofer. "Vernacular and Classical Ritual in Taoism," *JAS* 14.1:21–57 (November 1985).
Seaman, Gary. "The Chinese Cult of the Dead." Unpublished bibliography.
——. *The Chinese Cult of the Dead*, a series of films. Cedar Park, Texas: Far Eastern Audio Visuals, 1977.
——. Letters of 3 August 1978 and 5 August 1984.
——. "The Sexual Politics of Karmic Retribution." In Emily Martin Ahern and Hill Gates, eds., *The Anthropology of Taiwanese Society*. Stanford: Stanford University Press, 1981.
——. "Spirit Money: An Interpretation," *Journal of Chinese Religions* 10:80–91 (1982).
Shao Hung 邵紅. *Tun-huang shih-shih chiang-ching-wen yen-chiu* (A Study of the Buddhist Sutra Narration [*Chiang-Ching-Wen*] Found in the Tun-huang Caves)

敦煌石室講經文研究. Wen-shih ts'ung-k'an (History and Chinese literature series) 文史叢刊 33. Taipei: Ching-hua yin-shu-kuan, 1970.

Shao Jung-fen 邵榮芬. "Tun-huang su-wen-hsueh chung te pieh-tzu i-wen ho T'ang Wu-tai hsi-pei fang-yin" [Miswritten graphs and anomalous writing in the vernacular literature of Tun-huang texts and the local phonetic characteristics of the northwest during the T'ang and Five Dynasties periods] 敦煌俗文學中的別字異文和唐五代西北方音, *CKYW*, 3 (cumulative 124): 193–217 (22 June 1963).

Shih, Leei 石壘. Wen-hsin tiao-lung *yuan-tao yü Fo-tao i shu cheng* (A Comparative Study of Truth as the Source of Aesthetic Phenomena in the *Wen-hsin tiao-lung* and Buddhism) 文心雕龍原道與佛道義疏證. Honkong: Yun Tsai Book Study, 1971.

Shih-san ching chu-shu [The thirteen classics with commentaries and subcommentaries] 十三經注疏. Taipei: I-wen, 1976. reprint of 1896 ed. (1815 colophon given by publisher is incorrect.)

Shih Wei-liang 史惟亮. *Yin-yueh hsiang li-shih ch'iu cheng* [A study of music seeking verification from history] 音樂向歷史求證. Taipei: Chung-hua shu-chü, 1974.

Shih Yai [Yen] 史岩. *Tun-huang shih-shih hua-hsiang t'i-chih* (Chinese Inscriptions in the Caves of Tun-huang) 敦煌石室畫象題識. Chengtu: The Institute of Comparative Cultures, National Research Institute of Tun-huang and the West China Union University Museum, 1947.

Shionoya On 鹽谷溫. *Shina bungaku gairon* [An outline of Japanese literature] 支那文學概論. 2 vols. Tokyo: Kōdōkan, 1946–1947.

Shorto, H. L. *A Dictionary of the Mon Inscriptions from the Sixth to the Sixteenth Centuries*. London Oriental Series 24. London: Oxford University Press, 1971.

Simon, Walter. "Two Final Consonant Clusters in Archaic Tibetan," *CYYY* (Studies Presented to Yuen Ren Chao on His Sixty-Fifth Birthday) 29.1: 87–90 (November 1957).

Sivin, Nathan. "Preliminary Reflections on the Words *pien* 變, *hua* 化, and *t'ung* 通 in the Great Commentary to the Book of Changes." Unpublished paper, December 1977.

Soymié, Michel, ed. *Contributions aux études sur Touen-houang*. Hautes études orientales 10. Geneva and Paris: Librairie Droz, 1979.

——. "L'Entrevue de Confucius et de Hiang T'o," *JA* 242.3–4: 311–392 (1954). Published separately as no. 2 in Manuscrits de Haute Asie Conservés à la Bibliothèque de Paris (Fonds Pelliot).

——, ed. *Nouvelles contributions aux études de Touen-houang*. Hautes études orientales 17. Geneva: Droz, 1981.

——. "Un recueil d'inscriptions sur peintures: le manuscript P. 3304 verso." In Soymié, ed., *Nouvelles contributions*, plus plates 17–23.

Ssu Su 思蘇. "Shuo-shu yu-wu chiao-pen" [Do storytellers have promptbooks?] 說書有無脚本, *Ch'ü-i* [Song arts] 曲藝 52: 44–45 (18 July 1962).

Stein, Mark Aurel. *On Ancient Central-Asian Tracks: Brief Narrative of Three Expeditions in Innermost Asia and North-western China*. London: Macmillan, 1933.

——. *Ruins of Desert Cathay*. 2 vols. London: Macmillan, 1912.

——. *Serindia: Detailed Report of Explorations in Central Asia and Westernmost China*. 5 vols. Oxford: Clarendon Press, 1921.

——. *The Thousand Buddhas: ancient Buddhist paintings from the Cave-Temples of Tun-huang on the western frontier of China*, with an introductory essay by Laurence Binyon. London: B. Quaritch, 1921.

Stein, Rolf A. "Un ensemble sémantique tibétain: créer et procréer, être et devenir, vivre, nourrir et guérir," *BSOAS* 36.2:412–423 (1973).

Stevens Catherine. "Peking Drumsinging." PhD dissertation, Harvard University, 1972.

Strassberg, Richard E. "Buddhist Storytelling Texts from Tun-huang," *Chinoperl Papers* 8:39–99 (1978).

Su Pai 宿白. "Tun-huang Mo-kao-k'u chung te 'Wu-t'ai-shan t'u'" ["Pictures of the five terraces mountains" in the none higher caves at Tun-huang] 敦煌莫高窟中的『五臺山圖』. In *WW-TH* (B).

Su Ying-hui 蘇瑩輝. "Pa Hei-ch'eng so ch'u Hsi-hsia shih hsieh-pen Fo-chiao chich-ming chüan-tzu—chien lun Tun-huang shih-shih feng-pi nien-tai" [Postscript to the manuscript scroll of Buddhist Gāthā titles from Kara-khoto of the Hsi-hsia period—together with a discussion of the date of the sealing of the stone chamber at Tun-huang] 跋黑城所出西夏時寫本佛教偈名卷子—兼論敦煌石室封閉年代, *TLTC* 42.9:6–9 (15 September 1971).

——. *Tun-huang-hsueh kai-yao* (An Introduction to Tunhuang Studies) 敦煌學概要. Taipei: Chung-hua ts'ung-shu pien-shen wei-yuan-hui, 1964.

——. *Tun-huang lun-chi* (A Collection of Articles on Tunhuang) 敦煌論集. Taipei: Hsueh-sheng shu-chü, 1969.

Suen Kaedih [Sun K'ai-ti] 孫楷第. "T'ang-tai su-chiang chih k'o-fan yü t'i-ts'ai" (The Stating Procedure and Literary Forms of the Popular Buddhist Recitals of *Tarng* Dynasty) [Models and Styles of the Popular Lectures of the T'ang Period] 唐代俗講之科範與體裁, *Kuo-li Pei-ching ta-hsueh kuo-hsueh chi-k'an* (The Gwoshyue Jihkan: A Journal of Sinological Studies; National University of Peking) 國立北京大學國學季刊 6.2:1–52 (1936).

Sun Hsiu-shen 孫修身. "Bakukōkutsu no engi setwuwaga" (Paintings of Bud dhist Historical Accounts and Narrative Tales in the Mogao Grottoes) 莫高窟の縁起説話畫. In Tonkō bunbutsu kenkyūjo [Tun-huang wen-wu yen-chiu-so], ed., *Tonko Bakukōkutsu*, Vol. IV.

Sun K'ai-ti 孫楷第 (*see also* Suen Kaedih). "Chung-kuo tuan-p'ien pai-hua hsiao-shuo te fa-chan" [The development of the vernacular Chinese short story] 中國短篇白話小說的發展. In *TCC*. Originally written in 1951.

——. "Chung-kuo tuan-p'ien pai-hua hsiao-shuo te fa-chan yü i-shu shang te t'e-tien" [The development of the vernacular Chinese short story and its artistic features] 中國短篇白話小說的發展與藝術上的特點. In his *Su-chiang shuo-hua yü pai-hua hsiao-shuo*. Also in *Lun Chung-kuo tuan-p'ien pai-hua hsiao-shuo*. Originally appeared in *Wen-i pao* [Literature report] 文藝報 4.3 (1951). The first half of the article was reprinted in *TCC* (see preceding entry) without any mention that the second half (which contains valuable insights about the influence of Buddhist lectures on the Chinese fictional tradition) ever existed.

——. *Lun Chung-kuo tuan-p'ien pai-hua hsiao-shuo* [On the vernacular Chinese short story] 論中國短篇白話小說. Chung-kuo ku-tien wen-hsueh yen-chiu ts'ung-k'an [Studies on classical Chinese literature series] 中國古典文學研究叢刊. Shanghai: T'ang-ti ch'u-pan-she, 1953. 2nd printing.

——. *Su-chiang shuo-hua yü pai-hua hsiao-shuo* [Popular lectures, storytelling and vernacular fiction] 俗講, 說話與白話小說. Peking: Tso-chia ch'u-pan-she, 1956. A revised version of the author's *Lun Chung-kuo tuan-p'ien pai-hua hsiao-shuo, q.v.*

——. "T'ang-tai su-chiang kuei-fan yü ch'i pen chih t'i-ts'ai" [The rules for popular lectures of the T'ang period and the form of their texts] 唐代俗講軌範與其本之體裁. In his *Lun Chung-kuo tuan-p'ien pai-hua hsiao-shuo*. Also in *TCC* and *Su-chiang shuo-hua yü pai-hua hsiao-shuo*.

——. "Tu pien-wen" [On reading *pien-wen*] 讀變文. *TCC*. Originally written 1936. See also the same article under the next entry.

——. "Tu pien-wen tsa-chih" [Miscellaneous notes from reading *pien-wen*] 讀變文雜識, *HTFH* 1.10:3–6 (15 June 1951). Revised on 10 November 1957 and reprinted as "Tu pien-wen, erh tse" [On reading *pien-wen*, two aspects] 讀變文, 二則; in *LWL*, Vol. I.

——. "Tun-huang hsieh-pen Chang Huai-shen pien-wen pa" [Postscript to the *pien-wen* manuscript from Tun-huang on Chang Huai-shen] 燉煌寫本張淮深變文跋, *CYYY* 7.3:385–404 (November 1937).

——. "Tun-huang hsieh-pen Chang I-ch'ao pien-wen pa" [Postscript to the *pien-wen* manuscript from Tun-huang on Chang I-ch'ao] 燉煌寫本張義潮變文跋, *T'u-shu chi-k'an, chung-wen pen* (Quarterly Bulletin of Chinese Bibliography), Chinese Edition 圖書季刊, 中文本 3.3:97–105 (September 1936). Reprinted in *TCC*, and partially reprinted in Wang Chung-min, *Tun-huang ku-chi hsu-lu*.

Suzuki Kei 鈴木敬 and Akiyama Terukazu 秋山光和. *Chūgoku bijutsu* (Chinese Art in Western Collections) 中國美術. Vol. I, Painting. Tokyo: Kodansha, 1973.

Suzuki Torao 鈴木虎雄, ed. and comm. *Ri Chōkitsu kashishū* [The songs and poems of Li Ho] 李長吉歌詩集. 2 vols. Tokyo: Iwanami shoten, 1961.

Sweeney, (P. L.) Amin. "Professional Malay Story-Telling: Some Questions of Style and Presentation." In *Studies in Malaysian Oral and Musical Traditions*. Michigan Papers on South and Southeast Asia 8. Ann Arbor: Center for South and Southeast Asian Studies, The University of Michigan, 1974. Reprinted from the *Journal of the Malaysian Branch of the Royal Asiatic Society*.

——. *The Ramayana and the Malay Shadow-Play*. Kuala Lumpur: The National University of Malayasia Press, 1972.

Ta-t'ang San-tsang ch'ü-ching shih-hua [Tale interspersed with poetry on Tripiṭaka of the T'ang dynasty retrieving the Buddhist sūtras] 大唐三藏取經詩話 and *Ta-t'ang San-tsang fa-shih ch'ü-ching chi* [Record of the Dharma-Master Tripiṭaka of the T'ang dynasty *Retrieving the Buddhist Sūtras*] 大唐三藏法師取經記. Peking: Wen-hsueh ku-chi k'an-hsing-she, 1955. Also Shanghai:

Chung-kuo ku-tien wen-hsueh ch'u-pan-she, 1954. Facsimile reproduction in Vol. V of Lo Chen-yü, *Chi-shih an ts'ung-shu, q.v.*

Takakusu, J., tr. *A Record of the Buddhist Religion as Practised in India and the Malay Archipelago (A.D. 671–695) by I-Tsing (634–713)*. Oxford: Clarendon Press, 1896.

Takakusu, J. and Makoto Nagai, eds. *Samantapāsādikā: Buddhaghosa's Commentary on the Vinaya Piṭaka*. Vol. VI. London: Pali Text Society, 1947.

Takata Tokio 高田時雄. *Tonkō shiryō ni yoru Chūgokugo shi no kenkyū: kyū, jyū seiki no Kasei hōgen (A Historical Study of the Chinese Language Based on Dunhuang Materials: The Hexi Dialect of the Ninth and Tenth Centuries)* 敦煌資料による中國語史の研究—九・十世紀の河西方言 Tōyōgaku sōsho [Oriental Studies Library] 東洋學叢書, 33. Tokyo: Sōbunsha, 1988.

T'an Cheng-pi 譚正壁. *Chung-kuo hsiao-shuo fa-ta shih* [A history of the development of Chinese fiction] 中國小說發達史. Shanghai: Kuang-ming shu-chu, 1935.

——. "Pien-wen te ch'i-lai yü su-wen te i-liu" [The origins of *pien-wen* and the legacy of popular writing] 變文的起來與俗文的遺留. In his *Chung-kuo hsiao-shuo fa-ta shih.*

T'an Ts'ui 檀萃 (1725–1801). *Shuo man* [On "southern barbarians"] 說蠻. In *Chao-tai ts'ung-shu* [Luminous era collectanea] 昭代叢書, Vol. LVII.

Tanaka Ichimatsu 田中一松. *Emakimono* [Picture scrolls] 繪卷物. Tokyo: Dainihon yūbenkai kodansha, 1956.

Tanaka Kenji 田中謙二. "Henbunkyoku no ichi kuhō ni tsuite" (A Type of Verse Formation in *pien-wen* Style) 變文の一句法について. In *Tsukamoto hakase shojū kinen Bukkyō shigaku ronshū* (Essays on the History of Buddhism: Presented to Professor Zenryu Tsukamoto on his Retirement from the Research Institute for Humanistic Studies, Kyoto University) 塚本博士頌壽記念佛教史學論集. Kyoto: Tsukamoto Hakushi Shojū Kinenkai, 1961.

Teeuw, A., et al. *Śiwarātrikalpa* of Mpu Tanakuṅ: *An Old Javanese Poem, Its Indian Source and Balinese Illustrations*. Bibliotheca Indonesica (KITLV) 3. The Hague: Martinus Nijhoff, 1969.

Teng, Ssu-yü and Knight Biggerstaff. *An Annotated Bibliography of Selected Chinese Reference Works*. Harvard-Yenching Institute Studies 2. Cambridge: Harvard University Press, 1971. 3rd ed.

Thomas, F. W. and Sten Konow, eds. *Two Medieval Documents from Tun-huang*. Oslo: A. W. Brøgger, 1929.

Thompson, Laurence G. "Obiter Dicta on Chinese Religion as Play." In *Chung-yang yen-chiu-yuan kuo-chi han-hsueh hui-i lun-wen chi* (Proceedings of the International Conference on Sinology, Section on Folklore and Culture) 中央研究院國際漢學會議論文集. Taipei. 1981.

Tibetan Buddhist Canon.

a. Peking block-print edition kept in the Harvard-Yenching Library. Completed in the year 1700.

b. Lhasa block-print edition kept in the Harvard-Yenching Library. Perhaps completed under the 13th Dalai Lama in 1933 (?).

c. Derge block-print edition kept in the Harvard-Yenching Library. Completed in 1733.
Information from Kenneth Ch'en, dissertation. 1946.

Tochio Takeshi 栃尾武. "Tonkō henbun Kōshiden to Shunshi hen no hikaku" (A Comparison of "Hsiao Tzŭ Chuan" and "Shun Tzŭ Pian" in Pien-Wen of Tun Huang) 敦煌變文孝子傳と舜子變の比較, *Ōbirin daigaku Chūgoku bungaku ronsō* (The Journal of Chinese Literature) 櫻美林大學中國文學論叢 1:89–101 (March 1968).

Tökei, Ferenc. *Genre Theory in China in the 3rd–6th Centuries* (*Liu Hsieh's Theory on Poetic Genres*). Bibliotheca Orientalis Hungarica 15. Budapest: Akadémiai Kiadó, 1971.

Tonkō bunbutsu kenkyūjo [Tun-huang wen-wu yen-chiu-so] (The Dunhuang Institute for Cultural Relics) 敦煌文物研究所, ed. *Tonkō Bakukōkutsu* (The Mogao Grottos of Dunhuang) 敦煌莫高窟. *Chūgoku sekkutsu* (The Grotto Art of China) 中國石窟. 5 vols. plus index in supplement. Tokyo: Heibonsha, 1980–82.

Ts'ai-se Chung-hua ming-hua chi-lan [Color album of famous Chinese paintings] 彩色中華名畫輯覽. Taipei: Ho-le t'u-shu ch'u-pan-she, 1976.

Ts'ai-tiao chi, *See* Wei Hu.

Tsang Mou-hsun 臧懋循 (Advanced Scholar 1580). *Fu-pao t'ang chi* [Mushroom Hall collection] 負苞堂集. Shanghai: Ku-tien wen-hsueh ch'u-pan-she, 1958.

Tseng Yung-i 曾永義. "Kuan-yü pien-wen te t'i-ming, chieh-kou, ho yuan-yuan" [On the term *pien-wen*, its structure, and its origins] 關於變文的題名,結構和淵源, *Hsien-tai wen-hsueh* (Modern Literature) 現代文學 38:191–220 (1969). Reprinted in the author's *Shuo su-wen-hsueh* [On popular literature] 說俗文學. Taipei: Lien-ching ch'u-pan shih-yeh kung-ssu, 1980.

Tsukishima Hiroshi 築島裕. (*Kōfukuji hon*) *Daijionji Sanzō Hoshi den koten no kokugogakuteki kenkyū* [Studies pertaining to the Japanese language of the old punctuation marks on the Kōfukuji copy of the biography of the Tripitaka Dharma Master from the Temple of Great Compassion and Grace] (興福寺本)大慈恩寺三藏法師傳古點の國語學的研究. 3 vols. Tokyo: Tokyo University Press, 1965–1967.

Tu Yu 杜佑 (735–812), comp. *T'ung tien* [Comprehensive precedents] 通典. Shanghai: Commercial Press, 1935.

Tuan An-chieh 段安節. *Yueh-fu tsa-lu* [Miscellaneous register of ballads] 樂府雜錄. Chung-kuo wen-hsueh ts'an-k'ao tzu-liao hsiao ts'ung-shu [Small collectanea of reference materials for Chinese literature] 中國文學參考資料小叢書. Shanghai: Ku-tien wen-hsueh ch'u-pan-she, 1957.

Tuan Ch'eng-shih 段成式 (d. 863). *Ssu t'a chi* [Notes on monasteries and stupas] 寺塔記 (Ch. 5 and 6 of *Yu-yang tsa-tsu, hsu-chi* [A miscellany of rareties, additional collection] 酉陽雜俎續集). Concerning a visit to Ch'ang-an made in 843. Chung-kuo mei-shu lun-chu ts'ung-k'an [Collected works on Chinese art] 中國美術論著叢刊. Peking: Jen-min mei-shu ch'u-pan-she, 1964. Based on the edition in Chin-tai pi-shu [Secret books for crossing the ford] 津逮秘書.

——. *Yu-yang tsa-tsu* [A miscellany of rareties] 酉陽雜俎, c. 860. *SPTK* ed.

Tun-huang chüan-tzu [Tun-huang scrolls] 敦煌卷子. 6 vols. Taipei: Shih-men t'u-shu kung-ssu, 1976.

Tun-huang-hsüeh chi-k'an [Journal of Tunhuangology] 敦煌學輯刊, 1 (February 1980) and continuing. Published by Lan-chou ta-hsueh Tun-huang-hsueh yen-chiu-tsu [Research section for Tunhuangology of Lan-chow University] 蘭州大學敦煌學研究組.

Tung Tso-pin 董作賓. "Tun-huang chi-nien" [Chronology of Tun-huang] 敦煌紀年. In *P'ing-lu wen-ts'un* [Literary remains of Tung Tso-pin] 平廬文存, 2 vols. Taipei: I-wen, 1963. 1.2.31–62.

——. "Tun-huang chi-nien-piao" [Chronological chart of Tun-huang] 敦煌紀年表. *P'ing-lu wen-ts'un* 1.2.63–106. Also printed, with English title "A Chronological List of Dated Tunhuang Manuscripts," in *Tung-fang hsueh-pao* (Monumenta Orientalia) 東方學報 1.2:1–50 (1 December 1958).

Twitchett, Denis C. "Chinese Social History from the Seventh to the Tenth Centuries: The Tun-huang Documents and Their Implications," *Past and Present* 35:28–53 (December 1966).

Uchida Michio 內田道夫. "Chūgoku koshōsetsu no tenkai—Shinwa · densetsu · bungei— (The Development of the Old Chinese Novel—with Special Reference to the Problem of Myth, Legend, and Novel) 中國古小說の展開—神話·傳說·文藝—, *Bunka* (Culture) 文化 25.4:1–29 (625–653) (Winter 1961), plus English summary.

——. *Chūgoku shōsetsu no sekai* [The world of Chinese fiction] 中國小說の世界. Tokyo: Hyōronsha, 1970.

Umezu Jirō 梅津次郎. *Emakimono sōshi* [Collected essays on painted scrolls] 繪卷物叢誌. Kyoto: Hōzōkan, 1972.

——. "Hen to henbun: Etoki no kaiga-shi teki kōsatsu" (On *Pien* and *Pien-Wen*) 變と變文— 繪解の繪畫史的考察, 2, *Kokka* [Essence of the nation] 國華 760:191–207 (July 1955), plus English summary.

——. *Kegon engi* (Legends of the Kegon Sect) 華嚴緣起. Nihon no meiga [Famous paintings of Japan] 日本の名畫 7. Tokyo: Heibonsha, 1957.

——. "Pien and Pien-wen." In *The Japan Science Review* (Literature, Philosophy, and History), Vol. VIII. Tokyo: Union of Japanese Societies of Literature, Philosophy, and History, 1957.

Utsunomiya Kiyoyoshi 宇都宮清吉. *Daitō Daijionji Sanzō Hoshi den kōi* [Collation of the variants of the biography of the Tripitaka Dharma Master from the Temple of Great Compassion and Grace of the Great T'ang dynasty] 大唐大慈恩寺三藏法師傳考異. Kyoto: Hōyū shoten, 1979. Originally published 1932.

——. "Jion den no seiritsu ni tsuite" (The Formation of the "Tz'ŭ-ên-chuan 慈恩傳" or the Biography of "Hiuen-Tsiang 玄奘") 慈恩傳の成立に就いて, *Shi* 17.4:91–132 (October 1932).

Utz, David A. "Two Parthian Words in the Chinese Manichaean Tradition." Unpublished paper, 1985 (?).

Vandier-Nicolas, Nicole, tr. and comm. *Śāriputra et les six maîtres d'erreur*. Facsimilé du Manuscrit Chinois 4524 de la Bibliothèque Nationale. Mission Pelliot en Asie Centrale, Série in-Quarto, V. Paris: Imprimerie Nationale, 1954.

Vasu, Nagendra Nath. *The Modern Buddhism and Its Followers in Orissa*. Calcutta: By the author, 1911.

Velingerová, Milena. "The Art of Chinese Storytelling," *New Orient* 2.5:153–154 (October 1961).

de Visser, M. W. *Ancient Buddhism in Japan: Sūtras and Ceremonies in Use in the Seventh and Eighth Centuries A.D. and Their History in Later Times*. Leiden: E. J. Brill, 1935.

Vogel, Claus, ed. and tr. *The Teachings of the Six Heretics: According to the Pravrajyāvastu of the Tibetan Mūlasarvāstivāda Vinaya*. Abhandlungen für die Kunde des Morgenlandes (Herausgegeben von der Deutschen Morgenländischen Gesellschaft) 39.4. Wiesbaden: Franz Stein for Deutsche Morgenländische Gesellschaft, 1970.

Waley, Arthur, tr. *The Analects of Confucius*. New York: George Allen and Unwin, 1938; Vintage (Alfred A. Knopf and Random House) rpt.

——, tr. *Ballads and Stories from Tun-huang: An Anthology*. New York: MacMillan, 1960.

——. *The Real Tripitaka: and Other Pieces*. New York: Macmillan, 1952.

——. "Some References to Iranian Temples in the Tun-huang Region." *CYYY, Studies Presented to Hu Shih on His Sixty-Fifth Birthday*, part 1, Vol. XXVIII December 1956.

Wang Chen-min 王貞民. "Tu tseng-ting pen *Tun-huang pien-wen tzu-i t'ung-shih*" [A reading of the expanded and revised edition of *Comprehensive explanations of the meanings of characters in the* pien-wen *from Tun-huang*] 讀增訂本《敦煌變文字義通釋》, *LitHer, Suppl.* 8:231–236. Peking: Chung-hua shu-chü, 1961.

Wang Chi-lan 汪季蘭. *Chung-kuo min-chien i-shu te chin-hsi* [The old and new of Chinese folk arts] 中國民間藝術的今昔. Taipei: Ta-hua wan-pao she, 1972.

Wang Ch'i 王琦 (fl. 1758.), annot. *Li Ch'ang-chi ko-shih* [The songs and poems of Li Ho] 李長吉歌詩. *SPPY* ed.

Wang Chih 王質 (1127–1188). *Hsueh-shan chi* [Snow Mountain collection] 雪山集. *TsSCC*, 1990–92.

Wang Ch'ing-shu 王慶菽. "Shih-t'an pien-wen te ch'an-sheng ho ying-hsiang" [A tentative discussion of the production and influence of *pien-wen*] 試談 '變文' 的產生和影響, *Hsin chien-she* [New reconstruction] 新建設 3 (cumulative 102):21–26 (March 1957).

Wang Ch'iu-kuei. "The Transformation of the Meng Chiang-nü Story in Chinese Popular Literature." PhD dissertation, University of Cambridge, 1977.

Wang Cho 王灼 (fl. 1162). *Pi-chi man-chih* [Diffuse notes from the Ward of Blue-Green Fowl] 碧雞漫志. Shanghai: Ku-tien wen-hsueh ch'u-pan-she, 1957.

Wang Chung-min 王重民. "Chang I-ch'ao pien-wen" [The Chang I-ch'ao *pien-wen*] 張義潮變文. In his *Tun-huang ku-chi hsu-lu*. Originally appeared in *Ta-kung pao* (L'Impartial) 大公報, *T'u-shu fu-k'an* (Bookman) 圖書副刊 145 (27 August 1936).

——. *Pa-li Tun-huang ts'an-chüan hsu-lu* [Descriptive register of textual fragments of Tun-huang texts preserved at Paris] 巴黎敦煌殘卷叙錄, part 1. Peiping: Kuo-li Pei-p'ing t'u-shu-kuan, 1936.

——. "Pa Lun-tun pen Wang Ling pien-wen" [Postscript to the London text of the Wang Ling *pien-wen*] 跋倫敦本王陵變文, *Wen-shih chou-k'an* [Literature and history weekly] 文史周刊 75. *Nan-ching chung-yang jih-pao* (Nanking Central Daily) 南京中央日報 (5 January 1948).

——, ed. *Tun-huang ch'ü-tzu-tz'u chi* [Collection of Tun-huang cantos] 敦煌曲子詞集. Shanghai: Commercial Press, 1956, rev. ed. First published 1950.

——. *Tun-huang ku-chi hsu-lu* [Descriptive register of ancient manuscripts from Tun-huang] 敦煌古籍叙錄. Shanghai: Commercial Press, 1958.

——. "Tun-huang pen Tung Yung pien-wen pa" (Postscript to the *Pien-Wen* on Tung Yung, a Manuscript Copy from Tun-Huang)" 敦煌本董永變文跋, *T'u-shu chi-k'an* (Quarterly Bulletin of Chinese Bibliography) 圖書季刊, n.s. 2.3: 359–360 (September 1940).

——. "Tun-huang pen Wang Ling pien-wen" (Notes on the MS. "王陵變文" from Tun-huang) 燉煌本王陵變文, *Kuo-li Pei-p'ing t'u-shu-kuan* (Bulletin of the National Library of Peking) 國立北平圖書館館刊 10.6: 1–16 (November–December 1936). Subtitled "Chiao-lu" [Record of collations] 校錄.

——. "Tun-huang pien-wen yen-chiu" [Research on Tun-huang *pien-wen*] 敦煌變文研究. In *LWL*, Vol. I.

Wang Jen-chun 王仁俊, ed. *Tun-huang shih-shih chen-chi lu* [Register of actual handwriting from the Tun-huang stone chambers] 敦煌石室眞蹟錄 N. p.: Kuo-ts'ui t'ang, 1909. Rpt. in 2 vols., Taipei: I-wen yin-shu-kuan, 1974.

Wang, Jing. "The Mythology of Stone: A Study of Intertextuality of Ancient Chinese Stonelore and Three Classic Novels." PhD dissertation, University of Massachusetts, 1985.

Wang Kuo-wei 王國維. *See also* under pseudonym Ching-an 靜庵.

——. "Lu-ch'ü yü t'an" [Extra talks on recorded cantos] 錄曲餘談. *Tseng-pu ch'ü-yuan* [Florilegia of cantos, supplemented] 增補曲苑, *ts'e* 6. Shanghai and Hangchow: Liu-i shu-chü, 1932, 3rd ed. Also in his *Wang Kuan-t'ang hsien-sheng ch'üan-chi* [Complete works of Wang Kuo-wei] 王觀堂先生全集, Vol. XV. Taipei: Wen-hua ch'u-pan kung-ssu, 1968.

——. "Tun-huang fa-hsien T'ang-ch'ao chih t'ung-su shih chi t'ung-su hsiao-shuo" [Popular poetry and popular fiction of the T'ang dynasty discovered at Tun-huang] 敦煌發見唐朝之通俗詩及通俗小說. *Tung-fang wen-k'u* [Oriental library] 東方文庫 71. *K'ao-ku-hsueh ling-chien* (Essays on Paleography) 考古學零簡. Shanghai: Commercial Press, December 1923. 3rd ed., July 1925.

Wang P'ei-lun 王沛綸. *Hsi-ch'ü tz'u-tien* [Dictionary of drama] 戲曲辭典. Taipei: Chung-hua shu-chü, 1969.

Wang Shih-chen 王世禎 (1634–1711). *I-yuan chih-yen* [Goblet words from the garden of art] 藝苑巵言. In Vol. IX of Ting Fu-pao 丁福保, ed., *Li-tai shih-hua hsu-pien* [Continuation of poetry talks from successive periods] 歷代詩話續編. Shanghai: I-hsueh shu-chü, 1939.

Wang Ting-pao 王定保 (c. 870–955). *T'ang chih-yen* [T'ang gleanings] 唐摭言. Peking: Chung-hua shu-chü, 1959. Several other editions were consulted, including: *Hsueh chin t'ao yuan* [Seek the source of the Ford of Learning] 學津討源. Shanghai: Han-fen lou ed., *ts'e* 159–160. *Hsiao-yuan ts'ung-shu* [Whistling Garden collectanea] 嘯園叢書. Edition of 1883, *ts'e* 13–14. *Ya-yü t'ang ts'ung-shu* [Collectanea from the Hall of Elegant Rain] 雅雨堂叢書. Edition of 1756, *ts'e* 34. *TTTS* 8. *TsSCC* 2739. *SPPY* ed. Excerpts in *T'ai-p'ing kuang-chi*.

Wang Wei 王維 (701–761). *Wang Yu-ch'eng chi chien-chu* [Collected works of Wang Wei with commentary] 王右丞集箋注. Chao Tien-ch'eng 趙殿成 (1683–1756), annot. 2 vols. Shanghai: Chung-hua shu-chü, 1962.

Wang Wen-ts'ai 王文才. "Su-chiang i-shih k'ao" [An examination of orders of service for popular lectures] 俗講儀式考. In Kan-su sheng she-hui k'e-hsueh-yuan wen-hsueh yen-chiu-so [Research Institute for Literature of the Kansu Provincial Academy of Science] 甘肅省社會科學院文學研究所, ed. *Tun-huang-hsueh lun-chi* [A collection of articles on Tun-huang studies] 敦煌學論集. Lanchow: Kan-su jen-min ch'u-pan-she, 1985.

Wang Yi-t'ung, tr. and comm. *A Record of Buddhist Monasteries in Lo-yang*. Princeton University Press, 1984.

Wang Ying 王英. *Shih tz'u ch'ü yü-tz'u li-shih* [Illustrative explanations of words and phrases in poetry, lyric meters, and cantos] 詩詞曲語辭例釋. Peking: Chung-hua shu-chü, 1980.

Watson, Burton, tr. *The Complete Works of Chuang Tzu*. New York: Columbia University Press, 1968.

Watters, Thomas. *On Yuan Chwang's Travels in India 629–645 A.D.* Ed. T. W. Rhys Davids and S. W. Bushell. 2 vols. London: Royal Asiatic Society, 1904–1905.

Wei Hu 韋縠 (fl. Later Shu 蜀 [of the Five Dynasties and Ten Kingdoms, 934–965]), comp. *Ts'ai-tiao chi* [Collection of poems showing talent] 才調集. *SPTK* ed.

Wei T'ien-ts'ung. *See* Yu Tien-ts'ung.

Weller, Friedrich, ed. *Zum Lalita Vistara, I: Über die Prosa des Lalita Vistara*. Leipzig: G. Kreysing, 1915.

——. *Zum soghdischen Vimalakīrtinirdeśasūtra*. Leipzig: Deutsche Morgenländische Geselleschaft, kom. F. A. Brockhaus, 1937.

Weng T'ung-wen *See* last section of bibliography.

Wiese, E., tr. and intro. *Enter the Comics*. Rodolphe Töpffer's (1799–1846) Essay on Physiognomy and The True Story of Monsieur Crepin. Lincoln: University of Nebraska Press, 1965.

Wogihara, Unrai. *Bodhisattvabhūmi: A Statement of Whole Course of the Bodhisattva* (*Being Fifteenth Section of Yogācārabhūmi*). Tokyo: Published by the author, 1930.

Wogihara [Ogihara] Unrai 荻原雲來. *Bon-Kan taiyaku Bukkyō jiten* (The Sanskrit-Chinese Dictionary of Buddhist Technical Terms Based on the *Mahāvyutpatti*) 梵漢對譯佛教辭典. Tokyo: Sankibo, 1959, rpt.

—— and Tsuji Naoshiro 辻直四郎, eds. *Kan'yaku taishō Bon-wa daijiten* [Sanskrit-Japanese dictionary (with parallel Chinese translations)] (漢譯對照)梵和

大辭典. Taipei: Hsin wen feng ch'u-pan-she, 1979. Rpt. of Tokyo: Suzuki Gakujutsu Zaidan, 1968.

Wu Cheng-tzu 吳正子 (Sung). *Li Ch'ang-chi ko-shih* [The songs and poems of Li Ho] 李長吉歌詩. Kyoto: Kyoto University Library. Rpt. from original woodblock cut in 1818 by Shōheikō University 昌平黌, 1952.

Wu Ch'eng-en 吳承恩 (c. 1500–c. 1582). *Hsi-yu chi* [Record of a journey to the west] 西遊記. Peking: Tso-chia ch'u-pan-she, 1954. Tr. Anthony C. Yu as *The Journey to the West*, Vols. I–IV. Chicago and London: University of Chicago Press, 1977–1983. Tr. partially by Arthur Waley as *Monkey*. New York: Grove Press, 1958; originally published by John Day in 1943.

Wu Chi-yu "Les manuscrits de Touen-houang." In Vol. II of *Aspects de la Chine*. 2 vols. Musée Guimet Bibliothèque de diffusion 63. Paris: Presses Universitaires de France, 1959.

Wu Hsiao-ling 吳曉鈴. "Kuan-yü 'Su-chiang k'ao' yeh shuo chi chü hua; shang, hsia—chiu cheng yü Hsiang Chueh-ming hsien-sheng" [I, too have a few words to say about "An examination of popular lectures"; parts I and II: Inviting criticism from Mr. Hsiang Ta] 關於俗講考也說幾句話上下一就正於向覺明先生. In *SWH* supplements no. 1 and 11 of *Hua-pei jih-pao* [North China daily] 華北日報 (4 July and 12 September 1947), p. 6 of both issues.

Wu Ju-lun 吳汝綸 (1840–1903), comm. *Li Ch'ang-chi shih p'ing-chu* [Critical notes on the poems of Li Ho] 李長吉詩評注. N. p.: I-wen shu-chü, 1922.

Yabuki Keiki 矢吹慶輝, comp. *Meisha yoin* (Rare and Unknown Chinese Manuscript Remains of Buddhist Literature Discovered in Tunhuang Collected by Sir Aurel Stein and Preserved in the British Museum) [*The Reverberation of Howling Sands*] 鳴沙餘韻. Tokyo: Iwanami shoten, 1930.

Yamaguchi Susumu 山口益. *Yamaguchi Hakushi kanreki kinen Indogaku Bukkyōgaku ronsō* (Studies in Indology and Buddhology, Presented in Honor of Professor Susumu Yamaguchi on the Occasion of His Sixtieth Birthday) 山口博士還曆記念印度學佛教學論叢. Kyoto: Hōzōkan, 1955.

Yamazaki Hiroshi 山崎宏. *Shina chūsei Bukkyō no tenkai* [The development of medieval Chinese Buddhism] 支那中世佛教の展開. Kyoto: Hōzōkan, 1971.

Yang Chia-lo 楊家駱. *Hsiao-shuo yü chiang-ch'ang wen-hsueh* [Fiction and prosimetric literature] 小說與講唱文學. Tan-yuan shih kuo-wen hsuan-k'an [Selected whole works in the national language] 單元式國文選刊. Taipei: Shih-chieh shu-chü, 1953.

Yang Hsuan-chih 楊衒之 (d. 555?). *Ch'ung-k'an Lo-yang ch'ieh-lan chi* [Republication of the *Notes on monasteries* (*Saṃghārāma*) *of Loyang*] 重刊洛陽伽藍記, with notes and collation by Hsu Kao-juan 徐高阮. *CYYY* Special Issue 42. N. p.: Institute of History and Philology [Ching-hua yin-shu-kuan], 1960. I have also consulted the annotated edition of Fan Hsiang-yung 范祥雍. *Lo-yang ch'ieh-lan chi chiao-chu* [Collated and annotated *Notes on monasteries of Loyang*] 洛陽伽藍記校注. Shanghai: Ku-tien wen-hsueh ch'u-pan-she, 1958.

Yang Pin-kuei. "Praying for Rain: a *tantzu* Story," *Chinese Literature* 8:120–138 (August 1959). Reprinted in Walter J. Meserve and Ruth Meserve, eds., *Modern Literature from China*. New York: New York University Press, 1974.

Yang Yin-shen 陽蔭深. *Chung-kuo su-wen-hsueh kai-lun* [Outline of Chinese popular literature] 中國俗文學概論. Shanghai: Shih-chieh shu-chü, 1946.

Yao Wen-hsieh 姚文燮. *San chia p'ing-chu Li Ch'ang-chi ko-shih* [Poems and songs of Li Ho with critical notes by three commentators] 三家評注李長吉歌詩. Peking: Chung-hua shu-chü, 1959.

Yeh Sheng 葉盛 (1420–1474). *Shui-tung jih-chi* [Diary from east of the water] 水東日記. Chung-kuo shih-hsueh ts'ung-shu [Collectanea of Chinese historiography] 中國史學叢書 25. Taipei: Taiwan hsueh-sheng shu-chü, 1965. Reproduction of Ssu-shu lou ed. of 1680.

Yeh Te-chün 葉德均. *Hsi-ch'ü hsiao-shuo ts'ung-k'ao* [Collected studies on drama and fiction] 戲曲小說叢考. 2 vols. Peking: Chung-hua shu-chü, 1979.

Yen Keng-wang 嚴耕望. "T'ang-jen hsi-yeh shan-lin ssu-yuan chih feng-shang" [The T'ang fashion for pursuing studies at isolated Buddhist monasteries] 唐人習業山林寺院之風尙. Pp. 367–424 of the second following entry.

——. "T'ang-jen tu-shu shan-lin ssu-yuan chih feng-shang" (Studying at the Buddhist Cloisters as a Fashion During the T'ang Dynasty) 唐人讀書山林寺院之風尙, *CYYY* 30.2:689–728 (October 1959). Subtitled: "Chien lun shu-yuan chih-tu chih ch'i-yuan [Together with a discussion of the origins of the institution of the academy] 兼論書院制度之起源.

——. *T'ang-shih yen-chiu ts'ung-kao* [Collection of drafts related to studies of T'ang history] 唐史研究叢稿. Kowloon: Hsin-ya yen-chiu-so, 1969.

Yen Wen-ju 閻文儒. "Tun-huang shih-ti tsa-k'ao" [Sundry notes on the historical geography of Tun-huang] 敦煌史地雜考. In *WW-TH* (B).

Yoshimura Shūki 吉村修基, Tsuchihashi Shūkō 土橋秀高, Inokuchi Taijun 井ノ口泰淳. "Tonkō Bukkyōshi nenpyō" [Chronological table of the history of Buddhism in Tun-huang] 敦煌佛教史年表. In *MSI*, Vol. I.

Yu Tien-ts'ung [Yü (Wei) T'ien-ts'ung] 尉天驄. "T'ang-tai te su-chiang yü pien-wen" (Su-chiang and Pien-wen of the T'ang Dynasty) 唐代的俗講與變文, *Yu-shih hsueh-chih* (The Youth Quarterly) 幼獅學誌 5.1 (20 August 1966), 12th article.

Yü Chien-hua 兪劍華, annot. *Li-tai ming-hua chi* [A record of famous painters of successive dynasties] 歷代名畫記. Shanghai: Jen-min mei-shu ch'u-pan-she, 1964.

Yü Hsia-lung 于夏龍. "Tun-huang pien-wen 'shih'-tzu yung-fa fen-hsi" [An analysis of the usage of "*shih*" in Tun-huang *pien-wen*] 敦煌變文"是"字用法分析, *CKYW*, 4 (cumulative 137):293–295 (22 August 1965).

Yü T'ien-ts'ung. *See* Yu Tien-ts'ung.

Yuan Chen 元稹 (779–831). *Yuan shih Ch'ang-ch'ing chi* [The collected works of Yuan Chen] 元氏長慶集. *SPTK* ed.

Yuan Pin 袁賓. "*Tun-huang pien-wen chi* chiao pu" [Collation and supplements to *Collection of* pien-wen *from Tun-huang*] 《敦煌變文集》校補, *Hsi-pei shih-yuan hsueh-pao* [Journal of Northwest Normal College] 西北師院學報, She-hui k'e-hsueh pan [Social sciences] 社會科學版, Tseng-k'an [Expanded Issue] 增刊, Tun-huang-hsueh yen-chiu chuan-chi [Special issue on Tun-huang studies] 敦煌學研究專輯 (October 1984), pp. 38–45, (p. 45 includes a list of other recent supplemental annotations to T.)

Yūki Somei 結城素明. comp. *Saiiki-ga shūsei* [Collection of paintings from the western regions] 西域畫聚成. 15 vols. Tokyo: Shinbi shoin, 1940–1941.

Yuyama, Akira, comp. *Systematische Übersicht über die buddhistische Sanskrit-Literatur/ A Systematic Survey of Buddhist Sanskrit Literature*. Wiesbaden: Franz Steiner, 1979.

Zhao Jinming (Chao Chin-ming) 趙金銘. "Tun-huang pien-wen chung so chien te 'le' ho 'che'" (The evolution of the verbal suffixes *le* and *zhe* as seen in bian-wen from the Dunhuang Grottos) 敦煌變文中所見的"了"和"着," *CKYW*, 1 (cumulative 148): 65–69 (January 1979).

Zhelokhovtsev, A. N. and Yu. L. Krol'. "Ob Etimologii i Znachenii Termina Byanven'," *Narod'i Azii i Afriki* 3: 138–146 (1976).

Zürcher, E. *The Buddhist Conquest of China: The Spread and Adaptation of Buddhism in Early Medieval China*. 2 vols. Leiden: E. J. Brill, 1972, rpt. with additions and corrections.

ARTICLES AND BOOKS NOT SEEN

In this section are listed works which, to judge from their titles or from references made to them elsewhere, would appear to be germane to the subject of this study. The reader should be warned that the bibliographic information here provided has been culled from various sources, has not been verified, and is often incomplete. Several of the entries have been adapted in works listed in the main bibliography above.

Akiyama Terukazu 秋山光和. "Henbun to emaki—Perio shōraibon gōmahen zukan ni tsuite" [*Pien-wen* and picture scrolls—On the illustrated scroll of the subduing of demons retrieved by Paul Pelliot] 變文と繪卷—ペリオ將來本降魔變圖卷について, *Bunkashi kondan kaihō* [Bulletin of the cultural history discussion group] 文化史懇談會報 32 (1955).

Chou Tso-jen 周作人. Article on Mu-lien [Maudgalyāyana] 目連, *Min-chien* [Folk] 民間 6 (1931).

Fu Yun-tzu 傅芸子. "Su-wen-hsueh yen-chiu" [Studies on popular literature] 俗文學研究. Lecture notes, perhaps never published.

Hatano Tarō 波多野太郎. "Tonkō henbun jigi tsūshaku dokugo" [After reading *Comprehensive explanations of characters in Tun-huang* pien-wen] 敦煌變文字義通釋讀後, *Yokohama shiritsu daigaku kiyō* [The Bulletin of the Yokohama City University] 橫濱市立大學紀要 11.2 (1960).

Hsu Chia-jui 徐嘉瑞. "Tun-huang fa-hsien Fo-ch'ü su-wen shih-tai chih t'ui-ting" [A tentative establishment of the dating of the Buddhist cantos and popular writing discovered at Tun-huang] 敦煌發現佛曲俗文時代之推定, *Wen-hsueh chou-pao* [Literary weekly] 文學周報 199 (1925).

Hsu Ming-ya 徐鳴亞. "Ts'ung pien-wen tao chu-kung-tiao" [From *pien-wen* to *chu-kung-tiao*] 從變文到諸宮調, *Ch'ang-liu* [Free flowing] 暢流 21.8 (June 1960).

Hu Ku-huai 胡谷懷. "Ts'ung Mu-lien pien-wen shuo ch'i" [A discussion beginning with the Maudgalyāyana *pien-wen*] 從「目連變文」說起, *Kung-lun pao* [Public forum] 6 公論報 (8 April 1963).

Hung Liang 洪亮. "Tun-huang shih-shih li te min-su wen-hsueh" [Folk literature from the Tun-huang stone chamber] 敦煌石室裡的民俗文學. In Chapter 6, part 3 of *Chung-kuo min-su wen-hsueh shih-lueh* [Outline history of Chinese folk literature] 中國民俗文學史略. Shanghai: Ch'ün-chung, 1934.

Ju-chen, tr. 如眞譯 (?). "Tun-huang pien-wen yü Fo- [chiao] (?)" [Tun-huang *pien-wen* and Buddhism] 敦煌變文與佛[教], *Hsin hsueh-sheng* [The new student] 新學生 4.3 (16 March 1970).

Kanaoka Shōkō 金岡照光. "'Ō Ryō,' 'Ri Ryō' henbun tō ni tsuite—Tonkō-bon kōshi-rui no ichi-sokumen—" [On the Wang Ling and Li Ling *pien-wen*, etc.—An aspect of historical narrative texts from Tun-huang]「王陵」「李陵」變文等について—敦煌本講史類の一側面—. *Tōyōgaku kenkyū* [Studies of eastern culture] 東洋學研究 2:55–64 (1967).

——. "Pari zōhon Mokuren henbun sanshu fuchū" [Three manuscripts of the Maudgalyāyana *pien-wen* preserved in Paris, with notes] パリ藏本目連變文三種附註, *Ōkurayama gakuin kiyō* [Bulletin of Ōkurayama Academy] 大倉山學院紀要 3:169–193 (1959).

——. "Shunshi shikō henbun no shomondai" [Questions on the *pien-wen* of the utmost filiality of Shun as a boy] 舜子至孝變文の諸問題. *Ōkurayama gakuin kiyō* [Bulletin of Ōkurayama Academy] 大倉山學院紀要 2:167–190 (1956).

——. "Tonkō-bon Tō Ei-den shitan" [Exploratory discussion of the Tun-huang version of the story of Tung Yung] 敦煌本董永傳試探, *Tōyō daigaku kiyō* (Bulletin of the Faculty of Letters, Toyo University) 東洋大學紀要 20 (1966).

Kuan Te-tung 關德棟. "Ch'ou-nü yuan-ch'i ku-shih te ken-chü [The source of the story about the legend of the ugly maiden] 醜女緣起故事的根據. In *SWH* 9 (19 December 1947).

——. "Hsiang-mo pien-wen ya-tso-wen yü Mu-lien yuan-ch'i" [The *ya-tso-wen* for the *pien-wen* on the subduing of demons and the Maudgalyāyana *yuan-ch'i*] 降魔變文押座文與目連緣起. *Wen-i fu-hsing Chung-kuo wen-hsüeh yen-chiu hao* [Chinese literature studies issue of *Literary Renaissance*] 文藝復興中國文學研究號, Vol. II. c. 1949.

Mei Juo 梅若. "T'ang-tai te min-chien Fo-chiao wen-hsueh—pien-wen" [Pien-wen—folk Buddhist literature from the T'ang dynasty] 唐代的民間佛教文

學—變文, *Fo-hsueh yueh-k'an* [Buddhist studies monthly] 佛學月刊 1.12 (1942).

Ono Genmyō 小野玄妙. "Gōma jōdōzu no kenkyū" [Studies on pictures of the subduing of demons and achievement of the Way] 降魔成道圖の研究, *Shūkyōkai* [Religious world] 宗教界 5.10–11 (1909).

Ono Katsutoshi 小野勝年, annot. *Rekidai meiga-ki* [*Li-tai ming-hua chi*—A record of famous painters of successive dynasties] 歷代名畫記. 2 vols. Tokyo: Iwanami shoten, 1938.

P'eng Ch'u-heng 彭楚珩. "Pien-wen yü wo-kuo min-chien wen-hsueh chih yuan-yuan" [Pien-wen and the origin of Chinese popular literature] 變文與我國民間文學之淵源. *Hsueh-jen* [The scholars] 學人. *Taipei Chung-yang jih-pao* (Central Daily News, Taipei) 臺北中央日報. (24 July 1959?).

Tiao Ju-chün 刁汝鈞. "Pien-wen yen-chiu" [A study of *pien-wen*] 變文研究, *Wen-i hsien-feng* [Literary vanguard] 文藝先鋒 8.1 (1945).

Tung Ch'u 東初. "Tun-huang i-shu yü Chung-kuo wen-hua" [The manuscripts preserved at Tun-huang and Chinese culture] 敦煌遺書與中國文化, *Fo-chiao wen-hua* [Buddhist culture] 佛教文化 1.5 (19 September 1966).

Tung K'ang 董康. "Shun-tzu chih-hsiao pien-wen pa, Chao-chün pien-wen pa" [Postscript to the *pien-wen* on the utmost filiality of Shun as a boy and postscript to the *pien-wen* on Wang Chao-chün] 舜子至孝變文跋, 昭君變文跋. In his *Shu-po yung-t'an* [Common chatter from a book-laden junk] 書舶庸譚. Shanghai: Ta-tung shu-chü, 1920 (?) or 1928 (?).

Wang Ch'ing-shu 王慶菽. "Hsiao-shuo chih T'ang-tai shih ta ch'eng-li shih-ch'i chih yuan-yin" [The reason fiction attained maturity only upon reaching the T'ang period] 小說至唐代始達成立時期之原因, *Wen-shih chou-k'an* [Literature and history weekly] 文史周刊, 62 *Nan-ching chung-yang jih-pao* (Nanking Central Daily News) 南京中央日報 (6 October 1947).

Wang Chung-min 王重民. "Tun-huang pen Tung Yung pien-wen pa" [Postscript to the Tun-huang manuscript of the Tung Yung *pien-wen*] 敦煌本董永變文跋, *SWH* 3. *Pei-p'ing hua-pei jih-pao* [Peiping North China news] 北平華北日報 (18 July 1947).

——. "Tun-huang pen Wang Ling pien-wen pa" [Postscript to the Tun-huang manuscript of the Wang Ling *pien-wen*] 敦煌本王陵變文跋, *SWH* 8 and 9. *Pei-p'ing hua-pei jih-pao* [Peiping North China news] 北平華北日報 (22 and 29 August 1947).

Wang Wei 汪偉. "Ts'ung pien-wen tao t'an-tz'u" [From *pien-wen* to *t'an-tz'u*] 從變文到彈詞, *Min-to pan-yueh-k'an* [People's bell semi-monthly] 民鐸半月刊 3.

Weng T'ung-wen 翁同文. "Tun-huang shih-shih feng-pi nien-tai chih mi" [The puzzle concerning the period when the Tun-huang stone chamber was sealed] 敦煌石室封閉年代之謎, *Lun-heng* [*Weighing of Arguments*] 論衡. *Nan-yang shang-pao fu-k'an* [Supplement to the South Pacific commercial news] 南洋商報副刊 4.5 (?), or 5 April (?), 1971.

Wu Hsiao-ling 吳曉鈴. "Mu-lien chiu-mu ku-shih yen-pien yen-chiu" [A study of the evolution of the story of Maudgalyāyana rescuing his mother] 目蓮救母故事演變研究. *Yao-su yueh-k'an* [Folklore monthly] 謠俗月刊 5. *Pei-p'ing ch'en-pao* [The Peiping Morning news] 北平晨報 (4 July 1937).

Yang Kung-chi 楊公驥. *T'ang-tai min-ko k'ao-shih chi pien-wen k'ao-lun* [An examination and explanation of T'ang dynasty folk songs as well as an essay examining *pien-wen*] 唐代民歌考釋及變文考論. Changchun: Chi-lin jen-min ch'u-pan-she, 1962.

Yen Wan-chang 閻萬章. "Shuo chu-kung-tiao yü su-chiang te kuan-hsi" [An explanation of the relation between the medley and popular lectures] 說諸宮調與俗講的關係, *SWH* 68. *Pei-p'ing hua-pei jih-pao* [Peiping North China news] 北平華北日報 (15 October 1948).

Index

Note: A list of Tun-huang caves and manuscripts referred to in this book is available from the author.

Harvard-Yenching Institute Monograph Series
(titles now in print)

8 and 9. *The Ancient Na-Khi Kingdom of Southwest China*, 2 volumes, by Joseph F. Rock

11. *Han Shi Wai Chuan: Han Ying's Illustrations of the Didactic Application of the* Classic of Songs, translated and annotated by James Robert Hightower
12. *Money and Credit in China: A Short History*, by Liensheng Yang
13. *Civil Service in Early Sung China, 960–1067: With Particular Emphasis on the Development of Controlled Sponsorship to Foster Administrative Responsibility*, by E. A. Kracke, Jr.
16. *Sonq Dynasty Musical Sources and Their Interpretation*, by Rulan Chao Pian
17. *An Introduction to Sung Poetry*, by Kojiro Yoshikawa, translated by Burton Watson
18. *A History of Japanese Astronomy: Chinese Background and Western Impact*, by Shigeru Nakayama
19. *The Izumi Shikibu Diary: A Romance of the Heian Court*, translated and with an introduction by Edwin A. Cranston
20. *Miraculous Stories from the Japanese Buddhist Tradition: The* Nihon Ryōiki *of the Monk Kyōkai*, translated, edited, and with an introduction by Kyoko Motomochi Nakamura
21. *The Chinese Short Story: Studies in Dating, Authorship, and Composition*, by Patrick Hanan
22. *Songs of Flying Dragons: A Critical Reading*, by Peter H. Lee
23. *Early Chinese Civilization: Anthropological Perspectives*, by K. C. Chang
24. *Population, Disease, and Land in Early Japan, 645–900*, by William Wayne Farris
25. *Shikitei Sanba and the Comic Tradition in Edo Fiction*, by Robert W. Leutner
26. *Washing Silk: The Life and Selected Poetry of Wei Chuang (834?–910)*, by Robin D. S. Yates
27. *National Polity and Local Power: The Transformation of Late Imperial China*, by Min Tu-ki
28. *T'ang Transformation Texts: A Study of the Buddhist Contribution to the Rise of Vernacular Fiction and Drama in China*, by Victor H. Mair
29. *Mongolian Rule in China: Local Administration in the Yuan Dynasty*, by Elizabeth Endicott-West